Soviet Political Economy in Transition

Soviet Political Economy in Transition

From Lenin to Gorbachev

A. F. DOWLAH

Contributions in Economics and Economic History, Number 130

GREENWOOD PRESS
New York • Westport, Connecticut • London

Library of Congress Cataloging-in-Publication Data

Dowlah, A. F.
  Soviet political economy in transition : from Lenin to Gorbachev /
A. F. Dowlah.
      p. cm.—(Contributions in economics and economic history,
  ISSN 0084-9235 ; no. 130.)
  Includes bibliographical references and index.
  ISBN 0-313-27944-6 (alk. paper)
      1. Soviet Union—Economic policy—1917- 2. Soviet Union—Economic
policy—1986- 3. Marxian economics—Soviet Union—History.
4. Perestroĭka. I. Title. II. Series.
  HC335.D74 1992
  338.947—dc20   91-28147

British Library Cataloguing in Publication Data is available.

Library of Congress Catalog Card Number: 91-28147
ISBN: 0-313-27944-6
ISSN: 0084-9235

First published in 1992

Greenwood Press, 88 Post Road West, Westport, CT 06881
An imprint of Greenwood Publishing Group, Inc.

Printed in the United States of America

The paper used in this book complies with the
Permanent Paper Standard issued by the National
Information Standards Organization (Z39.48-1984).

10 9 8 7 6 5 4 3 2 1

Contents

Tables

Acknowledgments

This book deals with the contemporary crisis of transition in the Soviet Union. The advent of *perestroika* and the consequent breathtaking developments inspired me to take up this project, so first I wish to thank all the contributors to these events. A very special thanks, however, goes to Soviet leader Mikhail Sergeyevich Gorbachev. Seldom in history has an individual contributed so much to the welfare of mankind in so short a time.

My scholarly debt goes to Professor John E. Elliott, Director of Political Economy Program at the University of Southern California, who commented on several drafts of the book. I can do no more than reaffirm my gratitude to him. I owe special thanks to professors Carol Thompson and Mark Kann of USC, who also made critical and provocative comments. Professor Thompson, and Sonja Broomfield-Smith of the political economy program of USC also helped in subsequent revisions of the work. Also, I would like to thank the anonymous reader who reviewed the manuscript and made constructive suggestions for its improvement.

I have been able to draw extensively upon rich literature on the Soviet Union. I am grateful to those authors and scholars. I wish to thank specially professors Marshall Goldman of Harvard University, Ed A. Hewett of Brookings Institute, Stephen Cohen and Moshe Lewin of Princeton University, and Archie Brown of Oxford University for their longstanding scholarly influence.

I wish to thank Cynthia Harris, executive editor, and Kellie Cardone, production editor of Greenwood Press for the interest they have taken in this work and for their editorial assistance. At the State University of New York-Canton, I received support and assistance from Dean John McKean and Professor Donald Washburn, Canton College Foundation and its director Robert Raymo, and Dale Hobson.

Finally, I acknowledge a debt of gratitude to my wife, Shama, for taking pleasure in the involvement of her husband in this project.

All these, and many others, are responsible for whatever virtues this book may possess, but none is to be held accountable for its shortcomings.

Soviet Political Economy
in Transition

Introduction

The contemporary crisis in the Soviet Union threatens the economic, political and ideological foundations of its socialist system. In the late 1980s, similar crisis provoked explosions of people power throughout the countries of Central Europe, as well as the Soviet Union. The rapidity, magnitude, and comprehensive character of the unfolding events warrant their characterization as revolutionary, certainly as one of the most astounding phenomena of the twentieth century. In magnitude and import, this crisis has been compared with the Great Depression of the thirties.[1] The Great Depression struck at the very foundations of the capitalist system, bringing it to the breaking point; so does the current crisis in the socialist system. The capitalist system survived that crisis with the help of Keynesian economics and New Deal politics, but the fate of the socialist economies remains so far unclear.

Economists, social scientists, political leaders, and intellectuals, both in the West and East, commonly agree that existing economic theory offers little guidance for resolving contemporary problems in the socialist economies. Therefore, the slippery and hitherto uncharted road of transition out of a socialist economy deserves serious attention. In practice, socialist economies differ in terms of their respective situations, specific reform and transition strategies, priorities among objectives, and probable destinations. This study focuses on the Soviet Union, specifically on *perestroika*'s strategies for economic transition.

One of the root causes of the contemporary crisis lies in the inescapable need in the socialist countries for economic modernization. These countries have industrialized under the auspices of socialism, but require a transition to a post-industrialization phase of economic development. Such modernization requires a decisive shift from the dominant existing method of growth based on infusion of additional labor, capital, and material resources in the production processes (i.e., extensive methods of production) to growth based on improvements in productivity brought by new technologies and institutions (i.e., intensive methods of production). A significant component of Soviet leadership believes that this change calls for a departure from old-style forms of state ownership and comprehensive, centralized planning, moving instead toward greater decentralization, democratization, and a regulated market economy. Mikhail Sergeyevich Gorbachev and his advisers have apparently concluded that a successful transition from extensive to intensive methods of production is unlikely under the brand of centralized economy inherited from Joseph Stalin and Leonid Brezhnev, and with limited success have been grappling with alternative strategies to overcome this crisis since 1985.

The sweeping, fundamental, and rapid character of the unfolding events in the Soviet Union since the emergence of *perestroika* (Gorbachev's program of economic restructuring) in 1985 has captured the attention of the world community. The spirit of *perestroika* facilitated the dismantling of the Berlin Wall, the four-decade-old symbol of the cold war. *Perestroika* also contributed to what has been called the "Springtime of Nations" at the end of last decade, which brought the downfall of governments at breathtaking speed and led to the unprecedented humiliation and eventual ouster of communist regimes throughout the Central European countries. Gorbachev, the architect and exponent of *perestroika*, not only arrived on the world stage at a historically momentous time, but he has vigorously steered the wheel of history since his assumption of Soviet power in 1985. Regardless of its success or failure, *perestroika*, because of the monumental changes it has already caused in the Soviet Union and around the globe, will remain an incredible chapter in Soviet history, and will leave its indelible marks on the history of mankind itself.

According to Gorbachev (1987, 24), *perestroika* has joint aims: 1) recovery of the Soviet economy from "stagnation and other phenomena alien to socialism"; and 2) sustenance of "the great values born of the October Revolution and the heroic struggle for socialism." In sharp contrast with previous reform efforts, *perestroika* emerged as an "urgent necessity" to replace outdated structures of production with more efficient, socially oriented economic mechanisms. The leadership subscribes to the belief that society's superstructures are rooted in the economic base, so transformations of the other spheres of the society are also imperative for the successful transition out of the old economic system. Mainly to facilitate such a transition of the economy from an overly centralized, outdated command system of management to a more decentralized, democratically-oriented system, Gorbachev also initiated sweeping political programs, namely *glasnost* (openness) and *democratizatsiya* (democratization).

Glasnost, as an instrument of *perestroika*, is expected to expose the underlying root causes of dismal performance of the Soviet economy and bureaucracy. Major objectives of *glasnost* are to rejuvenate and reorganize the masses, to stimulate worker morale, and break the taboos that pose threats to changes and reforms. A major goal of *democratizatsiya* is to strengthen the democratic base of the society, establishing a genuine control from below in all levels of administration and economic management of the country. Under the Stalinist totalitarian command system, central planning machineries and dominant Communist Party control actually depoliticized the workers and alienated them from production processes. The program of *democratizatsiya*, therefore, aims to establish rule-of-law and promote democratic values, of course within the parameters of redefined socialist principles and beliefs. To Gorbachev, the three-prong programs of *perestroika*, *glasnost*, and *democratizatsiya* are inextricably interdependent.

To Gorbachev and his advisers, *perestroika*'s "new thinking" goes far beyond putting the economy back on the right track.[2] The essence of *perestroika* lies in a profound restructuring of the whole economy, in shifting the economic priorities and making the system work better, in reconstructing society's material, spiritual, and intellectual base, and in accelerating scientific and technological revolution in all spheres of the country. The principle priorities of *perestroika*, therefore, are to redirect the nation's economic and social preferences, to reactivate its human and material resources, and to inject into the economy the benefits of scientific and technological revolutions that heretofore have been concentrated in the military sector and in space exploration.

Perestroika emphasizes greater democratization and decentralization in economic relations. Under the new arrangements, the rights of the workers are substantially extended in all sectors of the economy, and central planning machineries are being effectively relieved from preparing and overseeing detailed blueprints of production and distribution. Initiatives toward greater privatization have been taken to reduce government control from above and to ensure individual initiatives, offering market relations a greater role in the organization and operation of the economy. But *perestroika* has, as of March 1991, which is when this study ends, largely been characterized by much talk and little action. The economy continues to stagnate and, in some indices, to contract. Arguably, an underlying cause for the apparent failure of *perestroika*'s economic programs (up to mid-1990) is that, so far, Gorbachev has tried to make the system work better without resorting to radical changes.[3] Despite exhortation and rhetoric by Gorbachev and his advisers, the Soviet Union still has a central plan that dictates blueprints for detailed functioning of the economy. Reform efforts have aimed at achieving greater growth rates without substantially changing the economic system and, until recently at least, without disturbing the internal balance of power. Initially, Gorbachev and his advisers believed that transition of the Soviet economy from extensive to intensive methods of production could be possible under the existing system dominated by central planning machineries and one-party rule.

Concrete steps, like institutional and organizational measures aimed at monetary and fiscal management suiting the needs of transformation from central planning to alternative systems, still need to be taken. Manifestly, the leadership has realized that further reform aimed at intensifying and accelerating production and growth is incompatible with the continued existence of an all-powerful party and negation of private ownership. Many Soviet leaders now believe that a transition from industrialization to post-industrialization will require decentralization of initiatives and entrepreneurial zeal for innovation and risk-taking, and especially large-scale privatization, none of which can be orchestrated by orders from above.

Perestroika is controversial. One cause of divergent assessment of *perestroika* is the discrepancy between actual and projected change under its banners. Moreover, *perestroika* is taking place in a context where prices of most consumer goods have remained essentially unchanged for years, where people have been trained to hate capitalist exploitation and government has been conceived as a provider of goods and services, where public enterprises have operated in an environment of "soft-budget" constraints for decades, and where inefficient enterprises have been regularly bailed out by paternalistic redistributive machineries.

Therefore, it is small wonder that *perestroika*'s programs seem unprecedented. To many, *perestroika*'s reform measures are so stunning and far-reaching as to appear to be genuinely revolutionary.[4] *Perestroika*, however, is best depicted as a unique program for the Soviet Union. It does not envisage privatization to the extent done by China. It insists on worker participation in the management of enterprises, but does not propose worker self-management, as practiced in Yugoslavia. It calls for widespread decentralization in economic management, but does not dismantle the central planning apparatus as in Hungary.

Therefore, we are faced with the following questions: 1) How can we best characterize the current crisis? Is it a cyclical crisis, like business cycles in the Western world? Is it a crisis of transition like that of the Great Depression? Or is it a systemic crisis that requires a systemic transformation in the socialist countries? If it is only a cyclical crisis, why has the Soviet economy not demonstrated its ability to recover? If it is a crisis of transition, is Soviet society capable of adapting to the challenges? 2) What is the fundamental character of *perestroika*? Is it a mere program of reform to tinker with the existing system to make it work better? Or is it a revolutionary phenomenon that aims at fundamental transformation of Soviet society and economy? 3) Is *perestroika* capable of transforming the Soviet economy? In other words, if contemporary crisis is systemic, are *perestroika*'s strategies capable of making needed systemic change.

Available literature does not provide persuasive answers to these questions.[5] First of all, although many of the writings are thought-provoking, few take Gorbachev seriously. Gorbachev claims that through *perestroika* an optimal balance between central planning and market in a socialist economy can be obtained. Moreover, he claims that his drive for more democratization of Soviet society and more decentralization of Soviet economic management is aimed at more socialism, not less. These claims certainly need to be taken seriously, but few writers have earnestly addressed these issues. One reason is the recency of the Gorbachev phenomenon. But it is time that his claims and actions receive serious academic analysis. Second, few writers examine *perestroika* as a transition strategy. Literature on the transition from capitalism to socialism is monumental, but little theoretical and empirical guidance exists for the transition of socialist economies toward market economy or market socialism. The literature on *perestroika* and Gorbachev has concentrated on describing policies and programs, adding little critical analysis of progress toward transition from extensive to intensive methods of production, and thereby, from the industrialization to the post-industrialization phase of economic development.[6]

Therefore, this study has two specific objectives: First, to examine *perestroika*'s strategies, to see whether they provide guidance toward an optimal balance between central planning and market mechanism in a socialist economy; second, to evaluate the programs and policies of *perestroika* for making a transition to a new variant of socialism. In other words, is *perestroika* capable of bringing about the transformation of Soviet economy which, according to Gorbachev and his advisers, it intends to accomplish?

For purposes of this study, we presuppose that characterizations of the Soviet economy, society, and politics as being "in crisis" are essentially correct. This crisis has two main aspects: systemic and transitional. A systemic crisis is deeply rooted in the basic institutions and modes of living in a society and thus requires, for its resolution, transformation to a different system. A transitional crisis, in contrast, refers to the process of transition from one system to another.[7]

In the Soviet Union, the crisis is both systemic and transitional. On the one hand, the contemporary difficulties are rooted deeply in the Soviet system itself, as bequeathed to the current generation by Joseph Stalin and Leonid Brezhnev, and only substantial changes in the institutional foundations of the society can resolve them. On the other hand, although it is problematic to stand still (much less to try to reestablish the institutional forms of the Stalin-Brezhnev years), it is equally difficult to move forward. The process of transition to the new society is itself filled with uncertainty and problems, because the old ways of doing things contain strengths as well as weaknesses. In addition, a transition of such magnitude involves dislocations, missing linkages, and dysfunctional and unintended consequences.

These problems bring us to the main hypotheses of our study. First, in contradistinction to common belief that socialism is sternly committed to a nondemocratic totalitarian political system and a centralized command economy, this study argues that two sharply opposed strands of socialist thought can be discerned from Marxian political economy: a centralized strand of socialist economic thought that emphasizes plan over markets, and a decentralized strand that emphasizes market forces over planning in a socialist economy. While the centralized strand of thought stands for lower ideals of socialism, such as nationalization of means of production and central planning, the decentralized strand of thought emphasizes higher ideals of socialism, such as democratization, higher standard of living, and qualitative improvement of common citizens.

Second, again in contradistinction to popular thinking, actually existing socialist societies also exhibit distinct forms, with diverse modes of organization and operation. Soviet society, in the course of its development and evolution, has experienced different stages or empirical models, as different, for example, as the New Economic Policy of the twenties and the Stalinist variant of centralized state socialism that followed. In each instance, advocates of that particular empirical model have claimed (with some truth) affinity with or inspiration from Marxian socialist theories.

Third, Gorbachev claims that *perestroika*'s programs embody more socialism, not less, and that he is looking within socialism, rather than outside it, for solutions to contemporary Soviet problems. On the one hand, his claim is supported by textual and empirical evidence, which shall be provided and discussed herein. On the other hand, Gorbachev is redefining socialism as well as working within the socialist tradition. New institutional modes (for example, "regulated market economy") need to be constructed if a genuinely democratic and decentralized form of socialism is to be established. Moreover, transition to a new form of socialism will also require innovation in institutions, structures, processes, and policies.

Fourth, traditionally, both Marxist and non-Marxist writers have contrasted capitalist and socialist societies. In this context, a transition from capitalism to socialism (or the reverse) would constitute a revolutionary transformation of the economic, social, and political system. Thus, the Bolshevik Revolution, which initiated the process of building socialism, is generally credited with constituting a transformation in systems. Similarly, it is popularly supposed that systemic trans-formation in the context of the contemporary Soviet society must consist in a counterrevolutionary transition from socialism to capitalism.

The contrasting characterization of *perestroika* as potentially revolutionary, but as working within the socialist tradition to establish more socialism, not less, suggests three partly overlapping claims. First, it suggests that centralized and authoritarian versus decentralized and democratic socialism are sufficiently differ-ent to constitute different systems, not merely different versions of the same system. We shall argue later that this suggestion is partly correct, partly incorrect. Second, it suggests that, in principle, a decentralized and democratic socialism is both possible and workable. We shall later support this claim, recognizing the contin-gency, however, that surrounds it in practice. Third, it is sometimes contended that Stalinism was itself antisocialist and that only now do existing socialist societies have the opportunity to build genuine socialism. We shall argue that this view is also partly true and partly false.

Succeeding investigation will be carried out with a fundamental premise that the economy and polity of a country are interdependent. In other words, the strategy will involve a political economy approach, in which mutual interdependence of politics and economics will constitute a guiding thread. The study will emphasize an open-system approach, oriented to both theoretical and empirical investigation. In fact, it will involve partially overlapping methods—descriptive, analytical, empirical, historical, and comparative. The comparative method is generally understood as cross-cultural and cross-national. This book will compare different theoretical and empirical models of socialism, primarily drawn from the experience of the Soviet Union.

The political economy approach will be supplemented by some of the parameters of the institutional approach. Like political economists in general, institutionalists envisage an economic system as an open and evolving goal-directed system, as a part of the larger social or cultural system that both influences and is influenced by the economic system. The distinguishing quality in institutionalist writings is the clear characterization of, and changes in, such institutions as markets, bureaucracy, and so on. Because the current transition in contemporary socialist economies involves nothing less than adapting to technological change, remaking social, economic, and political institutions, redesigning goals and priorities, and reorienting ownership and legal rights, an institutional approach is particularly relevant for our investigation.

Social scientists often become preoccupied with methodological tools at the expense of analysis. It seems better to have "imprecise or approximate answers to the right questions than to have precise answers to the wrong questions" (William Kapp quoted in Myrdal 1977). Moreover, the criteria for judging adequacy in causal explanations are often enormously conditioned by the insight and background of the would-be judge. Therefore, scope for debates and controversies will remain, precisely because our knowledge of the events under study, their correlations and causation, is never perfect or complete. I was limited by an inability to understand Russian; therefore the sources used are entirely from research, books, and articles already published in English by relevant scholars and analysts. However, because this study is more interpretive than descriptive, the lack of access to original Russian sources is perhaps not crucial. As the transition is still unfolding, reports in newspapers and magazines are also used as a source of current information.

This book is organized as follows: Chapter one addresses the decentralized strand of socialist economic thought and practice. It is argued that the decentralized and democratic strand of thought demonstrates not only the compatibility of democracy with socialism, but also the need for democracy to realize a socialist economy and society. The periods of New Economic Policy, Nikita Khrushchev's de-Stalinization and Aleksei Kosygin's reforms, drawn from Soviet experience, are elaborated as exemplars of decentralized approaches to socialism. Chapter two traces the centralized strand of socialist thought. It has been argued that centralized socialist's emphasis on planning and deemphasis on market forces conform to Karl Marx's dominant vision of socialist economic system, but depart from Marx's schema of the stages of economic development and the politics of the future society. The periods of War Communism, Stalinist command model, and Brezhnev's bureaucratic collectivism, again drawn from Soviet experience, have been elaborated as exemplars of centralized approaches to socialism.

Chapter three explores the immediate background of *perestroika* and focuses on the economic, social, and political conditions that made launching of *perestroika* an imperative for the new Soviet leadership. Chapter four evaluates Gorbachev's critique of pre-Gorbachev periods of Soviet socialism and his own vision of socialism. Documents, books, and other published materials in English concerning Gorbachev's statements, and opinions about the pre-Gorbachev period of Soviet experience and about the contending models of socialism are investigated. It is argued that Gorbachev's vision of socialism demonstrates a unique model of socialism and a revolutionary program for revitalization of Soviet person and mind, conforming to the needs and challenges of contemporary Soviet society, economy, and polity.

Chapter five examines the political and economic reforms undertaken by Gorbachev's regime and evaluates them from the perspective of the pre-Gorbachev reform efforts in the Soviet Union. Chapters six and seven analyze *perestroika* as a transition strategy. We have stated earlier that the Soviet economy is now undergoing both systemic and transitional crisis. If it is a systemic crisis, the economy will require compelling changes in the existing legal and functional ownership of the means of production, serious surgery of the central planning mechanism, and serious efforts to build and promote private initiatives. These will also require sweeping reforms in political processes and institutions, and above all, will call for national consensus on transition strategies and goals. How far *perestroika* can lead in this direction and what are the problematics and the forces for and against the transition strategies of *perestroika* will constitute the main subject matter of these chapters. Chapter eight offers a summary conclusion.

NOTES

1. See for example Nee and Stark 1989; Yakovlev 1989; Karol 1989 and Szelenyi 1989. Positions of the exponents of this strand of thought will be elaborated in Chapter Six.

2. Gorbachev (1988a, 420) declares, "*Perestroika* implies not only eliminating the stagnation and conservatism of the preceding period, and correcting the mistakes committed, but also overcoming historically limited, outdated features of social organizations and work needs."

3. Of course, to Soviet conservatives, especially to the Communist Party *apparatchiks*, *perestroika*'s reforms already constituted a counterrevolution to the October Revolution, and they, out of sheer desperation, orchestrated an unsuccessful coup in August 1991. Although this coup has caused far-reaching changes in the country, in terms of analysis of contending economic and political forces, ideological and historical transformation, and their complex interactions and interdependence, this study remains as current and relevant as can be expected.

4. Claiming *perestroika* as a "revolutionary process" aimed at consolidating socialism, not replacing it with capitalism, Gorbachev (1987, 36) asserts,

We are looking within socialism, rather than outside it, for the answers to all the questions that arise . . . Those who hope that we shall move away from the socialist path will be greatly disappointed . . . *perestroika* . . . is fully based on the principle of more socialism and more democracy.

5. The author has extensively reviewed the existing literature elsewhere. See Dowlah 1990a. 9-18.

6. Of course there are some exceptions, like Hewett 1989; Post and Wright 1989; Winiecki 1989a & 1989b; Nee & Stark 1989; Milanovic 1989; Joint Economic Committee's *Gorbachev's Economic Plans* 1987; Aganbegyan 1988a & 1989; Shmelev & Popov 1989; Aslund 1990; Gregory 1990; Desai 1990; Goldman 1987; Kornai 1990.

7. As shall be explained later, some writers differentiate between transitional and systemic crises in a manner that makes them mutually exclusive. Unless otherwise indicated, we shall use these terms in such a way as to permit a given society to experience both—and to do so, to some extent, at the same time.

1

The Decentralized Strand of Socialist Economic Thought and Practice

INTRODUCTION

This chapter examines the decentralized strand of socialist economic thought and practice that derives inspiration from or modifies the Marxian vision of socialist thought. Both Marxists and non-Marxists generally agree that Karl Marx concentrated his investigation on capitalism and its prospective destruction, and wrote little on the future socialist society. To Marx, writing on a non-existent society bordered on the utopianism for which he condemned his precursors. Therefore, he carefully refrained from offering detailed blueprints of future socialist society and discouraged others from such a project (Brus 1972, 12-15), leaving the task of developing socialist blueprints to future generations (Horvat 1982, 124). It is small wonder that there are divergences of opinion about Marxian socialist vision.

Socialism has been defined in numerous ways, and various socialist economic, sociological, and political models have been designed.[1] One reason for this is that although Marxism has never "at any time managed to take over, conquer the entire spectrum of socialism," attempts have persistently been made "to stretch Marx so as to accommodate new concerns and new departures" (Berki 1975, 71). Incorporation of such concerns and exploration of newer departures, "resulting from new discoveries and new ideas," however, constituted "the highest virtue rather than the greatest crime" (Bottomore 1975, 21), and it is argued, would be odd if such "extensions and applications" of Marxist socialism "were not to depart in some ways from Marx's original text" (Elliott 1976, 154). Indeed, Marxists believe theory derives from praxis, so it would be "un-Marxist" for the theory not to change according to historical praxis and diverse conditions.

Developments and revisions of the Marxian socialist vision can broadly be organized into two polar strands: the centralized and the decentralized strand of socialism.[2] Before embarking on the details of these strands of socialist thought, the concepts of the socialist economic system and its decentralized and centralized versions will be defined. Section three outlines Marx's incomplete vision of a socialist economic system. Section four explores the main postulates of a decentralized version of the socialist economic system as provided by Karl Kautsky, Rosa Luxemburg, Edward Bernstein and Nikolai Bukharin. Empirical illustrations of decentralized socialism, drawn from the Soviet experience of Vladmir Lenin's NEP period, Nikita Khrushchev's de-Stalinization, and Aleksei Kosygin's reforms will be discussed in sections five through seven. Section eight concludes. The centralized strand of socialist thought and practice will be taken up in the next chapter.

BASIC CONCEPTS

Socialist Economic System

An economic system, both as an economic model and as a living economy, involves two basic elements: (1) the ownership of the means of production, and (2) the method of resource allocation. The means of production can be owned individually or collectively. Private ownership of most means of production characterizes a capitalist economy, while overwhelming public ownership characterizes a socialist economic system. The resources of an economy can be allocated by markets through the use of prices, as done in capitalist economies, or administratively by physical planning, as done in socialist countries.[3] Moreover, every economic system must have methods to establish social goals or priorities, in terms of which economic decisions are made and resources are allocated; methods for comparing the gains and costs of alternative economic goals and programs; and social and political institutions to determine "the location and degree of concentration of economic power, or the capacity to make and enforce economic decisions" (Elliott 1985, 2-3). From the viewpoint of such institutional and organizational arrangements and processes, economic models and existing economies can be divided into two broad categories: command-oriented and market-oriented economic systems, although there is no denying that no economic system can be purely market- or command-oriented.

There exists no widely agreed upon framework or criteria for comparing economic systems.[4] But centralization versus decentralization of the system appears to be the most widely used framework in the study of socialist economic systems, and so we shall utilize this approach.[5] Of course, divergent criteria have been employed to measure and differentiate the degrees of centralization and decentralization of socialist economic systems, but we shall concentrate on the following four criteria:

1. Level of economic development, that is, the stage of economic development and its relation to socialist development and industrialization.

2. Ownership and control of the means of production, that is, the legal rights to own and dispose of property (ownership), and the ability to decide what, how, when, and for whom to produce, with legitimate authority to implement such decisions (control).
3. Markets and planning, that is, methods of resource allocation, organization of economic power, and processes of coordination, motivation, and control of economic activities.
4. Democracy and the state, that is, the locus of economic and political power, and political, social, and economic processes for the operation of the economy.

The next section sheds light on the concepts of centralization and decentralization, and centralized and decentralized versions of socialist economic systems.

Centralization and Decentralization

Although perfectly decentralized or pure market economies and absolutely centralized or pure command economies are often constructed for heuristic purposes, such economies have never existed and presumably never will. The meaning of the terms centralization and decentralization remains controversial. Ever since the controversy of socialism broke out in the early thirties, the debate over decentralized versus centralized institutions and processes in a socialist economy has remained at the core of any serious discussion on the viability of socialist economic systems. The debate encompasses such issues as how to measure the degree of centralization or decentralization in an economic system and how to prescribe what extent or combinations of centralization or decentralization could be feasible in a socialist economy.[6] Indeed, a variety of approaches have been employed to differentiate, measure, and quantify the degree of centralization and decentralization in a socialist economy.[7]

The roots of the controversy over centralization versus decentralization can be traced to the neo-Austrian critique of the economic theory of socialism. Neo-Austrians, especially Ludwig von Mises (1935) and Friedrich Hayek (1935) focused on the impossibility of adequate calculation in a socialist economy. They maintained that centrally planned economic systems fail to allocate resources effectively because rational calculation is constrained by the insurmountable problems emanating from gathering and processing information. Defenders of the practicability of socialism traditionally explained this phenomena in terms of a spectrum in which the opposite ends denoted centralization and decentralization, while the economic system or organization in question was placed in between the polar ends. In such schemes, movement towards Western-style price or market was invariably characterized as "more decentralization," and movement toward improving or strengthening of central planning was considered to be "more centralization."[8]

For Jan Drewnowski (1961, 110-127), whose terminology will be adopted for this study, the central question of centralization and decentralization in a socialist economy has to do with the determination of "the sphere of influence of state decisions as against that of individual decisions." Depending on the separate dominance of individual and state, and joint dominance of individual and state on economic activities, Drewnowski identifies three zones of socialist economy: (1) the zone of state interference, where state preferences are supreme; (2) the zone of individual influence, where individual preferences are most important; and (3) the zone of dual influence where state and individual preferences meet. According to these criteria, ideal capitalism can be considered as an economy exclusively composed of an individual zone and full-scale socialism can be characterized as a society without an individual zone.

Drewnowski maintains that in a socialist economy the state zone generally contains the investment goods industries, and the dual-influence zone encompasses the consumer goods sector, but the exact boundary between these two zones can be different in different cases. Based on the boundary between the state and dual zones, Drewnowski identifies two models of socialist economy: no market economy and market economy. No market economy, which is unrealistic and actually presents a limiting theoretical case of the institutional alternatives, refers to a socialist economy in which the whole national economy belongs to the state zone, that is, all decisions of production and distribution of goods are made by the state irrespective of consumer preferences. Drewnowski's market economy, on the other hand, represents an alternative institutional arrangement of a socialist economy in which consumer goods are sold in the market, with prices being determined by market forces but supply being determined by the state. Drewnowski further differentiates the degrees of socialist market economy depending upon the extent to which the state has influence over decisions involving the production and distribution of consumer goods.[9]

An extension of Drewnowski's zone of preference explanation can be seen in the writings of Wlodzimierz Brus (1973, 1989). Brus identifies two limiting cases of centralization and decentralization in a socialist economy: a minimum of centralization and a minimum of decentralization. Like Drewnowski, Brus, too, divides all economic decisions of a socialist economy into three schematic groups: (1) basic macroeconomic decisions; (2) current (or sectional) decisions; and (3) individual decisions. Brus's first category embraces macroeconomic decisions involving growth rates, shares of investment and consumption in the economy, distribution of investment outlays among sectors, and distribution of the consumption fund among various social and vocational groups. Brus's second category covers intermediate-level decisions concerned with size and detailed structure of output, sources of supply, sales, and personnel selection of an enterprise or branch of production. The third category involves individual decisions relating to the framework of household income, and choice of occupation and consumer-goods. Brus's minimum centralization in a socialist economy vests only the first group of decisions in the central authorities, and minimum decentralization entrusts the third group of economic decisions to individuals. According to this framework, a socialist economy is considered centralized if both the first and second groups of decisions are concentrated at the central level. On the other hand, a socialist economy is considered decentralized if it preserves central planning while emphasizing horizontal economic coordination between plans and multiple levels of decision-making units.

For this study, the centralized and decentralized strands of socialism will be examined primarily from the Lenin-Stalin-Dobb-Sweezy-Baran versus the Kautsky-Bernstein-Luxemburg-Bukharin-Lange perspectives. An economy will be considered more decentralized, "if the range of alternatives open to subordinates has increased" and more centralized when there is an increase "in the range of alternatives the authorities can impose on subordinates" (Ward 1967, 7). Thus, replacing public with private ownership and simultaneous initiatives to enhance enterprise autonomy can be considered as a movement away from central planning. A socialist economic model, following Drewnowski (1961), will be considered more decentralized as it reduces the role of the state zone and increases the roles of the dual zone and the individual zone of preferences. Following Brus's categories of economic decisions, an economy will be considered centralized when the jurisdiction of central authorities increases beyond the first group of decisions and encompasses the second category of decisions, and decentralized when there is an increase in the jurisdiction of individual decisions that encompasses the second and third category of decisions.

MARXIAN PERSPECTIVES ON THE SOCIALIST ECONOMIC SYSTEM

Although Karl Marx (1818-83) refrained from developing a rigorous analytical model of socialist economy, many believe he provided the broad outlines for the institutional and organizational structure of a socialist economic system.[10] Marxian vision is examined below in light of the criteria developed earlier.

Level of Economic Development

Marxian socialist economic vision is more intricate and extensive than is often realized, but it becomes further complicated when we consider the actual practices of socialism that claim inspiration from Marxian thought. While Marx postulated socialism as a successor to capitalism, socialist doctrines have actually been established in pre-capitalist economies, and then used as strategy for industrialization and modernization. Marx's scheme of economic development had five stages: the primitive economy, slavery, feudalism, a bourgeois revolution, then communism. To Marx, these stages emanate from a dialectic of changing relations of production—an immanent causal logic of the economic process itself. Marx's views in this regard are explained around three segments: utopian versus scientific socialism, crude versus true communism, and lower versus higher phases of communism.

Utopian versus scientific socialism. Marx and Friedrich Engels (1820-95) characterized earlier socialist doctrines as "unscientific", and "utopian."[11] By contrast, they claimed, their version of socialism was practical and scientific. Their precursors were utopian, Engels (1935, 140-89) claims, because they perceived society as merely evolutionary, and rested their arguments on reason or ideas, not on facts, and not on actual workers' movements. The utopians, Engels asserted, "appealed to reason as the sole judge of all that existed" and "everything that ran counter to eternal reason was to be relentlessly set aside." Marx and Engels also viewed society as evolutionary but attributed such evolution primarily to social processes, not to mere ideas. Moreover, many of their precursors such as Charles Fourier, encouraged rural cooperatives, and desired the demise of industrialism. Pierre-Joseph Proudhon despised property as theft, and believed in an extreme form of egalitarian individualism and anarchism. Jean Jacques Rousseau condemned the rich and envisaged republican virtues. Marx did not reject the industrial revolution. Instead, he eulogized its powerful creative abilities to accumulate capital, increase wealth, and industrialize, which he believed could lay the foundations for communism.

For Marx, acceptance of the industrial revolution alone, however, does not constitute scientific socialism. The followers of Comte de Saint-Simon, for example, believed that the scientific and industrial revolutions of the nineteenth century would bring universal prosperity for the whole of mankind. But like the followers of Auguste Comte, the Saint-Simonians emphasized the power of ideas, not economic forces, to bring about change.

Marx also departed from his socialist predecessors on the issue of the mode of social transformation. The Saint-Simonians emphasized a harmonious transformation to socialism. Fourier advertised for rich philanthropists to finance the establishment of phalansteries and expected that the "lion would lie down with lamb if spoken to nicely" (Crick 1987, 38). Robert Owen preferred federations of cooperative communities governed by producers. Louis Blanc conceived the state as an agency for social reform. John Stuart Mill (1985, 118-41) emphasized peaceful transformation of capitalism to socialism through a vigorous workers' cooperative movement. But instead of reliance on the generosity and philanthropic qualities of the capitalist class, Marx turned directly to the workers to replace the capitalist system.

Such distinction between utopian and scientific socialism has direct bearing on the level of economic development and industrialization. In the *Communist Manifesto* (1948), Marx and Engels rejected the idea of establishing a socialist economy in a pre-capitalist society that neither provides a solid industrial base, nor encourages a militant, politicized, alienated, and revolutionary working class to overthrow the capitalist mode of production. Therefore, the establishment of socialism in a pre-capitalist economy as a tool for industrialization is more reminiscent of the utopian socialist thought than of the Marxian vision of socialism as the successor of capitalism.

Crude versus true communism. In *Economic and Philosophical Manuscripts*,

Marx (1844) distinguished between crude and true communism. The crude form of communism, Marx explains, emerges in a pre-capitalist, pre-industrialized and underdeveloped economy, where the means of production might be nationalized or vested in the community and wages might be leveled by forceful elimination of differential talent and contribution to work, but capitalist vices like alienation and exploitation of workers cannot be done away with. According to Marx, the institutions of crude communism do not abolish the role of worker, rather they extend this role to all members of the community. Such a communism, Elliott (1976, 156) writes, is merely a primitive version, in which, lacking control over production and investment, "workers are both alienated—from their output, the work process, their own human nature to control and direct the forces of nature, and from other men—and exploited, and focus upon satisfactions from consumption rather than creative work."

Marx's true or genuine communism, by contrast, would emerge in a relatively developed industrialized economy when disciplined and skilled workers establish their control over the means of production, production relations that contribute to alienation and exploitation of workers are done away with, and satisfaction from consumption is replaced by satisfaction from the creativity and self-development of workers.

Lower versus higher phases of communism. In *Gotha Program*, Marx (1973, 13-30) differentiated between a lower phase versus a higher phase of communism. While the lower phase retains many birth pangs from the capitalist past, the higher phase of communism is expected to emerge in a distant future when a tremendous expansion of production and productivity will bring affluence and a dramatic alteration in individual and social psychology. During the first phase, inequalities of income, inequalities between higher and lower paid workers, and other inadequacies are unavoidable when the society "is just emerging after prolonged birth pangs from capitalist society." At this stage of socialist development, "no one can give anything except his labor . . . nothing can pass to ownership of individuals except individual means of consumption," and "a given amount of labor in one form is exchanged for an equal amount of labor in another form." Although this stage "tacitly recognizes unequal individual endowment," where "equal right is still constantly stigmatized by a bourgeois limitation," it does not recognize class differences. Marx believed that at this stage of communism such defects would be inevitable: "Right can never be higher than the economic structure of society and its cultural development conditioned thereby."[12]

But in the higher phase, during the post-capitalist socialism, such bourgeois rights and inequalities will disappear. At this stage, Marx envisioned a communist society where, with enormous increases in productive forces and development of the individual, "the enslaving subordination of the individual to the division of labor," and "the antithesis between mental and physical labor" will vanish. "Only then," Marx proclaimed, "can the narrow horizon of bourgeois right be crossed in its entirety and society inscribe on its banners: From each according to his ability, to each according to his needs."

The transition period between capitalism and the lower phase of communism (socialism) would be one of civil wars and national wars.[13] During this period, the dictatorship of the proletariat is expected to change the society so that the higher phase of communism, a classless society, can eventually be established. Marx maintains that dissolution of the capitalist mode of production does not create all the conditions for its succession by the socialist mode of production unless the political and ideological conditions for this succession are present as well. The transition period, as envisaged in the *Communist Manifesto*, included establishment of the political supremacy of the proletariat through winning the battle of democracy, and the gradual transcendence of politics into class struggles. Therefore, the lower phase of socialism will be primarily involved in the transformation of the capitalist mode of production to a mode of production that eventually facilitates the establishment of communism, the higher phase of socialism and the final stage of social development of mankind.[14]

Markets and Planning

Holding the capitalist economic system responsible for spreading market relations over the entire society, Marx associated his critique of capitalism profoundly with that of market relations. Marx's indictment of market relations, according to Selucky (1979, 7-11), took several forms: moral, philosophical, and economic. Marx found the fetishism of money—the universal form of capital—responsible for human misery, and saw in it "an expression of the dominance of things over people, of the objectification and reification of human relations." Marx's philosophic condemnation of money and market relations found ample expression in his concept of alienated labor, which reveals how human labor is reduced to a mere abstraction reflected in exchange value. Alienated labor, according to Marx, creates values not for the worker but for the capitalist who has purchased his labor power and reaps surplus value from the product. A capitalist class stands between workers in their capacities as producers and consumers.[15] Such alienation might be cured, Marx emphasized, by eliminating unequal distribution of the means of production, abolishing private property and substituting planning processes for market processes. For Marx, the capitalistic economic structure has grown out of the economic structure of feudal society. Similarly, the socialist system, in which capitalist ownership of the means of production will cease to exist, emerges out of capitalism, retaining important vestiges of the capitalist economy, notably the quid pro quo of the exchange processes. Under socialism, workers will be able to sell their labor to each other as cooperative associated producers. In exchange they will receive labor certificates which they can, in turn, use to obtain consumer goods from each other.[16] According to Marx, this constitutes an advance over capitalism because the inequalities in power and wealth (and their resulting alienation, exploitation, and crises) based on private ownership of the physical means of production are overturned. Despite this advance, the lower phase of communism exhibits some inevitable defects. One such defect is the sustenance of a process akin to market exchange in relations among workers, consumers, and enterprises. Another is the continuation, presumably for a significant period of time, of inequalities in labor income, based on unequal individual endowment of the capacity of labor. Thus, the equal right embodied in the "exchange of equivalents in commodity exchange" is "still constantly stigmatized by a bourgeois limitation." These defects can be overcome, Marx states, only in a higher phase of communist society (1973, 18-19).

Marx also criticized markets for their uneconomical allocation of factors of production. He maintained that by creating disproportions in supply and demand, market allocation of economic resources often results in wastage of social labor and unemployment. Therefore, Marx predicted that under capitalistic market conditions, periodical economic crises are unavoidable. By contrast, one of the major advantages of planning in a socialist setting is its ability to coordinate and balance aggregate demand and aggregate supply, thereby generating a higher level of activity and a more stable economy.

Thus, it is true that Marx envisioned the eventual transcendence of market relations. Abolition of the market system, in turn, would require abolition of its prerequisites, such as social division of labor, scarcity, and autonomy of producers (Selucky 1979, 10-14). But Marx and Engels, Selucky maintains, identified the concept of division of labor with different things at different times, ranging from private property to "direct domination of laborer by the instrument of labor." As to supersession of scarcity, Marx believed that man would someday achieve mastery over nature, free himself from his role as the principal agent of the production process and work at its side rather than within it.[17]

The third prerequisite for supersession of market relations is abolition of the autonomy of producers. The Marxist prescription for this problem is straightforward: abolish the autonomy of producers by expropriating private ownership of the means of production through wholesale socialization. With the subsequent worker-controlled state management of economic resources, capitalist market relations will soon prove to be redundant for all practical purposes. As markets are unpredictable and market relations are anarchic, they should be replaced by planning, to create "a community of free individuals, carrying on their work with the means of production in common, in which the labor-power of all different individuals is consciously applied as the combined labor-power of the community" and exchange among individuals is abolished altogether.

Marx's and Engels' positions on planning and markets remain controversial. This partly explains the genesis of controversies concerning different roles of planning and markets, centralization and decentralization in a socialist society. Two clearly discernible strands of thought can be identified in this context. One, envisaged and propagated by the exponents of a command, or centralized, model of socialism, maintains that Marx clearly excoriated market relations and preferred planning over markets. The other strand of thought maintains that Marx and Engels condemned the capitalist market exchange system, not markets themselves.

Ownership and Control

Common ownership and control of the means of production constitutes a fundamental feature of the post-capitalist economic system envisaged by Marx. It is the relations of production (i.e., ownership or nonownership of the means of production) that constitutes the basis for Marx's schema of historical class struggles. To Marx, "no facts are more threatening and heretical than the divorce of ownership from control," and nationalization of resources constitutes "the definition of socialism" (Wiles 1962, 50). Such an economic system would be characterized by common ownership and marked by the absence of private ownership and control over the means of production.

For Marx, private ownership and control of the means of production is primarily responsible for providing necessary social conditions for the sustenance and survival of commodity production (production for exchange, for markets). Therefore, an overwhelming goal for a socialist economy would be to bring an end to capitalist commodity production, to bring an end to the cash nexus, and to abolish private ownership as an essential precondition.[18]

It should be kept in mind that when Marx wrote of social, state, or national ownership, he presupposed a society of self-governance by the working class as "associated producers." Just as in capitalism private ownership and control of the means of production is capitalist, not merely private, so, too, for Marx, social ownership and control meant ownership and control by the working class through its public and collective agencies, not merely social or public ownership. Marx believed that capitalism had destroyed the preceding system of property, characterized by private ownership and control by individual, small producers. Capitalism, he claimed, maintained a regime of "private" ownership, but only for a tiny minority. The little private properties of peasants and small business proprietors were wiped out through depression and competition with larger and technologically superior capitalist enterprises. Therefore, reestablishment of a close association between producers and the ownership and control of the means of production could only occur through the collective action of a united working class.

Forms of control and ownership also remain a matter of controversy. Is state ownership, or wholesale nationalization of the means of production (i.e., statization or nationalization), a necessary or sufficient condition for socialization (social direction of the nationalized means of production) in a socialist economy? If the state is controlled by the proletariat, is statization or nationalization also required for socialization of the means of production? According to Bettleheim (1975, 45-48), state ownership is a necessary condition for socialization, but it is not by itself a sufficient condition. Nationalization is possible without socialization. Socialization requires conscious direction of commonly owned and controlled means of production toward fulfillment of socially agreed-upon objectives. By insisting on elimination of commodity production and abolition of private ownership, what did Marx prescribe? Nationalization, that is, a bureaucratically managed centralized economy, or socialization of the means of production with decentralized participative worker-managed political economy? Exponents of centralized and decentralized strands of thought also differ in their answers to these questions.

Democracy and the State

Marx's stand for political, economic, and social emancipation of human beings is pro-democratic and antitotalitarian.[19] He envisioned a future society in which human beings will attain mastery over nature, where conditions under which people are administered will be replaced by an administration of things, and where an environment will be created to enable human beings to achieve their full potential. Young Marx, as a radical democrat, was enthusiastic about human liberty (see Bottomore 1964). Young Marx also showed genuine enthusiasm about freedom of the press. Mounting "sweeping opposition to any and every control over opinions," he condemned censorship for punishing not opinions rather than crimes, and declared that human freedom "involves not only what but just as much how I live, not only that I perform a free act but that I perform it freely" (cited in Draper 1977, 42).

But Marx denounced the bourgeois approach to democracy and cautioned that democratic freedom must not be degraded into a mere instrument to advance the interests of the bourgeoisie. To Marx, bourgeois democracy masks a society of exploitation of both workers and consumers, at home and through foreign colonies, "of religious and cultural instincts by the artificialities of manipulated consciousness" (Cohen 1965, 6). Marx also censured bourgeois representative assemblies and advocated democratic control from below. Marx asserts, "A truly political assembly blossoms out only under the great protectorate of the public spirit, just as living things do only under the protectorate of the open air." While his precursors favored socialism from above and in some cases depended on the benevolence of elites for socialist transformation, Marx was the first socialist thinker who fused "the struggle for consistent political democracy with the struggle for a socialist transformation" (Draper 1977, 59), and called on the working masses to take an active role in the transformation of history and mankind.[20]

Marx's concept of freedom in the economic sphere contains the core of his concept of man's political emancipation. Marx maintained that as long as man is an economic being, he cannot be free at all. "The realm of freedom", Marx wrote, "actually begins only where labor which is determined by necessity and mundane considerations ceases" (quoted in Selucky 1979, 49). For Marx, both personal power (derived from the possession of money) and social power (derived from investment of capital by individuals) must disappear to guarantee economic freedom to the associated workers in a strictly nonmarket planned economy. Therefore, a demand for socialism is tantamount to a demand for democratization of economic power. Since the state is, by definition, a coercive force that establishes class rule, and since the economic power of the ruling class is a precondition for its political power, with the elimination of private property, the ruling class will be eliminated, and thus the need for a state's existence will cease.[21]

Marx's political theory of the state supplements his theory of historical materialism and class struggles. Discarding the contemporary theories of the state that emphasized the state as a necessary organization that represents the general interests of society, Marx conceived the state as an organized instrument of particular interest of the ruling class used to dominate and exploit the producers or the working class. For Marx, every state has its class content and governmental form, and to him the forms of state make little difference; what is important is its content. A state can impose class rule over society, or, in the presence of antagonistic social classes, the ruling class might attempt to present "its specific class interest as the general interest and its specific class ideology as the universal ideology," or the state's management might be entrusted to a professional meritocracy, "alienated and separated from the civil society." Whatever the form, the basic character of the bourgeois state remains bourgeois, and the proletariat must overthrow it to establish the dictatorship of the proletariat, that is, proletarian democracy.

The dictatorship of the proletariat, however, would still be a state, albeit a proletariat one. Democracy for all cannot exist under a class state. The proletariat will control, restrict, and repress the bourgeoisie until there is communism. It will be more democratic because the proletariat is the majority, but not totally democratic—it cannot be—given the nature of class rule. Because the state is by definition a coercive force that establishes class rule, and because the economic power of the ruling class is a precondition for its political power, with the elimination of private property the ruling class will be eliminated, and thus the need for a state's existence will cease.

For Marx the ultimate purpose of economic activity is the realization of human freedom and dignity. Marx's freedom contrasts sharply with the generally accepted liberal definition that refers to an absence of constraints on individual behavior. Marx was critical of this negative concept of freedom, because for him the distinctive character of humanity lies in its ability to plan conscious activity directed toward satisfying needs. The democracy Marx championed was aimed at establishing a classless society, where democracy would mean "effective exercise of power by the mass of the people in the interest of the mass," where the people, "having no interest in injustice" will have "no real interest in deception" (Aptheker 1965, 18-23). In contrast to the bourgeois conception of democracy, Marxian democracy stands for "an attempt to make democracy genuine, to make it fruitful of human goods, to take inequalities from human existence" (Cohen 1965, 15).

Marx's commitment to freedom, democracy and human emancipation is also profusely demonstrated in *Civil War In France*.[22] In the "Paris Commune" (cited in Elliott 1981, 409-16), Marx criticized centralized state power for "its ubiquitous organs of standing army, police, bureaucracy, clergy, and judicature." By contrast, he lauded the Commune as the "direct antithesis of the empire,... formed of the municipal councilors, chosen by universal suffrage" and "responsible and revocable at short terms." Marx eulogized the Paris Commune because most of its members were working men, or "acknowledged representatives of the working class." The Paris Commune, Marx maintained, not only made education accessible to all, but freed science itself from the chains of class prejudice and government. "Instead of deciding once in three or six years which member of the ruling class was to misrepresent the people in the parliament, universal suffrage was to serve the people."[23]

For Marx, men are "free to that extent that they consciously control both nature and their social conditions of existence to suit their needs and abilities" (Burkitt 1984, 38). Marxian socialism emphasized "the destruction of authoritarian state, communal decentralization, and producer's self-management" (Horvat 1982, 126). There is no denying that Marx and Engels stressed or implied eventual elimination of markets, money, and commodity relations, but they conceived that as integral to achieving self-governing socialism. By pinpointing the inhuman alienation of capitalist commodity relations, and entrusting the workers as the universal class for the emancipation of mankind, Marx brought the issue of human freedom and dignity to the center of the world agenda.

THEORETICAL UNDERPINNINGS OF DECENTRALIZED SOCIALISM

This section examines the theoretical underpinnings of the decentralized strand of socialism mainly from the perspectives of Edward Bernstein (1850-1932), Karl Kautsky (1854-1938), Rosa Luxemburg (1870-1919), Nikolai Bukharin (1888-1938), and Oskar Lange (1904-65).[24] Bernstein, the main protagonist of revisionist evolutionary socialism; Kautsky, the embodiment of Marxist Orthodoxy; and Luxemburg, who "combated both revisionists and orthodox centrists" (Kolakowski 1978, 31), jointly represent what Selucky (1979) calls the "Quasi-Revisions" of the Marxian vision oriented to democratic and decentralized socialism. Bukharin, a leading participant of the "Great Industrialization Debate" of the twenties, championed the case of democracy and economic decentralization, especially in challenge to Stalin's command economy and totalitarian regime. Lange (1938; 1952), by advancing the most influential and articulate argument in defense of socialism's feasibility and practicability during the Great Socialist Controversy of the thirties, provides the classic point of departure that intermingles the Great Revisionist Debate of the late nineteenth and early twentieth centuries with subsequent developments up to now. Discussion of their contributions, especially with respect to decentralized democratic socialism, is organized around the four criteria developed above.

Level of Economic Development

Following Marx, the pioneers of the decentralized socialist model considered socialism as a prospective successor to capitalism, and therefore expected its emergence in the economically developed and industrialized nations. To Bernstein, who believed in "organic evolutionism" and "socialism-in-capitalism," socialism was "not only temporarily but spiritually its [capitalism's] legitimate heir" (Gay 1952, 214). For him, "a definite degree of capitalist development" constituted "the first condition of the general realization of socialism" (Bernstein 1909, 97). Bernstein believed in the dynamic character of society and maintained that although adaptability of modern capitalism will be enhanced substantially, it will never be able to solve its own problems. For him, with the advance of capitalism, the workers, through the extension of democratic methods and movements, will gain more allies and more victories (Hook 1955, 67), and thus will steadily grow "in numbers, power and social importance" (Gay 1952, 215), and eventually accomplish the second condition for establishing socialism, "the exercise of political sovereignty by the class party of the workers" (Bernstein 1909, 97).

Kautsky also held that socialism can only be established in a post-capitalist society, in which economic maturity of capitalism and resulting polarization, and eventual "seizure of political power by the organized proletariat" will constitute an "essential and inevitable precondition" for socialism (Kolakowski 1978, 44). Although Kautsky differed from Marx with respect to some of the causes of the ultimate destruction of capitalism, he essentially believed in the inevitability of the self-destruction of the capitalist economic system. He maintained, however, that transition from capitalism to socialism required a revolutionary transformation of society. He insisted that mere transfer of political power from the capitalist class to the proletariat would not do any good to the proletariat "unless capitalism were economically and technically ripe for the change" (46).

Luxemburg, however, believed that capitalism will be overthrown long before its economic potentialities are exhausted, and thus indirectly endorsed Lenin's theories of "Law of Uneven Development" and "Law of Combined Development" (see Meyer 1957) which emphasize that socialism can well be established in a pre-capitalist society. In the words of Kolakowski (1978, 85), Luxemburg was "in agreement with Trotsky and Lenin: the party should seize power when it was politically feasible to do so, regardless of doctrinaire objection about economic maturity." However, strongly defending Marxist deterministic interpretation of history, she maintains that capitalism will collapse for "purely economic reasons" emanating from the destruction of the noncapitalist market, which is essential for its very survival (66). Following Lenin, Bukharin also called for laying the foundation of a new world even under the difficult conditions of a "backward, illiterate, impoverished, ruined" country with a "gigantic predominance of nonproletarian elements" (128). Lange's position oscillates between the two views. In his writings in the thirties, Lange (1938) essentially assumed socialism as a post-capitalist economic system. But in 1958, Lange presented "a kind of dialectical synthesis" (Elliott 1976, 159) characterized by a scheme of stages of economic development in which socialist revolution could be deemed feasible in a pre-capitalist economy.

Markets and Planning

Bernstein, Kautsky, Bukharin, and Lange all stipulated the existence of markets under a socialist economy. Although Luxemburg endorsed wholesale nationalization of the means of production, she very strongly excoriated and cautioned against centralized administrative control over enterprises and workers. Although Bernstein (1909, 187-88) maintained that bureaucracy and central government are indispensable in a future socialist state, he insisted that workers should be "left completely to themselves in their organization and government" of cooperatives that constitute "worthy and indispensable levers for the socialist emancipation." Bernstein did emphasize nationalization, but he insisted that this did not violate the principles of economic necessity and viability of democratic institutions. To him socialization of property was not an end, but a means. Therefore, extension of worker's political rights and their participation in economic and administrative bodies deserved greater importance.

Bukharin strongly opposed centralization of economic management, and emphasized a socialized public sector, a government-controlled private sector, and private enterprise coupled with free agricultural markets for the peasantry, as components of a socialist economic system. Bukharin anticipated that such an evolutionary process would eventually provide "a natural mechanism, the economic, political, social and psychological preconditions for socialism" (Elliott 1985, 364). Bukharin called for a careful balance between "the private interests of the small producers and the general interests of socialist reconstruction." Like Lenin, Bukharin envisaged "overcoming the market through the market," and maintained that the state sector "through its greater market competitiveness, efficiency, and resources" would gradually displace private capital. Whereas Lenin repeatedly described the NEP-type mixed economy as a transitional arrangement, or "breathing space," Bukharin not only strongly advocated its continuation, but also emphasized its vigorous expansion for decades (Cohen 1974, 180-81).

Bukharin, however, did not oppose planning altogether. He believed that planning should be a special applied science. By pointing out the limitations of even a "well-reasoned plan and the deleterious results of an ill-conceived one" he warned that with an "incorrect policy the cost of the process as a whole might be no less than the cost of capitalist anarchy" (Lewin 1974, 56- 57). Planning, for Bukharin, meant the maintenance of proportionality "between various branches of production within industry on the one hand, and the correct relations between industry and agriculture on the other" (Cohen 1974, 182).

Bukharin strongly denounced centralized planning orchestrated by the state. Such planning, he emphasized, would tend to establish a "strong-willed government imposed on a backward society." Its self-perpetuating bureaucracy would "engage in an overall drive to crush Russia's small people—the craftsman, small merchants, small industrialists, and small agricultural producers" (Lewin 1974, 62). He stressed pragmatic policies that would allow the private sector to prosper and to grow into socialism through market relations in an environment enveloped by a worker-controlled state. He pleaded for a pattern of development based on socialist humanism and emphasized "class collaboration, voluntary performances and reformist measures" (Cohen 1974, 201). Lewin (1974, 66) summarizes Bukharin's ideas: "less centralization, more party democracy, more rationality and scientific approach to problems, no mass coercion, less reliance on strictly administrative state measures, priority to gradualism and persuasion."

In his classic model, based on neoclassical formulations, Lange (1938) presented a sophisticated mechanism for coordination and allocation of resources under a socialist economy, which ever since has served as a reference point for a decentralized market model of socialism. Accepting the necessity of a price system for economic calculation and coordination, Lange claimed that a money price system based on market relations is not essential for efficient functioning of a socialist economy. Lange proposed two kinds of price systems: one, proposed for wages and consumers" goods prices, is similar to market price systems; the other, proposed for interest rates, rents, and prices of investment and intermediate goods, is determined by a central planning agency. Lange identified three major decision-making units in a socialist economy: households, enterprises, and a central planning board (CPB). Households can exercise their freedom with respect to consumption, saving, and occupation. Enterprise and industry managers, given market and accounting prices, determine the levels and composition of outputs and inputs within the framework prescribed by the CPB. The CPB's functions, in turn, included setting rules, supervising enterprises and industries, overseeing prices of investment and intermediate goods, determining aggregate levels of investment, social dividends, and composition of collective and quasi-collective goods, and coordinating the economy's monetary and fiscal policies. This model emphasizes a very high degree of decentralization and minimizes the role of planning, constituting a socialist "mixed" system that would embody significant decentralized and market elements.

In his postwar model, Lange (1958) emphasized greater centralization during the earlier phase of socialist economy and decentralization at a later stage. "The very process of the social revolution which liquidates one social system and establishes another requires centralized disposal of resources by the new revolutionary state." At this stage, Lange maintains, centralized allocation and disposal of economic and social resources will be needed for rapid industrialization of the economy and to "avoid dissipation of resources on other objectives which would divert resources from the purpose of rapid industrialization." But, he cautioned, centralized methods that are "necessary and useful in the period of social revolution and of intensive industrialization become an obstacle to further economic development when they are perpetuated beyond their historic justification." Continuation of such a centralized system beyond that point, Lange cautions, leads to inevitable wastage of resources resulting from rigidity, wasteful bureaucratic apparatus, and disregard to the changing needs of the population.

In his postwar model, Lange (1958, 174) also emphasized the direction of economic development as the minimum responsibility of central planning machineries in a socialist economy. For him, planning here accomplishes at least two tasks: (1) the division of national income between accumulation and consumption, primarily concerned with the general rate of growth of the economy; and (2) the distribution of investments among the different branches of the economy, primarily concerned with the direction of economic development. However, he cautions that administrative methods should be "limited to those fields where, for some reason or other, economic means are ineffective," and that economic methods must be embodied in a system of incentives that would "induce people to do exactly the things which are required by the plan." Lange also maintains that even when administrative measures are employed, general economic laws concerning the proportions necessary in the process of production and reproduction must be observed. "If the plan provides increase for steel, it must provide for certain additional output of capital."[25]

Ownership and Control

For Bernstein, socialism meant freedom through economic organization and greater freedom of society against economic factors. As opposed to capitalist enterprises and association of sellers, he emphasized cooperative production and genuine associations of purchasers. Bernstein (1909, 119) asserts, "All consume but all do not produce. Even the best productive association, as long as it is only an association for sale and exchange, will always stand in latent opposition to the community". Emphasizing the cooperative movement, he insists that "cooperative society is the easiest accessible form of association for the working class" (121). Bernstein maintained that by guaranteeing equal shares in profits, organizing buying power, and initiating democratic practices, consumer cooperatives will gain the capabilities to handle distribution in the socialist state (Gay 1952, 223). Under Bernstein's scheme, social legislation will gradually but surely bring an end to private ownership of the means of production, and he prescribed policies like nationalization, social insurance, housing and food distribution programs, leveling of differences in living standards, and even expropriation of private ownership by the socialist state. He insisted on the transfer of economic resources, that is, the means of production, into the hands of society, the operation of enterprises in the interest of the society as a whole, and the extension of social control to all fields of production (240-47; Bernstein 1909, 95-164). "Bernstein never doubted that large clusters of economic power represented by the trusts and cartels would have to be socialized" (Gay 1952, 187).

Kautsky held that sharpening class antagonism rather than increasing pauperization of the working class was the root cause of the socialist movement, and therefore concluded that nationalization and public ownership of the means of production and control of the production processes constitute preconditions for the eventual emancipation of the working class. He accused private ownership of contributing to concentration of capital and class polarization and preventing further development of technical progress (Kolakowski 1978, 51). For Kautsky, the imperatives of economic development place increasing significance on the state's role in the economy. "Economic development forces the state, partly in self-defense, partly for the sake of better fulfilling its functions, partly also for the purpose of increasing its revenues, to take into its own hands more and more functions or industries" (Howe 1986, 100).

Kautsky (1971), in *Class Struggle*, perceived the whole economic system as a cooperative commonwealth, but did not believe that every nationalization was a step toward the fulfillment of that objective. Neither did he endorse wholesale confiscation without compensation. Although Kautsky firmly maintained that the tendency of economic development and the necessity for larger production renders imperative the transfer of private ownership to collective, social ownership and operation of the means of production, he also insisted on the continuation of private ownership, notably in agriculture and small-scale trade.[26]

Luxemburg emphasized public ownership and control of the means of production. But in *Russian Revolution* (1961) she opposed the "dictatorial force of the factory overseer, draconic penalties, rule by terror" and sharply criticized replacement of the dictatorship of proletariat by a dictatorship of handful of a politicians that inevitably leads to bureaucratization of public life. Bukharin stood for an evolutionary process of economic development and emphasized economic policies "based on social harmony, class collaboration, voluntary performances and reformist measures" (Cohen 1974, 201). He pleaded for economic development based on "the principle of free, anarchistic competition, rather than squeezing everybody into the fist" (xii). For him, a socialist economy would be a mixed economy having both private and public ownership of the means of production, in which pragmatic policies would allow the private sector to prosper in an environment enveloped by a worker-controlled state. He expected private ownership to prevail in Soviet farming, trade, and light industry for an indefinite period of time. The Lange model placed no emphasis on worker ownership, and instead broadly vested the means of production in the hands of public authorities, without specifying the institutional arrangements for its administration.

Democracy and the State

For Bernstein (1909, 135-64), as mentioned before, socialism is a legitimate heir of capitalism/liberalism not only in "chronological sequence, but also in its spiritual qualities." He even described socialism as organizing liberalism to devise institutions to free individuals from "every economic compulsion in his action and choice of a calling" imposed by bourgeois liberalism. He asserts, "the formation of political and social organs of the democracy is the indispensable preliminary condition to the realization of socialism". To him, democracy is "at the same time means and end. It is the means of the struggle for socialism and it is the form socialism will take once it has been realized" (quoted in Gay 1952, 239). And the state, Bernstein (1909, 165-99) asserts, will guarantee rights of self-government to all local and national bodies, although "the law or the decree of the nation has to come from the highest legal authority of the community—the state," the rights and powers of state and municipalities should be clearly demarcated, and "regulations of the common law" must protect "the individual against the arbitrary action of accidental majorities."

Bernstein, articulator of the representative democratic state, according to Gay (1952, 243), "saw nothing but Utopian speculation" in Engels's "withering away of the state" and concluded: "It is impossible to jump out of the state: we can only hope to change it." Bernstein described the state "as a center of coercive power," but emphasized that the description of the state as the executive committee for managing the common affairs of the bourgeoisie underestimates the state's beneficial roles. In his scheme of the democratic socialist state, workers are expected to acquire experience with democracy and self-government through parliamentary practices, so that the concept of the dictatorship of the proletariat becomes meaningless (Kolakowski 1978, 107), and is rather understood as the "political sovereignty of the working class" (Lovell 1984, 101-2).

For Kautsky, "the Pope of Social Democracy," democracy and socialism are inextricably intertwined. Democracy is "the shortest, surest, and least costly road to socialism, just as it is the best instrument for the development of the political and social prerequisites for socialism" (quoted in Hook 1955, 55). Describing parliamentary practices as "one of the conditions prerequisite to a sound development of the proletariat," Kautsky (1971, 188) asserted that the parliamentary majority is "the most powerful lever that can be utilized to raise the proletariat out of its economic, social and moral degradation." To him, the state is primarily a class institution dominated by the bourgeois class; but he also maintained that "whenever the proletariat engages in parliamentary activity as a self-conscious class, parliamentarism begins to change its character" (188). To Kautsky, therefore, socialism does not mean the abolition of the state, but changing the class that rules it. For him, the dictatorship of the proletariat during the transition period from the lower to the higher phase of communism, is much like the Paris Commune, "based on democratic principles, a multiparty system, free elections, and the free expression of opinion," not "minority despotism imposed by force, which by its own logic was bound to intensify the rule of terror" (Kolakowski 1978, 50-51).

To Luxemburg democracy is more compatible with, and more feasible under, socialism than capitalism.[27] She maintained that although democratic institutions are not flawless, to abolish them is even worse. To her, the solution to the deficiencies and imperfections of democracy lies not in the wholesale elimination of democratic institutions, "as Lenin and Trotsky found," but in their improvement in making them more workable by guaranteeing the "active, untrammeled, energetic political life of the broadest masses of the people" that alone constituted "the very living source" of "the correction of all the innate shortcomings of social institutions" (quoted in Lovell 1984, 102). For her, "socialist democracy is not something which begins only in the promised land after the foundations of socialist economy were created, ... socialist democracy begins simultaneously with the beginnings of the destruction of class rule and of the constitution of socialism" (Hook 1955, 107). Her conception of democracy in a socialist state presumably would guarantee a free public opinion, freedom of elections and the press, the right to hold meetings and form associations, and to her the dictatorship of the proletariate is not a matter of abolishing democracy, but of applying it correctly (Kolakowski 1978, 87).

Luxemburg (1969, 33), also sided with Bernstein's evolutionary socialism, as she asserts, "extension of democracy, which Bernstein sees as a means of realizing socialism by degrees, does not contradict but, on the contrary, corresponds perfectly to the transformation realized in the nature of the state." In *Reform or Revolution* (1969) her strong opposition to capitalist parliamentary practices, and clear preference for active participation of the workers in the democratic processes can hardly be overemphasized. To her, unlike Bernstein and like Lenin, the state always represents a class organization, and as the existing state was a capitalist state, its parliament inevitably functioned as an instrument of the ruling class. Although the bourgeois parliament had a tendency to negate its class character, and could even represent general interest (33), any attempt to threaten bourgeois rule would be suppressed. Because the state intervenes only in the interest of capital, it can only pursue general policies insofar as those policies accord with the interests of the capitalist ruling class (Kolakowski 1978, 78). Therefore, to Luxemburg (1969, 61) parliamentary victory of the workers (reforms) under a capitalist state and parliament can bring no substantive victory [revolution] for the workers as "no law in the world can give to the proletariat the means of production."

Luxemburg, rather, emphasized democracy at the level of labor organizations, tha is, the conquest of political power by the proletariat, as an alternative to capitalist parliamentary reform. In "Problems of the Organization of Russian Social Democracy" (1972) she opposed the Leninist doctrine of centralization of social democracy that separates "the organized core of the party from the surrounding revolutionary milieu," and emphasized that "the agency of revolution must be the collective mind of the workers and not the consciousness of self-styled leaders" (Kolakowski 1978, 83). For her, only the active participation of the masses, of the self-conscious workers themselves, can guarantee real democracy. In the *Russian Revolution* (1986) she clearly emphasized that the greater the masses can control their representatives after the elections, the more democratic will be the system. She strongly believed that "actual first hand experiences of democratic participation and discussion of ordinary men and women in their daily living and working would broaden their imagination, make them more effective, and develop new, complex, and significant needs" (Hook 1955, 106), and there would be "no need of leaders to educate the masses or look after their consciousness for them" (Kolakowski 1978, 82).

Bukharin, on the other hand, "was not a democrat in a recognizable Western sense" (Cohen 1974, 202). Although he strongly advocated extension of the franchise, and protection of citizens from the state's power, he did accept the Leninist view that in an agricultural society with a peasant majority, a dictatorship of the proletariat would constitute rule by a minority unless accompanied by an alliance with the peasants, a despotism by the working class over the bourgeoisie, and a state as a class organization. Bukharin was, however, more interested in economic decentralization and reduction in the role of administrative decrees than in the political organization of socialism. Lange's contribution also remains mainly in the economic sphere. Logical extrapolations of Lange and Bukharin's positions, however, would presumably imply a more democratic and less authoritarian political system than that which was operative in the USSR, especially after 1928.

In the context of the decentralized stand on the state and democracy, Lenin's democratic, decentralized vision as manifested in *The State and Revolution* deserves mention. In his earlier work *What is to be Done?* (originally written in 1902), Lenin (1967, 91-256) emphasized the revolutionary vanguard role of the Communist Party and envisioned a stronger authoritarian state, and he categorically declared, "To belittle Socialist ideology *in any way*, to *deviate from it in the slightest degree* means strengthening bourgeois ideology." But in *The State and Revolution* (1974), which was written immediately before the October Revolution, Lenin softened his stand on the dictatorship of the proletariat, and, following Marx's position in the *Gotha Program*, envisaged a democratic and participative role for the workers during the stages of transition from capitalism to communism. Denouncing capitalist democracy as "democracy for an insignificant minority, democracy for the rich," "bound by the narrow framework of capitalist exploitation," Lenin envisaged a dictatorship of the proletariat that would expand democracy immensely and transform it into "democracy for the poor, democracy for the people."

To the Lenin of *The State and Revolution*, the state remained the product of class antagonisms, and he maintained that "the organization of the vanguard of the oppressed as the ruling class" alone cannot guarantee an expansion of democracy. While under capitalism, "exploiting minority" fiercely suppressed "exploited majority," during the transition period from capitalism to communism, the dictatorship of the proletariat would suppress the "minority of exploiters by the majority of exploited" by the "simple organization of the armed masses" and presumably with far less bloodshed. As capitalists disappear, class antagonisms disappear, and the state withers away, as there is further no need for the "*special apparatus* for compulsion which is called the state." Lenin, therefore, acknowledged a state of transition incorporating democratic principles, but he anticipated that formal democracy itself would also wither away, when "really full democracy, a democracy without an exceptions, will be possible and will be realized," because the "more, complete the democracy, the nearer the moment when it begins to be unnecessary." Similarly, the state withers away because there are no longer any capitalists or classes, so no class can be suppressed." Thus, for Lenin, both the state and democracy wither away at the ultimate stage of communism, but they both remain in force during the transition period.

The following section elaborates the empirical approaches to a decentralized socialist economic system based on Soviet experience. The Soviet Union has passed through a number of distinct periods of social, economic and political transformation. Reforms either attempted or actually carried out in different periods have often been spectacular and far-reaching, and obviously they responded to the realities of the day. The experiences of the NEP period, Khrushchev's de-Stalinization and Kosygin's reforms are explained below as exemplars of decentralized approaches to socialism.

NEW ECONOMIC POLICY (1923-28)

The New Economic Policy (NEP) came as a surprising negation and almost complete reversal of the policies and programs vigorously pursued during the War Communism period. While the War Communism was characterized by revolutionary and somewhat utopian expectations of breaking up "the old social-economic system completely at one stroke" (Tucker 1977, 81) and rapidly establishing a socialist system, the NEP envisaged a cautious and evolutionary strategy instead, and called for replacement of the revolutionary approach by a reformist one. In sharp contrast to the socialist goals and egalitarian principles of the War Communism period, the NEP sought to revive private business and trade, cooperatives, and petty proprietorship. Such a drastic policy shift in the positions of Lenin and the Communist Party of the Soviet Union (CPSU) was probably an inevitable result of the disastrous economic conditions of War Communism. In any event, the emergence of NEP was a sudden and complete about-turn.[28] As the economy was collapsing and the need for immediate rescue measures was felt widely, in March 1921, the Tenth Congress of the CPSU adopted the NEP almost unanimously. The main features of the NEP are discussed below.

Mixed Socialist Economy

Soviet leaders visualized the NEP as a mixed socialist economy that would blend the elements of private and public sectors in a competitive economic environment effectively controlled by a socialist government. Such an economic setting, in turn, was expected to generate lively competition between the private and public sectors. According to Preobrazhensky, the private sector would be regulated by "the law of value," while the state sector would be regulated mainly by "the law of primitive socialist accumulation." Preobrazhensky argued that with increased competition between these two sectors, the incompatibility of the two regulators would be widely manifested, and gradually with increased socialist accumulation, the public sector would flourish, while the private sector would eventually disappear (see Lewin 1974, 90).

The position of Preobrazhensky was challenged, however, by Bukharin, who maintained that a private-sector based on market relations and a state sector based on government planning should be seen as complementary, rather than mutually exclusive. Even for the state-owned enterprises, he emphasized, control through the market from below and supervision by the state machineries from above would create a conducive environment for the nation's economic development. The NEP strategies, therefore, blended the instruments of both planning and markets, and were intended to introduce a socialist version of mixed economy that combined, on the one hand, a large-scale industrial sector owned and managed by the state, and on the other hand, a private sector of agriculture, trade, and small-scale manufacturing.[29]

Agriculture as the Foundation

The NEP demonstrated a drastic policy-shift toward agriculture. During the War Communism period, agricultural production dropped alarmingly, and the agricultural surplus that was to feed the urban population and provide resources for urban industry became slimmer every year. Consequently, the CPSU found it extremely important to reverse the situation and ensure an adequate supply of grains. Lenin (1965, 225) proclaimed, "We must satisfy the middle peasantry economically and go over to free exchange; otherwise it will be impossible—economically impossible—to preserve the rule of the proletariat in Russia."

Accordingly, by March 1921, the War Communism policy of coercive requisitioning of grains was abolished and a tax-in-kind was introduced instead. The policies initiated under NEP allowed the peasants to increase their production as much as they wanted without worrying about the possibility of confiscation by the government. Once a small tax-in-kind on surplus production was paid, the farmers could sell the rest of their product at the prevailing market price and keep the profit for themselves. In order to boost the morale of farmers and to ensure further increases in agricultural production, the NEP encouraged private trade in agriculture, and by 1924 even replaced the tax-in-kind with a monetary tax.

Denationalization of Industry

NEP drastically revamped the whole industrial sector. Government retained its direct control over banking, foreign trade, and large-scale industrial enterprises, known as the "commanding heights," and encouraged private initiative in everything else. The nationalization order of the War Communism period was officially revoked, and many formerly nationalized enterprises were returned to private owners or to workers" cooperatives. Governmental regulations allowed private initiative in small-scale industries and handicraft production, however these enterprises were legally prohibited from hiring more than ten to twenty workers.

NEP drastically reformed the management structure and mechanism of the government-owned and government-managed industrial sector. Most of the administrative methods of management that were forcefully implemented during the War Communism period were thoroughly revamped. Industrial enterprises and the intermediary administrative units (like syndicates or trusts) were granted greater autonomy. An entirely different economic mechanism, blending methods of economic, administrative, and production-planning, was devised for the industrial sector.[30]

Currency, Price, and Financial Reforms

The NEP reforms went far beyond agriculture and industry, extending into foreign trade, joint ventures, prices, money, and banking. With the advent of the NEP, more and more monetary transactions, in terms of exchange of commodities and services, began to take place. During the War Communism period, attempts were made to do away with money and monetary transactions, and Soviet currency was not backed by gold. Under the NEP, measures were taken to put Soviet currency back on a gold standard, and several banks were established to extend credit to industry, agriculture, cooperatives, enterprises, and other activities. As mentioned above, the state retained monopoly over the large-scale industries, but limited free trade was legalized and small-scale manufacturing was allowed in the private sector. Lenin openly called for "state capitalism" and vigorously emphasized both public and private trade. Addressing the Ninth Congress of Soviets in December 1921 and emphasizing trade, Lenin (1965, 59) declared, "The proletariat state must become a cautious, assiduous and shrewd businessman, a punctilious wholesale merchant," and cautioned that otherwise the Soviet economy was destined to remain a backward and agrarian country. Private traders were allowed gradually to enter into trade deals of almost every kind.[31]

Ideological Justification of the NEP

Moving to the NEP constituted an almost absolute disenchantment with the policies of the War Communism period and therefore called for ideological justification by the Soviet leadership. Although the policies of War Communism brought victory in the civil war, they were also responsible for plunging the country's economy into chaos. The NEP emerged as a remedial measure for the economy, as a strategic retreat in the policies of the Communist Party. The NEP measures were aimed at granting concessions to the petty bourgeoisie and the peasants, and transforming Communist rule into what Lewin (1974, 96) called a "liberal dictatorship" aimed at healing the sufferings caused by a devastating civil war and the CPSU's overambitious dreams to establish communism at a stroke. The underlying rationale for introducing the NEP was to save the October Revolution itself by giving the economy an opportunity to rebuild, and by giving the Party leadership a breathing space to determine future strategy.

Lenin offered two arguments in justifying the NEP. First, he admitted that War Communism was a complete mistake and acknowledged that during this period "war stringencies erroneously had been mistaken for shortcut to socialism" (87). Second, Lenin argued that the NEP was actually a resumption of the policy of state capitalism that he had developed in the spring of 1918, but had been interrupted by the outbreak of the civil war. This standpoint presumably could mean that Lenin would have introduced NEP-type policies even in 1918, had there not been threats of internal and external aggression to the Revolution. Moreover, this position also justifies his claim that the authoritarian policies of War Communism period were the result of anarchistic situations in the country at the time in question. And as Nove (1969, 120) contends, if the NEP was a resumption of the strategy of 1918, that would clearly mean that the NEP was actually not a retreat, it was rather a return to the "status quo ante."

Lenin's policy of state capitalism meant an economy in which, under the dictatorship of the proletariat, a bridge between the petty-bourgeois individualist peasantry and socialism would be established. Beyond cooperation between the state and the private sectors of the economy, Soviet leaders saw an element of dialectical relationship in NEP policies; they envisioned both competition and struggle between these sectors. Under such a dialectical relationship, Lenin conceived a desperate life and death struggle between capitalism and communism, in which the commodity producing private sector was expected to disappear gradually as a result of increasing competition from the public sector.[32]

Therefore, NEP reforms could be considered as a tactical retreat, aimed at cleverly and cautiously utilizing capitalist instruments in order to promote socialistic goals. Growth of large-scale industry was seen as a necessary condition for the establishment of a full-scale communist economy; and the only way, the Soviet leadership visualized, that the relatively underdeveloped Soviet state could establish such large-scale industries was through partial restoration of capitalism.[33] Lenin underscored that the capitalists could be permitted to operate in a socialist economy, but he also cautioned that capitalist practices must be strictly controlled.[34]

Evaluation of the NEP

Economically, the NEP succeeded in fulfilling its immediate purpose. It rescued the Bolshevik Revolution from the possibility of ignoble failure and saved the Soviet economy from potential disintegration and collapse. Economic incentives for the peasantry did help to improve the agricultural sector. Soon the farmers began to produce grain and food in ever larger amounts. Within a year of the introduction of the NEP, the famine situation in the country was reversed, and by 1925, agricultural production had approached the prewar level.

The NEP's socioeconomic and political impacts were no less remarkable. The concessions to and compromise with the peasantry were made at an enormous cost to the industrial workers. Among the industrial workers, unemployment grew enormously. At the same time, the power of the "red managers" (drawn from traditional managerial sections) was massively increased and they were increasingly integrated into the CPSU hierarchy.[35] On the political front, the NEP imposed monolithic political order, although intra-party debates and discussions were allowed. In 1922, Stalin became general secretary of the CPSU and began to consolidate his power. While Lenin legitimated the monopoly of power in the CPSU, Stalin monopolized all power in himself.

The NEP was criticized for opening the door for a plethora of administrative and political abuses, nepotism, and discrimination. Although during the NEP period the standard of living of the industrial worker was definitely higher than during the harsh years of War Communism, according to Carr, "there had been no time since the revolution when discrimination was so overtly practiced against him, or when he had so many legitimate causes of bitterness against a regime which claimed to govern in his name" (quoted in Cliff 1979, 151).

Under the NEP, labor unions lost much of their importance. Earlier, labor unions played a coparticipatory role in the management of state-owned industries. The NEP, to the contrary, deprived labor unions of the right to intervene in the management of state-owned industries, and restricted intervention even in privately owned industries. As a result, union membership declined significantly during this period.[36] Also, the NEP experienced numerous unofficial strikes throughout the country. By the end of 1923, the status and influence of increasingly disorganized and dispersed trade unions were seriously eroded (see Carr 1952, 317-31). NEP was also accused of accelerating a process of class differentiation. Finally, under the NEP, the egalitarian atmosphere that was the hallmark of the War Communism came to an abrupt end. Cliff (1979, 152) remarks, "Inequality became widespread. Wealth and luxury became legitimate. There was no longer any need for concealing opulence."

KHRUSHCHEV'S DE-STALINIZATION (1957-64)

Nikita Khrushchev (1894-1971) consolidated his position in the CPSU and finally emerged as the new leader of the country in 1957.[37] Khrushchev orchestrated the sharpest break with the Stalinist model in the Soviet Union prior to Gorbachev by undertaking far-reaching reorganization of the country's economic and political system. By rejecting Stalinist personal tyranny and secret police terror, and by continuing central planning and one-party rule, Khrushchev made a transition from an "ideal totalitarianism" to a "classic form of authoritarianism," which was characterized by a law-governed state and freer intellectual activities (Migranian 1990b).

Khrushchev's consolidation of power also coincided with one of the brightest chapters in Soviet economic history, when "hopes ran high and accomplishments were not very far behind," and when the sixth plan (1956-60) boasted to overtake the United States in per capita output (Schwartz 1965, 85). It was a period of rapid and impressive economic growth; both industrial and agricultural sector growth increased by almost 50 percent during the period of 1955-58. The Soviet Union was developing at twice the rate of advanced capitalist countries, and "the gap in the level of economic and social development between the Soviet Union and the USA was rapidly closing" (Aganbegyan 1988a, 53). Coupled with an overwhelming increase in its nuclear and rocket strength, the Soviet Union appeared to be stronger, wealthier, and more influential than ever before. To Soviet leaders and citizens, nothing seemed impossible. The mood of this period is aptly described by Gorbachev (1988a, 418): "A wind of change swept the country, the people's spirit rose, they took heart, became bolder and more confident." The policies and reforms that Khrushchev initiated during his seven-year rule reflected this period's high optimism. A brief discussion of the major institutional and policy reforms that accompanied the mounting economic growth during Khrushchev's period follows.

Repudiation of the Stalinist Cult

Khrushchev's de-Stalinization campaign reached a climax when, in February 1956, he delivered a secret speech to the Twentieth CPSU Congress. Strongly denouncing the Stalinist personality cult, Khrushchev dramatically revealed the extent of the Stalinist purges and the costs of Stalin's repression. He accused Stalin of "rude violations of internal party and Soviet democracy, sterile administration, deviations of all sorts, covering up the shortcomings and vanishing of reality." He stated that during the Stalinist period, the Soviet nation "gave birth to many flatterers and specialists in false optimism and deceit" (quoted in Schwartz 1965, 75-76). Khrushchev pointedly criticized the extent of statistical distortions during Stalin's period and sketched a bleak picture of the state of collective farming in the Soviet Union. Nove (1969, 327) maintains that productivity in agriculture (per hectare, per cow, and per peasant) during the Stalinist period was much less than satisfactory, but that the truth was hidden by statistical distortions. Khrushchev's bold assault on Stalinist totalitarianism and limited openness to freedom and statistical information bolstered a very productive era of fresh thinking in Soviet society.[38]

Evidently, Khrushchev's period signified a distinctive qualitative change and a sharp discontinuity with the Stalinist model. Important changes initiated by Khrushchev included: eliminating the use of terror, and rejecting the notion of an inevitable war between capitalism and socialism. By eliminating the extensive use of terror, Khrushchev was able to provide a more congenial environment for unconstrained surfacing of new thoughts and ideas. Manifestation of such ideas and thoughts, especially concerning economic issues, was particularly significant in Khrushchev's period. Rejecting Leninist and Stalinist notions of an inevitable world war between capitalism and socialism, Khrushchev shifted the war to the economic front, and boasted that the Soviet Union would overtake the United States economically by 1980. He also called for relaxation of foreign policy tensions, and championed a detente. This fundamental shift meant a diversion of funds from defense spending to the expansion of the civilian economy.

Emphasis on Consumer Goods

Khrushchev abandoned and reversed many of the major policies of the Stalinist era. While Stalin strongly emphasized the preeminence of heavy industries over light industries, Khrushchev attached top priority to the production of consumer goods. Khrushchev emphasized more housing construction and food production and called for greater investment in the chemical industry to produce more fertilizer and consumer goods. In October 1958, Khrushchev reversed Stalin's policy to build expensive administrative buildings, stadiums, and palaces of culture, and diverted the funds to build schools, hospitals, and children's institutions. As a result, while urban housing completed in 1953 was 30.8 million square meters, in 1957 it rose to 52 million, and in 1960, it jumped to 82.8 million square meters (Schwartz 1965, 82). Nove (1969, 34) showed that state and cooperative housing more than doubled between 1955 and 1959, and private housing increased by more than 300 percent during the same period.

Reforms in Economic Management

Khrushchev undertook extensive measures to alter the entire system of industrial organization. Following the capital investment crisis of December 1956-May 1957, when with the slowdown of industrial production (see Table 1.1) it became evident that targets of the sixth plan were not attainable, Khrushchev accused the central ministries of taking a narrow departmental view of economic activity, making inefficient production and investment decisions, and thereby wasting scarce resources.[39]

Table 1.1
Slowdown in Soviet Industrial Production, 1952-55

Sector	1952 (actual)	1955 (plan)	1955 (actual)
Cotton Textiles*	5,044.0	6,267	5,905.0
Wool Textiles*	190.5	271	252.3
Silk Textiles*	224.6	573	525.8
Knitted Underwear**	234.9	382	346.5
Knitted Outerwear**	63.5	88	85.1
Hosiery†	584.9	777	772.2
Leather Footwear†	237.7	318	274.3
Sewing Machines††	804.5	2,615	1,610.9
Bicycles††	1,650.4	3,445	2,883.8
Motorcycles††	104.4	225	244.5
Watches/Clocks††	10,486.0	22,000	19,705.0
Radios/TVs††	1,331.9	4,527	4,024.6
Refrigerators††		330	151.4

*Million meters. ** Million units. †Million pairs. †† thousand units.
Source: Nove 1969, 325.

In May 1957, Khrushchev drastically reorganized both state and party machinery in the field of economic administration by initiating the *sovnarkhozy* reform, which replaced about twenty five major economic ministries with 105 regional economic units under the direction of newly created Councils of the National Economy. In most cases a separate *sovnarkhozy* was created for each province. In each of the fifteen republics, the regional *sovnarkhozy* were made subordinate to the republic authorities, and each republic's Council of Ministers supervised its *sovnarkhozy*. At the national level, coordination was placed in the hands of the *Gosplan* (State Planning Committee). These measures stripped power from central ministries and transferred responsibility for economic coordination to regional (and to some extent, local) bodies.

Table 1.2
Soviet Grain Production, 1953-62
(millions of metric tons)

Year	Total Grain Harvest	Basic Virgin Areas*	Rest of the Country
1953	82.5	26.9	55.6
1954	85.6	37.3	48.3
1955	106.8	27.7	79.1
1956	127.6	63.3	64.3
1957	105.0	38.1	66.9
1958	141.2	58.4	82.8
1959	125.9	55.3	70.6
1960	134.4	59.2	75.2
1961	138.0	51.3	86.7
1962	148.2	56.4	91.8

* Includes Kazakhstan, the Urals, Siberia, and part of the Volga region.
Source: Schwartz 1965, 107 & 131.

Agricultural Reforms

Khrushchev emphasized agricultural reforms. Immediately after Stalin's death, the new leadership lowered the tax burden and delivery quotas for peasants, and raised procurement prices for agricultural products. During succeeding years campaigns were intensified to manufacture chemical fertilizers and expand agricultural production in the virgin lands. In March 1955, *kolkhozes* were allowed to decide their production targets, and the planners' role was restricted to specifying the delivery obligations of the *kolkhozes*. Another important development was the amalgamation of *kolkhozes* into state farms. As a result, the number of *kolkhozes* dropped to 69,100 in 1958 from 125,000 in 1950. The number of state farms, on the other hand, grew from 4,857 at the end of 1953 to 6,002 in 1958. While in 1953 only 18.2 million hectares of land were sown, the area was increased to 97.43 million hectares in 1965. Also, while state and collective farms employed only 2.6 million people in 1953, the number increased to 8.6 million in 1965 (see Nove 1969, 336). Despite these changes and despite a massive campaign to send over 200,000 workers to the countryside to boost agricultural production, the harvest of 1960 fell short of expectations. By 1964, Khrushchev's seven-year crash program of agricultural development came to an end, but agricultural production had risen only 14 percent over its 1958 level, falling almost a third below its target level. Table 1.2 shows that, compared to 1953-55, bumper production was recorded in 1956 and 1958, but that otherwise production remained as low as before, except for 1962.

Another notable institutional change in agriculture was that in 1958 one of the basic features of the Stalinist system, the Machine Tractor Stations (MTS), was eliminated. Previously, government-owned MTSs controlled services of tractors, grain combines and similar heavy equipment on which *kolkhozes* were depended. Khrushchev also ordered the elimination of required compulsory deliveries from the private gardens of the peasants.

Reforms in the Incentive System

Khrushchev was preoccupied with raising labor productivity. In 1956, the Stalinist laws providing criminal penalties to freeze workers in their jobs were revoked, minimum wages and pensions were raised, and an effort was made to shorten the work week. Although the basic six-day workweek was retained, during 1957-58 a seven-hour workday was introduced generally and a six-hour workday was introduced primarily for underground or especially hazardous occupations. Khrushchev also revised the wage system in the economy. During Stalin's period, thousands of pay-scales were in vogue in factories, industries, ministries, and departments. The new wage system sought to simplify the complex wage structure by replacing it with a small number of scales, so that workers of a given occupation could receive the same wages regardless of where they were employed. The whole policy package was aimed at raising the wages of the lowest paid workers; making the wage system more effective in providing the needed incentives for higher worker productivity; and ensuring a steady rise in labor productivity. As a result, while the industrial worker's average annual income was 925 rubles in 1950, in 1961 it stood at 1,240 rubles (see Schwartz 1965, 101). This increase in workers' wages and salaries significantly reduced the inequality of income characteristic of the Stalinist command economy. According to Bergson (1989, 79), inequality in wages and salaries had been extraordinarily great in 1946, and by 1956, it had markedly decreased. As Table 1.3 shows, such decline continued throughout the Khrushchevian period, and continued until 1968.

Simultaneously, Khrushchev set up Communist Party control commissions in industrial and trade enterprises to check on the punctual fulfillment of delivery schedules and production quotas by enterprises. These commissions watched management decisions and illegal actions within the enterprises and reported to outside authorities. Khrushchev also initiated a number of measures to motivate workers and management to increase efficiency, reduce production costs, and make efficient use of productive resources. Success indicators used to determine managerial bonuses in non-priority industries were changed. Instead of reaching or exceeding output targets, bonuses were made dependent primarily upon a manager's ability to produce at lower costs. Attention was also focused upon managerial ability to turn out high quality goods, to deliver commodities on time, and other similar qualitative aspects of managerial work.

Table 1.3
Decile Ratios of Wage Earners and Salaried Workers in the Soviet Union, 1946-72

Year	Decile Ratios*	Year	Decile Ratios
1946	7.24	1964	3.69
1956	4.44	1966	3.26
1959	4.21	1968	2.83
1961	4.02	1972	3.10

*All sectors, monthly earnings.
Source: Bergson 1989, 79.

Khrushchev's period also enhanced the trade union's prestige and power. With the *sovnarkhozy* and the elimination of central ministries, it became necessary to restructure the trade unions, along with the *sovnarkhozy* in each area. Khrushchev expanded the power of the local union factory committees and established a permanent production conference in each enterprise with the power to exert worker influence upon the management of the plant. The factory trade union committees were even empowered to review, and if necessary to revoke or change, decisions on disputes between individual workers and management. Under the new provisions, all important decisions of the State Committee on Labor and Wages, which was responsible for basic labor policy, had to be approved by the national trade union leadership. Enterprise management was prohibited from firing any worker and appointing any new worker without the union's consent. Trade unions had the right to call for removal or punishment of production executives who failed to carry out obligations under collective agreements. Trade unions were also consulted over a wide range of other matters, from distribution of bonuses to the establishment of wage categories for different jobs. Trade union members representing workers were elected at general meetings of the work force.

Reforms in Prices, Wages and Finance

Khrushchev wanted to eliminate arbitrary bureaucratic control and stressed scientific calculation of costs for agricultural production and economic incentives to the farmers. He proposed a wage system that would permit collective farmers to receive monthly monetary payments. Previously, the same agricultural product could have three different prices; one for selling it to the state as a part of the compulsory delivery quota; another if it was an above-quota sale; and still another price if it was delivered to the MTS as a payment-in-kind. Khrushchev replaced this system by the principle of the same price for the same product grown in the same area. Thus, different agricultural products in different zones had different prices. Table 1.4 shows the indexes of average state prices paid for procurement from collective farms, collective farmers, and other workers and employees. Khrushchev instituted the same wholesale prices for both state and collective farms for purchasing farm machinery and other production essentials. Previously collective farms had been charged much higher prices than state farms for essentials of agricultural production.

Table 1.4
Indexes of Farm Prices Paid by the Soviet Government, 1954-58
(1952=100)

Product	1954	1956	1958
All farm products	207	251	296
All crops	171	207	203
Wheat	752	647	621
Rye	730	625	1047
Corn	564	572	819
Rice	243	887	957
Cotton	102	114	106
Flax fiber	166	213	239
Sugar beets	111	229	219
Sunflowers	626	928	774
Potatoes	369	814	789
All livestock	307	371	546
Cattle	476	508	1147
Hogs	786	976	1156
Milk/milk products	289	334	404
Eggs	135	155	297
Wool	146	246	352

Source: Schwartz 1965, 120.

Khrushchev also tried to reform the credit and banking system in the economy. The State Bank was separated from the Ministry of Finance, and entrusted with increased powers to extend credit to financially efficient enterprises and take appropriate measures to penalize those enterprises that incurred debts. In April 1959, the investment banking system that existed since 1932, was replaced by an all-union finance and investment bank, *Stroibank*, which took over most of its functions. The *Stroibank* was also entrusted with the responsibility to disburse state grants for capital investment in state enterprises, as well as the issuance of credit to collective farms, cooperatives, and other borrowers.

Evaluation of Khrushchev's Reform Measures

During his seven years of momentous rule, Khrushchev made decisive and bold attempts to reform the Stalinist economy. His period was marked by a remarkable improvement in the consumer sector and a significant decrease in income inequality, a characteristic feature of the Stalinist period. Greater availability of consumer goods, increase in housing construction and extension of educational and medical facilities were some of the hallmarks of this period. Gregory and Stuart (1986, 134) point out that during 1956-60 per capita consumption grew at a rate of 4.0 percent, and growth in housing construction exceeded growth of the urban population demanding housing. While in 1951 the housing growth rate was 2.6 percent, in 1959 the growth rate reached 5.9 percent. During Stalin's period, income inequality in the Soviet Union exceeded that of the United States, but during Khrushchev's period the situation improved remarkably. The average wage of the top 10 percent of wage-earners exceeded that of the bottom 10 percent by a factor of only 4.4 (343). Khrushchev also raised average wages. Increases in workers' income naturally threatened the market price; to keep the price level steady, price increases in food and drink items were balanced by cuts in prices of relatively abundant manufactured goods. Changes in the price structure improved the overall situation, but many anomalies remained. The process of price-fixing was not altered. As Nove (1969, 348) wrote, "there was still insufficient inducement to produce goods in demand or of high quality, or modern types of machinery."

Most Sovietologists conclude that Khrushchevian policies were erratic.[40] Khrushchev more than once announced a bold policy innovation from which he later retreated. For example, his dramatic reform of Soviet education in 1958 was repealed before he left power in 1964. Anticipating a labor shortage, Khrushchev in 1958 replaced the goal of a universal ten-year secondary education for all Soviets, with a goal of universal education through the eighth grade. In 1964 the decision was reversed. The much celebrated decentralization of economic administration, the *sovnarkhoz* reform of 1957, was abandoned in 1961. Khrushchev soon discovered that the *sovnarkhozy* was too small for efficient operation of the economy and merged the former one hundred or so *sovnarkhozy* into less than fifty. In 1961, seventeen Councils of Coordination and Planning were set up, each given wide powers over a large economic region, consisting, on average, of six or seven ordinary *sovnarkhozy*. Thus, the transfer of the *sovnarkhozy*'s power to the bureaucratic system was completed. Politically, Khrushchev initiated the most sweeping reform in the Soviet Union up to the 1960s. The whole Communist Party at all levels—local, provincial and republican—was vertically divided into two separate sections: an industrial communist party, exclusively dealing with industry;

and an agricultural communist party, concerned with agricultural issues. Such an organization actually resulted in three economic bureaus, one for industry and construction, one for agriculture, and one for the chemical and light industries. But soon Khrushchev had to eliminate the bifurcation of the CPSU in order to quell widespread criticism of party colleagues.

The most troublesome inconsistencies of Khrushchev's reforms, however, were manifested in his economic policies. For example, officially government gave priority to light over heavy industry, and promised that in two to three years Soviet industry would annually produce a million television sets, a half-million vacuum cleaners, over three hundred thousand refrigerators. Yet the actual economic indicators demonstrated an unmistakable priority to the producers' goods sector. In 1963, observes Schwartz (1965, 125), Soviet heavy industry accounted for almost 75 percent of all Soviet industrial production, while in 1952, Stalin's last full year of power, the corresponding share of heavy industry was less than 70 percent. In the field of capital investment, *Stroibank*'s authority was further consolidated by November 1959. Also in 1963, Khrushchev abandoned the seventh five-year plan, two years before the period's end, and redrew plans for 1964 and 1965.

Table 1.5
Annual Soviet Industrial Production Growth Rates, 1954 and 1958-64
(annual percentage increases)

Year	All Industry	Heavy Industry	Consumer Goods
1954	13.0	14	13
1958	10.0	11	8
1959	11.0	12	10
1960	10.0	11	7
1961	9.0	10	7
1962	9.5	11	7
1963	8.5	10	5
1964	7.5 *	10	2

* first half.
Source: Schwartz 1965, 124.

Consequently, growth of Soviet economy actually began to decline and numerous imbalances in the development of the country began to surface. For example, the rate of capital return in industry declined, reserves began to grow faster than production, and enterprises were having difficulty getting necessary inputs. While during the 1954-59 period the annual growth of agricultural production was more than 7.0 percent, it fell to 1.5 percent to 2.0 percent during 1960-64. In the agricultural sector, per capita production remained the same. Economic performance in the consumption sector was very strong in the late fifties. As Table 1.5 indicates, the rate of growth in the production of consumption goods ranged from 8 percent to 13 percent during this period. In the 1960s, the growth rate fell, however, to 7 percent, then 5 percent, and finally (in the first half of 1964) to only 2 percent. The rate of growth in heavy industry remained double -digit throughout the Khrushchev years, although, as Table 1.5 indicates, it dropped a bit in the late fifties and early sixties compared to the reference year of 1964. The all-industry growth rate, which combines performance in both heavy industry and in consumption, was 10 percent or above between 1954 and 1960, and ranged between 7.5 percent in the early sixties.[41]

Internationally, Khrushchev's de-Stalinization policy backfired; it fed East European unrest that culminated in revolts in Poland and Hungary. The conservatives used the revolts to press their demands for moderation of the de-Stalinization campaign and to curb Khrushchev's power. Khrushchev was ousted from power in 1964. With the sad end of his turbulent, momentous, and highly optimistic era, the dream of the Soviets to overtake the United States in a short time also came to a grinding halt.[42]

KOSYGIN'S REFORMS (1965)

A new turning point in Soviet economic policy came in 1965, immediately after Khrushchev was replaced by a collective leadership headed by Leonid Brezhnev (1906-82) as general secretary of the CPSU and Aleksei Kosygin (1904-81) as the chairman of the Council of Ministers. Declining overall economic growth rates and stagnation in agriculture were the main concerns of the new leadership. Khrushchevian reforms, such as weakening central control over the economy, reducing the power of bureaucracy, and scattering planning activities among regional authorities, were visualized by the new leadership as real or imagined chaos (Hewett 1988, 230). Less than a year after Khrushchev was unseated, Kosygin put forth a far-reaching proposal for reform.[43] The new leadership reversed some of Khrushchev's institutional changes. By October 1965, Khrushchev's bifurcation of the Communist Party and the *sovnarkhozy* reform were eliminated, central ministries were reestablished, and the stage was set for further economic reforms.

Reforms in Enterprise Management

Other than the structural changes aimed at recentralizing authority, Kosygin's reforms focused primarily on changes in planning and management at the enterprise level. To encourage enterprise managers, and thereby to enhance enterprise efficiency, Kosygin proposed to increase power and responsibility of enterprise managers by curbing the power of supervisory authorities and redesigning the incentive structure. Enterprise managers were granted more latitude in deciding how to utilize resources, and the number of success indicators was reduced. The only indicator handed down to the enterprises was the total wage fund. Kosygin also made clear that it, too, would be discontinued once the supply of consumers goods was adequately increased. The enterprise manager was also granted the right to determine which type of pay, that is, time rates or piece rates, was to be used (see Katz 1972, 136).

On the output side of the enterprises' operations, Kosygin brought about a major reform. Two success indicators came to the forefront: profitability (defined as the ratio of profits to fixed and working capital) and sales. While the sales indicator was expected to prevent profitability from rising at the expense of the quality of products, the profitability indicator was assumed to prevent production at any cost. These success indicators, in turn, governed the rate of deductions from enterprise profits into three funds: a material incentive fund for the payment of bonuses; a development fund in which the enterprise invested at its own will; and a social-cultural fund for worker housing and welfare. The distribution was done as follows: after meeting the first claims on enterprise profits, namely payment of the capital charge, differential rent, and interest on bank credits, deductions from the remaining profit into the three funds was made in accordance with the norms.

Hewett (1988, 231) points out that while previously thirty five to forty obligatory targets were handed down from above to the individual enterprises, Kosygin reduced the number of targets to only eight. The new targets were output of principal products (in physical units), sales volume, total profits, the rate of profit on capital, the total wage fund, the level of payments into the state budget, capital investments from centrally provided funds, specific tasks linked to introduction of new technology, and allocation of the most important material supplies. Moreover, Kosygin's reforms made a minor breakthrough in introducing cost accountability in state enterprises by levying about a 6 percent charge on the undepreciated value of assets. By making enterprise bonuses subject to achievement of target profits, state enterprises were enticed to undertake more ambitious production plans. The use of sales and profits as success indicators, along with the emphasis on reduction or elimination of subsidies, forced the enterprises to be more responsible in terms of financial accountability. The 1965 reforms also called for amalgamation of enterprises into large associations. Besides promoting research and development, amalgamation of enterprises was expected to promote *khozraschet* (financial accountability) in the whole industrial sector.

Reforms in Agriculture and Prices

Kosygin also tried to reform the agricultural sector. Following Khrushchev, he raised purchasing prices for agricultural products, lowered farmer tax obligations, and broadened the scope of farming on family plots. Kosygin sought to introduce a new form of agricultural planning to reduce administrative interference with collective and state farms. He fixed purchase prices for planned agricultural output for five years, and for many products the prices remained unchanged throughout this period. Moreover, agricultural products delivered in excess of the plan targets were sold for one and a half times the ordinary price.

Kosygin also sought to reform prices. He centralized the price-setting functions for the whole economy in *Goskomtsen* and revised most of the industrial prices. *Goskomtsen* stressed enterprise profitability by requiring full accounting of costs and linking prices to the goals of the reforms. However, Kosygin's price reforms ignored the possibility of a contradiction between central plan directives and the smooth functioning of prices.

Performance of the Economy

Kosygin's reforms received favorable evaluations from many Sovietologists. As a result of his agricultural reforms, the rate of growth of agricultural production almost doubled. In the period from 1966 to 1970, the volume of agricultural output increased at a rate of 21 percent above that of the previous five-year period. Such accelerated growth of agricultural production, in turn, allowed a substantial increase in the rate of production in light industries based on agricultural raw materials. As a result, production of consumer goods grew faster in 1966-70 than production in the heavy industry sector. All these significantly affected the growth of national income. During the eighth plan (1966-70) period, the rate of overall Soviet GNP growth increased to 5.3 percent while during the last plan period the growth was 4.9 percent (see Table 1.6). In the agricultural sector, the growth rate was 4.2 percent, while it was 2.4 percent during the preceding period. During the same period the consumption growth rate rose to 5.1 percent up from 4.0 percent during the previous plan period (1961-65). Growth in the industrial sector declined slightly from 6.6 percent in 1961-65 to 6.2 percent during the Eighth plan period. Overall, in terms of national income, labor productivity, and real per capita income, the performance of the Soviet economy during this period was somewhat better than in the immediate past. Hewett (1988, 308) shows that compared to the period of 1961-65, the period of 1966-72 also witnessed an increase in labor productivity (from 4.6 percent to 5.8 percent) and per capita income of Soviet people (from 3.5 percent to 5.5 percent).

Table 1.6
Soviet GNP by Sector of Origin (Factor Cost), 1956-70
(1970 prices)

Sector	1956-60	1961-65	1966-70
Industry	8.9	6.6	6.2
Civilian	11.4	7.9	6.9
Light	7.0	2.4	8.0
Agriculture	4.1	2.4	4.2
GNP	5.8	4.9	5.3
Consumption	5.4	4.0	5.1

Source: Wright 1980, 126.

According to Aganbegyan (1988a, 58), the whole reform movement of Kosygin was carried out without incorporating the activities of the ministries of planning and the financial authorities. Administrative methods remained predominant, even intensified, among the central economic institutions and branch ministries. With the progress of reforms, new departments and institutions expanded the size of bureaucracy. No significant effort was made to accelerate scientific and technological progress, or to increase efficiency or restructure the capital investment programs. Above all, Kosygin's reforms were not reinforced by corresponding measures in social life: no effort was made to democratize industrial management or to open up society. As Aganbegyan remarks, "working people and farmers had no role in working out the plans of their enterprises, or the ways that funds for incentives were to be used." Therefore, Kosygin's reforms remained, "a foreign body in the existing system of economic and social relations" and was "ultimately suppressed by the environment and assimilated by prevailing attitudes" (63). Still, Gorbachev (1988a, 419) maintains that Kosygin's reforms "changed the situation in the country for better." The economic and scientific potential of the Soviet Union increased, the defense capacity was strengthened, and the standard of living of the people improved. But untimely suspension of Kosygin's reforms, Gorbachev regrets, substantially retarded the growth of the Soviet economy.

Many Sovietologists, however, remain unconvinced that Kosygin's reforms constituted a sufficient departure from the practices and fabrics of command economy to really solve its dysfunctional consequences. Nove (1969, 23), for example, maintains that price revisions carried out under Kosygin's reform failed to "provide the scarcity signals, or the cash flow to enterprises, required to achieve the intended autonomy of industrial enterprises." Instead, he complains, the "comfortable practice of centrally allocating goods in chronic excess demand had been maintained and even strengthened." Undoubtedly, these inadequacies and inconsistencies in reform measures, coupled with continued centralized, administrative direction of the economy that hardly clarified the roles and responsibilities of enterprises, central planning, the respective ministries, and political bodies, resulted in the ultimate failure of Kosygin's reforms.[44]

CONCLUDING REMARKS

The preceding discussion leads us to two main conclusions. First, socialist literature provides a strong decentralized and democratic strand of thought that can serve as a rich arsenal of guidance for contemporary reformers in socialist countries. Writings of decentralized socialists, like Bernstein, Bukharin, Kautsky, Luxemburg, and Lange, as explained above, demonstrate not only the compatibility of democracy with socialism, but also the need for democracy to realize a socialist economy and society. Second, actual practice of socialism in the Soviet Union, as explained above, demonstrates decentralized and democratic approaches to the socialist economy. The periods of the NEP, Khrushchev, and Kosygin were characterized by more (compared to centralized approaches of socialism as will be explained in the next chapter) economic decentralization and political liberalization. Although, in the context of the Soviet Union, no correlation can be established between centralization/decentralization and better/poor economic performance, it can be safely concluded that the decentralized periods not only worked reasonably well, they were generally associated with higher standards of living and better fulfillment of the higher ideals of socialism: freedom, democracy, and rule of law. A fuller and comparative conclusion will follow in the next chapter.

NOTES

1. See Griffith 1924; Lindemann 1983; Berki 1975; Elliott 1976, 1984; Wilczynski 1970; Jameson & Wilber 1981; Pejovich 1987; Almond & Roselle 1989; Jones 1983; Shoup 1975; Welsh 1975; Montias 1970.

2. Elliott (1976) made a similar categorization.

3. Some scholars maintain that the only logical and useful distinctions between capitalistic and socialistic economic systems can be found in these two criteria, and all other institutional and behavioral dimensions are virtual offsprings of these (see Wiles 1962, 3). But there are others who believe that such institutional features serve at best as necessary, but not sufficient, bases for comparing socialist economic systems. For many Marxists, the essence of the socialist system has to do with the dictatorship of the proletariat consistent with the interests of the mass of the working population (see Fenichel & Kahn 1981, 813-24; Djilas 1955). Non-Marxist observers, by contrast, generally give priority to the institutions for making and coordinating economic decisions over ownership and control of productive facilities.

4. Based on the relations of production, that is, the way in which the producing and controlling classes relate to one another in the production process, Szymanski (1979) developed eight basic forms of economic systems ranging from state slavery as existed in the ancient Greek city-states to state capitalism as demonstrated in socialist countries where ownership and control of the means of production have been placed under state control and markets are replaced by the mechanism of central planning. On the basis of concentration of power in the Communist Party, ownership of means of production, central economic planning and distribution of national income, Wilczynski (1970, 21-25) developed four models of socialist economy: the bureaucratic centralized, the planometric centralist, selectively decentralized, and the supplemented market models. The first two provide highly centralized solutions, while the third and forth represent decentralized approaches of socialist economic system. Based on ten "system-traits," Montias (1970) developed four different models of the existing communist systems: mobilization, centralized, decentralized, and market socialism.

5. A partial list of scholars that use this approach includes the following: Dickinson 1933, 1939; Lerner 1934, 1944; Lange 1938, 1958, 1972; Baran 1952;

Baran and Sweezy 1966; Dobb 1955, 1966, 1969; Elliott 1976, 1985; Selukcy 1972, 1979; Sik 1976; Drewnowski 1961; and Roberts 1971.

6. See Sik 1967; Selukcy 1979; Liberman 1971; Nove 1983; Harrington 1989; Miller & Estrin 1989; Lange 1952.

7. The author discussed different approaches to centralization and decentralization in detail elsewhere. See Dowlah 1990a, 33-43.

8. According to Marschak (1973, 34-35), this approach in which the model of laissez-faire provides the guiding thread, also constituted the starting point for the classic debate of the thirties on the possibility of adequate calculation in centrally planned economies.

9. In Drewnowski's first degree market economy, prices are fixed by the state but quantities of supply are determined by consumers' preferences. In his second-degree market economy, the "next adjoining range of variables" are transferred from the state to the dual-influence zone. By adjoining variables he refers to "the quantities produced of particular consumer goods, the quantities of resources (excluding new investments) used in their production, and the distribution of resources among particular plants." In such a socialist market economy, presumably the role of the state zone will be squeezed to accommodate a larger role of dual-influence zone. In second-degree market model the aggregate volume of consumption goods and the quantities of investment goods remain in the state zone. But variables transferred to the dual-influence zone will be determined by adjusting production to consumers' demands and maximizing profits in the whole consumers' goods sector. Drewnowski's third-degree market economy refers to an arrangement in which "determination of the pattern of new investments" concerning both consumer and finished goods are transferred from the state to the dual-influence zone, but "aggregate quantities of produced consumer goods, of resources used, and of new investments remain in the state zone."

10. Some scholars, however, maintain that Marx went further than providing just a "pre-analytical vision" (Schumpeter 1950) for future socialist society. Bettleheim (1975, 13-30), for example, asserts that Marx "provided the conceptual tools by means of which the transition can be brought about, and supplied the scientific theory of transition". Similarly, Wiles (1962, 350) maintains that although Marx did not write a book titled *After the Revolution*, he indeed left a "blueprint for socialism" that dwelt on institutional and organizational transformations for post-revolutionary society. Based on *Capital, Critique of the Gotha Program, and Anti-Duhring*, Brus (1972, 12-41) derives the following five specific suggestions of Marx and Engels in regard to the functioning of future socialist economy:

(1) direct, ex ante, regulation of the social distribution of labor; (2) direct determination of labor input coefficients, for both living and embodied labor (a crystallization of labor time found in capital goods); (3) equilibrium of supply and demand in physical units; (4) the distribution of social product in accordance with the satisfaction of general needs, and at the same time the allocation of the fund intended for individual consumption according to the amount of labor contributed; (5) centralization of saving and investment decisions.

11. Although Marx was the most prominent socialist thinker, he was not the first. Socialist thinking and socialist movements were sporadic but persistent on the European continent, especially since the Industrial Revolution of the eighteenth century. Political thinkers and philosophers such as Robert Owen (1771-1859), Charles Fourier (1772-1837), Pierre-Joseph Proudhon (1809-65), Jean-Jacques Rousseau (1712-78), Comte de Saint-Simon (1760-1825), August Comte (1798-1857), John Stuart Mill (1806-73) and Louis Blanc (1811-82) propounded socialist doctrines prior to Marx and Engels. Moreover, historical records amply show that movements like those of the Weavers in Silesia, the Chartists in England, and other not-so-prominent working class movements often jolted the continent of Europe throughout the eighteenth and the nineteenth century.

12. Marx wrote in *Gotha Program* (1973, 17), "What we have to deal with here is a communist society, not as it has developed on its own foundations, but, on the contrary, just as it emerges from capitalist society; which is thus in every respect, economically, morally and intellectually, still stamped with the birthmarks of the old society from whose womb it emerges."

13. Marx (1973, 26) wrote, "Between capitalist and communist society lies the period of the revolutionary transformation of the one into the other. There corresponds to this also a political transition period in which the state can be nothing but the revolutionary dictatorship of the proletariat."

14. In such a society of material plenty, Engels claimed in *Anti-Duhring* (1939, 307), "The interference of the state power in social relations becomes superfluous in one sphere after another, and then ceases of itself. The government of persons is replaced by the administration of things." By solving the "riddle of history," such a society "organizes production anew on the basis of a free and equal association of the producers," and places the `whole state machine "in the museum of antiquities, side by side with the spinning wheel and the bronze axe" (quoted in Lenin 1969, 15).

15. Marx (1977, 216) wrote:

Therefore the worker himself constantly produces objective wealth, in the form of capital, an alien power that dominates and exploits him; and the capitalist just as constantly produces labor-power, in the form of a subjective source of wealth which is abstract, exists merely in the physical body of the worker, and is separated from its own means of objectification and realization; in short, the capitalist produces the worker as a wage-laborer. The incessant reproduction, this perpetuation of the worker, is the absolutely necessary condition for capitalist production.

The capitalist process of production, therefore, seen as a total, connected process, i.e., a process of reproduction, produces not only commodities, not only surplus-value, but it also produces and reproduces the capital relation itself; on the one hand the capitalist, on the other the wage-laborer (724).

16. As Marx (1973, 17-18) put it:

the individual producer receives back from society—after the deductions [for investment, depreciation, and social needs] have been made—exactly what he gives to it . . . his individual quantum of labor . . . He receives a certificate from society that he has furnished such and such amount of labor (after deducting his labor for the common funds), and with this certificate he draws from the social stock of the means of consumption as much as costs the same amount of labor.

Because of this market-like quid pro quo exchange process,

Here obviously the same principle prevails as that which regulates the exchange of commodities, as far as this is exchange of equal values. Content and form are changed, because under the altered circumstances no one can give anything except his labor, and . . . nothing can pass to the ownership of individuals except individual means of consumption. But as far as distribution of the latter among the individual producers is concerned, the same principle prevails as in the exchange of commodity-equivalents: a given amount of labor in one form is exchanged for a given amount of labor in another form.

17. Scholars, however, differ in their interpretations of Marx's position on the social division of labor and supersession of scarcity. Elliott (1980), for example, maintains that Marx clearly stipulated abolition of scarcity, but he understood scarcity as a "resource limitation relative to specified standards in particular socio-historical circumstances," not as limited resources relative to all conceivable wants. Elliott says Marx envisaged abundance or the potentiality of supersession of scarcity in terms of "basics or necessities, that will be capable of realization at normal or sufficient levels for all members of the society," and stipulated the principle, from each according to his ability and to each according to his needs, only for a distant future society of full-blown communism.

18. As Engels writes in *Anti-Duhring* (1939, 311), the "proletariat seizes the state power, transforms the means of production in the first instance into state property" and "the seizure of the means of production by society puts an end to commodity production." Engels, however, said, "State ownership of productive forces is not the solution of the conflict, but it contains within itself the formal means, the key to the solution" (306-7).

19. It is indeed ironic that although Marx wanted to free society from all kinds of inequality, exploitations, and miseries, most states that claim to practice his doctrine have demonstrated a rather contemptuous commitment to basic human rights and values of freedom and democracy. Indeed, much of the confusion that cloaks the Marxian stand on freedom, democracy, and the state has its roots in the practices of the so-called socialist states. Our concern, however, is not to pinpoint those deficiencies, but rather, to explore the classical Marxian concepts of freedom, democracy, and the state.

20. In the *Communist Manifesto* (1848), Marx asserted, "In place of the old bourgeois society, with its classes and class antagonisms, we shall have an association in which the free development of each is the condition for the free development of all". Also in the *Critique of the Gotha Program* (1973), Marx declared "freedom is when the state is transformed from an organ that is dominant

over society into an organ that is completely subordinate."

21. In *Anti-Duhring*, Engels (1939,307) wrote, "The first act in which the state really comes forward as the representative of society as a whole—the taking possession of the means of production in the name of society—is at the same time, its last independent act as a state."

22. Elliott and Scott (1986, 171) remark that in *The Civil War In France*, Marx examined the Paris Commune not only in its own right, but also "as the prototype of proletarian governments emerging in future revolutions."

23. In *Paris Commune* Marx emphasizes the need for bottom-up as opposed to top-down hierarchy, substantial role in decision-making by local and workers' organizations, and a more, rather than less, democratic process for control of political leaders than under capitalism. These provisions, adumbrated, for example, in *The Civil War in France*, imply a certain amount of autonomy for the associated producers in factories and localities as compared to planners at the center of the socialist system. To put the matter somewhat differently, Marx's critique of market processes suggests abolition of the autonomy of private capitalist producers and the reduction in autonomy of producers as compared, for example, with market-oriented proprietary economy. But his support of democracy and critique of hierarchy leads him to accept, especially in his political conceptualization of the future society, a substantial degree of decentralized decision-making, especially as compared to the theory and practice of centralized socialism in the twentieth century.

24. Subsequent developments in the context of decentralized or market socialism will be taken up in connection with evaluation of *perestroika* as a strategy for transition to decentralized and democratic socialism in Chapter 6.

25. Lange (174) also comments on the extent the decisions implied in the plan can be centralized or decentralized in a socialist economy. He recommends two criteria for determining the decentralization that economic planning requires: the possibility of decentralization, and the necessity of decentralization. Planning, Lange asserts, should be

decentralized so far as it is possible to set up economic incentives such that the decisions of the decentralized units are the same as the decisions which would be made centrally. Planning must be decentralized in all cases where the central decision responds to a situation too late, in such cases central planning becomes fictitious (178-79).

26. As he asserts:

Just as private property in the means of production is irreconcilable with cooperative work in large industry, so cooperative or social ownership in the means of production is irreconcilable with small production. This requires, as we have seen, private ownership in the means of production. The aim of socialism is to place the worker in possession of the necessary means of production. The expropriation of the means of production in small industry would mean merely the senseless proceeding of taking them from their present owner and returning them again to him (cited in Howe 1986, 107).

27. In *Reform or Revolution* she asserts:

democracy has become superfluous or annoying to the bourgeoisie, it is on the contrary necessary and indispensable to the working class. It is necessary to the working class because it creates the political forms (autonomous administration, electoral rights, etc.) which will serve the proletariat as fulcrums in its task of transforming bourgeois society (cited in Howe 1986, 142).

28. "Events," observes Nove (1969, 83), "rather than the central committee, provided a potent means of persuasion" to the Communist leadership to change the course of the country.

29. The concept of planning during the NEP period did not envisage tight state control as was later the case during the Stalinist period. NEP planning, instead, confined its role to providing control figures, which were "partly a forecast and partly a guide for strategic investment decisions," and the whole planning mechanism was designed to achieve some kind of "balance of the national economy" (Nove 1969, 101).

30. Nove (1969, 97) explains how the NEP's economic mechanisms for industrial management worked through different methods:

(1) Methods of an economic character: the financing of industry, the organization of industrial credit, price policy etc. (2) Methods of an administrative character: appointment and dismissal of responsible officials of trusts and other trading-and-industrial units, the transfer of material resources from one branch of industry to another, from enterprise to enterprise, and so forth, in conformity with the industrial plan. (3) Method of production-planning character: the drafting of production and disposal plans, inspection and checking on their execution, ensuring the conformity of the industrial plan with the general plan, etc.

31. Private trade in the Soviet economy during 1922-23 constituted 78 percent of all retail trade. In the field of wholesale trade, however, private trade controlled 14 percent of purely wholesale trade and 50 percent of mixed wholesale-retail trade, while the cooperative sector controlled 10 percent and the state sector controlled only 7 percent. In terms of retail trade the share of cooperatives jumped from 368 million rubles during 1922-23 to 6,838 million rubles during 1926-27. During the same periods, the state sector's role was increased from 512 million rubles to 1,817 million rubles. More strikingly, the private sector including cooperatives produced 97.8 percent of total output during 1923-24, 97.4 percent during 1924-25, 97.5 percent during 1925-26, and 97.7 percent during 1926-27. Conversely, the state sector's contribution to total output was only 2.2 percent, 2.6 percent, 2.5 percent, and 2.3 percent, respectively, during these periods. Quite naturally, the private sector, including cooperatives and small scale/craftsman industries employed bulk of the Soviet work force during the NEP period (based on Nove 1969, 103-5;

Dowlah 1990b, 72-74, 93-94).

32. As Lenin asserts:

Inasmuch as we are as yet unable to pass directly from small production to socialism, some capitalism is inevitable as the elemental product of small production and exchange; so that we must utilize capitalism (particularly by directing it into the channels of state capitalism) as the intermediary link between small production and socialism, as a means, a path, and a method of increasing the productive forces (quoted in Cliff 1979, 143).

33. Discarding the contradiction of communism and trade, Lenin (1974, 641) told the Third Congress of the Communist International:

Within the limits indicated, however, this is not at all dangerous for socialism as long as transport and large scale industry remain in the hands of the proletariat. On the contrary, the development of capitalism, controlled and regulated by the proletarian state (i.e., 'state' capitalism in this sense of the term) , is advantageous and necessary in an extremely devastated and backward small-peasant country.

34. As Lenin announced, "We shall make as many concessions as possible within limits, of course, of what the proletarian can concede and yet remain the ruling class." He asserted, "The proletarian state may, without changing its own nature, permit freedom to trade and the development of capitalism only within certain bounds, and only on condition that the state regulates (supervises, controls, determines the forms and methods of) private trade and capitalism" (Cliff 1979, 144). The meaning is clear: Capitalists would be allowed to participate in the economy as long as the state and state-supported public sector remains dominant in the economy.

35. According to Dobb (1948, 143), whereas in 1922, 65 percent of the managing personnel were officially classified as workers and 35 percent as nonworkers, a year later in 1923, these proportions were almost exactly reversed: only 36 percent were workers and 64 percent were nonworkers.

36. For details on the excruciating conditions of workers during the NEP period see Carr (1952, 317-31).

37. During the period of transition of power from Stalin to Khrushchev, Premier Malenkov announced his "New Course" in March 1953. Malenkov's New Course emphasized a rise in the standard of living of the people by increasing the supply of consumer goods, even at the expense of heavy industry. That turned the Stalinist strategy of building up heavy industry at the expense of the consumer sector literally upside down. Malenkov also announced a comprehensive series of price cuts in consumer goods and food, seeking also to achieve an abundance of food within a few years, and an improvement in the quality of goods. Another important measure taken during Malenkov's premiership was a 50 percent cut in the amount of compulsory state bonds that Soviet people were required to purchase annually. Malenkov supplemented the reduction in bond-purchase requirements with a 3

percent increase in average wages. These moves contributed to an increase in the purchasing power of the Soviet population. Ironically, the situation in the consumer market worsened further as the supply of goods available for sale hardly matched the increased purchasing power of the people.

Malenkov also spelled out drastic changes in the government's agricultural policy to decrease the agricultural tax, increase procurement prices for agricultural goods, and substantially reduce quotas for compulsory deliveries of garden produce to the state. As regards the industrial sector, Malenkov publicly acknowledged the disparity between the goods produced and the demands of the population and officially substantiated the fact that the economy was producing many unwanted goods. Malenkov attached greater priority to the production of consumer goods.

But Malenkov's reforms did not constitute a break with the Stalinist model. Neither did he propose any measure to change the course of Soviet political economy. His reform measures are largely considered to be derivatives of Stalin's thought as outlined by Stalin (1952). Indeed Malenkov promised continued expansion of heavy industry, too. He described heavy industry as "the foundation of foundations" of socialist economy.

The short-lived Malenkov period bears historical significance, at least for making a few new and remarkable beginnings. Never before had the poor living standards of the vast masses of the Soviet people figured so prominently in the agenda of the Soviet leadership. Never before did the Soviet leadership admit the debacle in Soviet agriculture and stress the need for reform. Most importantly, Malenkov's purge of KGB chief N. Beria was a great relief from the absolute power and terror of the secret police. But by 1957, Khrushchev was successful in ousting Malenkov from power.

38. Thirty years later, Gorbachev (1988a, 418) appreciated the moment by declaring at the seventieth anniversary of Bolshevik Revolution, "It required no small courage of the party and its leadership, headed by Khrushchev, to criticize the personality cult and its consequences, and to reestablish socialist legality."

39. He criticized the central ministries for producing great waste of resources, the build-up of parallel bureaucratic structures, incomplete utilization of existing productive facilities, irrational hauling and cross-hauling of freight, and a series of other economic losses. To eliminate these weaknesses, he ordered a major reorganization in economic administration and a partial decentralization of authority (see Schwartz 1965, 87-88).

40. After the fall of Khrushchev, a *Pravda* editorial on October 16, 1964 described Khrushchev's reforms as "harebrained scheming, immature conclusions and hasty decisions and actions divorced from reality ... unwillingness to take into account the achievements of science and practical experience." A careful examination of the policies and programs of Khrushchev, indeed, reveals that most of his reforms were "inconsistent and self-contradictory" (Draper 1988, 292), and "voluntaristic", "insufficiently thought-out" and simply "unrealistic" (Aganbegyan 1988a, 53-56).

41. According to the Joint Economic Committee Report of the U.S. Congress

(1982), Soviet GNP grew by 5.4 percent during 1955-65. Sectoral growths were as follows: industry 7.5 percent, agriculture 3.5 percent, services 4.0 percent, consumption 4.7 percent, and investment 9.1 percent.

42. Many Sovietologists, however, argue that Khrushchev's downfall in 1964 was at least in part based on declining economic growth in th early 1960s (see Gregory & Stuart 1990, 139-45).

43. It should be noted here that Kosygin's reforms were based on Professor Evsey Liberman's proposals. Briefly, "Libermanism" emphasized overall macroeconomic control of central planning, substantial flexibility, and autonomy for public enterprises and nonprivate profitability as a criterion for enterprise performance. For details see Liberman 1971.

44. Hewett (1988, 240-44) identifies three specific causes for the ultimate failure of the 1965 reforms. First, the Kosygin reform program gave the ministries contradictory responsibilities. It entrusted enterprises with greater autonomy and restricted ministries' control to eight indicators, but at the same time it held the ministries responsible for gross output. Second, expected enterprise performance was clearly unrealistic. Under the provisions of Kosygin's reforms, bonus payments were determined out of profits, but the formula was so faulty that if an enterprise economized on labor and lowered wages, that would automatically reduce available bonuses. Third, with the price system remaining crippled, the planning system was left to coordinate the economy. Because the ministries did not have the authority to interfere in the activities of the enterprises, the planning system failed to coordinate the nation's economic activities adequately. Prescriptions for limited indicators, therefore, did not work, and subsequently the number of indicators was substantially increased.

2

The Centralized Strand of Socialist Economic Thought and Practice

INTRODUCTION

This chapter examines the centralized strand of socialist economic thought and practice that derives inspiration from or attributes its origin and development to Marxian socialist vision. The following section traces the theoretical underpinnings of the centralized socialist model mainly in the writings of: Vladimir Lenin (1870-1924), the founding father of the Soviet socialist system; Joseph Stalin (1879-1953), architect and executor of the command model; Leon Trotsky (1879-1940), a leading participant of the "Great Industrialization Debate" of the twenties; Maurice Dobb, Paul Sweezy, and Charles Bettleheim, leading Western neo-Marxists, and Michal Kalecki, prominent Polish economist, who defended the planned, centralized model by challenging the rationale and viability of the decentralized (market) model of socialist economy. Section three contrasts the basic principles of the centralized and decentralized models, and then examines the pressures for centralization and decentralization in existing socialist economies. Sections four through six present empirical illustrations of centralized models drawing from the Soviet experiences of the War Communism period, the Stalinist Command Model, and Brezhnev's Bureaucratic Collectivism.

THEORETICAL UNDERPINNINGS OF CENTRALIZED SOCIALISM

A centralized model replaces market processes with central planning and vests ownership of the means of production in the public sector. As a result, private ownership and market processes in the economy are severely circumscribed, if not eliminated. In a centralized model, "economic control is exercised as a function of government" and "essential choices are made by a political agency representing the state" (Solo 1967, 11-12). Therefore, in a centralized model organization, allocation, production, and distribution of resources are carried out at governmental discretion. It is, observes Wiles (1962, 19-20), a form of socialist economy in which the "state takes over all main initiative and economic bureaucracy does administratively the things that the free market does automatically."[1]

The protagonists of the centralized model generally envisage Marxian prescriptions for the abolition of private ownership and establishment of public ownership of all means of production.[2] Opposing Walrasian/neoclassical analysis of consumer sovereignty or Lange type analysis of decentralized socialism, they advocate ex ante planning—macroeconomic decisions concerning allocation and distribution of a nation's resources taken by a central planning authority. Deriving their ideological inspiration largely from the Marxist critique of property, market, and money relations, these scholars argue that a socialist economic system is incompatible with private ownership, market, and money processes. Marx and Engels provided penetrating critiques of capitalist property and market relations on numerous occasions, so the advocates of central planning find no lack of quotations to cite.[3] According to them, Marx rejected market exchange as an effective guide to resource allocation and heavily emphasized planning in a post-capitalist economy. They maintain that centralized economic management is not inconsistent with an association of free producers, and that in a socialist economy, ownership of the means of production must be placed under state control. To facilitate the discussion, we shall utilize the four criteria we have developed earlier.

Level of Economic Development

In contrast to the Marxian schema of stages of economic development and the stand of many exponents of decentralized socialism, the centralized socialists view socialism as a substitute for, not a successor to, capitalism. According to them, socialism usually emerges in underdeveloped countries far back in the Marxian series, which in turn uses socialism for rapid industrialization and modernization of the economy. To them, the actual evolution of socialism is a matter of the interrelationship between underdevelopment and socialism (see Ellman 1984; Post & Wright 1989).[4] By denying the necessity of capitalism as the only historic route to industrialization, the centralized socialists "conceive of the major problems of socialist planning to bethose of fostering rapid economic growth" (Elliott 1985, 336). Therefore an overarching goals of socialism, for them, would presumably be the utilization of a socialist economic system and state apparatus for transforming economic underdevelopment into industrialization and economic development.

Lenin, the founder of the first socialist country in an underdeveloped economy, and the original architect of the above argument, developed the "law of uneven development" and the "law of combined development" to justify the emergence of socialism in economically less advanced countries. These laws, Bellis (1979, 27) argues, emphasize that capitalist social relations of production "interpenetrate and subordinate the pre-existing socio-economic forms" in backward countries like the

Soviet Union. Taking a similar position, Trotsky (1965) held that transition to socialism could be possible by consolidating two separate revolutions (one against feudalism, and the other against capitalism) into one. He argued that in a real historical setting a logical distinction between the two revolutionary stages could not be transposed into a chronological succession.

Trotsky envisaged rapid industrialization, a high rate of economic growth, and diversion of resources from the private sector for the development of the state sector. He called for sweeping measures for rapid industrialization in order to create the necessary foundations for a socialist transformation (see Day 1973; Dowlah 1990b, 191-200). Stalin, too, recommended dramatic measures to force the pace of industrialization; his preoccupation with forced collectivization and rapid industrialization virtually turned the Soviet Union into a forced-labor-camp economy (Shmelev & Popov 1989, 64). With hindsight, contemporary critics criticize such measures as reckless and unrealistic (Medvedev 1979, 64).

Emphasis on central direction and coordination of economic decisions by neo-Marxist writers stems from their overwhelming belief that a centralized socialist economic system is more capable of achieving rapid industrialization, full employment stability, and economic growth than its alternatives, especially in a pre-capitalistic economy, and can better protect society from regressing towards monopoly capitalism (Nuti 1986, 333).[5]

Markets and Planning

Centralized socialists, as mentioned above, take Marx's critique and condemnation of capitalist market relations literally, and thereby call for elimination of production for market exchange and emphasize ex ante planning, or conscious coordination and direction of the economy. To them, alienation of the individual can be overcome only when atomistic competition is replaced by a collective economy, characterized by an "economic plan as its expression" (Dobb 1970, 132). To them, men are free to the extent that they consciously control both nature and their social conditions of existence to suit their needs and abilities.

Centralized socialists are particularly critical of market processes and consumer sovereignty as envisaged by neoclassical/Walrasian analysis. Dobb (1970, 135), for example, maintains that neoclassical economists, because of their "particular and habitual modes of thought" and "perhaps by reason of their preoccupation with conditions of stationary equilibrium," are particularly unaware that prices perform many distinct functions in a socialist economy, not only one, as the neoclassical theory of equilibrium envisages. He criticized neoclassicals for their failure to realize that economic equilibrium might be reached by other instruments than that of continually fluctuating market-prices, and censured them for treating "any price system that does not provide for complete, almost day-to-day, flexibility (like an organized stock or produce market) as *ipso facto* irrational." The kinds of prices that Dobb (136-40) emphasizes in a socialist planned economy include: (1) accounting prices used as a basis for planning or for administrative decisions; (2) accounting prices used purely for recording and accounting purposes without having any direct influence on planning and decisions; (3) shadow prices that perform the function of summarizing information to provide an evaluation of a complex situation; (4) special cost-prices of inputs, used primarily for price comparisons; (5) transaction or actual prices, which govern incentives payments made to individuals or gropus of individuals (such as an enterprise); and finally (6) retail prices of consumer goods, "which must be true market prices, equilibrating demand with current supply."

In his scheme of centralized socialism, Dobb maintains that prices paid to producing units and suppliers need not always be identical with those charged to users, and recommends that "either some compromise between different functions" or "some combination of different kind of prices", must be worked out for the successful operation of the economy. To Dobb, planning's character and objectivity provides "suitability for easy and fairly rapid systematization and digestion" with respect to "supply and conditioning of information, for controlling the creation of new productive equipment."

In defense of planning over market in a socialist economic system, Dobb's arguments can be recapitulated as follows: In an economy beset with problems of underdevelopment and backwardness, a blend of centralized planning with minimal use of market mechanisms will be superior to atomistically competitive markets, especially for attaining full-capacity utilization, making major investment decisions, checking economic fluctuations, ensuring desired growth-rates and effectuating required structural changes. Furthermore, Centralized planning is more capable of dealing with social effects of production and consumption, that is, external economies or diseconomies, by taking into consideration social costs and benefits that self-interested decision-making does not incorporate. Planning provides a better income distribution than markets; under planning, distribution of income will be a "constant preoccupation of policy both from the side of production and from the side of money income." Planning can guard against monopolistic tendencies of enterprises by prohibiting arbitrary decisions involving fixation of output and price of goods and services. Finally, under centralized planning, readjustment processes can be speedier and smoother than in a competitive atomistic system. Central planning, Dobb maintains, presumably offers "a richer arsenal of weapons" than competitive markets, as it can utilize, alternatively or in combination, both the weapon of direct intervention or command and a variety of market interventions.[6]

Taking a similar stand, Sweezy (1949, 236) argues that comprehensive planning is all but inevitable in a socialist economy. He envisages a Central Planning Board that designs a general plan for the overall development of the economy by "consolidating the investment and consumption schedules" and "comparing them with current and prospective supplies." To Sweezy it is the CPB that can guarantee that "what is needed will be ready at the right time, at the right place, and in the right quantities," not price and market systems. He also stressed that once a plan has been adopted by a central planning authority, "it cannot be left to the discretion of individual industry and plant managers whether or not they will conform to it; rather it must be their first duty imposed by law, to carry out their part of the plan to the best of their ability."

For Sweezy (Bettleheim & Sweezy 1971, 26), transition from capitalism to socialism is "a one-way street", and "whoever acts to strengthen the market instead of struggling against the market is, regardless of intentions, promoting capitalism and not socialism" (8). Sweezy even remarks that increasing reliance on the "discipline of market and the incentive of profit" is tantamount to putting the economy "on the road back to essentially capitalist societies" (9). For him, the transition period (between socialism and capitalism) "does not lead to socialism in a linear fashion; it can also lead to renewed forms of capitalism, notably to state capitalism" (25). Therefore, the existence of market processes (money and prices) in a socialist economy constitutes a "standing danger to the system" and, unless the market forces are "strictly hedged in and controlled, will lead to degeneration and retrogression" (27). Sweezy, however, does not believe in "absolute contradictions" between markets and planning, and, indeed, emphasizes that coexistence of the two forces will be "inevitable under socialism for a long time." But he insists that markets and planning are not only "in opposition to each other," they are also "necessarily locked in an uninterrupted struggle for dominance," the magnitude of which actually "determines whether the society moves forward to socialism or backward to capitalism" (27-28).

Baran (1957) maintains that the evolution of capitalism into socialism requires an unremitting struggle against the principle of equivalent exchange. Although socialism does not imply dispensing with rational calculation, it necessarily involves profound changes in economic calculation.[7] Bettleheim (Bettleheim & Sweezy 1971, 44) maintains that the existence of a commodity relationship under a socialist economy "is a condition of possibility of bourgeois domination." To him, the continuation of some form of commodity exchange under a socialist system constitutes "a process which increasingly subjects the laboring masses to the requirements of a process of reproduction which they do not control, and which ultimately, therefore, can only serve the interests of a minority which uses the state apparatus."

Under Kalecki's scheme, economic functions of the most important financial, industrial, and public utility enterprises of the country would be subject to central planning, but private enterprises engaged in small-scale production of consumption goods and distributive services would operate in markets. Kalecki emphasized restructuring large-scale organizations along vertical lines, tightening control by central planning, especially with respect to employment, investment, price controls and providing physical targets to state enterprises. However, he also emphasized the wisdom of the non-interference in the internal operations of enterprises (see Nuti 1986).

In sum, both the centralized and decentralized socialists emphasize coexistence of markets and planning in coordinating economic decisions. While centralized socialists tend to replace market processes with central planning, decentralized socialists tend to replace central planning with a market price system as the dominant social process for organizing and coordinating economic decisions.

Ownership and Control

The proponents of the centralized model of socialism generally envisage nationalization/socialization of the means of production and degrade the role of private ownership in a socialist economy. As mentioned above, Marx and Engels repeatedly reprimanded private ownership. To them nationalization of the means of production was "the definition of socialism," and "an indispensable prerequisite of planning" in a socialist economy (Wiles 1962, 57). For Engels, the first task of a victorious proletariat is the "seizure of the means of production." By emphasizing central planning, the centralized socialists assume governmental control and ownership of the means of production almost as an indisputable factor. Centralized socialists "find it logical contradiction that a proletariat state should plan production, the instruments of which are owned by bourgeoisie" (50). Elliott (1985, 336) remarks that just as defenders of capitalism treat private ownership as an end in itself, the centralized socialists consider state ownership as if it were itself a goal of economic policy.

For Ward (1967, 7), the concept of socialism itself implies social ownership of the means of production in industry and trade, and state control of the directions of economic change. To Dobb (1970, 133), state ownership of the means of production constitutes the crucial basis for a centrally planned socialist economy. Kalecki's socialist model envisages a dominant centrally planned state sector, a liberalized cooperative sector, and private handicrafts (see Nuti 1986).

Lenin's position on ownership and control oscillated between the extremes of complete nationalization of the means of production, as in the War Communism period, and allowing substantial private and cooperative ownership along with a state sector controlling the commanding heights of the economy, as demonstrated during the NEP period. For Stalin (1952, 14-16), the only difference in commodity production under a capitalist and a socialist economy is the existence of private ownership of the means of production under the former and its absence under the latter; therefore, elimination of private ownership and subsequent nationalization of the means of production is essential for a socialist economy. Stalin also maintained that relations of production must necessarily conform with the character of the productive forces; therefore, the means of production must be socialized, the nation's property must be owned by the whole people, and abolition of all kinds of exploitation is a prior condition for a socialist economy. Stalin, however maintained that commodity production will not disappear with the nationalization of all means of production, and such production has to be continued, especially with respect to international trade and agriculture, until the final stage of communism is reached.

Trotsky emphasized conscious planning by the socialist state. He insisted that decisions like what to import, what to export, and what to produce, should be planned and coordinated by a central planning agency, but that international trade plans should be devised using a system of comparative coefficients, so that linkages between socialist production and world standards of price and quality can be established (Day 1973, 140-41). Adopting Marx's principle of "primitive capitalist accumulation," Trotsky proposed rapid industrialization at the expense of the private sector, specifically at the cost of the peasantry. Realizing that an underdeveloped economy lacks colonies for primitive capitalist accumulation and necessary capital would not be provided by internal savings, Trotsky called upon the state to finance the socialist industrial sector by pumping resources out of the private sector. Denouncing the idea of mutual development of both agriculture and industry, Trotsky asserted that "it would indeed be impossible simultaneously to fight the *kulaks*, raise prices charged to peasants, increase off-farm surpluses and greatly to raise the levels of capital accumulation" (Nove 1969, 127).

Democracy and the State

Centralized socialists generally envisage greater state control from above than democratic and popular control from below. By emphasizing central planning, state ownership of the means of production, centralized coordination and direction of the national economy, and organized and goal-directed channeling of national resources for rapid industrialization and modernization, the centralized socialists stress the state's dominant role in the economy. Marx, although emphasizing overall planning, never proposed replacement of consumers' sovereignty by planners' sovereignty. To most centralized socialists, by contrast, central planning and the state's overwhelming authority are preconditions for socialist modernization. Marx analyzed the working people as the universal class, clearly stipulating that emancipation will come "by the working class itself"; that the working class "will itself become the ruling class," and that the post-capitalist society will be a society of associated producers and the state, along with exploitation and worker alienation, will wither away. The expositors of the centralized strand of socialism, in contrast, emphasize authoritarian state control.

Lenin was the first to discover that Marxian prescriptions of the state and workers' democracy were impracticable in the context of economic backwardness. The authoritarian cast to Lenin's thought was revealed specifically in his arguments for the vanguard role of the Communist Party and in his perceptions of state and democracy in practice. Lenin argued that social change led by the proletariat itself could well end up as a trade union movement. To Lenin, to give the workers' movement a revolutionary character and to lead it to its logical destination was the task of a revolutionary vanguard party consisting of professional revolutionaries (see Lenin 1967, 91-256).[8]

In *The Proletarian Revolution and the Renegade Kautsky* (1965), Lenin maintained, opposing Marx, that the important thing is not the content, but the form of the state.[9] To Lenin the character of the state "is determined not by its representative institutions, but by its `machine', the people who work in it and the interests it serves" (Lovell 1984, 170). For Lenin the dictatorship of the proletariat constitutes the very essence of their revolution and Marx's doctrine, and proletarian democracy is "a million times more democratic" than the most democratic bourgeois state.[10]

Lenin's position during War Communism with regard to the need for an authoritarian state was softened during the NEP period, when, as mentioned before, efforts were made to denationalize industries, deconcentrate and decentralize economic management, and reintroduce trade and market relations, and price, money, and credit systems. NEP policies officially tolerated "social pluralism in economic, cultural-intellectual, even [in local soviets and high state agencies] political life" (Cohen 1977, 21).

Although Trotsky emphasized central planning and thereby the state's dominant role in the socialist economy, he condemned bureaucratic proliferation. In *The New Course* (1965), Trotsky provided his seminal critique of Soviet "bureaucratic degeneracy," which he thought could be remedied by increasing intra-party democracy and by promoting more proletarians to administrative positions. He was also a pioneer of worker self-government. In his "search for guarantees against bureaucratization and opportunist deviations of mass working class organizations" Trotsky sought to establish worker councils as a form of direct democracy in which bourgeois democracy's "barriers between passive voters and active participants in the business of government" would wither away with the elimination of the division of labor between the governor and the governed (Mandel 1979, 53-62). Describing worker organizations as "the new wave of the future," Trotsky anticipated that a democratically elected workers' council, by handling its own finances, self-defense, food supply, public relations and so on, would constitute an embryonic future workers' state in which the workers' (or socialist) democracy would be greater than the most advanced form of bourgeois democracy (57-58).[11]

Stalin's preoccupation with catching up with the West, massive industrialization drive, coercive collectivization of agriculture, and building of a bureaucratic state apparatus and gigantic politico-economic police empire, vividly demonstrate his focus on totalitarian state power and the resultant subordination of democratic processes in the economy and society. In the words of Tucker (1977, 83), Stalin's revolution from above was "indeed state-initiated, state-directed, and state-enforced revolution." Emphasizing the principle of "socialism in one country," he proclaimed at the December 1925 CPSU Congress that to make the Soviet Union economically self-dependent and a center of attraction for other countries that gradually quit capitalism and enter the channel of socialist economy (Bideleux 1985, 117), the Soviet Union must develop large-scale heavy industry under the unified and strict command of the state.

To such Western centralized socialists as Dobb, Sweezy, and Baran, the central government and its associated decision-making and administrative bodies, especially the CPB, constitute the "dominant social processes for making, coordinating, and enforcing economic decisions"; and the "major dynamic motive force" for the economy "is the aspirations of and direction given by political leaders and central planners" (Elliott 1985, 336-37). Consequently, the role and autonomy of local governments, workers' councils, trade unions, enterprises, and consumers will diminish, and physical targets and incentives manipulated by bureaucratic machinery will replace market mechanisms in the operation of the economy. By emphasizing comprehensive government ownership and centrally planned and administered allocation and distribution of income, the centralized socialists, "relegate worker control to a lower rank in their priority system" (337).

To Bettleheim (1975, 19), what distinguishes socialism from capitalism is not "the existence or non-existence of market relationships, money and prices, but the existence of the domination of the proletariat;" which can only be accomplished by exercising this dictatorship in all areas—economic, political and ideological. For Sweezy (Bettleheim & Sweezy 1971, 49-51), socialism involves a movement "as rapidly as possible from a commodity-producing to a fully planned economic system" under a dictatorship of the proletariat committed to repressing counter-revolutionaries and bringing the "oppressed segment" of the population "up to the proletarian level." Kalecki's centralized economic system emphasizes the state's dominant control and the pressure of the workers' councils from below, as a workable formula for efficient and accountable operation of socialist enterprises. Under Kalecki's scheme, workers' councils in each enterprise would make decisions about the organization of production (working conditions, overtime pay, etc.), and would guard against excessive bureaucratization and centralization tendencies at the enterprise level.[12]

COMPARISON OF CENTRALIZED AND DECENTRALIZED MODELS

Comparison of the centralized and decentralized models of socialism occupies a prominent position in the relevant literature, and relative superiority of one over the other remains controversial. As mentioned previously, customarily the "socialist controversy" is traced to the writings of Mises-Hayek-Robinson (who concentrate on socialism's impossibility/impracticability), and Lange-Lerner-Taylor (who articulated decentralized market models).[13] Subsequently, the debate extended to Dobb/Sweezy/Baran and others who concentrated on centralized socialism. Herein, the major similarities and differences between the contending models of socialism will be elaborated first, then pressures or imperatives for centralization and decentralization in a socialist economy will be explored.

Major Similarities and Differences

Decentralized socialists envisage the emergence of socialism in an economically advanced country where "capitalist economic relations have outlived their time and . . . those denoted as socialist are, *ipso facto*, more progressive and altogether superior" (Sik 1976, 24). They perceive socialism as a new economic system in which both forces of production and economic relations are mature enough to make possible a gradual, democratic, peaceful transition out of capitalism. Compared with exponents of centralized socialism, decentralized socialists rely more heavily on democratic principles, and ascribe a greater role to private ownership of the means of production, the role of markets in the economy, the power and autonomy of workers' councils, and decentralization in economic management. Decentralized socialists are critical of the bureaucratic management of an economy, generally emphasize neoclassical ideals such as price-mechanisms and free competition, and presuppose such liberal democratic principles as human rights and freedom of speech and of the press, both in the transition to and operation of the future socialist society.

Although none of the decentralized versions provides an integrated and coherent ideology, generally they agree that allocation of resources is more efficient through market forces than by administrative methods, and that central ownership and control of the means of production goes hand in hand with political authoritarianism (see Rakovski 1978). Decentralized socialists find no incompatibility between socialism and democracy.[14] Decentralized socialists believe not only that socialism and a flourishing and robust democracy can coexist, they can actually be mutually supportive (Yunker 1979, 9). To many decentralized socialists, even large-scale private ownership of the means of production is not incompatible with a socialist economic system.

Centralized socialists criticize decentralized socialists for their emphasis on consumers' sovereignty and political democracy. Because the divergence of opinions with respect to political democracy has been elaborated above, we shall concentrate here on the dispute surrounding consumer sovereignty. Centralized socialists challenge the concept of consumer sovereignty and strive to show how irrational consumers' preferences are in the real world. Dobb (1970, 220) maintains that there is no justification for the belief that the consumer is capable of deciding what best contributes to his/her own welfare.[15]

Criticism of the alleged rationality of consumer preferences and consumers' sovereignty is not unique to centralized socialists. Albert (1987, 68-69), for example, maintains that consumers' sovereignty in a market economy does not mean actual involvement of the consumers in making production decisions, it rather means providing a platform for testing the solutions adopted by the entrepreneurs and indirectly influencing the future activities in the sphere of production. Many main stream economists are also critical of the concept of consumer sovereignty (see Hansen 1960; Dahl and Lindblom 1953).

What are the basic differences between the economic behavior of the centralized socialist model and that of the Lange model? While in the centralized model the CPB commands the economy and brings equilibrium in the market through administrative methods, in Lange's model, the market is given a significant role to play, but the CPB instructs and coordinates the economy. Lange's CPB is primarily concerned with growth and overall direction of the economy, not with technical problems such as fixing production targets for certain commodities. On the other hand, centralized socialists emphasize physical planning, detailed and overall blueprints by the CPB that will literally coordinate all economic decisions involving production, consumption and investment of an economy. Sweezy's (1949, 236) CPB will not only estimate consumer demand for all products that compete for resources with the investment plan, it must "ensure that what is needed will be ready at the right time, at the right place, and in the right quantities" to fulfill planned investment objectives. For Baran (1957), the CPB's primary preoccupation is accumulation and mobilization of the planned economic surplus to accelerate economic growth and eliminate irrational wastage of economic resources.[16]

Pressures for Centralization and Decentralization

Socialist economies are subject to pressures for both centralization and decentralization, for at least two reasons: (1) the character of the economy; and (2) the stage of its economic development. Every socialist state by definition requires central coordination, monitoring, and direction of the economy; therefore, Brus (1973, 3) says that central level decision-making, is indispensable to a socialist economy, regardless of its centralized or decentralized character. A socialist state, because it owns most of the means of production, and because of its preponderant preoccupation with macroeconomic decisions involving growth, investments, savings, consumption and distribution, will have to maintain what Brus and Lange (1958) have called a "minimum of centralization." Even Lange (1958, 174) emphasized that effective direction of economic development is the minimum responsibility of central planning in a socialist economy. For him, such minimum centralization involves division of national income between accumulation and consumption, determination of the general rate of growth of the economy, and distribution of investments among the different branches of the economy.

At the same time, any socialist economy, whatever the degree of central control, will have some freedom of choice or market relations involving decisions pertaining to personal consumption, occupation, and place of work that would constitute the opposite end, "the minimum of decentralization." Even Dobb (1970, 144-45) seems to have recognized the necessity for some decentralization in any socialist economy by indicating that "short period" questions concerning day-to-day plant utilization could be based on marginal operating cost and could presumably be decentralized. Of course, there had been some periods during which such minimum of decentralization was disrupted in existing socialist economies.

Secondly, pressures for centralization and decentralization in a socialist economy might depend on the stage of its economic development. Dobb (140), for example, maintains that with the growth and development of a centralized socialist system, "feasible limits on efficient centralized decision- making become more evident," and, correspondingly, the need to decentralize economic decisions becomes more pressing. According to him, as the economy grows, societal complexities multiply, the standard of living of the population improves, and the demand for consumption goods increase. The decentralization of economic decisions will become imperative, especially to raise productivity of labor, encourage innovation and rationalization of working methods, and stimulate initiative at lower levels of production.

Similarly, Lange's (1958, 172-74) postwar model outlined greater centralization during the earlier phase of economic development, since a centralized authority is better suited to achieving rapid and efficient industrialization. However, with the development of economy, centralized economic management will lead to bureaucratic rigidity and disregard of public needs, and decentralization will be in order.[17] The following three sections deal with empirical examples of centralized approaches to socialism.

WAR COMMUNISM (1917-21)

The War Communism period was characterized by a centralized dictatorship, in which an authoritatively organized Communist Party extended its dominant and decisive control over the whole economy and society. In the absence of any blueprint or prior experience of an economic system under socialism, and largely stimulated by revolutionary zeal and expectations of the immediate establishment of socialism, Soviet leaders of this period attempted to promote egalitarian government policies and programs. This newly born and only worker-run country in the world had to fight external aggression and internal civil war simultaneously. Given this desperate situation, the CPSU adopted drastic measures to organize the country's pre-industrial economy using principles intended for establishing communism in a highly industrialized society.

Nationalization of Industry

War Communism adopted wholesale nationalization of the country's industry, trade and land. Within one month of the Revolution, in November 1917, all Soviet land was brought under state control, and the owners of industrial enterprises were ordered to oblige the decisions of the workers' control organs. As early as January 1918, virtually all means of production were brought under the control of the "workers and peasants" state. Revolutionary measures like these, however, came as an "urgent necessity, both to combat attempts at sabotage [by bourgeoisie] and to ensure priority for military supplies" (Cliff 1978, 82). In most cases workers themselves took over the control of the enterprises.[18] The nationalization spree went so far that by the end of 1920, out of the 37,000 enterprises nationalized by the CPSU, almost half were nonmechanical and more than 5,000 employed only one worker (83).

The sweeping nationalization measures of the War Communism period, however, were not backed by rational planning or an efficient administrative machinery.

Nationalization measures quite logically necessitated centralization of economic management, but the existing administrative machinery obviously had neither the experience nor the efficiency to handle responsibilities of such a magnitude. As a result, in many cases orders from the center were often confused and contradictory. Clearly a thoroughly inefficient and unexperienced administrative system, in the absence of rational economic planning to manage the nationalized industries, further aggravated the already disastrous economic condition of the country. The whole economy, especially the industrial sector, almost totally collapsed. This period also witnessed tremendous decline in labor productivity resulting from acute shortages of raw materials, fuel, and food. Worker productivity compared to 1913 dropped to 85 percent in 1917, 44 percent in 1918, and 22 percent in 1919 (see Nove 1969, 47). Table 2.1 shows the dismal picture of the Soviet economy resulting from the catastrophic decline of industrial production during this period. As manifested in the table, industrial production ranged between 0 percent and 43 percent of 1913 production level.

Table 2.1
Soviet Industrial Production in 1920
(1913=100)

Products	Index	Products	Index
Petroleum	42.7	Electric bulbs	10.1
Tobacco	42.5	Sugar	6.7
Leather	38.0	Electrical Engineering	
Linen Yarn	38.0	machinery/apparatus	5.4
Salt	30.0	Cotton yarn	5.1
Wool Yarn	27.0	Railway Carriage const.	4.2
Coal	27.0	Paper and pulp	25.0
Hemp spun yarn	23.0	Vegetable Oils	3.0
Locomotive		Cement	3.0
construction	14.8	Pig Iron	2.4
Matches	14.0	Bricks	2.1
Ploughs	13.3	Iron Ore	1.7
Accumulators	12.5	Copper	0.0

Source: Cliff 1978, 86.

Compulsory Requisitioning of Food

The collapse in industrial production was accompanied by a serious famine and chronic shortages of other consumer goods. As initial attempts to procure food from the peasants at official prices failed, the CPSU introduced a policy of forced requisitioning of grain to ensure the supply of food mainly for the military forces and the urban population. The policy, known as *prodrazverstka*, made it mandatory for peasants to deliver their surplus grains to the state. Under the provisions of the *prodrazverstka*, the state confiscated, at a nominal price, "all that the peasant had over and above an ill-defined minimum requirement for himself and his family" (Nove 1969, 60). Collected food was then distributed by the state according to a rigid class criteria. For this purpose the whole population, was divided into four classes: manual workers, heavy physical workers, light workers, and professionals. Available food supplies were distributed to these four categories in the ratio 4:3:2:1(see Cliff 1978, 88).

But forced requisitioning of grain did not help to mitigate the problem. Instead, food shortages remained at chronic levels throughout the War Communism period. Widespread hunger, even mass starvation, remained a constant threat to the Revolution. Because forced requisition policy gave little or no incentive to the peasants to increase their production, grain production fell sharply and it became even more difficult to find surpluses that could be requisitioned. Indeed, peasants actually "resented *prodrazverstka* deeply, and numerous riots broke out" (Nove 1969, 60). Thus, coupled with the collapse of industrial production, food shortages brought the country to a state of complete chaos. The massacres of the civil war, exodus of people from the urban areas to the countryside, and booming illegal markets were some of the dangerous signs of chaos in the country's economy.[19]

Attempts to Abolish Markets and Money

War Communism sought to do away with the markets and monetary system. To the socialist revolutionaries, capitalist market paraphernalia such as private owner-ship, money, prices, wages, and profits were intolerable enemies of socialist economy. Thus, policies like nationalization of the means of production, centralized planning, and abolition of the monetary system were accepted by all Bolsheviks as indispensable principles for establishing socialism. While Marx called for leveling up of economic inequality during the mature stage of communism, presumably in an industrially and technologically developed country, the Soviet leaders called for immediate practice of such egalitarian principles in the War Communism period.[20] The logic of such a utopian expectation, according to Lewin (1974, 81), went like this: "The more nationalization, the narrower the market, the nearer the advent of socialism, or the larger the socialist market." Even Bukharin (1982, 146), the widely known protagonist of left communism, saw the distribution of rations in kind (instead of wages in terms of money) as the disappearance of wage labor. He, therefore, concluded that as an inevitable consequence, the monetary system, and with it the commodity system in general, would collapse during the transition period.

Hence, normal economic mechanisms and incentives were disrupted in order to eliminate money and abolish the market system; instead, the whole economic system was "activated by a combination of coercion and an appeal to enthusiasm and moral commitment" (Lewin 1974, 78). By 1919-20 workers' wages were largely paid in kind, and industrial enterprises did not pay for their raw materials and other services because bookkeeping took care of all transactions, even the transfer of working capital allocations from one account to another. Consequently, money and market mechanisms, in effect, were eliminated.[21]

Evaluation of the War Communism Period

An overall evaluation of the War Communism period requires a proper understanding of the existing situation in the Soviet Union at the time. The entire period of War Communism was subject to chaos, anarchy, civil war, and foreign aggression. On the other hand, the socialist principles enunciated by the CPSU were at a rudimentary stage, and expectations of the revolutionary leaders to establish socialism in the Soviet Union were running high. Therefore, policy measures of this period resulted in a substantial breakdown of the economy and brought excruciating suffering for the people.

We have seen above how inefficient and disorganized the state distribution system was during this period. Food requisitioning from the peasants and distribution of the grain to the urban and military force, is an example. There was no rational economic plan, no uniformity in administrative decisions, and no coherence in the decrees issued by the government. Lenin himself said, "such is the sad fate of our decrees: they are signed, and then we ourselves forget about them and fail to carry them out" (quoted in Nove 1969, 47). The forced requisition of grain, along with efforts to dismantle monetary mechanisms, suppressed the foundations for the commercial exchange of grain and industrial goods.

Nevertheless, the policies of War Communism brought victory for the Soviet state. By nationalizing the means of production, centralizing production and distribution processes, and militarizing administrative machinery, the CPSU succeeded in mobilizing the revolutionary masses to secure victory over a coalition of domestic and foreign enemies. But the victory in the civil war was earned at a very high cost. War Communism's policies, such as introducing single managers in enterprises to replace the committee system, entrusting ever more power to the appointed administrators, weakening the position of the trade unions, and increasing domination over local party organizations, were considered by many as clear deviations from socialist principles. After the civil war, as elaborated in Chapter 1, Lenin admitted that mistakes were committed during the War Communism period, but at the same time also argued that both internal and external situations of the Soviet Union necessitated such measures.

Evidently, the Soviet economy was in shambles. Destruction and ruin, misery and suffering in the Soviet Union were overpowering. National output dropped below pre-War levels, and industry and agriculture almost totally collapsed. Thousands of people perished from sickness and starvation, and millions left the starving cities for the countryside. The working class was "physically and spiritually exhausted, strikes were commonplace" (Medvedev 1981, 59). Worse still, towards the end of 1920, a crisis of increasing disenchantment and growing worker-peasant opposition was threatening the very foundations of the October Revolution. Lenin himself admitted "the revolution is on the brink of precipice which all previous revolutions reached and recoiled from" (quoted in Elliott 1985, 363). Workers supported industrial mobilization and militarization of labor enthusiastically during the civil war, but now that the civil war ended they became more assertive about their rights and privileges. The peasants, although they resented the policy of forced requisitioning of grain throughout the civil war period, "on the whole tolerated the Bolshevik regime as the lesser evil compared with White restoration" (Cliff 1978, 101).

Besides plunging the country's economy into virtual collapse and making the Revolution equally vulnerable, the policies and programs of War Communism left behind two other very significant legacies. Besides earning victory in the civil war, it left administrative and political legacies that still dominate life in the Soviet Union. Some of the far-reaching consequences of this period include centralized planning, bureaucratic administration, coercive mobilization of labor, the forced requisitioning of peasants for armed squads, and the elimination of regular markets.

THE STALINIST COMMAND MODEL (1929-53)

Lenin died in January 1924. The next Soviet leader, Joseph Stalin, consolidated his position in 1929, after a five-year-long succession struggle.[22] In 1921, the Communist Party had to compromise with the peasants for the very survival of the state and the Revolution. By 1926, the Soviet economy had recovered significantly and an opportune time came to stop "treading water ...to take hold of the economy and move it forward ...to begin the march toward greater industrial production" (Adams 1972, 43). Therefore, through revolutionary measures such as collectivization and industrialization, Stalin embarked on a massive modernization drive to lift an overwhelmingly peasant society out of its backwardness and transform it into an industrialized society in step with the twentieth century. Stalin's drive for rapid industrialization, coercive collectivization of agriculture, radical transformation of the society itself, and destruction of old social institutions, under the strictest control of the Communist Party and government and his own totalitarian rule, has come down in history as the "Stalinist Revolution."

Mass-Collectivization

Revolutionary transformations in the agricultural sector began in 1929 when Stalin called for elimination of the *kulaks* as a class and initiated the coercive process of mass collectivization. Stalin (1945, 305) described the agricultural revolution as "a leap from an old qualitative state of society to a new qualitative state, equivalent in its consequences to the revolution of October 1917." Out of the one million *kulak* farms in 1928, the *dekulakization* drive, according to Bideleux (1985, 121), resulted in the deportation of 240,000 *kulak* families, and forced expropriation of another 600,000 *kulak* farms.[23] The collectivization of agriculture, achieved at the cost of untold sufferings of millions of people, displaced millions of household farms that had been functioning on nationalized land, and forcefully brought them under four new rural institutions; (1) state farm (*sovkhoz*), (2) collective farm (*kolkhoz*), (3) Machine Tractor Station (MTS), and (4) private plot. Among them the *kolkhoz*, or collective farms, were dominant; they combined cooperative ownership with tight government control. The *sovkhoz*, or state farm, was reserved for very large or experimental farms. The MTS pooled farm machinery and was in charge of conducting all heavy machine operations on nearby collective farms.[24]

These changes brought an end to the private ownership of agricultural land and private markets in the countryside that had been so earnestly encouraged during the NEP period. While in 1928 only 1.7 percent of total cultivated land of the Soviet Union was in the collectivized sector, the percentage rose to 93.0 percent by 1937 (see Table 2.2). Again, as the table shows, while the collectivized sector contributed only 3.3 percent to the gross agricultural product of the country in 1928, by 1937, the share was increased to 98.5 percent.

Table 2.2

Stages of Collectivization and Contribution of Socialized Sector to Soviet Economy, 1927-37

A. Stages of Soviet Collectivization, 1927-37

Year	Number of kholkozy firms	Collectivized Firms as percentage of Total	Percentage of Total Cultivated Area Occupied
1927	14,800	0.8	---
1928	33,300	1.7	2.3
1929	57,000	3.9	4.9
1930	85,950	23.6	33.6
1931	-----	52.7	67.8
1932	211,100	61.5	77.7
1937	240,000	93.0	---

B. The Socialized Sector as a Proportion of the Soviet Economy (%), 1924-37

	1924	1928	1937
National income	35.0	44.0	99.1
Gross national product	76.3	82.4	99.8
Gross agri. product	1.6	3.3	98.5
Retail trade Turnover	47.3	76.4	100.0

Source: Lavigne 1974, 17.

Thus, from the Stalinist perspective, the collectivization campaign could presumably be considered as a great success. Stalin's ruthless drive for mass collectivization succeeded in accomplishing a sweeping transformation of the backward institutions of Soviet countryside, and therefore, fully attained its avowed objective of setting the foundations for collectivized agriculture. Collectivization gave Soviet leaders control over agricultural production, consumption, and surplus. Evidently, the primary impetus for Stalin's collectivization campaign came from the demonstrated failure of the agricultural sector to produce a sufficient surplus to feed the urban population and to provide the raw materials for industries. The philosophy, as prescribed by Preobrazhensky and Trotsky, was that in a largely agrarian economy like the Soviet Union, a "primitive socialist accumulation" was needed and the expansion of state sector producer goods should be attained at the expense of the peasant community.[25] But Munting (1982, 83) maintains that the coercion and suffering of the people under Stalinist collectivization was so enormous that even Trotsky himself condemned forced collectivization and liquidation of the *kulaks*. However, to Stalin, breaking the backbone of the *kulaks* was a necessary condition for laying the foundations for modern, productive and collectivized agricultural production, a prerequisite for exacting surpluses to achieve rapid industrialization of an underdeveloped economy. Evidently, Stalin's collectivization strategy was aimed at establishing centralized state control, direction and coordination over rural labor, food, raw materials, and exports for industrialization and urbanization. Such a strategy eventually resulted in massive class transformation in Soviet society: Peasantry was largely transformed into working class.

Industrialization Drive

Stalin embarked on a massive industrialization program exceeding in scope and rapidity the proposals of Preobrazhensky and other pro-industrializers of the twenties.[26] The Stalinist drive for rapid industrialization was strictly coordinated by central authorities—especially by the *Gosplan* (the state planning commission), and the Council of People's Commissars. With the enthusiastic goal of catching up with the West within a decade, Stalin preferred to build up heavy industry first, speculating that by concentrating on heavy industry, he would be able build up a much larger productive capacity in the long run. Therefore, Stalin's drive for industrialization came to be understood as development of heavy industry, especially machine-building. Stalin anticipated that once the instruments and means of production are produced locally, the economy would be able to produce consumer goods at a record rate. Stalin also opted for the policy of "socialism in one country," and emphasized that to make the Soviet Union economically self-dependent and an attractive model for other countries the Soviet Union must develop large-scale heavy industries at any cost. To Stalin, a principle purpose of industrialization campaign was to guarantee economic and political independence to the country.

Stalin believed in the Leninist view that foreign aid signifies colonialism and the loss of the nation's independence to creditors. Therefore, accumulation of capital for rapid industrialization of the country must come from internal sources. One source, as Preobrazhensky and Trotsky suggested before, was to transfer the agricultural surplus for industrial development. Besides channeling resources from the agricultural sector to the industrial sector, Stalin's strategy for industrial development of an agrarian Soviet economy envisaged greater emphasis on heavy industry, and a commensurately lesser emphasis on the consumption sector.[27] Stalin increased capital investment to 30 percent of the gross national product and set production targets at ever higher levels every year. The Stalinist strategy also involved a transfer of private sector savings to government savings and investment.

Under Stalin's iron rule, enterprise managers were transformed into faithful executors of operational plans that specified production levels, supply allotments, delivery schedules, and prices. The central planning agencies assigned highest priority to the rapid development of heavy industry, and gave secondary importance to agriculture, housing, and other consumer goods. During the first plan period, 86 percent of all investments went to heavy industry. Increasing emphasis upon heavy industries meant that light industries, those producing textiles, shoes, and other consumer items, or processing food and making furniture, as well as smaller industries like handicrafts, trades and shops, were hardly encouraged by government.

Establishment of a Totalitarian State

Stalin's programs and policies of rapid industrialization and coercive collectivization were supplemented by a draconian and all-pervasive political and administrative rule, usually characterized as Stalinist "totalitarianism."[28] In fact, totalitarianism actually became a synonym for Stalinism. Following the famine of 1928-29 (that culminated in the terrible famine of 1932-33), Stalin started to roll back the NEP policies of peaceful and cooperative coexistence of agriculture and industry, and thus began the process of destruction of the NEP institutions and processes. However, the final triumph of Stalinism over the Bolshevik tradition was achieved by 1936-39 (Cohen 1977, 24-25).[29]

Stalin orchestrated his programs of massive industrialization and mass collectivization by establishing what Rigby (1977, 53-76) calls a "mono-organizational society," a society-wide organization that not only ran the production and distribution of nearly all goods and services, but also monopolized "the socialization and moral guidance of its members." The global range of functions of the society-wide single organization was marked by "distinctive characteristics of ideology and repression" in which "the organizational culture, the political legitimation and the socialization of individuals came together in a single purportedly comprehensive ideology."

Stalinist totalitarianism, according to Tucker (1977, 95), was a "state-building process, the construction of a powerful, highly centralized, bureaucratic, military-industrial Soviet Russian State." Elliott (1989) identifies five interrelated characteristics of Stalinist totalitarianism: (1) dictatorship by the CPSU over the state; (2) personal tyranny of Stalin over the CPSU; (3) a closely knit set of institutional innovations for control and coordination of the economy, namely, collectivization of agriculture, social ownership of the means of production, central planning, and hierarchically structured bureaucracy; (4) rapid industrialization with emphasis on investment in heavy industry and shifting of resources from agriculture to industry; and (5) a comprehensivity of control by the Dictator, Party, and State over society orchestrated by monopolization of control over the armed forces, mass communication, ideology, education, and systematic use of secret police terror.

The dictatorship of the CPSU over the state was inherited from Bolshevism. Lenin, as we have seen before, both theoretically and practically, stood for political monopoly of the CPSU. He, however, allowed substantial debate, discussion, and opposition within the Communist Party, whereas Stalin in the late thirties ruthlessly eliminated those practices. We have elaborated how Stalin won out over both the right and left opposition and consolidated his absolute power over the party throughout the five-year period of 1924-29, and over the state itself throughout the period of 1929-39. While Lenin consolidated power in the Communist Party, Stalin succeeded in transferring it to himself. Stalin, a shrewd politician and organizational tactician, also became the general secretary of the CPSU in 1922, and persistently filled party positions with people personally loyal to him.

A closely integrated bureaucratic apparatus of central planning, hierarchically organized party and state machineries—Rigby's mono-organizational society was necessitated by the programs of rapid industrialization and mass-collectivization. To accomplish the goals of centrally planned rapid industrialization, to suck resources from the agricultural sector by force, to direct investments to heavy industry and mobilize savings at the cost of consumption, Stalin had to resort to a rollback to NEP policies of gradual and peaceful economic development, and resort to a hierarchically organized and centrally commanded party and state. Tucker (1977, 82) remarks that instead of proceeding gradually and by means of persuasion, Stalinism "proceeded at breakneck speed and wielded state power coercively to smash popular resistance." Under Stalin's bureaucratic leviathan, the state and the CPSU established its comprehensive and totalitarian control over the whole society by eliminating all opposition, ruthlessly using secret police, and commanding and coordinating virtually every aspect of Soviet life. Consequently, the state, the society, and the CPSU all came under the absolute control of Stalin's personal tyranny.

Performance of the Stalinist Model

The performance of the Soviet economy under the Stalinist model was extraordinary. Between 1928 and 1937, Soviet industrial production, labor force and capital stock grew at unusually high rates. Steel output between 1928 and 1940 increased by 326 percent, coal extraction by 367 percent, and hydraulic generation went up 866 percent (see Table 2.3). Dependence of the Soviet economy on import was substantially curtailed. For example, the percentage of machine tools that had to be imported fell from 78 percent in 1932 to less than 10 percent in 1936 and 1937. Overall growth of the economy was among the highest in the world during the first eight years of Stalin's rule. In 1937, however, growth began to slump due to a growing defense burden that rose from 3.4 percent of the budget in 1933 to 16.1 percent in 1936 and 32.6 percent in 1940.

Table 2.3
Outcome of the Soviet Industrialization Drive of 1928-37

Indicators	1928	1937
A. Changes in Manufacturing		
Heavy /overall manufacturing		
Net product share (1928 prices)	31	63
Labor force share	28	(1933) 43
Light/overall manufacturing		
Net product share (1928 prices)	68	36
Labor force share	71	(1933) 56
B. Changes in Major Economic Sectors		
Share in net national product (1937 prices)		
Agriculture	49	31
Industry	28	45
Services	23	24
Share in labor force		
Agriculture	71	(1940) 51
Industry	18	(1940) 29
Services	12	(1940) 20
C. Rates of Growth and Capital Stock (1928-37)		
GNP (1937 prices)		4.8%
Labor Force		8.7%
Industrial Production (1937 prices)		11.3%
Agricultural Production (1958 prices)		1.1%
Livestock		-1.2%
Gross Industrial Capital Stock		
(1937 prices, billions of rubles)	34.8	119
D. Changes in the structure of GNP by end use		
(1937 prices)		
Household consumption/GNP	80	53
Annual growth rate (1928-37)	--	0.8%
Communal Services/GNP	5	11
Annual growth rate (1928-37)	--	15.7%
Government Administration and defense/GNP	3	11
Annual growth rate (1928-37)	--	15.6%

Table 2.3 (continued)

Indicators	1928	1937
Gross Capital Investment/GNP	13	26
Annual growth rate (128-37)		14.4%
E. Foreign Trade Proportions		
(Exports + imports)/GNP	6%	1%
F. Prices		
Consumer goods prices		
(state and cooperative		
sector, 1928=100)	100	700
Average realized prices of farm products		
(1928=100)	100	539
G. Urbanization		
Rural population (mill.)	(1926) 147.0	(1939) 114.4
Percent of total	82%	67%
Urban population (mill.)	(1926) 26.3	(1939) 56.1
Percent of total	18%	33%

Source: Elliott 1985, 369.

Stalin's overwhelming focus on heavy industry was accompanied by neglect of light industries. This resulted in large shortages of consumer goods and consequent suffering and hardship of the masses. On the other hand, the Stalinist revolution brought a transformation of social patterns, the most visible being rapid demographic change. During Stalin's period, the urban population nearly doubled, from 28.7 million at the beginning of 1929 to 56.1 million at the beginning of 1939, jumping from 18 percent to 33 percent of the total population. The proportion of the · population represented by workers and their families more than doubled from 12.4 percent in 1928 to 33.7 percent in 1939. The annual graduation of specialists from higher educational institutions increased 157 percent during 1938-40 compared to the period of 1928-32. During the same period, specialized secondary institutions rose by 210 percent.

The Stalinist revolution, however, buried the egalitarian aspirations of the Leninist period and replaced it with a society with differential access to power, income and privileges. In June 1931, Stalin legitimized wage differentials, describing wage equality as "Petty-bourgeois egalitarianism". Introduction of closed shops and a system of authorizations to ensure supplies of scarce goods to a select few made the situation worse. Lastly, the Stalinist model made extensive use of terror, from uprooting the kulaks to hounding dissident CPSU leaders.[30]

Evaluation of the Stalinist Command Model

The Stalinist model, at least on its own terms, was overwhelmingly successful. It "did what it was initially expected to do" (Goldman 1983, 2). Under Stalin's ruthless leadership, a backward and agrarian Soviet economy was swiftly transformed into an industrial and military giant within a decade. Stalin himself gave his period very high marks. As early as 1933, in his address to the Seventeenth Congress of the CPSU, Stalin asserted that he transformed "an ignorant, illiterate and uncultured country" into a giant industrialized and modern country, and increased the national income of the country from 29,000 million rubles in 1929 to 50,000 million rubles in 1933. Stalin did not attribute the credit for these achievements to any miracle; rather he held "expanding socialist reconstruction" as responsible for the tremendous success (see Franklin 1972).

After Stalin's death, however, it was discovered that the Stalinist model did not fit the changed needs of the society. The Stalinist model fostered rapid development of heavy industry, but it was not responsive to popular wants and sophisticated industrial needs. It kept on producing steel and basic machine tools, when what was needed was food, consumer goods, and modern technology (Goldman 1983, 2). Therefore, after the death of Stalin, as Tucker (1977, 173) points out, the question was not "Who shall replace him?" but "What shall take the place of Stalinism as a mode of rule and pattern of policy and ideas?"

There is no doubt that subsequently the Stalinist model lost most of its usefulness, but this uselessness was also the one of the inevitable results of its unprecedented success. The Stalinist system, having built an industrial society, Meyer (1957, 51) maintains, "was poorly equipped by its own structure and operating methods to maintain, manage and improve" the fundamentally changed Soviet society. Stalin replaced the previous oligarchic dictatorship of the CPSU with a personal dictatorship and totalitarian rule, reducing the CPSU to a ruling bureaucracy and making it (like other bureaucracies, such as the secret police, army, and state apparatuses) directly accountable to him. Stalin transformed a predominantly peasant society into a predominantly working-class society under the vanguard leadership of the CPSU. In the absence of a capitalist class, Stalin vested the responsibility to organize and direct the economy in the hands of the Party leadership. This small class of Party elites, in turn, derived their authority and power from Stalin himself, and remained accountable to him.

Because of its overwhelming emphasis on target fulfillment, the Stalinist model repressed creativity, innovation, and initiative, and most certainly lacked the "flexibility to adjust plans and decisions to rapidly changing domestic and international conditions and to unanticipated opportunities and problems" (Hoffman & Laird 1982, 26). Stalin's command economy was also criticized for inefficiency and wastage. Therefore, after the death of Stalin, his policies and programs increasingly faced thorough scrutiny, and in many cases formidable challenges and drastic attempts at reversal.

BREZHNEV'S BUREAUCRATIC COLLECTIVISM (1964-82)

In sharp contrast to the turbulent period of Khrushchev and the short interregnum of Kosygin's tantalizing experiment with "Libermanism," Brezhnev's two decades of rule over the Soviet Union brought fewer changes and demonstrated more commitment to proceduralism, institutional continuity, and gradual transformation of the society, which earned him the reputation as the leader of bureaucratic collectivism. Brezhnev's conservative strategy emphasized primacy of central planning and centralized control. He focused on discipline and order in economic management and sought to preserve and reinforce central command through the Communist Party and governmental apparatuses. Brezhnev retreated from Kosygin's decentralizing reforms of the planning and administrative system and broader role for enterprises. To Brezhnev, Leung (1985) believes, "economic reform did not qualify as an issue area." Therefore, it is hardly surprising that the Brezhnev era contributed little to economic decentralization, and indeed ended up with the worst economic stagnation in Soviet history. Apart from the restoration of the central ministries and elimination of bifurcation in the CPSU, the most important reforms of the Brezhnev era can be discussed as follows.

Mergers and Reorganizations

In March 1973, Brezhnev sought to reorganize the central administrative apparatus by streamlining the decision-making hierarchy in the ministries and by promoting mergers of enterprises into production associations. Measures were taken to merge industrial enterprises under one decision-making authority, apparently with the objectives of promoting administrative efficiency and redirecting resources from the least to the most productive enterprise. Brezhnev replaced the *Glavki*, a division that supervised all enterprises involved in closely related products within each ministry, with All-Union industrial associations (VPOs), whose authority generally covered similar enterprises throughout the country. Newly created VPOs, which also included research and design organizations and technical institutes, were planned to work on a *khozrashet* (self-accounting) basis.

While in 1970 the VPOs accounted for 6.7 percent of total industrial output, by 1975 the share was increased to almost a quarter (24.4 percent) of total industrial output of the economy. Those figures, Hewett (1988, 245) maintains, continued to climb in the second half of the 1970s. By the early 1980s, VPOs represented almost one-half of total industrial outputs. The nonmember enterprises contributed the other half of the industrial output and, in most cases, were directly supervised by VPOs. The VPOs, however, lacked the authority and incentive for effective management of the enterprises, and ironically ended up exercising administrative control over the enterprises much as the *Glavki* did before.[31] Merger efforts were not successful, and actually represented the tendency of the Soviet leaders to look to supply-side solutions, instead of at the demand-side consequences of their problems.[32]

Reforms in the Economic Mechanisms

In 1979, Brezhnev's relatively stereotyped administration initiated another reform, apparently with the objective of bolstering efficiency and effectiveness in state enterprises. Although many of the proposals were not implemented, and the initiative clearly lacked commitment and support from the central administration, for heuristic purposes we briefly describe it in the following paragraphs. Brezhnev's 1979 reform, known as the Program to Improve the Economic Mechanism (PIEM), came in response to the dismal performance of Soviet economy. Apparently, Brezhnev's administration was disturbed by the slowdown of the economy, low level of labor productivity, and shortages of productive inputs resulting from extensive methods of production, and attempted to correct the situation by introducing PIEM. PIEM emphasized planning and supply elements as well as performance indicators of the enterprises. PIEM mainly emphasized: collection of more accurate information on factor inputs; application of a larger number of more precise input-output norms; closer approximation to "optimal tautness" in the planning of supply, production, and investment; better coordination of plans across time and space; and a greater role for enterprise contracts (Bornstein 1985, 2-8). In addition, every enterprise was asked to prepare an annual report providing detailed information on almost every aspect of its life, ranging from production capacity to financial flows.

PIEM's performance indicators envisaged more efficient use of human resources, fuel and other inputs, and designated labor productivity (calculated as net, rather than gross output per worker) as a key indicator. Use of technology for improving product quality or producing new products was recognized as an important performance indicator. In addition, fulfillment of contract delivery obligations (covering volume, assortment, quality and timeliness) constituted another important performance indicator for enterprises. Besides these, other indicators, such as total cost, profit, and gross or marketable output, remained significant.[33]

PIEM also attempted to strengthen incentives for the achievement of plan assignments, primarily by altering arrangements for enterprise material incentive funds and by promoting the use of the brigade as a form of work organization. PIEM's biggest change was the designation of labor productivity and the share of highest-quality output in total output as the "main fund-forming indicators" for enterprises. By tying the size of the enterprise's material incentive fund for personal bonuses to top-quality-grade output, a linkage was established between growth of labor productivity and growth of output. Besides, promotion of the brigade as a form of work organization was expected to provide incentives to production workers. The brigade system indeed attained a moderate level of success for a short period of time. By the beginning of 1983, 75.1 percent of construction workers and 59 percent of industrial workers were organized in brigades. PIEM also envisaged efficiency in investment and promotion of self-financing and financial responsibility among the ministries and enterprises.

Reforms in Agriculture

Brezhnev's preoccupation with agriculture is reflected in the fact that of the eight Central Committee plenary sessions devoted to specific economic issues since 1965, six were concerned with agriculture. He initiated a number of capital-intensive strategies for revitalizing agriculture. Consequently, investment in the agricultural sector steadily increased. From 1961–65, on average about 19 percent of total national investment was devoted to agriculture. This rose to 27 percent for the five years between 1976 and 1980—possibly over 33 percent, if investment in related industrial fields is also considered (see Kurtzweg 1987).

This huge influx of capital naturally allowed Brezhnev to pursue massive programs aimed at upgrading agricultural production and mending previously neglected infrastructures. Ambitious programs were undertaken to increase the supply of fertilizers, tractors, electricity, water, and so forth, to rural areas. In addition, Brezhnev promoted individual household plots, extended regular monthly payments and provided better pension benefits to the *kolkhozniki*. Also, efforts were made to reduce urban-rural income gaps. But like other reform attempts, Brezhnev's agricultural program essentially involved policy changes; few substantive structural modifications were initiated. No attempt was made to significantly revamp an overcentralized and truncated agricultural administration, nor to do away with huge food subsidies. The Brezhnev regime also failed to stamp out the serious rural exodus of badly needed youth and talent to the urban centers.

Bureaucratic Collectivism

Economically, Brezhnev's period was characterized by proceduralism and incrementalism, and politically, Brezhnev demonstrated a commitment to the continuation of the system, often attempting to revive elements of Stalinism that were earlier discarded by Khrushchev. Of the five elements of Stalinist totalitarianism, Khrushchev orchestrated a sharp break with the Stalinist model by rejecting personal tyranny of dictator and eliminating secret police terror. But, as pointed out before, Khrushchev found continuation of central planning and one-party rule to be indispensable for the system. Thus, Khrushchev made a transition from an "ideal totalitarianism" characterized by "complete state control" over the economy, politics and intellectual activity to a "classic form of authoritarianism" in which state control over all these were softened (Migranian 1990b). But, inheriting Khrushchev's classic form of authoritarianism, Brezhnev has been charged with establishing a "bureaucratic collectivism" of the political process itself.

Moreover, Brezhnev's movement from "stability to immobility" (Nove 1980, 371), as demonstrated in the establishment of bureaucratic collective leadership, showed inclinations more toward Stalinist totalitarianism than away from it. Neither in his address to the Twenty-third Party Congress in 1966, nor in the Twenty-fourth Party Congress in 1971, did Brezhnev demonstrate his disassociation with Stalinism, and in both cases he defended Stalinist excesses under the pretext of an early stage of economic development (see Evans, Jr. 1986). But in the Twenty-third Party Congress, Brezhnev reversed the previous position of the CPSU not to permit the same individual to hold both the top Party and government positions simultaneously, and not only got the position of general secretary of the CPSU reinstated, but also was able to elevate the position's authority and responsibility substantially. Nevertheless, although the collective leadership at the top... vested preponderant authority in the post of the general secretary, Brezhnev's position was largely "first among equals" in the politburo.

Goldman (1983, 18) remarks that Brezhnev did not abuse power as Stalin did, nor was he as "psychotic as Stalin was," but nevertheless, his hard-line policies, "apologia for the status quo," and support for the orthodox theorists (Brown 1989, 6) succeeded in replacing "inspiring hopes for reforms and visions of the future" with conservative defense of "bureaucratic positions of power against all liberalizing influences from within the country and from without" (Holt, Rinehart & Winston 1974, 194). But although Brezhnev ended up with a conservative, immobile, and status-quo type regime, and although no substantive change took place in other spheres of the Soviet Union, the Brezhnevian period did not reinvoke Stalinist totalitarianism. Brezhnev sided with hardliners and orthodox socialists, but he did not indulge in secret police terror or personal tyranny as Stalin did. Therefore, subsequent leaders could take up the task of de-Stalinization where Khrushchev had to stop: in central planning's monopoly control over the economy and the CPSU's monopoly control over the state and society.

Evaluation of Brezhnev's Period

From the above discussion, one can surmise how timid Brezhnev's reform efforts were, and how modestly they were implemented. The decrees of 1973 and 1979 were not even adequately backed by governmental administrative and political support. In the agricultural sector, for example, Brezhnev hardly attempted to resolve structural defects in planning and management. As a result, capital-intensive agricultural programs started to show signs of diminishing returns by the mid-1970s. Compounded by unfavorable weather conditions, the average annual growth of gross agricultural output, as shown in Table 2.4, plummeted from a respectable 3.4 percent for 1966-70 to -2.3 percent during 1971-76 and then rose to a meager 1.2 percent during 1976-80.

The consequences of Brezhnev's conservatism, bureaucratic management, and commitment to proceduralism were simply disastrous. The most visible manifestation of this disaster was economic stagnation, the catastrophic decline in actual economic growth of the Soviet Union in the late seventies and early eighties. Economic growth declined to an annual rate of perhaps 1 percent by 1979 and 1980. Compared to the eighth plan, industrial and agricultural output sharply declined during the ninth plan, national income fell alarmingly, and efficiency was reduced to one-third of the previous plan level (see Table 2.4). All these called for serious and immediate action for the whole economy.

Table 2.4
Soviet Economic Performance (sector-wise), 1966-85
(Average annual rate of growth)

Sector	1966-70	1971-75	1976-80	1981-85
GNP	4.9	3.1	2.1	1.9
Agriculture	3.4	-2.3	1.2	1.2
Industry	6.0	5.6	2.4	2.0
Construction	5.4	5.6	2.5	2.1
Transportation	7.1	6.5	3.6	2.2
Communication	8.6	6.4	4.7	3.9
Trade	7.1	4.7	2.7	1.8
Services	4.3	3.4	2.7	2.2
Others	3.6	2.1	1.7	1.1

Source: CIA Handbook of Economic Statistics, 1989.

Brezhnev's death, according to Goldman (1987, 69), was overdue by four years. Under Brezhnev's eighteen years of conservative leadership the Soviet economy reached a near-crisis situation. Although Brezhnev channeled almost one-fifth of the nation's total investment to agriculture, in 1979 Soviet Union experienced the largest drop in its grain harvest in its entire history. Consequently, in the early eighties formal food rationing was introduced in several major cities. In the industrial sector the situation was equally puzzling. Industrial production declined terribly; moreover, shortages of human resources, fuel and other industrial inputs reached chronic levels. Drunkenness, alcoholism, absenteeism, and corruption had decisive effects on worker morale and productivity. To the Soviet people, the end of Brezhnev's regime of unchallenged corruption, stagnant economy and sterile leadership came as a relief.[34]

CONCLUDING REMARKS

The evolution of the Soviet political economy, as explained above, clearly demonstrates centralized/decentralized and democratic/authoritarian approaches to socialist economy and society. The periods of the NEP, under Khrushchev and Kosygin, were characterized by economic decentralization and political liberalization, while the periods of War Communism, Stalin's command economy, and Brezhnev's bureaucratic collectivism were characterized by more economic centralization and political authoritarianism. It can also be argued that the Soviet Union started with an extremely centralized, and nonmonetary socialist economy and gradually moved away from extreme centralization towards greater decentralization. The movement toward decentralization was neither unidirectional nor smooth, however. There have been twists and turns, and bold initiatives for reform have often been reversed and abandoned in midstream. But generally, economic reforms contributed to further decentralization and softening of control of central planning and direction.

Discussions in Chapters 1 and 2 demonstrate how waves of reforms, that is, centralization and decentralization, influenced the performance of the Soviet economy. The highest rate of economic growth was experienced during the NEP period, and a relative decline took place during the Stalinist period. Also, the growth rate of the economy was very high in the fifties as compared to the sixties and onward. Therefore, no correlation between higher degrees of decentralization and higher growth rates can be generated. The growth rate was higher during the Stalinist model, when economic administration was extremely centralized, and the rate has been extremely low during the late seventies and early eighties, when the economy was greatly decentralized. Still, one cannot conclude that decentralization is invariably associated with lower rates of economic growth, because the relatively more centralized Brezhnevian period was associated with a relatively lower rate of economic growth than that of the Khrushchevian period, which was characterized by relatively greater decentralization. The previous discussion also shows that the decentralized periods worked reasonably well, and were generally associated with higher standards of living. They certainly outperformed centralized approaches in terms of "higher ideals of socialism" while not lagging behind the centralized models in terms of "lower ideals of socialism."[35]

NOTES

1. Ward (1967, 105) identifies four necessary (and, according to him, sufficient) conditions of a centralized economy: (1) integrated hierarchic organization: (2) separation of rewards and short-run performance by the use of instructions; (3) strong and generalized sanctions against disobedience of instructions; and (4) promotion within the hierarchy as the major interest-oriented incentive. According to Asselain (1984, 13-30), three fundamental elements of a centralized socialist economy are: (1) concentration of economic power in the hands of the central authorities; (2) a passive role of money; and (3) an elaborate incentive system, based either on an a priori assessment by the authorities or on comparison with the previous year's performance.

2. Although a high degree of centralization has been one of the most striking characteristics of the Soviet economy ever since the October Revolution, theories of a centrally planned socialist economic system are rather a recent phenomenon. Besides owing their origins to the Marxian vision, three separate factors can be held responsible for the outgrowth of centralized socialism: (1) actual experience in the socialist economies especially in the Soviet Union; (2) responses to the "Great

Socialist Controversy" of the thirties; and (3) defense of central planning and challenge to the decentralized (market) model of socialism.

3. Defenders of centralized socialism usually cite such quotations as the following from the writings of Marx and Engels:

- Within the cooperative society based on common ownership of the means of production, the producers do not exchange their products; just as little does the labor employed on the products appear as the value of these products, as a material quality possessed by them, since now, in contrast to capitalist society, individual labor no longer exists in an indirect fashion but directly as a component part of the total labor. (Marx 1973, 17).

- The national centralization of the means of production will become the natural base for a society which will consist of an association of free and equal producers acting consciously according to a general and rational plan. (Marx, quoted in Selucky 1979, 47).

- State ownership of the productive force is not the solution of the conflict [between the social character of the productive forces and private ownership of means of production], but it contains within itself the formal means, the key to the solution. This solution can only consist in the recognition in practice of the social nature of the modern productive forces, in bringing, therefore, the mode of production, appropriation and exchange into accord with the social character of the means of production. And this can only be brought about by society, openly and without deviation, taking possession of the productive forces. (Engels 1939, 304-5).

- No society can permanently retain the mastery of its own production and the control over the social effects of its process of production unless it abolishes exchange between individuals (Engels quoted in Selucky 1979, 9).

- In communist society it will be easy to know what is being produced and what is being consumed. As we know what each individual needs, on the average, it will be easy to calculate what a definite number of individual needs, and since production will no longer be in the hands of any private producers but in those of the Commune and its administration, it will not be at all difficult to regulate production according to needs. (Engels quoted in Bettleheim 1975, 32).

- The life process of society, which is based on the process of material production, does not strip off its veil until it is treated as production by freely associated men, and is consciously regulated by them in accordance with a settled plan (Marx 1967, I:80).

4. While Robinson (1965, III:158) sees a "clear connection between backwardness and socialism," Baran (1957, 26) asserts that the "establishment of a socialist planned economy is an essential, indeed indispensable, condition for the attainment of economic and social progress in underdeveloped economies."

5. Arguing in the same line, Sweezy (Bettleheim & Sweezy 1971, 52-53) remarks that although "actually drawn from several classes and struggling with the

life and death tasks of running the economy" the dictatorship of the proletariat "molded into a revolutionary force" in an underdeveloped economy has not only the potentiality to overthrow the old system, but also to transform society "culturally, politically, even technologically." Mainly based on the Soviet experience, Dobb (1961) concludes that socialism, by transforming economic underdevelopment into a basis for material prosperity, in fact provides a platform for making the transition to communism at a later stage.

6. Although Dobb (1970, 187) strongly maintains that "one cannot carry over from capitalism the advantages of an automatic decision-making mechanism without importing its principal defects as well," he nevertheless emphasized autonomy of production units in "discretion as to what and how much to produce, choice of inputs and sources of supply, problems of employment and personnel on the basis of given plant and equipment" (140). He did not rule out the possibility of having retail prices of consumer goods reflecting market prices (137). Emphasizing a blend of market and planning, he stipulated that "even if planning embraces a multitude of detail, [it] does not preclude the necessity for operational commands at various levels concerned with execution and with the complex of particular decisions associated therewith" (133). To Dobb (1966, 245), the crucial test for a socialist economic system is not "the attainment of perfect equilibrium in any given situation," but a successful transition from "one economic situation, with its given combination of resources and configurations of demand to another."

7. In *The Political Economy of Growth*, Baran (1957) distinguished three varieties of economic surplus—actual, potential and planned. Actual economic surplus referred to the difference between actual consumption and actual output of an economy. Potential economic surplus was the difference between what could be produced and essential consumption, and planned economic surplus stood for the difference between optimum output and optimal consumption. Based on such differentiation of economic surplus, Baran concluded that mobilization and allocation of the planned economic surplus was the key strategy for centrally planned economic development in an underdeveloped economy. He, therefore, emphasized a 'rational plan' that would stipulate what a society wished to produce, consume, save or invest in order to mobilize the potential economic surplus.

8. In *What is to Be Done?* Lenin (1967, 97-256) condemned trade-unionist politics of the working class as "precisely bourgeois politics of the working class" (167), and maintained that "Class political consciousness can be brought to the *workers only from without*, that is, only from outside the economic struggle, from outside the sphere of relations between workers and employers" (163). Expressing serious doubts in the ability of trade unionists to organize and lead all classes of the population, Lenin emphasized "organic contact" with the proletarian struggle of all strata of the population (168). He asked the Social Democratic Party to organize "an all-round political struggle" in such a manner as to make it possible for all oppositional strata to render their fullest support to the struggle and to the party (168). But he emphasized that "the party is organized strongly along the principles of hierarchy and iron discipline; that it relies on centralism rather than on autonomism,

on bureaucracy rather than on democracy" (Selucky 1979, 98-99). No doubt, this reflected the harsh, autocratic conditions of Czarist Russia, wherein any radical or democratic organization perforce had to be underground. Luxemburg (1961, 84) excoriated Lenin's strict centralism as "a mechanical transposition of the organizational principles of Blanquism into the mass movement of the socialist working class".

9. Marx's position in this context deserves mention here. Marx maintained that during the transition period the dictatorship of the proletariat would operate through the state to smash the defeated exploiting class. To many scholars, as described above, Marx's emphasis on winning the battle of democracy in *The Communist Manifesto* indicates his concern that the content of the dictatorship of the proletariat be "rule of the majority, by the majority and for the majority" (Selucky 1979, 63).

10. According to Sik (1976, 370-78), by developing the theory of two phases of socialism in the *State and Revolution* Lenin claimed that the proletarian state will not wither away immediately after the revolution. He rather tacitly shifted the emphasis from the transitional role of the proletarian state "in repressing remnants of the defeated classes to that of control over labor and distribution throughout a lengthy period of socialist development," and thereby extended the concept of dictatorship of the proletariat to cover the entire phase of transition to communism. Lenin's position in this regard has been elaborated in Chapter 1.

11. Trotsky was undeniably in favor of central planning, but he simultaneously underscored the necessity for continuation of market processes. Undoubtedly Trotsky was less enthusiastic than Bukharin in defending a harmonious relationship between industry and agriculture, but unlike Preobrazhensky, another defender of leftist arguments of the debate of the twenties, he strongly denounced the idea of suppressing agriculture to promote industry.

12. In the context of the viewpoints of Western centralized socialists on the state and democracy, it should be noted that they emphasized the state's paramount role in a socialist system established in an underdeveloped economy. Given the backwardness of the economy, they argue, the primary role of the state would be to plan the allocation and distribution of economic resources for rapid industrialization and modernization. This, in turn, would require the state to actively direct economic resources/investments to selected sectors. However, in the context of a socialist system operating in economically advanced conditions, Western centralized socialists would emphasize a circumscribed role for the state so as to accommodate greater democratization of society and decentralization of economic mechanisms.

13. Samuelson (1976, 642) observes that long before the "great socialist controversy" of the 1930s, around the year 1900, Italian economist Valfredo Pareto showed that "an ideal socialism would have to solve the same equations as competitive capitalism" and "rational economic organization was logically impossible in the absence of free markets." Representing the other side of the debate, Lange (1938), Lerner (1944), Taylor (1929), and Dickinson (1939) have argued, based on neoclassical analysis, that decentralized socialism is not only possible, it

might even be superior in economic performance to the capitalist competitive model. Subsequently, numerous decentralized socialist models have been developed that showed that markets, socialism, and democracy are compatible (see Selucky 1979; Miller and Estrin 1989; Harrington 1989b; Sik 1976; Brus 1972 & 1973; Yunker 1979; Vanek 1970).

14. Centralized socialists do not oppose democracy per se. However, in certain contexts (e.g., revolution in an autocratic regime (Lenin), or industrialization in a peasant-based society (Dobb)), democratic practices might be impracticable to a greater or lesser extent.

15. Dobb asserts:

We have seen that there are numerous cases .... where there is good reason for supposing that his individual verdict is not to be trusted, either because he is insufficiently rational or lacks the experience and sophistication needed to adjust his desires to real satisfactions, because he lacks sufficient information, or because there are effects of his own consumption on others of which he takes no account (or insufficient account). There seems to be no reasonable ground for treating individual desires as an ultimate beyond which there can be no appeal, or consumers' sovereignty as possessing some kind of value per se. (ibid., 220-21).

16. Elliott (1985, 337) recapitulates the major differences and similarities between the main economic postulates and principles of centralized and decentralized socialism:

Centralized socialism shares with decentralized socialism: government ownership and control of capital and natural resources, a central government planning body and government hierarchy as a social process for making and coordinating economic decisions, and smaller income inequality through the reduction of private property, coupled with wage differentials as a source of incentives. Centralized socialism diverges from decentralized socialism: in its assumption that socialism will typically emerge in underdeveloped economies with a precapitalistic or only rudimentary capitalist resource base; in its critique of consumer sovereignty and its concentration of economic power in government and a highly centralized governmental planning body, with responsibility for the formulation of plans for the promotion of governmentally-determined goals; in its sharp restriction of the price system and its correspondingly heavier reliance on hierarchically structured governmental bureaucracy as the dominant social process for making and coordinating economic decisions; and in its determination of wage differentials by governmental planning rather than market bidding.

17. It is indeed interesting that Lange originally articulated the decentralized market model as a rebuttal to the neo-Austrian critique of socialism's possibility/feasibility during the great debate of socialist controversy; then in the postwar period, influenced mainly by actual experience in socialist countries, he came up with the compromise formula of centralization during the earlier stages of economic

development and decentralization at the later stage. Dobb, who originally favored decentralized socialism, also changed his position later in view of the actual experiences in socialist countries, and became a prominent protagonist of a centralized model of socialism.

18. Cliff (1978, 83) maintains that out of the 1,208 industries nationalized by the end of 1918, less than 30 percent were expropriated by state decree, the rest were taken at the initiative of local organizations.

19. According to Kritzman (quoted in Cliff 1978, 88), out of a total of 136 million pud of cereal that reached the consumers in 1919, only 40 percent was distributed by the state; a booming illegal market did the rest.

20. Shmelev and Popov (1989, 7) maintain that because of the principle of "leveled distribution" of War Communism, in 1917, a highly skilled worker was paid 2.3 times more than an unskilled worker, in 1918, he was paid 1.3 times more, and in 1920, his payment was only 1.04 times more than an unskilled worker.

21. Policies of the period made money virtually worthless. For the magnitude of printing and depreciation of money during 1916-21, see Shmelev and Popov 1989, 5-6.

22. During the five years after Lenin's death, Stalin faced a tremendous challenge from both left-wing opposition, led by Leon Trotsky, and right-wing opposition, led by Nikolai Bukharin. A master politician, Stalin succeeded in eliminating both oppositions, and established himself as the unchallenged leader of the CPSU. Both Trotsky and Bukharin were members of the CPSU Politburo at the time of Lenin's death. Stalin exiled Trotsky, and, later, executed Bukharin. (see Dowlah 1990b, 191-200; Bideleux 1985).

23. Exact human and material cost of Stalin's collectivization drive remains controversial. Few scholars doubt that collectivization was brutally imposed on an unwilling peasantry. According to some authors, 3.5 million *kulaks* (vaguely, including any resisters on the part of peasantry as a whole) were thrown into labor camps, 3.5 million were resettled, and another 3.5 million lost their lives. Stalin himself admitted that about 10 million perished during the forced collectivization drive (see Shmelev & Popov 1989, 48). Nonhuman costs of the collectivization drive were equally appalling. Peasant resistance to the drive for forced collectivization resulted in the devastation of livestock and agricultural implements. By January 1931, the number of cattle had decreased 30 percent, sheep and goats had decreased 37 percent, and the number of hogs had declined 50 percent (see Adams 1972, 60). Such devastation not only induced bitter peasant hatred, especially by *kulaks*, toward collectivization of agriculture, but also had disastrous effects on Stalin's regime and the Soviet economy. As a result, during the early 1930s agricultural production dropped alarmingly and a severe food crisis crippled the Soviet economy.

24. Stalinist agricultural policy, however, allowed each household to hold approximately one acre of land to work for its own needs and for sale in local markets.

25. Marx pointed out that exploitations based on conquest, enslavement, robbery, murder, and force, were historically demonstrated "secrets" of primitive

capitalist accumulation. For Stalin and other "super-industrializers," in the absence of such opportunities, the only feasible and possible arena for "primitive socialist accumulation" appeared to be exploitation of the peasantry, to establish control over their labor, food output, raw materials, and exports, and to channel them for industrialization under strict governmental planning and management.

26. Stalin's (1955, 312) famous declaration in this regard is worth quoting: "We are fifty or a hundred years behind the advanced countries. We must make good this distance in ten years. Either we do it or we go under."

27. Stalinist capital accumulation sources included the reduction in rental, interest, and royalty charges on industry and the state; the profits of state industry and banks; the state monopoly of foreign trade; taxation; public borrowing; retail price increases; reduction and simplification of the State and cooperative apparatus; a crackdown on absenteeism, and mass participation based on shop floor production conferences (see Bideleux 1985, 117).

28. Totalitarianism, both as a concept and empirical phenomenon, is essentially a twentieth-century phenomenon and has been a widely studied topic, especially since the early fifties. In common parlance, however, totalitarianism is widely understood as negation or elimination of democracy or popular participation in the governmental processes, elimination of the rule of law and separation of powers, ruthless and combined use of terror, coercion, and propaganda. Friedrich and Brezezinski (1956) identified six characteristics of totalitarianism: an official, monopolistic ideology; a single political party; pervasive police terror; monopoly over communication of ideas; monopoly over weapons; and a centrally directed economy. Of course, many other theoretical definitions, characterizations, and empirical varieties of totalitarianism can be found in the relevant literature. (see Moore, Jr. 1967; Arendt 1966; Hayes 1939; Jones 1985; Skocpol 1983; Almond & Roselle 1989).

29. It should, however, be noted that whether the Stalinist "full-blown totalitarian regime" was a product of a Bolshevik "totalitarian embryo" (Fainsod 1963) or a "triumph over Bolshevism" remains widely debated in Sovietology (see Tucker 1977). The controversy between continuity/discontinuity theorists will be taken up in greater detail in Chapter 4.

30. Shmelev and Popov (1989, 58-64) maintain that at the time of Stalin's death alone there were 12 million people in forced labor camps.

31. Goldman (1987, 57) maintains that VPOs turned out to be "nothing more than a disguised version of the old, pre-reform administrative units," and in most cases, "the change involved nothing more than calling in a painter to put a new title on the old door."

32. According to Hewett (1988, 245), mergers initiated by 1973 decrees were actually a bureaucratic attempt to imitate financially successful mergers in the United States.

33. Another notable feature of 1979 reforms was Normative Net Output (NNO), calculated as the product of the quantity of output and the net output normative per unit of each item. Replacement of traditional gross output by NNO as an indicator

of enterprise performance was apparently aimed at facilitating transition from extensive to intensive methods of production. Requiring greater use of inputs extensive methods contribute to gross or marketable output, but not to net output. Hence, NNO was expected to discourage the enterprises from using greater inputs of material, fuels, and energy.

34. Brezhnev's death, as Hewett (1988, 257) observes, "created a long-awaited opportunity for the Soviet elite to rethink their approach to the economy, and to introduce new reforms in an effort . . . to get the country moving again." During the two-and-a-half years between the death of Brezhnev in November 1982 and the appointment of Gorbachev as general secretary of the CPSU in March 1985, the Soviet Union had two leaders: Yuri Andropov (November 12, 1982-June 16, 1983), and Konstantin Cherenenko (February 13, 1984 - March 10, 1985). Both Andropov and Cherenenko were old when they assumed power, and their short tenures were not marked by any profound changes in the Soviet economy and society.

35. Higher ideals of socialism refer to greater democratization of work places, public participation in the governmental processes, liberation of human mind, creativity, and enthusiasm. Lower ideals of socialism, on the other hand, refer to factors like nationalization of the means of production, higher employment, and economic growth.

3

The Immediate Background
of *Perestroika*

INTRODUCTION

This chapter examines the immediate economic, political, and social problems that made the launching of *perestroika* an imperative for Mikhail Gorbachev. Gorbachev became the general secretary of the CPSU in March 1985, and within a month the campaign of *perestroika* was inaugurated and its main principles were enunciated by the Plenary Meeting of the CPSU Central Committee. Gorbachev and his advisers, however, maintain that *perestroika* was not instantaneous. The Soviet Union, asserts Gorbachev (1987, 17), had long been yearning for *perestroika* to emancipate a sleeping crippled society and reactivate a sluggish economy that was "verging on crisis." The new leadership comprehended that the whole nation—its economy, society, and culture—was deteriorating alarmingly (see Gorbachev 1988a).

By the early eighties, both the Soviet leadership and the citizenry came to realize that the existing economic and political infrastructures failed to respond to the needs of a mature, industrialized, and urbanized society (Zaslavskaya 1988), was hopelessly out of joint with reality (Kagarlitsky 1990b, 283-326), and was inconsistent with the needs and demands of the future (Yakovlev 1989). Indeed, a fundamentally transformed Soviet society demanded a thorough overhaul of every aspect of the country, both at the macro (national) and micro (individual and family) levels. Aganbegyan (1987, 6) asserts that rapidly worsening economic and political conditions in the country required a revolutionary reconstruction of society's economic and social bases and superstructures. Gorbachev (1987, 24) himself observes that there was "a growing awareness" in the public consciousness that things could not go on indefinitely as they were and any delay in beginning *perestroika*, he declares, "could have led to exacerbated internal situation."

Before embarking on the study of the radical and sweeping reforms initiated by *perestroika*, it will be useful first to see what went wrong in the Soviet economy and society. What are the underlying causes of the emergence of *perestroika*? Why was the Soviet economy at the verge of crisis? Why did the economy that Gorbachev inherited fall short in meeting the demands of new conditions? What were the new societal conditions that made revolutionary changes inevitable in the Soviet Union? How did the structure of production that once accomplished monumental success became so obsolete by the eighties? These questions are addressed in this chapter. Section two explores the economic background that Gorbachev inherited, Section three examines the socio-political background of *perestroika*, and Section five analyzes the implications of those economic, social and political backgrounds on the new Soviet leadership and *perestroika*.

ECONOMIC BACKGROUND OF *PERESTROIKA*

Gorbachev and his associates literally inherited the Soviet Union in crisis. In the early eighties, Soviet economy had been experiencing significantly low performance, if not failure. While in the fifties "the main arguments tended to center on when, not whether" (Miller 1987, 114) the Soviet economy would overtake that of the United States, in the early eighties the situation took a diagonal turn. The economic stagnation of the Brezhnevian period not only virtually shattered the dream of surpassing the capitalist countries, but also perilously punctured the very legitimacy of "real socialism" (Ellman 1986, 530).[1]

Indeed, the disappointing economic performance of the Soviet Union sent alarms around the globe. Many anticipated that if the trends of decline were not reversed soon, "the USSR will slide down the economic-league table of nations" (Hanson 1987, 10). Economic destabilizers like "stagnation, low productivity, low morale, and technological backwardness" were dragging the economy, "into the last quarter of the twentieth century" (Friedberg & Isham 1987, ix). Describing the existing economic situation as counterproductive, and suggesting that only urgent reforms could put the system back to work, Goldman (1983, 3) cautions that "the longer economic and political change is postponed, the more violent it is likely to be when it eventually comes." Birman (1988) agrees that the Soviet economic system was caught in a "vicious cycle" that could even lead to collapse. What really went wrong in the Soviet economy that could be held responsible for such a bleak situation?

Six major economic factors are pertinent to the emergence of *perestroika*: (1) a grand slowdown in the economic growth during the late seventies and early eighties; (2) strikingly low labor productivity in most Soviet industries; (3) the consistent failure to meet consumption needs and living standards; (4) a slowdown in demographic growth; (5) a conspicuous absence of economic incentive systems; and (6) other major problems to be explained below.

The Grand Slowdown in Economic Growth

The slowdown in the economic growth of the Soviet Union started in the latter part of the 1970s and was particularly significant in the early 1980s.[2] For heuristic purposes, we begin our investigation into the Soviet economy in the early sixties. Between 1960 and 1975, the Soviet Union's economic performance was unquestionably strong. During this period, the Soviet gross national product (GNP) doubled and annual rates of increase in GNP averaged over 4 percent.[3] Growth of the Soviet GNP began to decline during the late seventies (see Table 3.1). Kurtzweg (1987, 26) calculated that during the late seventies, GNP growth fell to an average of 2.3 percent a year, while the decline in the average growth in GNP actually fell to about 2 percent during 1975 to 1986. According to Aganbegyan (1988a, 2), the rate of growth of Soviet GNP (based on Soviet official statistical data) actually fell nearly 2.5 times during the three five-year plan periods between 1971 and 1985. Worse still, more accurate estimates indicate no growth at all during this period.

Table 3.1
USSR: Growth of GNP, MNP, and Factor Productivity, 1961-86

	GNP*	Adjusted GNP† (1) (2)	NMP‡	Difference Between 1 &2	Factor Productivity
Average annual growth in percent					
1961-65	4.8	5.0	6.5	1.5	0.3
1966-70	5.1	5.4	7.8	2.4	0.8
1971-75	3.0	3.3	5.7	2.4	-1.3
1976-80	2.3	2.3	4.3	2.0	-1.2
1981-85	1.9	1.8	3.6	1.8	-1.0
1986 preliminary	3.8	--	--	--	1.2

* GNP growth is based on estimates of value added at 1982 factor cost. † The weights used to calculate growth of adjusted GNP are estimates of 1982 value added in established prices rather than at factor cost. ‡ NMP is measured using a series of linked price bases (1958, 1965, and 1973), all earlier than that for GNP.
Source: Kurtzweg 1987, 135.

A comparison of growth of GNP and net material product (NMP)—the official Soviet measure closest to GNP—shows similar patterns over this period. During the period between 1960 and 1986, the rates of NMP growth exceeded GNP growth in the Soviet Union. This conforms to Aganbegyan's position and to traditional Western estimates of Soviet economic growth, on which we shall focus in a moment. Subbstantial omission of disguised inflation in the calculation of Soviet NMP accounts for the discrepency in its estimation.

The growth of GNP in the agricultural sector was negative during 1979-82, while during the years of 1984 and 1985 this sector registered no growth at all (see Table 3.2). It is precisely during this period that the Soviet economy, according to

Table 3.2
USSR: Selected Indicators of Soviet Economic Performance, 1971-85
(in percent per annum)

	1971-75	1976-78	1979-82	1983	1984	1985
Growth of GNP	3.7	3.7	1.6	3.2	2.0	--
Growth in Industry	5.9	3.8	2.4	3.4	4.3	3.9
Growth in Agriculture	-0.4	5.2	-0.9	6.3	0	0
Growth of national income used in consumption		(1976-80)	(1981)			
and accumulation	5.1	3.8	3.2	3.1	2.6	3.1

Source: Miller 1989, 115.

Aganbegyan (1988a, 3), plunged into an unprecedented stagnation and crisis situation. Soviet GNP in the fields of consumption and accumulation declined from the annual growth rate of 5.1 percent during 1971-75 to only 3.1 percent during 1985. However, a modest recovery in the industrial sector could be observed during 1984 and 1985. But as Miller (1987, 114) points out, this improvement was made possible at a very high cost. According to him, during the late seventies and early eighties both the level of investment growth and the rate of return per ruble of investment substantially declined. Therefore, during 1984 and 1985, the level of investment was increased, exceeding the original five-year plan targets, to prevent further decline in overall productivity. As the last column in Table 3.1 shows, Soviet economy experienced negative growth in factor productivity during 1971-85.

Table 3.3
Comparison of GNP Growth in USSR and Western Countries, 1961-85

	USSR	US	FRG	France	Italy	UK
Average annual growth in percent						
1961-65	4.8	4.6	4.8	5.8	5.2	3.2
1966-70	5.1	3.0	4.2	5.4	6.2	2.5
1971-75	3.0	2.2	2.1	4.0	2.4	2.2
1976-80	2.3	3.4	3.3	3.3	3.8	1.6
1981-85	1.9	2.4	1.3	1.1	0.9	1.9

*US GNP calculated in 1982 prices. GNP growths of FRG, France, Italy and UK are calculated from GDP in 1980 prices.

Source: Kurtzweg 1987, 136.

Table 3.3 compares GNP growth in the Soviet Union with that of several countries of the Organization for Economic Cooperation and Development (OECD). During 1976-85, the average annual rates of GNP growth in the Soviet Union were smaller than those of the United States. However, the rates of GNP growth were much higher in the USSR during 1961-75. During the periods of slowdown of the Soviet economy, between 1976-85, the increase in the growth of GNP in the OECD countries were also slower. For example, during 1981-85, the Soviet Union's economic growth equalled that of the United Kingdom, each registered at 1.9 percent growth. The performance of the industrial and agricultural sectors have been highlighted below.

Table 3.4
USSR: Growth of GNP by Sector of Origin, 1961-86*
(Average annual rates in percent)

Sectors	1961-65	1966-70	1971-75	1976-80	1981-85
Industry	6.5	6.4	5.5	2.7	1.9
Construction	4.7	5.4	4.5	2.9	2.9
Agriculture	2.8	3.4	-2.3	0.2	1.2
Transportation	10.2	7.2	6.6	3.6	2.3
Communication	7.3	8.6	6.4	4.7	3.8
Trade	5.0	7.3	4.5	2.7	1.6
Services†	4.4	4.3	3.5	2.7	2.2
Military Personnel‡	2.0	3.7	2.0	1.5	0.3

* Based on estimate of value added at 1982 factor cost. † Includes consumer services like housing and utilities. ‡ Includes military wages

Source: Kurtzweg 1987, 138.

Industrial Sector. Table 3.4 projects sectoral growth of total GNP in the Soviet economy for 1961-85. Economic performance in almost every sector of the Soviet economy declined over the last twenty five years. While the industrial sector grew 6.5 percent during the 1961-65, its growth fell to 1.9 percent during 1981-85. Moreover, for most of the post–1960 period, the growth in the industrial sector exceeded the overall growth rate of the economy.[4]

Part of the slowdown of industrial growth is explained by a declining growth in labor and capital inputs. The so-called extensive method of production that calls for putting more and more labor and capital inputs into production processes eventually resulted in diminishing returns by increasing the cost of extraction of raw materials and fuels and by causing a decline in labor productivity. Besides, the continued emphasis on heavy industry at the cost of light and consumer industry led the country toward an agonizingly wrong destination. As an inevitable result of the misplaced priorities based on the Stalinist model, developments in the manufacturing industry and the processing of raw materials were deplorably slow, and the service sector, according to Aganbegyan (1988a, 4), was the worst hit. It is indeed difficult to imagine a situation in which desperate Soviet people are forming ever larger queues on the streets for consumer goods, while the Soviet economy vigorously continues to produce steel and other industrial goods. Blunders of such character have caused the Soviet Union not only distressful consumer dissatisfaction, but have also charged to it the high cost of bypassing much needed scientific and technological revolutions.

Agriculture Sector. The performance of the Soviet economy has been most frustrating in the field of agriculture. For a long time the agricultural sector received almost a fifth or more of the total national investment, yet it had been a drag on both long-term and short-term growth of Soviet GNP. The contribution of the agricultural sector to the growth of Soviet GNP actually increased by about 40 percent during the period between 1960 and 1986. But, as Kurtzweg (1987, 143) points out, most of the gains were achieved before 1970 and since then, positive growth in some years has been followed by setbacks in others.

In fact, agriculture has consistently been a burden on the Soviet economy.[5] Although the Soviet Union was one of the world's largest grain exporters in the twenties, since the Stalinist period, it has become the world's largest grain importer. More than 20 percent of the Soviet labor force is employed in agriculture (compared to only 3-5 percent in the United States); yet, the Soviet Union every year imports as much as 25 percent of its grain requirements (see Table 3.5). Also, the Soviet Union throughout the 1970s imported almost 300 million tons of meat a year, even though one of the largest grazing lands of the world belongs to the country.

Table 3.5
Soviet Grain Harvest, Exports, and Imports, 1950-82
(Million metric tons)

Year	Harvest	Export	Import	Year	Harvest	Export	Import
1950	81	2.9	0.2	1968	170	5.4	1.6
1955	104	3.7	0.3	1969	162	7.2	0.6
1956	125	3.2	0.5	1970	187	5.7	2.2
1957	103	7.4	0.2	1971	181	8.6	3.5
1958	135	5.1	0.8	1972	168	4.6	15.5
1959	120	7.0	0.3	1973	223	4.9	23.9
1960	126	6.8	0.2	1974	196	7.0	7.1
1961	131	7.5	0.7	1975	140	3.6	15.9
1962	140	7.8	--	1976	224	1.5	20.6
1963	108	6.3	3.1	1977	196	3.0	10.5
1964	152	3.5	7.3	1978	237	1.5	23.0
1965	121	4.3	6.4	1979	179	3.0	25.5
1966	171	3.6	7.7	1980	189	2.0	30-35.0
1967	148	6.2	2.2	1981	160	3.0	43.0

Source: Goldman 1983, 65.

Aganbegyan (1988a, 83-84) observes that at the start of the 1980s the situation in agriculture was worse than at the beginning of the 1960s. At the end of the eighth plan (1966-70) agricultural output of the country increased by 21 percent, but during the ninth plan period the output went up only 13 percent. During the tenth plan period (1976-80) agricultural output increased by only 9 percent, while during the eleventh plan period (1981-84) the agricultural sector made no progress at all.[6]

Evidently, one of the chronic problems of Soviet agriculture is undercapitalization. Relatively less favorable natural conditions in the Soviet Union calls for a higher level of capital intensity in agriculture. But Soviet agriculture relative to the United States and to the specified output targets for the sector remains undercapitalized. For the poor performance of agriculture in the Soviet Union, three factors can be held responsible: low investment in rural infrastructure, adverse composition of labor, and faulty procurement prices for agricultural goods (see Miller 1981). We have seen above that agriculture absorbs more than 20 percent of Soviet investment annually.[7] But the Soviet agricultural labor force is composed mainly of non-working-age people, and their productivity level is low.[8] Another formidable problem emanates from procurement prices for agricultural goods, which, like other prices in the Soviet Union, do not reflect real economic trade-offs.

Besides the legacy of the Stalinist model, the organizational, planning, and administrative practices could be held substantially responsible for the systemic failure of this sector. Another systemic constraint on Soviet agriculture, Bornstein (1981, 270) maintains, is its very large size and lack of specialization: "They get assignments for the delivery of too many products to permit them to specialize in what they can best produce." Other major constraints on the agricultural sector include the tendency to overcentralize decision-making, to overcommit resources in the planning process, and to restrict private initiative in agriculture.

Low Productivity

The Soviet Union's strategy for economic growth traditionally relied heavily on rapid infusion of productive resources—increased use of labor, fixed capital, and raw material inputs. The Soviets call this the "extensive" method of development; Western writers often call it a "classical" or "traditional" strategy for economic growth. Given the context of its enormous resources, this extensive method of production has had little difficulty in accelerating the growth rate of the country. In fact, since 1960, the Soviet Union achieved the highest growth of employment, and was second only to Japan in the growth of fixed capital stock. But, unfortunately, the Soviet Union made too little effort to increase the productivity of its productive resources. As Table 3.6 explicates, the Soviet Union has the lowest combined rate of increase of labor and capital productivity among the industrialized economies.[9]

How, then, was the Soviet economy moving faster than any industrialized economy in the world, except perhaps Japan? The secret of the initial overwhelming success of the extensive growth strategy lies in the country's resource endowment and in institutional factors. Until the 1960s the Soviet economy could draw upon an unusually large pool of unemployed agricultural labor, so industrial employment of labor could be increased easily. The high rate of growth of productive capital stock was made possible by mobilizing an unusually high national savings. The investment/GNP ratio in Soviet economy reached 26.0 percent, second only to that of Japan (32.0 percent); the U.S. rate during the same period was 18.2 percent (see Cohn 1987). The high rates of investment for growth were then reinforced by an investment policy that favored heavy industry over consumer goods production. Aganbegyan (1988a, 7) points out that in any typical postwar five-year plan period, "the basic application of funds and capital investment increased 1.5 times, the extraction of fuel and raw materials by 25-30 precent, and a further 10-11 million people were recruited" into the Soviet economy.

Table 3.6

Comparison of Soviet and Western Real Gross Product, Factor Inputs, and Productivities, 1960-78

(Average annual percentage rates of change)

Country/yrs.		Real Gross Product	Factor Inputs			Factor Productivities		
			Total	Labor	Capital	Total	Labor	Capital
US	1960-73	4.4	2.3	1.3	4.1	2.1	3.1	0.3
	1973-78	2.9	2.3	1.5	3.6	0.6	1.4	-0.7
Japan	1960-73	10.8	4.7	0.9	12.2	6.1	9.9	-1.4
	1973-78	3.8	2.5	0.2	7.2	1.3	3.6	-3.4
UK	1960-73	2.9	0.8	-0.9	3.9	2.1	3.8	-1.0
	1973-78	0.4	0.1	--	4.7	1.8	4.0	-1.7
France	1960-73	5.8	1.9	-0.1	5.1	3.9	5.9	0.7
	1973-78	3.0	1.2	-1.0	4.7	1.8	4.0	-1.7
USSR	1960-73	5.2	3.6	1.4	8.8	1.5	3.7	-3.2
	1973-78	3.6	3.3	1.3	8.1	0.3	2.3	-4.5

Source: Cohn 1987, 12.

But the extensive growth strategy started to face challenges after 1975, when growth in the use of resources in the economy began to decline dramatically. By the late seventies, the Soviet economy actually began to face diminishing returns, and in the early eighties a "near-crisis situation or stagnation" became pronounced. Birth rates declined sharply, exhaustion of surplus rural labor became widely manifest, and a startling drop in the growth of plant and equipment dismayed the politicians. By Soviet measurements, the return on investment has fallen by half in the past thirty years and by a third in the past decade.

Slowing growth of resources is, however, a typical phenomenon for the industrialization process. What is peculiar about the Soviet Union is that the level of Soviet "productivity fell from levels that were below those in market economies at similar stages of economic development" (Cohn 1987, 13). Another crucial factor is that while market economies utilized modern technology to improve the productivity of labor and capital, the Soviet Union largely ignored it. Technological progress has proceeded considerably more slowly in the Soviet economy than in other advanced industrialized economies (Table 3.6).

The discrepancies in the degree of intensification of resources in Soviet-type economies and the industrialized West European market economies can be gauged from Table 3.7. In none of the major industrialized economies of the world did technological progress account for less than 50 percent of growth of output between 1950-62. But in the Soviet Union, as Berliner (1981, 296) points out, technological progress contributed only 42 percent of its growth of output during the same period.[10] Soviets also lag far behind the United States in key technologies. A CIA and DIA report (1989, 16) estimates that the Soviet Union is lagging behind the United States eight to ten years in advanced microcircuits, four to ten years in minicomputers, nine to fifteen years in mainframe computers, and eleven to fifteen years in supercomputers.

Table 3.7
Resource Intensity of Soviet-type Economies and Industrialized West European Market Economies: Energy and Steel, 1979-80

Countries	Energy Intensity*	Steel Intensity **
Soviet-type Economies		
Bulgaria	1464	87
Czechoslovakia	1290	132
Hungary	1058	88
GDR	1356	88
Poland	1515	135
USSR	1490	135
West European Market-Economies		
Austria	603	39
Belgium	618	36
Denmark	502	30
Finland	767	40
France	502	42
FRG	565	52
Italy	655	79
Sweden	713	44

* Energy intensity in 1979 in kg of coal equivalent consumption per 1,000 US dollars of GDP. ** Steel intensity in 1980 in kg of steel consumption per 1,000 US dollars of GDP.
Source: Winiecki 1986, 327.

Failures of Soviet Consumption

By the standards of the Western industrialized countries, per capita consumption

in the Soviet Union remains low and largely unsatisfactory, and according to many
Sovietologists, is out of proportion to the Soviet Union's industrial, scientific,
technological, and educational achievements.[11] Besides forced diversion of an ever
larger share of national resources to heavy industry and defense during the thirties
and forties, the lag in the consumer sector can also be traced to "the negative
tendencies in economic development that surfaced during the last fifteen years"
(Aganbegyan 1988a, 81). By applying the so-called leftover principle (i.e., preference of industry, defense and agriculture above the consumer sector), past regimes
in the Soviet Union aggravated the economic situation of the country.

Although the consumer sector accounts for 37 percent of national accumulation,
because of the leftover principle, it receives only 8 percent of capital investment.
The steady reduction of Soviet GNP share to the consumer sector is clearly visible
from the following figures: Outlays on housing construction dropped from 23
percent in 1960 to 14-15 percent in the early eighties; expenditures in the educational sector during the same period dropped from 10 to 7 percent; and national
income allocated to medical services dropped to less than 4 percent (see Aganbegyan
1988a, 75-88; 1987, 103-7). Low quality of goods, frequent unavailability of
necessities, and poor delivery systems often compounded the situation further.

Table 3.8
USSR: Consumption Per Capita, 1928-75

Year	1950 = 100	Interval	Growth (in Percent)
1928	88.0	1928-37	-0.3
1937	85.3	1937-40	-1.0
1940	82.8	1940-44	-10.0
1944	56.7	1944-50	9.9
1950	100.0	1950-55	5.3
1955	129.3	1955-60	4.2
1960	159.2	1960-65	2.5
1965	180.5	1965-70	4.6
1970	226.8	1970-75	3.2
1975	264.9		

Source: Aboucher 1979, 29.

Per capita consumption in the Soviet Union declined through the 1930s and then
marked an annual increase of 5.3 percent during 1950-55, and then again registered
an annual increase of 4.2 percent between 1955-60 (see Table 3.8). In the early
sixties the growth declined to 2.5 percent but again increased to 4.6 percent during
1965-70. In the early seventies the growth again dropped to a rate of 3.2 percent.[12]

The food problem remains a great concern for the Soviet Union. Aganbegyan
(1988a, 80-85) estimates that while in other developed nations per head meat
consumption a year is 75-80 kg or even 85 kg, in the Soviet Union it is 62 kg.

Moreover, Aganbegyan points out, the Soviet population annually consumes only 33 percent of the medically recommended level of fruit. Because of the low quality of domestically produced goods and scarcity of imported goods, consumers have little to buy, and eventually end up with huge savings. Such enormous savings in individual hands naturally promotes an enormous private illegal market (the second economy) that, according to some estimates, could be as big as 25 percent of Soviet GNP (see Goldman 1983, 55-56; Grossman 1977, 25).

Slowdown in Demographic Growth

The problems discussed above are further compounded, Soviet leaders believe, by a sharp decline in the growth of the labor force in the eighties. Soviet leaders consider the rapid decline in the annual increment of the working-age population (for women 16-55 and for men 16-60) as an "extremely adverse factor" (Kostakov 1988, 22) to the growth of the Soviet economy.[13] Between 1971 and 1978, the Soviet Union's working-age population increased by more than two million each year, but since 1976 the annual net increment to the working-age population has been steadily falling, from 2.7 million in 1976 to 0.4 million in 1985 (Ellman 1986, 536). This decline in the working-age population during the late seventies and early eighties has been further compounded by a falling birth rate and a sharp increase in the number of pension-age population.

Another dimension of the Soviet Union's current labor shortage is that it shows a clear trend to be highly regionally specific. Recent demographic figures indicate that the labor shortage is acute in the traditionally industrialized regions like Ukraine, Russia, Belorussia, and the Baltic republics, where the working-age population is expected to remain constant or decline in the 1980s. On the other hand, an increase in the working-age population is expected in the industrially less developed regions.[14] Overall projection of the working-age population growth in the Soviet Union, to the end of the century, however, is particularly alarming. The increase in working-age population during the fifteen-year period 1981-95 is expected to be less than during the five-year period 1976-80, which in turn registered less than the 1971-75 period. All these indicate that the traditional abundance of industrial labor in the USSR has ended, and the labor problem is going to affect the growth of the economy.

The thesis of the demographic nature of the labor problem, however, faces an uphill challenge from many Sovietologists. Kostakov (1988), for example, rejects this interpretation as a "superficial explanation without foundation." He argues that what the country is facing now is not a labor shortage, but rather, "an overabundance of manpower" resulting from the extremely ineffective utilization of labor power in the economy. Kostakov maintains that the problem originates from a low level of labor productivity. He claims that during the period 1961-70, on an annual average, national income per worker in material production rose by 6.4 percent; while during 1981-85 the rate dropped to 4.5 percent. In most organizations, Kostakov asserts that often two or even three people are employed to do a job that could be handled by one worker. Mikulsky also denounces the demographic explanation of labor shortage as an illusion created by the economic mechanism and stipulates that superfluous industrial employment in the Soviet Union ranges far above the currently believed rate of 15-20 percent (see Ellman 1986, 536). These authors believe that with an effective economic mechanism, Soviet labor productivity could rise sharply, and much present employment can be exposed as unnecessary.

Ineffective Economic Incentives

Conspicuous absence of economic incentives is almost a universally accepted cause of slow growth of the Soviet economy. Western and non-Western writers, even Soviet leaders, single out this factor to explain the poor performance of the Soviet economy. Of course other factors, like consumer supply conditions, food shortages, and corruption, have had serious effects on worker morale, discipline, and productivity. Under the Stalinist system, the central government agencies were mainly responsible for providing enterprises with necessary inputs and disbursing their outputs. The administrative machinery favored sovereignty of producers over consumers by fixing prices from above and assuring the sale of enterprise outputs. By ignoring the demand side altogether, the Stalinist system not only "perpetuated an economy of shortages" but also "set a tradition whereby the interests of the enterprises and their workers were in conflict with that of the higher authorities" (Aganbegyan 1988a, 159).

Troubles with central planning stem from the fact that the whole incentive system was geared to the fulfillment or overfulfillment of government plans. Such an incentive system, according to Winiecki (1986a, 330), strongly mitigated against innovation by orienting the success indicators and bonus payments to the fulfillment of plan targets. The emphasis on plan targets led to many serious unintended and undesirable consequences, including production of unwanted consumer goods and continuation of technologically distorted producer goods. Most importantly, as new innovation requires time to attain mastery over new techniques, and involves the risk of delaying production, enterprise managers continued to concentrate on doing things they had learned to do well (Miller 1987, 117). The whole economic structure of the country, remarks Berliner (1981, 382), attached "maximal encouragement to decision makers, favored established products and processes and discriminated against innovations."

A second major problem of the incentive system emanates from Soviet price structure. Based on the Marxian labor theory of value, pricing policy is designed according to the principle of cost-plus-standard-profit. Such a pricing policy discriminates against innovation both by ignoring any reward for innovative ideas and products and by placing pressure on enterprises to maximize the current rate of output at the expense of other considerations.

Other Major Problems in the Soviet Economy

Other major problems of the Soviet economy include: lack of specialization, material shortages, high surplus inventories, huge subsidies, non-productivity of capital, and obsolescent machinery and equipment.

One of the biggest problems of the Soviet-type economies has been the lack of sufficient specialization. For example, Stalin attached little importance to the potential advantages from international division of labor and foreign trade. He believed that the benefits derived from obtaining independence from capitalists and the vagaries of the capitalist world market exceeded those from foreign trade. Moreover, each Soviet industry or collective farm was driven by the yearning to produce everything it required.[15] Shmelev and Popov (1989, 134-35) show how huge surpluses of inventories troubled the Soviet economy over decades," much heavier than those that weigh on a capitalist economy during the most destructive recessions." In 1982, during "the most severe recession in recent United States history," the authors maintain, the average inventory/sales ratio was 1.7 in the manufacturing industry, 1.2 in wholesale trade, and 1.4 in retail trade; while in the Soviet Union in 1985, this ratio was 2.4 in industry and 3.6 in trade. At the end of 1985 joint inventories of the sectors of material production and collective farms totaled more than 90 percent of the national income of the year.[16]

Another problem is the existence and continuation of huge subsidies in the Soviet economy. Enterprises are constrained by "soft budgets", that is, paternalistic bureaucratic control and patronage; and "hard budgets", that is, economic account-ability for performance, has received secondary or no importance at all. Conse-quently, state subsidies to enterprises and price subsidies to consumer goods grew in socialist economies as a rule. State subsidies totaled about 20 percent of the state budget in 1988, and subsidies on wholesale and retail prices grew 20 times between 1965 and 1989 (169). The exact size of subsidies in Soviet economy, however, remains controversial.

Nonproductivity and underutilization of capital constitute another major prob-lem in the Soviet economy. The ratio of growth of national income to capital investment, or capital productivity in Soviet economy was two times smaller during the eleventh five- year plan (1981-85) than it was during the eighth five-year plan (1966-70). Underutilization and immobilization of capital stock and machineries have also plagued the economy since the mid-seventies. Between 1960-85, each percent of growth in labor productivity was based on a 2 percent increase in the capital employment ratio in agricultural sector; in the construction sector, 20 percent of construction equipment stood still, and 70-90 percent of the capital investment remained unfinished; in the industrial sector, 20-30 percent of the equipment stood idle, only 35-55 percent of all investment went into the expansion of capital stock, whereas only 7 percent of the profit has gone to production development funds (137-47).

A corollary of the above is the obsolescence of machinery and equipment, a significant element in the slowdown of the Soviet economy. Menshikov (Galbraith

& Menshikov 1988) believes that one of the main reasons for the grand slowdown of the Soviet economy is that it has been undergoing a kind of Kondratiev cycle. He maintains that most of the industrial potential of the Soviet Union was built by the fifties, and by the beginning of the eighties, all these are nearing the end of physical life cycle and need substantial reconstruction. Arguing in the same vein, Hasbulatov (1989, 7) also points out that most of the production facilities, machine tools and other machinery and equipment in the Soviet Union were growing increasingly obsolescent for years.

SOCIOPOLITICAL BACKGROUND OF *PERESTROIKA*

In addition to an inefficient economy and in contradistinction to pervasive degeneration in the economic sphere of the country, from the societal perspectives, Gorbachev inherited an educated, industrialized, and urbanized population with sophisticated economic and political demands and high levels of expectations. By the eighties, forces of modernization, industrialization and urbanization had indeed radicalized demands and aspirations of the Soviet population. Interdependent factors responsible for such societal transformation can be identified under two headings: urbanization and modernization.[17]

Urbanization

In 1926, 18 percent of the Soviet population lived in cities. The number increased to 32 percent in 1939, 49 percent in 1960, and 52 percent by 1972. Thus, by the late sixties/early seventies, transformation of a predominantly peasant population into an industrial, urban, working-class population was accomplished. By 1985 the urban population accounted for 65 percent—the whole society became predominantly urbanized. Of more than 2,000 formally designated cities in the Soviet Union, by the early eighties 272 had more than 100,000 population, while only 88 cities had such population in 1959 (see Harris 1970, 240; Lewin 1988, 30-31). Such proliferation of big cities not only indicated an internal regrouping of urban population into the "biggest agglomerations" as Lewin (1988, 32) observes, it also resulted in "ungovernable agglomerations" from the viewpoint of law and order (Kagarlitsky 1990b, 286). Until the sixties the majority of the urban population were born in the countryside, but by the seventies the majority of the urban population had been born in the cities. Therefore, although before the seventies peasant outlook and mentality survived even in the cities, by the eighties rural traditions began to disappear and a qualitatively different new urban class, which Kagarlitsky calls a new generation "shaped by the conditions of Europeanized city life," emerged. Such urbanization resulted in a "cultural revolution" that not only demonstrated new urban norms of living, but also exhibited "a great variety of forms and specific problems, replete with different cultural features, standards of living, and new inequalities of status, culture, and national roles" (Lewin 1988, 40). Such a cultural revolution, in turn, not only intensified pressures on the authorities for better and more effective articulation of qualitatively different and sophisticated demands,[18] but also demonstrated differential access to education, professions and social mobility.

Modernization

Djilas (1990) remarks that Gorbachev also inherited a highly skilled, educated, and modernized population. Even in 1959, the overwhelming majority of the Soviet population (91.3 percent of workers and 98.2 percent of *kolkhoz* peasants) had four years of elementary education. Only two decades later, in 1979, 86.3 percent of urban and 69.3 percent rural population achieved higher and secondary education. An interesting dimension of Soviet education is that although women constitute 51 percent of the total population, they constitute 54 percent of university students and 58 percent of students in secondary specialized schools.

According to Lewin (1988, 50-56), the urban employed population in the Soviet Union consists of three groups: workers (almost 60 percent), officials and specialists (almost 40 percent), and *kolkhoz* peasants (1-5 percent). Among the workers, 10-12 percent are unskilled or poorly skilled, 44-46 percent are physical workers—the backbone of the industrial labor force, and 3-4 percent are highly skilled workers involved in physical and intellectual activities. The relatively smaller employment of highly skilled workers reflects the fact that there are too many educated workers, but insufficient employment opportunities and many skilled workers, but not enough challenging, demanding jobs.

In the second category, the officials-cum-specialist group, 11-12 percent are poorly trained or untrained, 17-18 percent are in professional jobs (requiring secondary and specialized schools or university training), 2.4-3 percent are in medium-rank managerial and professional positions (requiring university level and higher training)[19] and 2 percent in upper-rank leadership positions who perform largely intellectual functions. Lewin maintains that in the contemporary Soviet Union the professional classes and intellectuals direct all spheres of economic, political, and social life.

But the Soviet educational system has produced doctors, engineers, and other specialists outnumbering their demand in the economy. While during 1960-86, the overall employed population in the Soviet Union increased by 155 percent, the number of specialists grew fourfold. As a result, according to Kagarlitsky (1990b, 287-301), in 1969 alone, 28,000 engineers were employed as industrial workers, and throughout the Brezhnev period many doctors were employed as agricultural labor.

Denial to the well-educated majority of the opportunity to realize their learning resulted in a decline in the economy's growth rate and a deceleration in technical progress. But a decrease in the series of intellectual professions helped to stabilize the working class. Because professionals like doctors and engineers are paid less than workers, and also because of "inequality in real opportunities,"[20] intelligent young people in the working class, "who previously had an absolute desire to join the intelligentsia," more frequently remained within their own social milieu (287). Second, those peasants who are moving out of the countryside to join the urban industrial work force have a different social and cultural outlook than those of the early phase of industrialization. Third, because "hereditary proletarians" in the cities came to constitute about 70 percent of the working population, the level of consciousness among the urban working class sharpened throughout the Brezhnev era.

Gordon and Komarovskii (1986) provide an excellent study of the transformation of Soviet society and culture throughout the twentieth century.[21] These authors' "vocational x-ray" of three generations of Soviet society—(1) those (men) born around 1910 who entered the work force in the thirties, (2) those (sons) born in the thirties who joined the labor force in the fifties, and (3) those (grandsons) born in the fifties who entered the labor force in the seventies—captures the underlying dynamics and mobility of Soviet society during the transition from a predominantly peasant to an industrial, then to a service and information-oriented society. The authors point out that the first generation was predominantly employed in "preindustrial" peasant jobs that required no schooling. The second generation, mainly employed in industry, required skills. A modest portion of this generation also moved to the service and information sectors. The third generation is substantially employed in service and information sectors that require intellectual training. Throughout the intergenerational changes, the work force first moved from agriculture to industry, then to the service sector. The authors forecast that during the period of the third generation, in the 1990s, the agricultural and industrial labor force will decline to 10 percent, 40 percent will be employed in intellectual professions, and 30-40 percent will be involved in professions related to information creation and processing.

These undercurrents of transformation (urbanization, industrialization and mobilization), in turn, resulted in profound changes in Soviet society. First, the composition and structure of both the working and the professional classes have dramatically changed. Second, patterns of occupational and job structures were radically transformed, and third, these transformations resulted in dramatic alterations in intergenerational attitudes and outlooks.

Political and economic consequences of such profound changes, which began to surface in the eighties, are no less dramatic. First, as Kagarlitsky (1990b, 288) observes, "a more intellectual and civilized labor force, rendered unavoidable the Europeanization of thought." This educated, Westernized labor force not only demonstrated a distinct cultural stage in the development of Soviet society, but also radically altered the qualitative economic demand structure of the society. What was "an unnecessary luxury" for the old generation, became "an unavoidable shortage" for the young generation. Politically, raising wages or relaxing bureaucratic control no longer satisfied a more conscious working class. What was required was to broaden the "rights of workers qualitatively, to humanize and democratize production relations as a whole" (305). Pressures for such sweeping political and economic changes mounted everyday because of incredible social, economic and political transformations, and also brought about revolutionary changes in the psychological arena of the country. Attention shifted from macrodimensions like economic development, national education system, and large-scale problems to microdimensions like personal and human relations and small-scale community welfare (Lewin 1988, 63-65). The new environment, coupled with the contemporary technical and scientific revolution, intensified demands for autonomous activity of creative individuals, which clashed head-on with the existing authoritative and coercive administrative-political-economic system.

IMPLICATIONS FOR *PERESTROIKA*

In sum, one can surmise that most of the Soviet Union's contemporary problems stem, one way or another, from the type of economic and political system developed during the Stalin and Brezhnev eras. The Stalinist model was tremendously successful in its early years, notably in its remarkably rapid pace of industrialization, but it has proven inappropriate to meet the demands and needs of a more mature economy and society.

The new leadership realized that the extensive methods of production that helped the Soviet economy achieve industrialization in record time had lost their usefulness. The Soviet economy of the eighties has neither enormous raw materials as it did during the Stalinist period, nor surplus agricultural labor to direct to industrial expansion. Moreover, as mentioned above, the demographic slowdown has made transition from extensive to intensive methods of production imperative for Soviet leaders. The new leadership also realized that years of bureaucratic and central management of the economy had cost the Soviet Union benefits of scientific and technological revolutions. The Soviet Union now lags behind the newly industrialized countries of Asia and the Pacific in terms of technological development.[22]

Another important concern of *perestroika*, especially in its overwhelming importance to shifting priorities of economy, emanated from a disproportionately higher allocation of GNP to military build-up; this might have contributed to the slowdown of growth in other sectors of the economy. The leadership also realized that efforts to reform the economic environment and improve consumer satisfaction without reforming the economic system itself are doomed to failure. Earlier reform attempts, both in the Soviet Union and elsewhere, convincingly demonstrated that the existing Stalinist system either rejects or is unreceptive to such efforts (see Gorbachev 1990b, 32; *New York Times*, June 2, 1990; *Time*, June 4, 1990). Therefore, to the new leadership of the Soviet Union, it became imperative to embark on a massive, revolutionary program of *perestroika* to salvage the economy and society.

Finally, we should consider briefly the issue of the relative role of systemic versus nonsystemic factors in the Soviet growth slowdown just prior to Gorbachev's ascension to power. Montias (1973) has usefully observed that economic performance of a society depends on three factors: the (economic and noneconomic) environment; economic goals and policy priorities; and the structure of the economic system itself. In practice, these factors are difficult to separate and quantitatively assess. In principle, the growth slowdown could have been caused more by unwise policies (e.g., the heavy emphasis on the military sector relative to investment and consumption) or by intractable aspects of the economic environment (e.g., demographic factors causing the growth in the labor force to decrease) than by the system itself. Thus, it is difficult for Gorbachev and his advisers to prove, especially to his conservative critics, that dramatic reforms in the Soviet system are imperative, as contrasted to making policy and environmental adjustments within the system of centralized state management.

Gorbachev's response, insofar as it can be filtered out of his speeches and writings (and that of his associates), runs something like this. First, there is little that can be done to elicit dramatic changes in the economic environment, especially in the short run. Focus must therefore be placed on reforming policies and structures and institutions. Second, unwise policies undoubtedly have contributed to the current malaise in the Soviet economy, and better policies no doubt must be an integral part of a positive program for reform. However, on the other hand, bad policies might emanate, in significant measure, from the overcentralized system of state management and authoritarian system of politics bequeathed to Gorbachev and his supporters from the Stalin-Brezhnev years. Dramatic demilitarization, for example, with its potential for releasing massive resources for nonmilitary sectors of Soviet society, might require vigorous openness, decentralization, and democratization. On the other hand, sufficient evidence has accumulated to render plausible the double hypothesis that the model of Soviet economy inherited from Stalin and Brezhnev, especially in a mature economy, itself contains deficiencies, and these deficiencies are serious. Thus, policy changes, even if they could be engineered somehow in an unchanged politicoeconomic structure, would be insufficient.

CONCLUDING REMARKS

The preceding discussion demonstrates that Gorbachev's claim that in the early eighties Soviet economy and society were inflicted with serious troubles requiring immediate remedial measures is hardly an exaggeration. Economic downswing was threatening the perceived legitimacy and hence the authority of the Soviet government and exercise of authority by the CPSU. The system itself was failing demonstratively to meet the altered demands and modern challenges of a qualitatively changed, that is, urbanized, and modernized population. Indeed Gorbachev (1987, 24) rightly concluded:

The need for change was brewing not only in the material sphere of life but also in public consciousness. People who had practical experience, a sense of justice and commitment to the ideals of Bolshevism criticized the established practice of doing things and noted with anxiety the symptoms of moral degradation and erosion of revolutionary ideals and socialist values . . . There was a growing awareness that things could not go on like this much longer.

NOTES

1. As a result of such a deteriorating situation, the economic potential of the Soviet Union, according to Hohmann (1987, 29),

"came under pressure from all sides of the polygon of economic policy goals—the assurance of adequate capital formation, the stabilization of progress in the standard of living, the guaranteed ability to maintain the aspired military capacities, the provision of an economic basis for Soviet hegemony policy, the restoration of legitimacy to the Soviet system."

2. Aganbegyan (1988a, 81) traces manifestations of the stagnation and pre-crisis trends in the economy to the beginning of the 1980s. According to Hohmann (1987, 29), the Soviet economy reached "crisis-scale slowdown in economic growth" at the end of the seventies. Hanson (1987, 10) traces the origin of the stagnation to the mid-1970s, while Miller (1987, 114) argues that there has been a marked decline in the rate of growth of the Soviet economy since the days of Khrushchev. Even some Sovietologists believe that economic decline was partly responsible for the downfall of Khrushchev in 1964 (Gregory & Stuart 1990,139).

3. The actual performance of the Soviet economy, however, remains controversial. According to many Western and non-Western authorities, Soviet-type economies systematically overstate or misreport economic statistics. According to IMF estimates (1990, 65), Soviet GNP registered 5 percent growth during 1951-73 and 2.1 percent growth during 1974-82. For non-Western estimates, see Winiecki 1989a.

4. IMF estimates (1990, 66), however, show 5 percent and 2.5 percent growth rates respectively, for the periods of 1961-80 and 1981-88.

5. According to IMF (1990, 66) estimates, Soviet agriculure grew at a rate of 1.0 percent during 1961-80 and 0.6 percent during 1981-88.

6. Such disappointing performance of agriculture, especially during the late seventies and early eighties, presumably could be partially attributed to extremely unfavorable weather conditions. Kurtzweg (1987, 145), however, maintains that even the Soviet leaders acknowledge that problems besides weather contributed substantially to low growth and poor returns in the agricultural sector.

7. Such rates, however, might not be sustainable for long, because other sectors of the economy, especially technological progress in the industrial sector and expansion of the poorly attended service sector, will demand bigger amounts of

national investment in the future.

8. According to Bornstein (1981, 269), output per worker per day on Soviet farms is only 5-10 percent of the U.S. level.

9. Productivity of labor and capital was also low in other socialist countries. Bergson (1987, 342-57), has shown that output per worker in socialist countries in 1975 was 30 percent below that in the western mixed-economy countries. Shmelev and Popov (1989, 128-30) point out that in terms of materials and capital inputs of production, the Soviet Union is less productive than other developed countries. According to the Soviet Institute of World Economy and International Relations, the Soviet Union uses 1.5 times more materials and 2.1 times more energy per unit of national income than the United States. Soviet machines and machine tools are 15 to 25 percent heavier than foreign models, and Soviet agriculture, which uses 3.5 time more energy, produces 15 percent less than the United States. According to these authors, during 1960-86, Soviet national income (in current prices) rose by a factor of 4 to 4.4, while material input (also in current prices) increased almost 5 times.

10. The IMF (1990, 66) estimates that total factor productivity in the Soviet Union increased 0.5 percent during 1951-73 and actually registered a negative growth (-1.4 percent) during the 1974-84 period.

11. Gorbachev (1987, 5) put it more flagrantly:

"Our rockets can find Halley's comet and fly to Venus with amazing accuracy, but side by side with these scientific and technological triumphs is an obvious lack of efficiency in using scientific achievements for economic needs, and many Soviet household appliances are of poor quality."

12. Household consumption in the Soviet economy, according to Gregory and Stuart (1990, 361) grew at a rate of 3.3 percent annually between 1970-84.

13. Aganbegyan (1987, 67) maintains that the process of demographic slump in the Soviet Union in the early seventies occurred as a direct consequence of World War II. On the other hand, Ellman (1986) argues that the process of decline in the working-age population in the Soviet Union began precisely in 1976.

14. Campbell (1989, 69) estimates that between 1980 to 1990 the working-age population in the Soviet Union will increase by less than 6 million in contrast to 10 to 11 million during the sixties, and most of the increase will take place in the Central Asia and Kazakhstan regions, where industry is relatively underdeveloped.

15. Winiecki (1986a, 329) explains how the "vicious circle" of shortages of supply and drives for self-sufficiency perpetuated lack of specialization in Soviet-type economies:

This lack of specialization was manifest in two ways: these countries have an overgrown share of industries turning out intermediate products in GDP; secondly, given the chronic and endemic shortage of everything, enterprises display an extreme do-it-yourself bias, to reduce the uncertainty of supply, they tend to produce as much as possible within their own enterprise. The enterprises tend to do all phases of processing, to make all parts and components of the final product, as a result the scale of the enterprise does not equal the scale of production. Labor is spread over too many activities, while intermediate goods are produced at higher costs than would have been the case in specialized enterprises.

16. In an earlier work, Kornai (1984) has shown how heavy demands for resources by enterprises, both for current inputs and for investment resources, create chronic shortage under the centralized system of economic management in the socialist countries. Also see Kemme (1989); Winiecki (1989a); Staniszkis (1989).

17. Understood as developments in education, skill, and profession of the population.

18. Sophistication in the demands of urban population is not an unusual phenomenon in the urbanization process. What is peculiar about Soviet urbanization is that, unlike the experience of other urbanized countries, it was achieved fairly rapidly. Moreover, as Lewin (1988, 42) observes, the Soviet Union was "already a superpower even before urbanization was consummated."

19. According to Lewin (1988, 48), 60 percent of all specialists with both higher and secondary education, 56 percent of educated specialists, and 40 percent of scientists in the Soviet Union are females.

20. Kagarlitsky (1990b, 286-90) maintains that children of intellectuals had greater advantages in entering institutions of higher education, as "though the intelligentsia is reproducing itself."

21. This study is in Russian. This author analyzes their findings on the basis of discussions in Lewin (1988, 52-56).

22. As Draper (1988, 295-96) remarks:

If any one factor may be said to have shaken the leadership out of its accustomed self-satisfaction and inertia, it is this—the failure to meet the competition of what Gorbachev has referred to as "the capitalism of the 1980s, the capitalism of the age of electronics, and the informatics, computers and robots." It was not simply that the Soviet Union had fallen behind the United States or Western Europe in the new technology, it could not produce what Japan, South Korea and even Taiwan were turning out in mass production and with which they were flooding world markets.

4

Gorbachev's Critique and Vision
of Soviet Socialism

INTRODUCTION

Mikhail Gorbachev inherited a Soviet economy literally in shambles and found Soviet society ravaged by "braking mechanisms." His predecessors bequeathed to him a stagnant, wasteful and technologically backward economy, which, in Gorbachev's (1987, 19) words, was wavering "at the brink of near-crisis situation," and a degenerated and apathetic society where "the great values born of the October Revolution and the heroic struggle for socialism were being trampled underfoot" (24). Therefore, he launched a "red square reformation" (Conot 1990) against ideological dogmatism in the Soviet Union. Just one month after assuming power, in April 1985, Gorbachev initiated the programs of *perestroika* (restructuring) for rapid recovery of the economy and society from "stagnation and other phenomena alien to socialism" (Gorbachev 1987, 24).

To facilitate the implementation of *perestroika*, programs of *glasnost* (openness) and *demokratizatsiya* (democratization) have been initiated simultaneously. Gorbachev's vision of a freer socialism, an "unabashedly antimonopolistic, antiauthoritarian" (Talbott 1990, 31) and humanitarian socialism, has already accomplished a herculean task in the contemporary world. Reorganization and restructuring measures undertaken so far to revitalize the stagnant economy and reenergize the Soviet people constitute one of the most fascinating phenomena of modern times.

Details of those programs and policies will be taken up in Chapter 5. This chapter concentrates on Gorbachev's critique of pre-Gorbachev Soviet political economy and explores Gorbachev's own vision of socialism. Gorbachev's socialism is characterized as a distinctive, unique, and revolutionary phenomenon, as a revolution within socialist revolution. As a context for the discussion, in the next section contending perspectives on the Soviet political economy are reviewed both from Western and Soviet viewpoints. Section three analyzes Gorbachev's own critique of the pre-Gorbachev Soviet political economy. Section four explores Gorbachev's vision of "socialism with a human face" and section five outlines basic features of Gorbachev's decentralized, democratic and market-oriented socialism.

CONTENDING PERSPECTIVES ON SOVIET POLITICAL ECONOMY

Western and Eastern scholars, even Soviet leaders themselves, have interpreted Soviet political economy from different, and often contrasting and contradictory, perspectives. Therefore, the nature of Soviet socialism remains controversial, which often has resulted in reinterpretations of Soviet history itself. Before embarking on Gorbachev's own critique and vision of Soviet socialism, a brief overview of contending perspectives on Soviet socialism is in order.

The Western Critique

Two broad approaches can be identified in Western interpretations of Soviet socialism.[1] The first approach conceives Soviet society as a nonexploitative society in which the proletariat is the ruling class in either a de facto or a direct sense. The second approach interprets Soviet society as an exploitative society in which a class other than the proletariat rules. Based on these approaches, four distinct positions can be identified in Western interpretations of Soviet economy and society.

To the first group, the Soviet Union is a non-exploitative socialist society that combines state ownership of the means of production with central planning.[2] To these scholars, state ownership of the means of production and centrally directed economy are essential preconditions for socialism. To them the Soviet economic system, predominantly characterized by state ownership and central planning, has been overwhelmingly successful in achieving overall economic growth and emancipation of the proletariat. These scholars find hardly any evidence of exploitation or class in Soviet society; rather, they believe, Soviet society is characterized by limited but effective and active participation of the working people in management and decision-making processes. They believe the Soviet Union is pursuing a socialist road that needs reforms, but only gradual ones.

A second group conceives the Soviet Union as a nonexploitative transitional society, in which the proletariat has de facto power over the means of production, but lacks political rights and decision-making power in the management of the economy (Mandel 1981). By describing Soviet socialism as a transitional one in which, although the means of production are nationalized, effective control of the economy lies essentially with the state bureaucracy, Mandel actually extends the argument put forward originally by Trotsky (1936) in *Revolution Betrayed*.[3] Mandel (1981), however, rejects the idea that Soviet socialism (because the workers lack effective control over decision-making) actually constitutes a "state capitalist" society. He describes the Soviet Union as a contradictory society characterized by disproportions and imbalances in social and industrial policies, as a degenerated workers' state, in which the bureaucracy exercises monopoly over political and economic power. But he maintains that the Soviet economy lacks many crucial elements of capitalism, such as the privilege of legal ownership of private property. This group implies radical political reforms to dislodge the bureaucratic stratum that denies workers' control over the economy and the state machinery.

A third group theorizes the Soviet Union as a new and distinctive, neither socialist nor capitalist society, in which the state-run economy is staffed by a bureaucracy that is not only unresponsive to the workers, but is also inconsistent with socialist principles.[4] Exponents of this strand of thought argue that the Soviet Union: (1) is a post-revolutionary society at a higher stage than capitalism, but qualitatively at a lower stage than socialism (Bettleheim & Sweezy 1971); (2) is an exploitative society, in which the bureaucracy as a class dominates the working class through its monopoly over power and privilege (Schachtman 1971); (3) is an essentially independent state power, which dictatorially directs society's vast resources according to its own laws (Hilferding 1971).

A fourth group of Sovietologists hypothesizes the Soviet Union as a state-capitalist society, which is different from monopoly or competitive capitalism but similar to capitalism in many respects, notably separation of workers from control over the means of production.[5] To these scholars, formal juridical relations such as the ownership of the means of production are less important than actual control exercised at the point of production, and they are critical of the apparent reemergence of market processes in the Soviet Union (see Bettleheim 1976, Bettleheim in Bettleheim & Sweezy 1971). These scholars find similarities between Stalinist institutional processes for the mobilization and allocation of an economic surplus (such as one-party rule, collectivization of agriculture, turnover tax and emasculation of labor unions and the nineteenth century capitalist accumulation that was based primarily on ownership and control over the means of production by the capitalist class (see Elliott 1984, 43-47).

A fifth strand of thought interprets the Soviet Union as a state socialist economy.[6] These scholars provide a kind of synthesis of the competing perspectives mentioned above. To them, the Soviet Union is a state socialist economy, in which Marxism-Leninism serves as official ideology, the Communist Party provides dominant institutional support to the state, and the state, in turn, owns, controls, and mobilizes the means of production. Drawing a line between nationalization and socialization of the means of production, they maintain that state ownership is a necessary but not a sufficient condition for socialism.[7] They insist on two conditions for transformation of nationalization into socialization: the means of production must be employed in the interests of society, and the society, in turn, must have effective disposition over the means of production it owns (see Brus 1973).

All these perspectives on Soviet socialism are controversial. In many areas they overlap in their arguments and emphases, and none of these perspectives constitute perfect representation of Soviet society. All have merits and demerits in terms of emphasis, approach, and explanatory power and appeal. But the arguments of the state socialist perspective that Soviet socialism is pre-eminently controlled by the state, that it has achieved statization of the means of production, not socialization, profusely reflect the reality. Conception of the Soviet Union as a state socialist society enables direction of future reforms to transforming statization into socialization. Gorbachev's views come close to this standpoint. He believes the Soviet economy so far has remained largely a state socialist economy that alienated workers. Therefore, socialization of the means of production constitutes one of the fundamental aims of *perestroika* (see Gorbachev 1988a).

A corollary of the above controversy involves Western perceptions about the different periods of Soviet socialism. The Soviet Union passed through a number of distinct periods of social, economic, and political transformations. Each of these periods, as discussed in previous chapters, endeavored to reconcile the ideological and practical goals of socialism with the centralized/decentralized and authoritarian/democratic elements of socialism. It is this process of reconciliation that differentiated these periods from each other so distinctively.[8]

The Western controversy surrounding Lenin and his perceptions of socialism boils down to two main questions: Was the NEP a temporary retreat from War Communism or was it a decisive break to be sustained for a long and indefinite period? Was Lenin authoritarian, as he appears to be in *What is to be Done*? or less authoritarian, as *The State and Revolution* portrays? Two strands of thought can be identified in this respect.

To the exponents of the first strand of thought, the NEP constituted an absolute disenchantment with the policies of War Communism and called for a new set of governmental and party policies for transforming Communist rule into a "liberal dictatorship" (Lewin 1974, 46). They maintain that NEP was actually a resumption of the policy of state capitalism that Lenin developed in the spring of 1918, and that had been interrupted by the outbreak of the civil war. To these writers, NEP was not a temporary, but a strategic retreat aimed at granting concessions to the petty bourgeoisie and the peasants. According to Nove (1969, 120), it was not even a retreat, it was rather a return to the "status quo ante," to the resumption of the strategy already planned in 1918. Howe (1988, 511) maintains that from November 1917 to the summer of 1918, "Bolsheviks favored what we'd now call a mixed economy," in which "large areas of private ownership of industry would continue, but production and investment decisions would be controlled by the leftist state together, presumably, with working class institutions." This strand of thought believes Lenin foresaw NEP for as long a period as needed to catch up with capitalist countries.[9]

A second strand of thought envisages NEP as a temporary retreat, "an interval between two phases of the Russian revolutionary processes" (Tucker 1977, 79), which was aimed at giving the CPSU a breathing spell to save the October Revolution and cleverly manipulate capitalist instruments for recovery from the disastrous economic situation of War Communism (see Kolakowski 1978, 485-91).

The second question involves authoritarianism in Lenin. In this respect both strands of thought rely upon "an exclusionary selection of references" (Cohen 1977,

13). Those who highlight authoritarianism in Lenin point to *What is to be Done?* while minimizing *The State and Revolution*, and those who deemphasize authoritarianism in Lenin do the opposite (Stojanovic 1988, 153-59). Those who underline authoritarianism in Lenin contend that the NEP was essentially economic in character and it hardly affected the monolithic one-party state structure that Lenin bequeathed to Stalin. Also known as "continuity theorists", the protagonists of this strand of thought draw a political straight line between Bolshevism and Stalinism.

The other strand of thought emphasizes Lenin of *The State and Revolution* and 1922-23 and downplays Lenin of *What is to be Done?* and 1919. According to them, not only were the official economic policies of NEP distinctly unlike Stalin's, but "the social-political order of NEP, with its officially tolerated social pluralism in economic, cultural-intellectual, and even (in local soviets and high state agencies) political life, represents a historical model of Soviet Communist rule radically unlike Stalinism" (Cohen 1977, 21). Indeed, Tucker (1977, 92) maintains that the NEP culture found expressions "in institutions, ideas, habits of mind, and conduct" of Soviet life and in the "primacy of persuasion and educative methods in the regime's approach to the people." According to Lewin (1977, 114), the NEP policies "produced a remarkable set of compromises, between plan and market, political monopoly and social and cultural diversity, state and society, ideology and expedient."[10]

Stalin's period marks a watershed in Soviet history and in the Western analysis of Soviet socialism. The five perspectives on Soviet socialism described above are preponderantly based on the Stalinist period. Besides, the Stalinist phenomenon has been variously interpreted in Western literature. One reason for this is that Stalin dominated the Soviet stage for three tumultuous decades. Although many authors find strong elements of continuity between Stalinism and Leninism, and indeed believe that there is "absolutely nothing in the worst excesses of the worst years of Stalinism that cannot be justified on Leninist principles" (Kolakowski 1978, 516), discontinuity theorists maintain that not only Leninism, but the project of socialism itself suffered "enormous damage wrought by Stalinism" (Howe 1988, 512).[11] Essentially, Gorbachev's position conforms to that of the discontinuity theorists; he consistently differentiates Leninism from Stalinism and claims that *perestroika*, which aims at repudiating Stalinism, derives inspirations from Leninism, especially from the NEP Lenin.

A major controversy on Stalinism involves the so-called success of the Stalinist model in achieving economic progress and catching up with the West. One strand of thought maintains that the Stalinist model, at least in its own terms, was overwhelmingly successful in transforming a semi-feudal, semi-colonial backward country into a highly industrialized society in a record time. The proponents of this theory contend that having built industrial society, the Stalinist model began to take on a life of its own and gradually became inappropriate for a subsequent period of post-industrialization. Therefore, they conclude, failure of the Stalinist model was indeed "failure born of success" as visualized by Schumpeter's concept of creative destruction (Elliott 1989). The other strand of thought maintains that Stalinist economic achievements were less than real. Szelenyi (1989), for example, asserts that growth based on extensive methods of production was attained by appropriating private wealth and by depressing living standards; moreover, growth did not create real productive capacity upon which future growth can be built. Nove (1969, 1987) also concludes that Stalin was not necessary for Soviet industrialization, and the Stalinist command economy was indeed responsible for the contemporary crisis in the Soviet economy. Although Gorbachev (1987, 38-49) initially approved Stalin's programs of collectivization and industrialization and only criticized "forms and methods" of those programs, gradually his position has shifted more toward this standpoint.

Among the post-Stalin and pre-Gorbachev Soviet leaders Khrushchev's de-Stalinization campaign was marked by enthusiasm in Western literature. Khrushchev has been especially credited for: dismantling Stalinist totalitarian control over society and the state and making a shift to authoritarianism, eliminating terror of the state police and the personal tyranny of the dictator. Economically, he is credited with shifting emphasis from heavy to light industry, from the production to the consumption sector, and for emphasizing decentralization and restructuring of the economy.[12] Brezhnev's era, as discussed before, was mainly characterized by bureaucratic collectivism, commitment to proceduralism, and prolonged economic stagnation.

The Soviet Critique

According to the official Soviet view, Lenin was both theorist and practitioner of socialism. As theorist, he popularized and interpreted Marxism; as practitioner, he put into practice the doctrines propounded by Marx and Engels.[13] Soviet historian Medvedev (1981, 14), however, emphasizes that Lenin was not a mere "practitioner of the working class movement." He says Lenin was also a "genius in the realm of history."[14]

Lenin leaned heavily on Marx and Engels in developing his own ideas. But Leninism was also influenced by ideological legacy from the Russian revolutionary tradition, especially the lively debates on social democracy that sprung up in Tsarist Russia during the late nineteenth century. In addition, the revolutionary writings of A. I. Herzen (1812-1870), N. G. Chernyshevsky (1828-1889), and others that contributed to the core of the Narodnik movement of the 1870s (which called for the revolutionary transformation of Russian society), influenced Lenin's life and work. Therefore, Leninism can be understood as a powerful blend of the Russian revolutionary-democratic tradition of the latter half of nineteenth century, the revolutionary teachings of Marx and Engels, and Lenin's own analysis of the revolutionary transformation of an underdeveloped economy to socialism. Leninist revisions of socialism involve two fundamental aspects: his reliance on a vanguard party; and his interpretation of the concept of the dictatorship of the proletariat.

Lenin, as discussed previously, found the Marxian prescription for the working class to become the ruling class impracticable, and argued that social change led by the proletariat itself would end up as a trade union movement. To him, giving the workers' movement a revolutionary character and leading it to its logical destination required a vanguard party consisting of professional revolutionaries (see Lenin 1967, 91-256). Second although Marx used the term dictatorship of proletariat no more than five times in his works and emphasized "rule of the majority, by the majority and for the majority," Lenin interpreted the term as "authority untrammelled by any laws, absolutely unrestricted by any rules whatever, and based directly on force" (Selucky 1979, 62-63). However, in *The State and Revolution* Lenin softened his stand on this concept and admitted that transition to socialism could be possible through peaceful means, through active participation of the masses as suggested by Kautsky.[15]

Another important revision in Lenin's thought concerned the NEP. On numerous occasions Lenin proclaimed that the NEP had been established "seriously and for long time," that the NEP policy "is being adopted in earnest," and that NEP policies will continue "until we fully restore large-scale industry" (see Lenin 1974, 635-93). Cohen (1977, 21-22) maintains that even during the momentous industrialization debate of the late 1920s, "NEP was for the Bukharinists a viable development (not static) model." He argues that even the economic proposals of Trotsky were based on the NEP and its continuation.

In *Testament*, Lenin criticized Stalin for his rude and authoritarian character; indeed Lenin called for Stalin's removal as general secretary of the CPSU. Stalin subsequently repudiated Lenin's NEP policies, but officially depicted himself as a bona fide follower of Lenin. Stalin himself proclaimed on numerous occasions his unshakable belief in Leninist principles, but unmistakably his emphasis was on the Lenin of War Communism and *What is to be Done?* To him, Leninism was "the theory and tactics of the proletarian revolution in general, the theory and tactics of the dictatorship of the proletariat in particular." And Lenin's *What is to be Done?* provided the "theoretical foundations for a truly revolutionary movement of the Russian working class" (Stalin cited in Franklin 1972, 91-107). He therefore stressed the Communist Party's vanguard role. In practice, he gradually concentrated its monopoly power into his own hands, extended its directive role throughout the Soviet polity and economy, and ended up with a totalitarian politico-economic system, as discussed previously.

Regarding Lenin's intention for continuation of NEP, Stalin took Lenin's words literally. Stalin characterized NEP as a temporary breathing space, a tactical means to cleverly utilize the capitalist elements for socialist construction, to be dismantled once it outgrows its usefulness. At the Fifteenth Congress of the CPSU in 1927, Stalin condemned the emergence of capitalism, new forms of landlordism, small capitalists, and rich peasants under the policies of NEP, and prescribed collectivization as the only way out for a movement toward socialism in the Soviet Union (see Franklin 1972, 17).

Discarding the NEP strategy of gradual and peaceful transition to industrialization, Stalin, in 1929, launched a massive, forceful, ambitious, state-planned, state-dictated, state-mobilized and state-coordinated programs of rapid industrialization to catch up with the West within ten years. Stalin also championed Leninist theory and practice of socialism in one country, that is, the view that socialism could (and should) be established within the USSR by essentially internal resources and efforts as opposed to large-scale assistance from successful Western socialist revolutionary movements. At the Seventeenth Congress of the CPSU in 1934, he claimed that socialism had been achieved in the Soviet Union. In his last work *Economic Problems of Socialism in the U.S.S.R* (1952), Stalin categorically asserted the existence of contradictions and inevitability of war between socialism and capitalism.[16]

As in the West, in the Soviet Union too, Stalin's programs and policies faced tremendous criticisms. Bukharin (1964, 1967), who also championed the principle of socialism in one country, wanted continuation of NEP for decades, being aware of grave but inevitable consequences of a state-imposed rapid industrialization program. He cautioned that such a program would lead to centralization of economic management, proliferation of bureaucratization, and inordinate domination of administrative machineries on society. Bukharin (1982) also condemned the Stalinist strategy of exploiting the peasants for capital accumulation and investment, and stressed mutually supportive industrialization strategies between industry and agriculture.

Trotsky, who championed an "integrationist approach" in his *New Course* (1965), cautioned about bureaucratic proliferation under a centrally planned and directed economy. In *Revolution Betrayed*, Trotsky even asserted that Stalin betrayed the basic tenets of the October Revolution. Trotsky denounced the idea that Leninism was in any way responsible for Stalinism, and asserted that the Leninist conception of the vanguard party was incompatible with the excesses and dictatorial character of the Stalinist regime (Howe 1986, 202-12). Trotsky proclaims, "Bolshevik revolution, with all its repressions, meant an upheaval of social relations in the interest of the masses, whereas the Stalinist Thermidorian upheaval accompanies the transformation of Soviet society in the interests of a privileged minority" (212). To him the Stalinist period was neither capitalism nor socialism, but an economic society in between, where workers are separated from ownership and control of the means of production and society is thoroughly bureaucratized, but the bureaucracy lacks the privileges associated with private ownership of the means of production or official rights.

Khrushchev's denunciation of Stalinism and the consequent break with the Stalinist period came with his famous address at the Twentieth Congress of the CPSU. In this address, Khrushchev dramatically revealed the extent of the Stalinist purges and costs of Stalin's repression and accused Stalin of "covering up the shortcomings and vanishing of reality." Khrushchev repudiated Stalin's personality cult, brought an end to the use of terror, eliminated the party and state's totalitarian control over society, and rejected the conception of an inevitable war between capitalism and socialism. But he continued Stalinist one-party control and the central planning apparatus. In the Twenty-second Congress of the CPSU in 1961,

Khrushchev not only boasted to overtake the United States in economic production by 1970, but, declaring nonexistence of contradictions in Soviet socialism, proclaimed that full communism would be achieved in the Soviet Union by the early eighties. In practice, the mission of establishing communism remained unaccomplished. Shortly after that announcement, Khrushchev was overthrown and retired for "hairbrained scheming, immature conclusions and hasty decisions and actions divorced from reality."[17]

Khrushchev's successor, Brezhnev, in the Twenty-fourth Congress of the CPSU in 1971, backed off from the ambition of immediate establishment of communism, and introduced the concept of "developed socialism" into Marxist-Leninist ideology. Brezhnev maintained that by the late sixties Soviet socialism had reached a stage in which relations of production were solidly based on socialist principles, and thus all contradictions inherent in the transition from capitalism to socialism had been overcome. Commending the accomplishment of "superiority of socialist way of life," imbued with "moral principles such as collectivism, humanism, democratism and internationalism," Brezhnev declared that Soviet socialism was moving in the right direction and aimed at construction of full-scale communism (quoted in Evans, Jr. 1986, 11). Justifying the Stalinist policies of collectivization and industrialization, Brezhnev asserted that in the early stage of socialism, "single-mindedness in the allocation of economic resources were inevitable." But he maintained that the logic of such strategies expired at the stage of developed socialism which is characterized by a higher level of industrialization and application of Stalinist strategies in such a society was "not only unnecessary, but also irrational" (3).

Gorbachev's own evaluation of pre-Gorbachev Soviet political economy will be taken up in the next section. Soviet critique of Soviet socialism was never confined to the Soviet leadership. Even during the Stalinist totalitarian period, criticisms surfaced through different instruments of communication. But especially since Khrushchev's bold assault on the Stalinist personality cult and totalitarian rule at the Twentieth Congress of the CPSU, a new era of fresh, innovative, and reform-oriented thinking began in the Soviet Union. Cohen (1980) identifies two broad strands of thought in the Soviet Union since Khrushchev's period: the reformists who condemn the Stalinist command model and emphasize decentralization in economic management and democratization in political arena; and the conservatives, who defend Stalinism, the orthodox values of central planning, authoritarianism, and continuity of the system.

But during and in the immediate aftermath of Brezhnevian period, as Shlapentokh (1988, 108-10) points out, three major ideological currents surfaced in the country: conservative (Brezhnevian), neo-Stalinist, and liberal-Marxist. The conservative ideology was characterized by negative attitudes toward the liberal movement, consolidation of dominance of the Communist Party in all spheres of social life, emphasis on power and stability of the system, protection of party leaders, both past and present, and sporadic efforts to restore Stalinist cult, especially in connection with commendation of the authoritarian state and dominant political system. The neo-Stalinist ideology rejected Stalin's methods of repression and terror, and incorporated some elements of liberalism and a scientific approach to economics and other spheres of life. They denounced Brezhnevian authoritarian ideology of stability for the ruling class. But their ideology, like Stalinism, has also been characterized by strong antidemocratism and deep mistrust of common citizens, and endorsement of the principle that any serious achievement justifies its high cost and human sacrifices. Unlike Stalinism, however, the neo-Stalinists glorify statehood, not the cult of party or leader, and are extremely critical of the *apparatchiks* (the state bureaucracy).

According to Shlapentokh, the liberal-Marxist ideology had its real precursor in the Soviet Union in Khrushchev, and had most recent manifestations in the Soviet sociologist Zaslavskya's *Novosibirsk* memorandum (1984), which identified the *apparatchik* as the main enemy of economic and political reform in the Soviet Union. Liberal-Marxists emphasize democracy both inside and outside the party, call for bolder private petty-bourgeois activities in industry and agriculture, and are willing to go beyond the Leninist tradition in their quest for political democratization and economic liberalization. Shlapentokh claims that Gorbachev belongs to the latter group.

Debate between reformism and conservatism in the Soviet Union, however, has undoubtedly reached its zenith with *glasnost* and *demokratizatsiya*. Because *perestroika* demonstrates an unmistakable continuation of the reformist strand of thought in the Soviet Union (see Dowlah 1990b, 99-163), Gorbachev's own position largely concords with the broad spectrum of arguments of reformist of thought. Therefore, while evaluating Gorbachev's critique of pre-Gorbachev Soviet political economy, the viewpoints of pro-reform forces will be taken into consideration.[18]

GORBACHEV'S CRITIQUE OF SOVIET POLITICAL ECONOMY

Immediately after assuming power, Gorbachev (1987, 40) insisted on "a really truthful and scientific" scrutiny of Soviet political economy in order "to pay due credit to all the heroism in the past, and to draw lessons from mistakes and miscalculations" (Gorbachev 1988a, 411). Discussion of his critique of pre-Gorbachev Soviet political economy has been organized as follows.[19]

Lenin and the NEP Period

Available literature and Gorbachev's own statements and speeches indicate that Lenin, the founder of the Soviet Union, is Gorbachev's idol and mentor. Although policies such as initiation of political pluralism and a greater private initiatives have led many to conclude that Gorbachev is going beyond Lenin's legacy (see Talbott 1990; Baum 1989; Brown 1989), scholars generally agree that he derives ideological inspiration from Lenin, and many of his programs and policies are vividly reminiscent of Lenin's NEP period (see Dowlah 1990b, 165-205). It can therefore be argued that the genesis, if not subsequent development, of Gorbachev's *perestroika* lies with NEP-Lenin. While Stalin cited Lenin of the War Communism period, Gorbachev consistently cites Lenin of the NEP period to enlist doctrinal support for *perestroika*'s programs and policies.[20]

Gorbachev praises Lenin's NEP principles to build socialism "on the basis of personal interests, personal incentives and business principles," for encouraging cooperatives and involvement of the working masses in processes of running the state, for organizing the state apparatus on the principle of "better fewer, but better," and for insistence on "the cultural development of the entire people" and the consolidation of the federation of free nations "without lies or bayonets" (Gorbachev 1988a, 410-11). He deplores how, after 1928, belief in "universal effectiveness of rigid centralization," in "methods of command" led to the development of a "party and government leadership system of administrative command" in the Soviet Union, "even though Lenin had warned about its danger in his day" (414). Yakovlev (1988) maintains that Gorbachev's moral and ideological inspirations from Leninist principles are especially reminiscent in his emphasis on cooperative and market ventures. Yakovlev argues that Lenin, like Marx before him, rejected the idea that capitalism could be peacefully transformed into socialism through the cooperative movement, as envisaged by many non-Marxist socialist scholars, but regarded cooperatives "as the high road to Socialism in the condition of post-revolutionary Russia."

Gorbachev repeatedly invokes Leninist practices of the NEP period to exonerate his vision of decentralized, democratic, and market-oriented socialism. Staunchly defending Lenin's stand for democratic and decentralized values, Gorbachev (1987, 47) condemns portrayal of Lenin "as an advocate of authoritarian methods of administration" as a "sign of total ignorance of Lenin's ideas and, not infrequently, of their deliberate distortion." He maintains that to Lenin, socialism and democracy were indivisible principles for organizing and operating a socialist economy. Gorbachev also compliments Lenin for valuable ideas on self-management, profit-and-loss accounting, and on linking of public and personal interests" (48). To Lenin, the market was "the most democratic mechanism of social accounting" (Yakovlev 1988, 65).

But arguments to the effect that Gorbachev too, like his predecessors, has manipulated Lenin's image and legitimacy in support of his aspirations for establishing socialism with a human face cannot be easily overruled. Tarasulo (1989, 4) identifies three reasons for Gorbachev's focus on Lenin: first, Gorbachev is unwilling to undermine the legitimacy of the entire system that Lenin helped to establish; second, Lenin provides an appropriate figure to juxtapose against Stalin; and third, Lenin's writings, that total fifty-five volumes, provide an arsenal of quotations that can be conveniently and suitably cited to justify practically any political or economic course. In addition, it can be presumed that Lenin and the NEP provide Gorbachev with invaluable guidance to develop a workable program of economic restructuring.

Stalin's Period

Gorbachev challenges the fundamentals of command-oriented economy and the challenge encompasses both the Stalinist and the post-Stalinist perspectives of Soviet socialism. While other post-Stalin leaders repudiated Stalin's personality cult and made cosmetic efforts at economic decentralization but continued the CPSU's monolithic, authoritarian control over the nation's political power and central planning's unbridled authority over the economy, Gorbachev denounces the Stalinist totalitarian model in toto: for the encrusted political and economic system that was bequeathed to him, the stagnation of the economy, the deeply corroded social and moral fabric of Soviet society, and for "enormous reinforcement of the most dogmatic strands of Marxism-Leninism" in Soviet history (Brown 1989, 4).

According to Lapidus (1989, 123), the basic thrust of *perestroika* is to alter the fundamental premise of the Stalinist system from "all that is not permitted is prohibited" to the principle that "all that is not prohibited is permitted." *Perestroika* is, in fact, an antithesis of the Stalinist command model. While Stalin iron-handedly established a totalitarian model of socialism through a "revolution from above," Gorbachev is orchestrating a more politicized, less bureaucratic, more decentralized, more pluralistic socialism, mainly through a spectacular revolution from below. Gorbachev is indeed redefining Stalinist concepts of party and state, and by promoting greater reliance on markets, competition, and self-regulation, he is repudiating Stalinist principles of state control and central planning. Zemtsov and Farrar (1988) maintain that Gorbachev has waged an war against both the subjective and objective traits of the Stalinist model, and one of the fundamental objectives of *perestroika* is to make sure that the Soviet system lacks the ability to generate new Stalins. Gorbachev has officially reinstated Stalin's "enemy of socialism," Bukharin, rehabilitated many Stalinist victims, and declassified many documents that exposed terror, coercion, and lawlessness during the Stalinist period to the people and to the press.

Gorbachev's criticism of Stalin and the Stalinist model demonstrates an evolutionary character. In *Perestroika* (1987, 38-49), although he sternly censured Stalin for orchestrating an "emasculated image of socialism," "exaggerated centralism," "neglect for the rich variety of human interests" and "serious excesses and blunders", he finally approved Stalinist collectivization policy as "a great historic act, the most important social change since 1917." He praised the program of collectivization for providing foundations for modernization of the agricultural sector of the economy, for enhancing productivity, and increasing agricultural output, thus releasing substantial amounts of material resources and workers for other sectors of the economy, and above all, for creating a solid basis for rapid industrialization of the country. Gorbachev also characterized Stalin's industrialization program as indispensable, without it, he argued, the country would have been "unarmed before fascism."

Subsequently, Gorbachev's criticism and rhetoric against Stalinist policies were sharpened. At the seventieth anniversary of the Bolshevik Revolution, Gorbachev

(1988b, 410-25) accused Stalin of resorting to methods and forms that were not "always [in] accord with socialist principles, with socialist ideology and philosophy." He criticized Stalin for restricting "the development of the democratic potential of socialism" and holding back the "progress of socialist democracy." Gorbachev denounced Stalin for erecting a hierarchical command system and charged him with "real crimes stemming from an abuse of power" and "enormous and unforgivable" offenses against the nation. However, until the seventieth anniversary of the Bolshevik Revolution, even though Gorbachev criticized Stalin strongly, and even described some of his actions and policies as crimes and offences against the nation, his stand on Stalin remained largely neutral and compromising (Tarasulo 1989, 5).[21]

In March 1989, addressing the CPSU Central Committee extended plenum on agriculture, Gorbachev denounced Stalin's peasant policies as the "most flagrant departures from the Leninist course," which manifested the "ugliest form in forcible methods" and "voluntarist intervention in the processes of production, exchange, and distribution," which led to "great social, economic, ethical costs" (FBIS, March 16, 1989, 32). Gorbachev strongly denounced Stalin's "methods of extra-economic coercion," denial to the peasants of their legitimate aspirations to be masters of their own land, and implanting of "a ramified bureaucratic apparatus" to dominate the collective and state farms and the peasantry. Gorbachev also condemned Stalin for adopting Trotsky-Preobrazhensky's concept of primary socialist accumulation that emphasized transfer of resources from agriculture to industry, for curtailing commodity-money relations as introduced by NEP, and for resorting to a "diametrically opposed road" to that of the NEP and Leninist principles. Gorbachev also accused Stalin of making a "serious strategic miscalculation and departure from Marxist views and notions concerning ways of solving the agrarian-peasant question" (29-31). Subsequently, in an interview with *Time* (June 4, 1989, 34), implicitly referring to Stalinist excesses, Gorbachev asserted "no matter how noble and attractive" a program may seem, it "never justifies indiscriminate means."

Therefore, in Gorbachev's current view, Stalin did not only depart from the Marxist-Leninist path, by resorting to orthodox values and indiscriminate means, forms, and methods. Stalin, as Soviet sociologist Zaslavskaya describes, was actually engaged in an "antidemocratic and antisocialistic" project (FBIS, Jan 19, 1989, 75). Gorbachev and his associates believe that Stalin, in fact, derailed the development of Soviet society from the trajectory that had been planned by Lenin for establishing democratic socialism, and thereby imperiled further progress of socialism.

The Post-Stalinist Period

Gorbachev's critique encompasses the post-Stalinist periods of Khrushchev and Brezhnev as well. Although the campaign of de-Stalinization began immediately after Stalin's death with the introduction of premier G.M. Malenkov's "New

Course," Gorbachev and his associates strongly believe that earlier efforts were half-hearted and piecemeal in nature; they merely tinkered with the system and ultimately accomplished nothing substantial. Attempts at reforms aimed at de-Stalinization and greater decentralization of Soviet economy were never comprehensive and never backed by societal or democratic reforms. Gorbachev and his associates maintain that although Khrushchev and Kosygin made appreciable efforts to reform the Stalinist system, Brezhnev not only stalled the process, but also reintroduced many Stalinist legacies.[22]

Gorbachev (1987, 43) described the Twentieth Congress of the CPSU in 1956 as a "major landmark" in the Soviet history and praised it for its "great contribution to the theory and practice of socialist construction" and for imparting "an impulse to liberation from the negative aspects of sociopolitical life engendered by the Stalin personality cult". In a similar spirit, at the seventieth anniversary of the Bolshevik Revolution, Gorbachev admired Khrushchev's courage for attacking Stalin's personality cult. But at the same time, Gorbachev maintained that Khrushchev's reforms, except for bringing in temporary "sound results," actually accomplished nothing of significance. Gorbachev (1988b) identified two basic faults with Khrushchev's reforms: (1) they were started at the top, ("no small number of subjectivist errors were committed"); and (2) they were nondemocratic in nature ("not backed up by a broad development of democratization processes").

In his book *Perestroika* (1987, 43), Gorbachev accuses Khrushchev of not fully utilizing the possibilities that emerged with the new spirit of the people. According to Gorbachev, Khrushchev dominated economic management by "improvisation," resorted to "ambitious and unfounded promises and predictions" and demonstrated a "gap between words and deeds." Gorbachev also accused Khrushchev of giving currency to "superficial notions of communism and various prophecies and abstract views," detracting from "the historical significance of socialism," and weakening "the influence of socialist ideology" (Brown 1989, 6).[23]

To Gorbachev (1987, 44), Kosygin's reforms of the mid-sixties were "more considered and better substantiated" and could bring "positive changes in the economy." But he regrets that having produced temporary but substantially sound results, the reforms dissipated and thus, further progress of socialist development was retarded. Gorbachev acknowledges that Kosygin's economic reforms succeeded in raising aspirations, improving the standard of living of the Soviet people, promoting productivity and enhancing the economic and scientific potential of the country, and indeed changed "the overall economy for the better" and enhanced the "international prestige of Soviet state." The gains of those reforms were short-lived because, Gorbachev observes, the leadership had neither the necessary political will nor the competence to put resources into productive work. Therefore, "much of what had been decided remained on paper, was left suspended in mid-air" (Gorbachev 1988b, 419). As a notable example, the CPSU continued to command the economy as before, and no appreciable measures were undertaken to democratize the nation's economic mechanism or industrial management.

Gorbachev strongly condemns Brezhnev for substantially inhibiting the nation's development potential during his eighteen-year rule. He holds Brezhnev responsible for the braking mechanisms in the economy, for their social and ideological consequences that led to "bureaucracy-ridden public structures," and for allowing bureaucracy to acquire "too great an influence in all state, administrative and even public affairs" (1987, 47-48).[24]

GORBACHEV'S VISION OF SOVIET SOCIALISM

Mikhail Gorbachev, born in 1931, is essentially a product of the Soviet system. He belongs to the post-Stalin generation that was brought up in an industrialized, modernized, and materially advanced society. Gorbachev is the second youngest general secretary of the CPSU,[25] and has heralded a revolution in the Soviet Union to create a "new individual" suiting the needs of a qualitatively different stage of sociopolitical and economic development of the Soviet Union, to meet the standards of today's scientifically and technologically advanced world. Instead of emphasizing traditional Soviet socialist values of collectivism, democratic centralism, dogmatism, and so on, like some of his predecessors, Gorbachev struggles to create a characteristically different and qualitatively modified model of socialism. Gorbachev envisions a radical, wholesale transformation of Stalinist "command socialism," Khrushchevian "goulash communism," and Brezhnev's "developed socialism" into a humanitarian, democratic, decentralized market socialism that can effectively influence world development "along ennobling and humanistic lines" (Yakovlev 1988, 54), and lead the Soviet Union into the twenty-first century as a "profoundly democratic state," the economy of which will constitute "an important and integral part of a new global economy" (*Time*, June 4, 1989, 34). Gorbachev's socialism presents the most decisive blow to the dogma that Soviet socialism continues to represent an unbroken continuum of ossified Leninist monocracy or Stalinist totalitarianism.

Marx predicted the emergence of socialism in a post-capitalist, industrialized, and advanced economy. In contrast, Soviet socialism emerged in a backward, semi-colonial, and semi-feudal Russian empire. In a remarkably short time, it transformed that backwardness into one of the mightiest economic, political, and military powers on the earth. As noted earlier, while other nations, under different economic and political ideologies, took a hundred or more years to attain industrialization, the Soviet Union accomplished the same goal within a matter of a decade or two. But the spectacular achievements of the Soviet socialist economy, especially since the late seventies, have become a matter of the past. The wheels of progress that once stunned people around the globe have halted. Economic stagnation, social alienation, and political lethargism—conditions long believed to be alien to socialism—have become pronounced. Aspirations and dreams to move forward to establish a post-capitalist communist society have reached a critical stage. Many conclude that in the fifties the socialist economies looked for ways "to socialism," now they are desperately looking for ways "from socialism" (Prybyla 1990; Reagan 1989).

Does this mean that a socialist system is, in fact, conducive for achieving industrialization, but not capable of realizing post-industrialization, as Djilas (1990) claims? Can the evolution of socialist economies be explained as a matter of interrelationship between socialism and underdevelopment, as Post and Wright (1989) claim? Is socialism's potentiality exhausted, as many scholars such as Fukuyama (1989) and Heilbroner (1989) claim? Is socialism unreformable, as Brezezniski and Huntington (1965) concluded in the early sixties? Is Gorbachev moving away from socialism, as western media often report (Kaiser 1988; Unger 1989)? Is Gorbachev merely tinkering with the Stalinist centralized socialism to make it work better, as Hewett (1988 & 1989), Zemtsov & Farrar (1989), Lenches (1990), and many others conclude? Are Gorbachev's reforms as reversible as previous reforms in Soviet history, as Jermakowicz (1988) theorizes?

Answers to these questions, according to Gorbachev, are categorically negative. His rhetoric and statements, the astounding pace of change, and the breathtaking events in the Soviet Union and other socialist countries since his assumption of power in 1985, overwhelmingly support the view that indeed socialism is reformable and *perestroika* is actually a revolutionary phenomenon. Certainly Gorbachev is optimistic concerning socialism's potentiality and believes socialism is capable of post-industrialization. For solutions to the problems of Soviet socialism, Gorbachev is looking within the orbit of socialism, not outside it.

Denouncing claims to the effect that socialism's potentiality has been exhausted, Gorbachev (1987, 29) asserts that socialism is "the living creativity of the masses," not an "a priori theoretical scheme"; therefore, it is capable of evolving into "the most progressive forms of social organization" that can accommodate the "fullest exposure of the humanist nature" of crucial economic, political, and moral aspects of a society. At the Twenty-seventh Plenary Session of the Central Committee of the CPSU, Gorbachev condemned orthodox socialists for regarding socialism as "immutable," and for "leaving no room for objective scientific analysis" within it (*Current Digest of Soviet Press*, Feb. 25, 1987, 3). Proclaiming unshakable belief in socialism's capacity of "self-perfection," Gorbachev (1987, 44) writes,

Socialism as a social system has proved that it has immense potentialities for resolving the most complex problems of social progress. We are convinced of its capacity for self-perfection, for still greater revelation of its possibilities, and for dealing with the present major problems of social progress which arise as we approach the twenty-first century.

Challenging the thesis that the Soviet Union represents a frozen, unreformable society, Gorbachev asserts that a practical demonstration of "socialism's inherent capability of constant self-improvement" can be ascertained by accelerating the process of restructuring the economy and society, by arresting the processes of stagnation and alienation, by providing guarantees against the recurrence of past mistakes, and by "fuller use of the possibilities inherent in the socialist system" (CDSP, Feb. 25, 1987, 2-3). Also contesting the arguments of those who claim that his reforms are piecemeal, half-hearted, and a mere repetition of past experiences,

Gorbachev repeatedly claims that *perestroika* envisages a radical and "comprehensive reform," and "revolution both from above and below." Gorbachev and his advisors claim *perestroika* as a revolutionary transformation in contrast to an evolutionary form of change (Aganbegyan 1988a, 6). The fact that most of Gorbachev's policies and programs are virtually irreversible has become so clear by now that it can hardly be disputed.

Gorbachev's socialism is not orthodox socialism as centralized socialists or Stalinists envisage. His is rather a unique and distinct vision of socialism that envisions effective democratic participation of the masses in the governmental and work processes, an optimal balance between market forces and central planning in economic mechanisms, which he calls a "regulated market system," decentralization of authority, and acceleration of scientific and technological progress in the industrial spheres, creation of a qualitatively new man, new mind, and new thinking in the societal processes. Unquestionably, Gorbachev did not start with a comprehensive blueprint of his own vision of socialism. This is an evolving process, and time and events, naturally, will shape and reshape it. A careful analysis of Gorbachev's writings, addresses, and statements published in English so far strongly indicate that Gorbachev's vision of socialism is a distinct and unique phenomenon in Soviet history and socialist literature, tantamount to a revolution within the socialist revolution. Before embarking on the details of Gorbachev's socialist vision, a few words on our claims of its unique, distinct, and revolutionary characters are in order.

Distinct Character

Gorbachev envisages a socialist system that is distinctly different from other models of socialism in Soviet theory and practice. The previous models, Gorbachev claims, possessed "lower socialist ideals," such as nationalization of the means of production, an official ideology committed to the working class and its welfare, and so on. But they commonly lacked, although to different degrees, what Rosefielde (1981, 5) calls "higher socialist ideals" pertaining to humanitarian values, democratic principles, due legal processes, civil liberties, and authentic social consciousness. Gorbachev not only minimizes the importance of the lower socialist ideals, and emphasizes the higher socialist ideals, he has actually ushered in a revolution for accomplishing these objectives on a priority basis. Gorbachev's socialism, in his own words, stresses "vital creativity of the masses, the all round democracy and socialist self-government, the encouragement of initiative and independent activity, the strengthening of discipline and order, and the expansion of openness, criticism in all spheres of the life of society; it means respect, raised on high, for the value and worth of the individual" (CDSP, Feb. 25, 1987, 6).

As we have seen above, Gorbachev has actually waged a war against Stalinist and post-Stalinist models. According to Yakovlev (1989, 47), *perestroika* "is actually a complete rejection of the Stalinist legacy in all spheres of life." Gorbachev proclaims that an administrative command system might be useful for a period of industrialization, but is no longer appropriate in a post-industrialized society. While the post-Stalin Soviet leaders discarded Stalinist personal tyranny and control over society, they essentially continued the Stalinist traditions of one-party dictatorship and central planning. Gorbachev challenges the whole Stalinist tradition. He has already done away with the traditional dominance of central planning and introduced multi-party-based political pluralism, has emboldened private initiative, and has called for a substantially increased role of markets and prices in the economic processes.

Gorbachev's socialism also goes beyond Lenin's NEP policies in many respects. While Lenin's NEP allowed small-scale private ownership and markets in the agricultural and consumer goods sectors only, Gorbachev's socialism extends private initiative and ownership to industrial enterprises, and envisages a greater role for market processes and price mechanisms. Although Gorbachev and many others claim that *perestroika*'s programs and policies are reminiscent of NEP, they do not necessarily conform to NEP in all details, and of course such conformity is not expected of a society that is at the threshold of the twenty-first century. Therefore, it can be concluded that describing Stalinism as "Super-War Communism" is as wrong as describing Gorbachev's *perestroika* as Super-NEP. Indeed, Gorbachev widens the horizon of Soviet models, and he effectively repudiates the traditional argument of polarity of choices in the Soviet Union between war communism and NEP. Even Lewin, who championed such polarity in *Political Undercurrents in Soviet Economic Debates* (1974), in his later work *Gorbachev Phenomenon* (1988, 152) concludes that Gorbachev provides an escape from "the seemingly fatal bi-model pendulum."

Gorbachev's break with the post-Stalinist legacy has also been manifested in his ideological standpoint. Soviet society demands ideological justification of programs and policies enunciated by its leaders, and Gorbachev is no exception. Schneider (1989, 24-39) maintains that, historically, Marxist-Leninist ideology performed at least five functions in the Soviet Union. It: (1) served to justify the existence of the Communist Party and the Soviet political system; (2) worked as a legitimizing instrument; (3) provided additional avenues for cohesion of the political party; (4) filtered information through the eyeglasses of ideology; and (5) furnished a framework for political discussion and conflict resolution. As no Soviet political system can "survive intact with a fundamental contradiction between practical policies and ideology," virtually every Soviet leader, including Gorbachev, adjusted ideology according to practical political requirements.

But Gorbachev's adjustments of Soviet ideology constitute a "comprehensive socialist renewal" (Yakovlev 1989, 34), a "redefinition of socialism" (Lapidus 1989, 123), and a "new socialist revolution" (Scanlan 1988, 50). At the Twenty-second Congress of the CPSU, Khrushchev proclaimed that full communism would be achieved in the Soviet Union by the early eighties, but in the early eighties, the Soviet economy experienced the worst stagnation since the early twenties. Gorbachev squarely blames Khrushchev for "superficial notions of communism and various prophesies and abstractions" that dwindled the historical significance of socialism and seriously crippled the socialist ideology. Brezhnev also made similarly boastful claims at the Twenty-fourth Congress of the CPSU.

But to Gorbachev, Soviet socialism is yet far from overcoming contradictions (see Woody 1989). Like Andropov and Chernenko before him, Gorbachev believes it is inappropriate to describe contemporary Soviet society as developed socialism or mature socialism, but, rather, recognizes the existence of widespread "negative processes" in the society, and stresses that a fundamental transformation of existing production and social relations is necessary for perfecting socialism in the Soviet Union (Meissner 1987, 63). Gorbachev proclaims, "No achievements, even the mightiest ones, should obscure contradictions in the development of society," and believes that the root cause of "all those contradictions that occur in life" lies in the "theoretical notions about socialism in many ways remained on the level of the 1930s and 1940s," when "lively discussion and creative thought disappeared from theory and social sciences and authoritarian assessments and judgments became indisputable truths subject only to commentary" (CDSP, Feb 25, 1987, 1-4).

Therefore, by denouncing the Stalinism that rationalizes authoritarianism, Gorbachev emphasizes "moving away from dogmatism" (FBIS, March 14, 1990, 6) to create a solid democratic foundation for qualitatively new social processes of socialist rejuvenation. Gorbachev consistently emphasizes that the individual and his potential, *demokratizatsiya*, and *glasnost* are the core of his socialism, not orthodox dogmas, such as central planning, collectivism, the Communist Party, or the leadership dictatorship over society. He wants to remake the individual "the master at production, through democratic forms and new methods of economic management," to elevate man "as the main motive force in every field of restructuring, in every sphere of life" (FBIS, April 27, 1989, 35). He wants to open a "real path toward the renewal of society, to its assumption of new quality, and to the creation of truly humane and democratic socialism" (FBIS, Sept. 11, 1989, 27).

Gorbachev, "the Soviet plenipotentiary" (O'Brien 1990) decisively discards cold war politics; instead, he envisages trust, peaceful coexistence, humanized international relations in a nonviolent world where people will "hasten enlightenment and broaden mutual understanding" (Gorbachev 1988b, 23). Gorbachev has brought a decisive end to the cold-war period, and envisions an end of Soviet isolationism, giving up the dogma of an inevitable war between socialism and capitalism. As in his earlier address at the United Nations General Assembly in 1988, he reasserted his global vision in his interview with *Time* (June 4, 1990, 31): "The countries and peoples of the East, the West, the North and the South—however different their social systems and levels of development, and however dissimilar their cultures, beliefs and ideologies—are parts of a single world and have basic, vital interests in common." In the Twenty-eighth Congress of the CPSU, Gorbachev (1990c) outlined three key premises of international relations: (1) every people's freedom of choice is a "fundamental precondition for building up a new type of world order"; (2) contemporary imperatives are "co-development, co-creativity and cooperation"; and (3) incorporation of the Soviet economy into the world economy is a "necessary condition" for modernization of the Soviet economy and for the construction of the "material foundation of an irreversibly peaceful period of history."

Gorbachev's socialism attacks "the equation of Stalinism with socialism" and portrays Stalinism as a "response to specific conditions at a particular historical moment rather than a universally valid approach to economic, social, or political dilemmas" (Lapidus 1989, 131). Gorbachev struggles to recreate socialism, recognizing that Soviet society cannot "endure the challenges of modernization, technical specialization, and state bureaucratization" without significantly altering Marxist-Leninist institutions and values" (Miller 1989, 430). Indeed, Soviet society needs a state that can encounter its present level of development and complexity, and Gorbachev's socialism is precisely it. On the basis of careful evaluation of Gorbachev's domestic and international policies and views on overall socialist project, Schneider (1989, 24-32) argues that in contrast to the previous Soviet perceptions of socialism, Gorbachev's vision of socialism is distinguished by its lack of a claim to the absolute truth; its allowance for antagonistic contradictions in socialism; its preference for world-peace over class-struggle; and its postponement of worldwide victory of socialism into history's far future. Miller (1989, 430) concludes that Gorbachev's socialist vision confronts the forces of conservatism by "sweeping away the dogmas which have passed for theory up to the recent past" under the pretense of developed socialism, and provides positive guidance for shaping the concrete social and economic policies of *perestroika*.

Unique Vision

Gorbachev's modernized version of socialism also provides a unique model of socialist economy, which is not only distinguishable from earlier practices in the pre-Gorbachev Soviet Union, as we discussed above, but is also significantly different from other socialist models.[26] Gorbachev's socialism visualizes private initiatives, competition, profit, market pricing, and serious reform of central planning, but it does not stand, at least so far, for dismantling the mechanisms of central planning as has been done in Hungary. Gorbachev's *perestroika* envisages privatization and liberalization, but not to the extent done in China. Deng Xiaoping's Chinese socialism can afford to be less careful of the color of the cat and more concerned with its efficiency in catching mice, and it can afford to discard orthodox Marxism to justify greater permissiveness of privatization under the pretext of an early stage of socialism. Although Gorbachev rejects previous claims of developed socialism or mature socialism in the USSR, and he most certainly cannot use the excuse of the existence of early socialism in the Soviet Union. His freedom to manipulate the official Soviet ideology of Marxism-Leninism is further constrained by "global responsibilities and the attendant institutional and psychological limitations" (Miller 1989, 444), which do not equally constrain the Chinese leadership.

Gorbachev's socialism also can be distinguished from the Yugoslav model of workers' self-management. Gorbachev insists on decentralization, market social-ism, workers' participation in the management processes, and democratization of overall society, but not worker self-management, self-governance of communes, or socialized (as opposed to state) ownership of the means of production, that constitute the cardinal tenets of the Yugoslav model. Claims are often made that Gorbachev's vision of socialism derives inspiration from the Swedish experience. The Swedish model has been enormously successful in nullifying the postwar Keynesian proposition of an inevitable trade-off between full-employment and inflation. Whereas Yugoslav self-governing socialism demonstrates enormous contradictions and provides both shortcomings and opportunities, Swedish experi-ence provides a rich example of how socialists can combine elements of democratic planning and market efficiency and attain full employment under an economic system in which "the plan decommodifies the labor market and treats workers as human beings but it does so in response to signals from the labor market" (Harrington 1989b, 64-70). Although Gorbachev has made favorable reference to Sweden, he consistently maintains that he is looking within Soviet socialism, not outside it. To him, one of the major reasons that the Central European countries are rejecting the socialist system is that it was imposed from outside, and it has done "violence to their national character and national rights" (*Time*, June 4, 1990, 34). Despite aberrations under Stalin and his successors, it should be noted that socialism has deep roots in Soviet experience.

Revolutionary Phenomenon

Gorbachev's vision of socialism is not only distinctly different from the previous models of Soviet socialism, is unique among various versions of existing socialist systems, it is indeed a revolutionary phenomenon that can only be next to the October Revolution in historical significance.[27] Gorbachev intends to redefine socialism, reinvent democracy, restructure its social, economic, cultural, and political base, suiting the needs, demands, and concerns of post-industrialized society. Gorbachev's socialism visualizes a complete replacement of the Stalinist command model to repair what Howe (1988, 512) calls the "enormous damage wrought by Stalinism" to the socialist project, and he vividly demonstrates that even a "long-established socialist society can be wrongly established, can exhibit stagnation and a retardation mechanism" (Scanlan 1988, 56). By envisaging a thorough and comprehensive radical reform aimed at eliminating the dictatorship of the Communist Party—promoting genuine, meaningful, and active participation of the masses in the governmental processes by invigorating the unprecedented policies of *glasnost* and *demokratizatsiya*—Gorbachev unleashed forces that have the potential to revolutionize the whole society. Gorbachev emphasizes profound restructuring of the economic mechanism to bolster worker morale and participa-tion in public enterprises, and has initiated sweeping measures to liberalize the state economy, to encourage private, individual, and cooperative sectors, and allow international economic cooperation. Each one of these steps alone constitutes a radical transformation of Soviet society; each of these sweeping measures challenges the fundamental tenets of the Soviet Union of the last seven decades. Together, they constitute a revolution that fundamentally challenges the established system, and therefore, bears the potentiality of replacing it altogether.

Especially since the beginning of 1990, Gorbachev's strategies are more resolutely targeted at the discontinuation of the CPSU monopoly political power, and more aggressively aimed at laying the foundations for political pluralism in the Soviet Union, which marks a demonstrative break not only with the Stalinist totalitarian system, but also with the Leninist authoritarian tradition of one-party rule. Moreover, by initiating a bona fide process aimed at vigorous privatization and a regulated market system, Gorbachev very clearly moves away from the orthodox Soviet Marxian values that insist on abolition of private ownership of the means of production as one of the major preconditions for socialism.

During an earlier stage, Gorbachev adhered to the existing system and wanted to put the economy in order by restructuring it, mainly through improvements in the central planning machineries, changing personnel and injecting scientific and technological developments into the economy. Neither control of central planning, nor the monopoly power of the CPSU was seriously challenged. NEP-Lenin provided him with ideological inspiration. He repudiated Stalinism but wrestled with post-Stalinism. More recent policies show unambiguous signs of moving away from Lenin, too. Gradually, emphasis has shifted to laying the foundations of legal, political, and economic steps aimed at dismantling the existing system and building a new system that in the words of Gorbachev himself, "is a shift in direction comparable in magnitude to the October Revolution, because we will be replacing one economic and political model with another" (Time, June 4, 1990, 27).[28]

Among the typologies of revolution, perestroika could be approximated to either Stone's (1971, 44-56) typology of Jacobin Communist Revolution, or Wallace's (1956, 264-65) notion of a revitalization movement or Tucker's (1977, 79-81) concept of "full-scale sociopolitical revolution." The Jacobin Communist Revolution, according to Neumann (quoted in Stone 1971, 47), signifies "a sweeping fundamental change in political organization, social structure, economic property control and the predominant myth of a social order," thus indicating a major break in the continuity of development. Certainly, a dominant goal of perestroika is to demolish Stalinism and its command model. The changes contemplated in perestroika are indeed sweeping and fundamental, and might thereby overturn the so-called "Stalinist Revolution." Wallace's concept of a revitalization movement or Tucker's notion of a sociopolitical revolution can take place from below by involving the masses or from above, orchestrated by the new political leadership brought to power by the revolution. Such a revolution, according to Tucker, can take place over years or decades as a "historically protracted process" instead of in a "short time of spectacular social change." Such a sociopolitical revolution reconstitutes society's institutions, symbol systems, behavioral patterns, rituals, art forms, and habitual mode of life.

Therefore, *perestroika* can be understood as a revolutionary process aimed at social, economic, and political transformation in the Soviet Union. Implemented properly, it should create a robust democracy both in society and in the work places, and thereby Stalinist totalitarianism and post-Stalinist authoritarianism will be replaced by a system in which the democratic and participative role of Soviet citizens will be enhanced.

According to Gorbachev, revolutionary changes as orchestrated by *perestroika* are manifested in the processes of: (1) replacement of the "Stalinist model of socialism by a civil society of free men and women"; (2) transformation of an authoritarian political system by genuine democracy based on free elections, beginnings of a multi-party system, human rights, and rule of law; (3) replacement of production relations based on "alienation of the working people from property and from the results of their work" by conditions for "free competition of socialist producers"; (4) replacement of an overcentralized state by a "genuine Union based on the self-determination and voluntary association of peoples"; and above all, (5) replacement of ideological domination by "freedom of thought and *glasnost*, by an openness of society to information" (*News and Views From the USSR*, July 5, 1990, 2).

BASIC FEATURES OF GORBACHEV'S DECENTRALIZED SOCIALISM

The basic features of Gorbachev's vision of a freer, market-oriented, democratic, decentralized, and modernized "socialism with human face" have been elucidated below following the four criteria developed earlier. Gorbachev's vision of socialism not only resembles those of the decentralized socialists, but also elevates that vision to a newer, pragmatic, and emboldened stature conforming to the needs and concerns of the day.

Level of Economic Development

Gorbachev's socialism is preponderantly concerned with transition from extensive to intensive methods of production; in other words, from the industrialized to the post-industrialization phase of Soviet economy and society. Therefore, it could presumably be argued that Gorbachev's position with respect to level of economic development will be similar to that of the decentralized socialists, that is, socialism is a successor of capitalism that emerges in an advanced and industrialized economy. However, Gorbachev realizes that Soviet economy has been transformed to a socialist stage from a backward, semi-colonial, and semi-feudal stage of economic development, and has thereby skipped the stage of capitalism completely and feudalism at least partially. But like Bukharin and Luxemburg, Gorbachev approves of the emergence of socialism in pre-capitalist economic conditions. He (1987, 42) asserts that "a strict and impartial" analysis of history leads to the conclusion that the socialist option taken during the October Revolution was primarily responsible for bringing the Soviet Union to the "right place—the place the Soviet Union now occupies in human progress."

Therefore, although *perestroika* envisages a complete negation of Stalinism, and although he is highly critical of the methods and forms of Stalinist programs, Gorbachev has acknowledged that Stalin's programs of collectivization and industrialization were historically indispensable and legitimate decisions. Gorbachev justifies these programs on the grounds that early Soviet socialism, which broke the historical sequence of transition, necessitated such ordering of priorities, and found such single-mindedness in the allocation of economic resources indispensable for the development of Soviet economy.

By justifying command economy at the initial stages of socialism, Gorbachev comes closer to postwar Lange (1958) and Dobb's positions (1970), which prescribe that socialist economy may be centrally planned and organized at the initial stage of industrialization when national resources need to be directed consciously for the development of priority sectors of the economy. Gorbachev also subscribes to Lange's position that because of the dialectic nature of development, the centralized planned economy becomes useless, unproductive, even counterproductive, once industrialization has been achieved (FBIS, July 11, 1989, 39).

Gorbachev's stand concerning collectivization and industrialization, however, remains controversial. Many of *perestroika*'s staunch supporters believe that Stalin's "antidemocratic" and "antisocialist" measures constituted a deviation of the actual development of Soviet society from the trajectory that had been planned by Lenin (FBIS, January 19, 1989, 75). Western scholars find Stalin's collectivization and industrialization programs to be fatal and nightmarish decisions, which indeed were enormously responsible for counter-productive and dysfunctional consequences in subsequent periods of Soviet history (see Draper 1988; Howe 1988; Nee & Stark 1989; Winiecki 1989a).

Planning and Markets

Gorbachev and his advisers, like traditional protagonists of decentralized socialists,[29] find the inseparable association of market with capitalism, on the one hand, and planning with socialism, on the other, as erroneous and misleading. Gorbachev and his associates do not hesitate to acknowledge that commodity production and market relations were indeed universalized under the capitalist system, but they firmly maintain that the market is a pre-capitalistic phenomenon that was used even in earlier stages of economic development. The fact of the matter is, the capitalist system used it, and the socialist system, intentionally or inadvertently, either used it less or attempted to ignore it altogether.

Gorbachev and his advisers express their conviction on markets as a historically formed "objective economic and social reality" and as "the only known reliable anti-waste mechanism" (Yakovlev 1988, 66-67), which has nothing to do specifically with capitalism or socialism. Like Harrington (1989b), they tend to blame capitalist manipulation of markets, not the market itself, for social, political, and economic consequences that are commonly believed to be offsprings of markets. To Gorbachev and his associates, the market is an objective and neutral phenomenon. They maintain that even Lenin, by emphasizing "social accounting," and business-like behavior, sought to utilize market instruments, and thereby sought to reduce the bureaucratically organized, centrally planned direction of socialist economy. They maintain that a decentralized socialist economic system cannot function devoid of commodity production and market and money relations. For them such relations inevitably emerge when producers are individualized and there is a division of labor. A decentralized socialist economic system, by putting public enterprises on the basis of self-financing and self-management, by encouraging cooperative enterprises, self-employment, and private initiatives, inescapably assumes development of market parameters like "separation of producers, the division of labor, and the exchange of commodities" (Aganbegyan 1988a, 127).

Moreover, Gorbachev and his advisers are aware of the past experiences of detailed planning and understand that planning, whether directive (determining volumes of production) or indicative (determining prices), will fall far short of meeting the needs and concerns of the contemporary Soviet economy. For them an unbalanced plan "entails far more waste than automatic market regulation," and an "unsubstantiated plan is far more costly than market self-adjustment" (Shmelev & Popov 1989, 215). But Gorbachev and his associates are equally aware that the market is blind and cannot provide for the long-term interests of society. Therefore, they envisage simultaneous existence and interplay of market and planning in the economy. Gorbachev's socialism, therefore, does not stand for dismantling central planning altogether, it rather envisages a regulated market in which "planning for the development of the economy will in part be realized through the market" (Aganbegyan 1988a, 132). Therefore, measures to reform price, market, credit and other financial resources and mechanisms are being taken gradually and with extreme caution. Gorbachev repeatedly emphasizes development of "constructive and businesslike character" among the citizenry so that "alienations that have been developed between the people and the authorities" (FBIS, Sept. 11, 1989, 27) over the last seven decades can be overcome, and an optimal balance between market mechanisms and central planning by state control, as Bukharin envisaged, can be developed.

But many Western scholars point out that Gorbachev's emphasis on market relations and dismantling of the planning mechanism falls far short of market socialism, as envisaged, let us say, by Lange. Apparently, Gorbachev and his associates do not even claim that they are marching forward to the establishment of Lange-type decentralized market socialism, although they clearly stress proper understanding of economic reforms, and, thereby, lessons, from different countries. Aganbegyan (1988a, 132) maintains that *perestroika* envisages a "government-regulated market," it does not envisage "universalization and general spread of the market place, an economic system in which everything is bought and sold."

Perestroika's market reforms, as outlined by Gorbachev at the Twenty-eighth Congress of the CPSU, appear to be carefully circumscribed; they do not extend to a free market for land and natural resources, and do not provide for a stock exchange, or other capital resources.[30] Subsequently, the Five Hundred Day program, introduced in October 1990, provided a timetable and detailed schedule for comprehensive economic reforms aimed at a grand transition to a market economy.[31] Clearly the direction is toward market economy, although the expectation is that it will take a long time.

Ownership and Control

Like decentralized socialists, Gorbachev rejects the notion of wholesale nationalization of the means of production as a precondition for socialism. His vision of socialism stresses promotion of private ownership side by side with the dominant and necessary existence of public ownership of the means of production, and consequently, aims at curbing control and domination of the state and the CPSU over the country's economic sphere. Gorbachev's emphasis on private ownership, however, apparently is more pervasive than that of other decentralized socialists. For example, Kautsky, Bernstein, Luxemburg, and Lange, in general, emphasized gradual but extensive public ownership and control along with private ownership. Lenin and Bukharin, in their versions of mixed economy, emphasized a careful balance between private ownership and public ownership, and a strong role of state and party to overcome the market through the market and keep private ownership limited mainly to agricultural and household sectors. Gorbachev has already extended conspicuous privatization into the industrial sector, and he emphasizes not overcoming the market through the market, as Bukharin and Lenin did, but realizing planned objectives through the market.

To Gorbachev and his associates, all-encompassing central planning and its essential offshoot, extensive, unresponsive bureaucratization and predominance of administrative methods over economic methods in the economic mechanism, is not only an alienable and disposable feature of socialism, but indeed, it has also historically proven to be an essentially counterproductive feature in an economic system. Therefore, Gorbachev (1987, 34) emphasizes "universal introduction of economic methods, the renunciation of management by injunction and by administrative methods, and the overall encouragement of innovation."

Gorbachev emphasizes extensive changes in the relations between enterprise and central management organs, and calls for new economic methods and levers to stimulate efficiency, initiative, and productivity in enterprises. As he asserts, "It is impossible to boost up collective" interest unless we switch to new forms of organizing economic life, unless we pave the way for economic accountability, self-financing, contracts, leasing, cooperatives" (FBIS, August 21, 1989, 40). In order to put enterprises on "economically substantiated prices," on economic methods and economic accountability, Gorbachev also emphasizes major reforms in the structure of prices (as will be explained in Chapter 5).

Indeed, *perestroika* envisages "universal" rather than restricted introduction of economic methods of incentives, as seen during the NEP period. It stresses innovation and productivity rather than target fulfillment, greater individual initiatives rather than passive obedience of the workers, and bolder privatization rather than massive collectivization and nationalization, as seen during the Stalinist and post-Stalinist periods. In sharp contrast to the legacy of the command economy, Gorbachev intends a radical restructuring in ownership and control by introducing extensive and diversified ownerships, including private ownership of the means of production. Condemning "dogmatic approaches to the choice of ways of running the economy and organizing management" and demanding a revision in "orthodox theory and practice" on ownership, Gorbachev underscores equality of various forms of socialist ownership of the means of production and of economic management based on them (FBIS, March 16, 1989, 36; also see *New York Times*, June 2, 1990). He pleads for an expanding role of private business and producers' cooperatives and calls for a new approach to family and individual work and commodity-producing farms based on the farmer's own work. Such promotion of private initiative based on individual labor contradicts the orthodox belief that socialism means negation of private initiative and ownership. Roucek (1988, 49) comments that to orthodox Soviet socialists, it comes as "an attack on the ideological purity of socialist economic model."

To Gorbachev, however, a fundamental transformation in the ownership of the means of production is an imperative to make "it possible to overcome man's alienation from the means of production," to create "incentives for independent creative work," to offer "possibilities for economic independence and for displaying initiative and enterprise," to institute "equal conditions of economic operation for state and cooperative enterprises," and to establish "diverse forms of socialist ownership" (FBIS, Sept. 11, 1989, 29). Gorbachev's associates defend the drive for privatization with no less enthusiasm (see Aganbegyan 1988a, 27-30; Roucek 1988). They maintain that a combination of private and public ownership and management will significantly help to put the economy back on the track. Principal arguments put forward by the protagonists of a viable private sector in the Soviet economy include: (1) private enterprise has existed in the Soviet Union since its inception, so it's not an entirely new phenomenon; (2) especially during the NEP period, private ownership played a significant role in rejuvenating the economy ravaged by the policies of War Communism period; (3) it helps to legalize the vast "second economy" in the country; and (4) other socialist countries have promoted private initiatives that have made positive contributions to those economies (see Zaslavskaya 1989; Gorbachev 1990c).

Democracy and the State

To Gorbachev, democratization of the society, economy, and state—every sphere of the country—is a sine qua non for successful operation of the socialist system. Issacson (1989, 57) remarks that while in other socialist countries forces of people challenge the state authority from below, in the Soviet Union they are marshalled by the leader from above. Like Bernstein, Gorbachev believes democracy is an "indispensable precondition for realization of socialism." Like Kautsky, Gorbachev believes democracy is "the most powerful lever" for social, economic and political revitalization of the country. Like Luxemburg, Gorbachev is aware that democratic institutions are not flawless, but at the same time maintains that to abolish (or forbid) them would be even worse. Like her, Gorbachev also believes in freedom of press, free elections, free public opinion, and freedom of association. Gorbachev's democracy is much more robust than that envisaged by Lenin and Bukharin. Nonauthoritarian Lenin envisaged discussions and freedom within the Communist Party, not outside it, and Bukharin emphasized reduction in the state's dominance on economy, but Gorbachev's democracy envisages a multi-party system, real political pluralism, *glasnost*, and *demokratizatsiya*, which not only call for reduction in the role of the state, but also effectively stimulate the people to take up initiative and responsibility, and to curb bureaucratization.

To Gorbachev, *perestroika* stands for "more socialism and more democracy." His democracy stands for "more culture and humanism in production, social and personal relations among people, more dignity and self-respect for the individual" (Gorbachev 1987, 37). His profound belief in democratic practices is amply manifested in his concepts of *glasnost*, political pluralism, and *demokratizatsiya*. Gorbachev (1987, 75-76) emphasizes *glasnost* to instigate a "normal and favorable spiritual and moral atmosphere in society," to nourish it as an "effective form of public control over the activities of all government bodies," to ensure "the greatest possible openness in the work of government and mass organizations and to enable working people to express their opinion on any issue of social life and government activity without fear."

The policies of *glasnost* and *demokratizatsiya*, Gorbachev (1988b, 282) asserts at the Ninteenth All Union Conference of the CPSU, release "a powerful flood of thoughts, emotions and initiatives" that purifies "the social atmosphere, giving people wings, emancipating consciousness and stimulating activity." Gorbachev asserts,

Perestroika has opened a real path toward the renewal of society, to its assumption of a new quality, and to the creation of a truly humane and democratic socialism. It has restored to our great country a sense of dignity and has given the Soviet person a feeling of freedom. It is a powerful source of social and spiritual and, I would say, patriotic energy for decades to come (FBIS, Sept. 11, 1989, 27).

The notion of political pluralism acknowledges the diversity of groups and interests, and makes a decisive shift from the notion of "single truth" to the recognition of the legitimacy and necessity of divergent opinions (Lapidus 1989, 131-32). It encourages new thinking in political, economic, and social spheres, and above all, gives up the ideological dogmatism of the past. Gorbachev (1988b) proclaims, "We start from the fact that socialism is a society of growing diversity in opinions, relations, and activities of the people."[32] Besides giving opportunity to challenge the orthodox dogmatism, *demokratizatsiya* is also aimed at strengthening the support base for Gorbachev's vision of reformed socialism. He says: "It is within the framework of *glasnost* and democracy that those who try to insinuate alien values and alien banners and slogans must be put in their place. Rejection of *glasnost* and democracy would testify to lack of confidence and mistrust in people" (FBIS, August 21, 1989, 42). Brown (1989, 9) identified three fundamental principles that were previously elevated in the Soviet Union to a "higher pinnacle than the rest": the fundamental importance of class consciousness and of the class struggle; the leading role of the Communist Party; and democratic centralism. All three are fundamentally challenged by Gorbachev.[33]

CONCLUDING REMARKS

Gorbachev's vision of socialism is distinctly different from the previous models of Soviet socialism and is unique among the existing socialist systems. It constitutes a revolutionary phenomenon in Soviet history comparable to the October Revolution. Gorbachev has been striving to redefine socialism and restructure the social, economic, cultural, and political bases to suit the needs and challenges of post-industrialized Soviet society. Gorbachev's reforms are aimed at replacing the Stalinist model, restructuring the economic mechanism, and liberalizing the economic and political system. We conclude, therefore, that *perestroika* ushers in a genuinely revolutionary process of social, economic, and political transformation in the Soviet Union. *Perestroika* not only challenges Stalinism and post-Stalinism, especially in terms of its direction and progression, it even goes beyond orthodox Soviet Marxism-Leninism.[34]

The comprehensive character of *perestroika* has no full parallels or precedents in Soviet history or elsewhere. Moreover, its transformations do not necessarily lead to a movement away from socialism; they reinforce Gorbachev's commitment to socialism. Gorbachev reiterated his claim, "As we dismantle the Stalinist system, we are not retreating from socialism but are moving toward it" (*Time*, June 4, 1990, 31). Nixon insightfully comments, "As a Communist he [Gorbachev] is publicly dedicated not to renouncing Marxism, like millions of demonstrators in Eastern Europe, but to rejuvenating it" (*Time*, Dec 18, 1989). Indeed, *perestroika* envisages a revolution within socialism that aims at replacing a Stalinist system by a more democratic and decentralized socialist system. And this new experiment has not only brought an irrevocable end to Stalinism, both internally and externally, it also provides a "positive point of reference" for the socialist project around the globe (Miliband, Panitch and Saville, 1988). Indeed, Gorbachev's revision of socialism demonstrates an escape from age-old efforts to seek "answers to all contingencies of life in quotations from the classics" and in the Marxist "scriptures," and demonstrates a bold new step toward a "creative approach to theory and practice of socialism and to the comprehension of the historical experience of the twentieth century and the heritage of Marx, Engels, and Lenin and other eminent exponents of revolutionary and progressive thought" (Gorbachev 1990c, 34).

NOTES

1. *Review of Radical Political Economics* in its Spring 1981 issue summarized contrasting viewpoints of Western scholars about the nature of Soviet political economy.

2. Main proponents of this strand of thought include Szymanski 1979; Dobb 1966; and Drewnowski 1961.

3. We shall take up Trotsky's position in a moment.

4. Main protagonists of this strand of thought include Hilferding 1971; Sweezy in Bettleheim & Sweezy 1971; Schachtman 1971; and Tucker 1977.

5. Scholars that can be identified in this group include: Bettleheim 1976 and Bettleheim in Bettleheim & Sweezy 1971; Cliff 1974; Marcuse 1958; and Corrigan, Ramsay, and Sayer 1978.

6. Major protagonists of this strand of thought include: Lane 1979; Brus 1973 & 1975; Bahro 1978; Nee and Stark 1989; Nove 1979; Sik 1976; Selucky 1979; Szelenyi 1989; Milanovic 1989; Berki 1975; and Kalecki 1972.

7. Nationalization, Howe (1988, 514) asserts, is a "somewhat neutral device, available to just about every kind of government; but, whatever else, it is surely not a sufficient condition for a socialist transformation."

8. Elliott (1985, 373-74) maintains that the different periods of Soviet economic development not only represent distinguishable institutional characteristics, but also provide "alternative versions of Soviet communism" having empirical analogues in different parts of the world.

9. Draper (1988, 287), for example, maintains that Lenin "introduced it in March 1921, defended it to his last breath, and died in January 1924, while the NEP was still untouchable."

10. Many Western scholars including Howe 1988; Harrington 1989a; Draper 1988; Lewin 1974 & 1988; Elliott 1985 & 1989; and Remington (1989) share this viewpoint. Gorbachev (1987 & 1988a) also sides with this strand of thought and denounces Stalinism for resorting to "indiscriminate," and "coercive" forms and methods.

11. Like Carr 1952; Tucker 1977; Deutscher 1960; Brezeziniski 1967; Hilferding 1971; Kolakowski 1978; Lovell 1984; Polan 1984; and Stites 1989.

12. Draper (1988, 292) observes that one of the main contributions of the Khrushchev era is that "Khrushchev showed that it was possible to repudiate at least the worst excesses of the Stalinist heritage and die in bed."

13. The anonymous writers of *The Basics of Marxist-Leninist Theory* (1982, 9) claim that Lenin, the "heir to the teachings of Marx and Engels," developed

Marxism-Leninism under new conditions, "in the age of imperialism and proletarian revolutions" to aid the working people "in their struggle against the domination of bourgeoisie, against the exploitation of man by man and social inequality."

14. Medvedev (1981, 14) observes: "Lenin alone had to come up with first solutions to all problems of proletarian revolution, theoretical and practical—the Soviets as a new form of power, the union between the proletariat and the peasantry, the building of new society in post-revolutionary Russia, the new economy and the new state itself."

15. But, as mentioned before, he cautioned that "nowhere has the bourgeoisie ever voluntarily ceded its power and privileges" and "such peaceful possibilities have so far presented themselves very rarely in the course of history."

16. As Stalin asserts:

At the time when the New Economic Policy was being introduced, Lenin said that there were elements of five forms of social and economic structure in our country: (1) patriarchal economy (largely natural economy); (2) small-commodity production (the majority of the peasants who sell grain); (3) private capitalism; (4) state capitalism; and (5) socialism. We can now say that the first, the third, and the fourth forms of social and economic structure no longer exist; the second form has been forced into a secondary position, while the fifth form— the socialist form of social and economic structure—now holds undivided sway and is the sole commanding force in the whole economy (Franklin 1972, 245-46).

17. Comments in *Pravda*, after ouster of Khrushchev, October 16, 1964.

18. There are ultra reformists who disagree with Gorbachev's opinions and conservatives who are critical of Gorbachev's *perestroika*. Contending positions of both strands will be taken up in Chapter 6.

19. Gorbachev (1988b) believes that policies of War Communism were the outcome of "war and dislocations" caused by "concrete conditions," "Civil War and intervention from outside." As an almost identical position was taken by his predecessors, we refrain from elaborating Gorbachev's stand in this regard

20. Hundreds of quotations can be cited in which Gorbachev's focus on Lenin and Lenin's NEP period have been manifested. Here are just a few:

• These days, we turn ever more often to the last works of Lenin, to Lenin's New Economic Policy, and strive to extract from it all the valuable elements that we require today (Gorbachev 1988a, 410).

• The essence of *perestroika* lies in the fact that it unites socialism with democracy and revives Leninist concept of socialist construction both in theory and practice (35).

• The new economic policy stemmed logically from the objective development of the revolutionary process and was conceived in all earnestness and for a long period of time. It was based on the grassroots initiative, on democracy, cost-accounting and diverse forms of cooperation (FBIS, March 16, 1989, 31).

21. By accusing Stalin only for forms and methods, but at the same time justifying the policy contents of collectivization and industrialization, Gorbachev not only sidestepped Stalinist distortions of socialism, but disappointed many *perestroika* supporters (see Selyunin 1989, 11-27; Hazan 1990).

22. For details see Shlapentokh 1988, 87-104; Goldman 1987.

23. Aganbegyan (1988a, 54), Gorbachev's former chief economic adviser, points out three deeper reasons for the failure of Khrushchev's de-Stalinization efforts: (1) preservation of the administrative system of management; (2) lack of democratic principles in the direction of the country; and (3) hasty and unthought-out measures.

24. It should be noted that among his predecessors since Lenin, Gorbachev, however, does not fail to praise Khrushchev's efforts to reorganize and restructure the economy, curb the power of the secret police, and reduce bureaucratic proliferations. According to Shlapentokh (1988, 127), Khrushchev was the only "real precursor" of Gorbachev's liberal ideology. Also Gorbachev admires Kosygin's reforms aimed at decentralizing the economic mechanism of the country. As a matter of fact, Gorbachev takes over where Khrushchev and Kosygin left off. Gorbachev (1990c) said, "The concept of reform is not an offhand discovery by a particular group of individuals. The quest for it [*perestroika*] has been going on in the party and in the community ever since the Twentieth Congress of the CPSU [1956]. Unfortunately, it received no support and was even suppressed in most cases.

The reform efforts of *perestroika* are more vigorous, more comprehensive, and more radical than previous efforts. Presumably *perestroika*'s programs and policies are also reinforced by the lessons of previous reform efforts in the Soviet Union and elsewhere.

25. Not the youngest as many claim—at the time of appointment as general secretary of the CPSU Gorbachev was 54. Stalin was 43.

26. Goldman (1987) identified "Two Roads to Economic Reform: Hungary and the German Republic." He noted Gorbachev's reservations about the Hungarian model because of its shortcomings pertaining to the economic growth rate, inflation, balance of trade, and poor morale, but observed that Gorbachev has demonstrated his preference for the East German model because of its discovery of "a way of making central planning work." A similar conclusion was reached by Brezezinski (1989). Of course, circumstances have dramatically changed since those assessments were made. Neither Goldman nor Brzeziniski presumably would argue now that Gorbachev's vision of socialism is analogous to East Germany, which relinquished its independent identity by merging with capitalist West Germany.

27. The term "revolution" remains controversial because "each revolution reopens and creatively changes the very views that we have previously had on the subject" (Mazlish, Kaledin & Ralston 1971, 3). Commonly, it is conceived as a sweeping, comprehensive and rapid transformation of a society and polity. Scholars, however, debate how comprehensive, and sweeping the changes must be to be truly revolutionary, and one may also debate the question of rapidity. After all,

history provides many examples of social, economic, and political changes that emerge over a period of several hundred years, that taken as a whole, constitute a revolution. The Industrial Revolution and the Modern Capitalist Revolution provide good examples of such revolutions. In addition, when human beings are in the grip of profound and widespread changes, they may well expect or believe that the end result of the dynamic events they are witnessing will be revolutionary, even if, strictly speaking, an objective observer at the time remains unconvinced. Such a situation can well be understood as a revolutionary process.

28. Addressing the CPSU Central Committee plenum, Gorbachev claimed that *perestroika* aims at 'decisive reevaluation of obsolete theoretical concepts, a revolutionary renewal of society' (FBIS, Sept. 19, 1989, 40). Also in *perestroika* (1987, 50-51) he said, "Historical experience has shown that socialist society is not insured against the emergence and accumulation of stagnant tendencies and even against major socio-political crises. And it is precisely measures of a revolutionary character that are necessary for overcoming a crisis or pre-crisis situation".

29. Such as Bernstein 1909; Kautsky 1964; Luxemburg 1961; and Bukharin 1982; and Western scholars like Howe 1985 & 1988; Harrington 1989a; and Galbraith 1979.

30. Gorbachev (1990c, 12) described his vision of market economy at the Congress as follows:

We regard the market not as a goal in itself, but as a means of making the economy more effective and improving the standard of living. The market must facilitate a speedy solution to the problem of giving our economy greater social orientation and gearing it to people's interests.

State-owned enterprises, the collective ownership of a cooperative or joint-stock association, the work-earned property of the farmer, artisan or family all serve to strengthen the democratic pillars of society since the working people become genuine masters of the means of production and the results of their work, and have a personal stake in efficient performance and good ultimate results. Here there is no basis for exploitation.

This means that by moving toward market we are not swerving from the road to socialism but are advancing toward a fuller realization of society's potential.

31. This program had the potential to make sweeping changes in Gorbachev's position. But Gorbachev and his advisers, as will be explained in Chapter 5, believe that the existing Soviet economy will not be able to withstand such a major transition. Also, they are hesitant to extend rights of private ownership to land. These are some of the issues that in early 1991 resulted in sharp differences with Boris Yeltsin, who champions such reforms. As a result, as of March 1991, the program still remains in a state of flux. The compromises made on more radical proposals prepared by academician S.S. Shatalin and relatively less sweeping proposals orchestrated by Gorbachev and his close advisers have not only damaged the prospects for the program, but also made the whole enterprise unworkable and uncertain. But it does not necessarily indicate that Gorbachev is reversing his

reforms or defending the conservatives. He might be temporarily siding with conservatives.

32. Such diverse interests and views in Soviet society has long been claimed by Zaslavskaya (1988, 255-280).

33. As he asserts:

Perestroika will be successful provided we really involve people in all affairs of state and society through democracy, through political reform. Only thus. And only thus will *perestroika* become irreversible, only thus will nobody succeed in halting this process. This will be ensured within the framework of democracy and *glasnost* (FBIS, August 21, 1989, 41).

34. In this context the remarks of Gorbachev's ideological adviser Vadim Medvedev is worth quoting:

Today it is no longer enough to simply return to the Leninist concept of socialism. The main difficulty is to interpret Leninist ideas in light of contemporary conditions, contemporary experience, and contemporary tasks, and in the general context of contemporary world development and the present stage of civilization (FBIS, Feb. 3, 1989).

5

Perestroika's Economic
and Political Reforms

INTRODUCTION

This chapter examines the economic and political reforms that have so far been initiated under the banner of *perestroika*. In contrast to previous reform efforts in Soviet history, *perestroika* was launched to salvage the Soviet economy from "stagnation and other phenomena alien to socialism" (Gorbachev 1987, 24), and to replace an outdated structure of production with a "more progressive, efficient and socially oriented" economic and political system (Aganbegyan 1988a, 5). Specifically, the programs of *perestroika* were launched to transform the Soviet economy "from an overly centralized command system of management to a democratic system based mainly on economic methods and on an optimal combination of centralism and self-management" (Gorbachev 1988a, 420). This involves a profound structural reorganization of the economy, redirection of the nation's economic and social preferences, reactivation of its human and material resources, and injection into the economy of the benefits of scientific and technological revolution that apparently bypassed Soviet society during previous regimes.

Perestroika visualizes a thorough and vigorous reconstruction of both the micro and macro management of the economy, sweeping transformations in its material base, and amelioration of the scientific and technological foundations of Soviet society. In contrast to the half-hearted, piece-meal reforms of the past that "attempted to remedy the symptoms of the disease rather than worry about the causes" (Goldman 1987, 46), *perestroika* stands for a revolutionary transformation of Soviet economy. It also emphasizes similar transformations in other spheres, notably in the political and ideological frameworks, as preconditions for successful implementation of *perestroika*. Therefore, sweeping political reforms, namely, *glasnost* (openness) and *demokratizatsiya* (democratization), were also initiated.

This chapter is organized as follows: Section two explores four stages in the evolution of *perestroika*, section three outlines its goals, and section four examines the economic and political reforms that have been initiated so far. Section five evaluates Gorbachev's reforms in the context of previous reform efforts in Soviet history.

STAGES OF *PERESTROIKA*

Mikhail Gorbachev and the new leadership did not start with a grand blueprint of reforms. Indeed, the economic and political reforms launched under the auspices of *perestroika* have largely been responses to the challenges and imperatives posed by the constantly redefined objectives of *perestroika*. Therefore, *perestroika*, from the perspective of its changing directions and shifting emphases, can be visualized as an evolutionary phenomenon. At least four distinguishable stages can be discerned in the evolutionary process of *perestroika*: (1) the initial stage, characterized by tinkering with the system, from March 1985 to early 1987; (2) the second stage, which can be called the stage of moderate reforms, from the June 1987 plenum of the CPSU Central Committee to late 1989; (3) the third stage, characterized by radical reforms, from late 1989 to late 1990; and (4) the fourth stage, characterized by a triumph of pragmatism over radicalism, beginning October 1990 when Gorbachev backed away from the so-called Five Hundred Day program, remaining open-ended. Up to the third stage, transition from one stage to the other was characterized by resolute efforts to change the inherited system more fundamentally and more decisively. But the fourth stage, although not marked by major retreats or reversals, as of March 1991 shows more gradualism than radicalism.

Tinkering with the System

The initial stage, which covers the period from Gorbachev's assumption of power in March 1985 until early 1987, was characterized by economic and political measures that somewhat resembled earlier reform efforts that tinkered with the system to make it work better, not to dismantle it. During this stage, Gorbachev had not yet grasped "the full implications of his ambitious economic goals and his very general commitment to economic reform," and although he vigorously emphasized *intensifiatsiya* (intensive as opposed to extensive methods of production), and *uskorenie* (acceleration of social and economic development), he was still searching for "the right combination of policy changes and reforms to actually get the acceleration going" (Hewett 1988, 304). At this stage the focus was on the labor discipline and anti-alcoholism campaigns initiated by his predecessor Yuri Andropov.[1] The policies of *glasnost* and *demokratizatsiya* were also initiated during this period, which led to vigorous debates among intelligentsia and the Soviet press and induced even stronger calls for reforms. But reforms remained impressive in appearance, not in practice.

Moderate Reforms

The second stage, which began with the June 1987 plenum of the CPSU Central Committee and extended until late 1989, has been characterized by Gorbachev and his advisers as "radical" or "revolutionary" *perestroika*, and by Western writers as "possibilities of radical reform" (Hardt & Kaufman 1987). The proposed reforms were radical in rhetoric, but were actually carefully circumscribed in practice. Transition to this stage was prompted by failure of the anti-alcoholism program, and by the unsatisfactory performance of the economy. The June 1987 Plenum approved "Basic Provisions for Fundamentally Reorganizing Economic Management," which called for sweeping and far-reaching structural transformations of the economy—covering labor wages to price structures, cooperatives to private enterprises, agriculture to international trade.

Still, the programs and policies of the second stage too were found deficient in accomplishing the professed objectives of *perestroika*. During this stage, Gorbachev wanted to put the economy in order by restructuring it mainly through improvements in the central planning machineries, changing personnel, and injecting scientific and technological developments into the economy. Despite the exhortations and rhetoric of Gorbachev and his associates, neither control of central planning nor the monopoly power of the CPSU were seriously challenged, and only very limited private ownership was allowed, with *glasnost* and *demokratizatsiya* being adroitly managed by leadership from above. During this period, Lenin provided Gorbachev with ideological inspiration, and repudiation of Stalinism remained indecisive and incomplete. Apparently the leadership believed that transition of the economy from extensive to intensive methods of production would be possible under the existing system dominated by central planning machineries and one-party rule. The leadership thus continued a conservative program replete with administrative measures.[2]

Radical Reforms

The third stage of *perestroika* emerged in late 1989, marked the beginning of radical reforms, both political and economic. Several factors demonstrate a new turning point in the direction of *perestroika*. First, Gorbachev and his associates realized that the existing system was unreceptive to *perestroika*'s reforms, and the economy continued to stagnate, political turmoils mounted, and an alarmingly deteriorating overall internal situation called for more radical reforms.[3]

Second, Hewett (1989b, 48-49) points out that debate over economic policy within the country became "much more sophisticated" than it had been before, and unprecedented ties between policy makers and economists were established. Also, in late 1989, the replacement of Abel Aganbegyan by Leonid Abalkin as chief economic adviser to Gorbachev, and the appointment of Abalkin as a deputy prime minister and as head of the newly created twenty-two-member high-level Commission on Economic Reforms contributed to a radical shift in the direction of *perestroika*.

Third, a radical shift was manifested in two very dramatic policy changes: In December 1989 the CPSU gave up its monopoly and opened the door for multi-party political pluralism; and in February 1990 state monopoly ownership of all means of production was abolished, and genuinely diversified, large-scale private and cooperative ownerships were allowed. Of these policies, the former marks a demonstrative break with the Leninist authoritarian tradition of one-party rule, and the latter challenges the Marxist doctrine of abolition of private ownership of the means of production as an essential precondition for socialism. Therefore, it is at this stage that the gap between rhetoric and reality narrowed and the radical character of *perestroika* was exposed.[4]

Triumph of Pragmatism over Radicalism

The fourth stage began in October 1990 when the Supreme Soviet approved the "Basic Guidelines for the Stabilization of the National Economy and the Changeover to Market Economy," the so-called Five Hundred Day program. Among other things, the program provided a detailed schedule for comprehensive economic reforms, including liberalization of prices and destatization of enterprises, aimed at a grand transition to a market economy. The program granted republics economic sovereignty, enterprises freedom of economic activity, and citizens consumer choice and social guarantees (CDSP, vol. 35, 1-19). Policies of this stage envisage bolder private enterprise, genuine market and price reforms, foreign investments, and even stock exchanges. But it should be noted that as of March 1991 the program remained in a state of flux. The compromises made on more radical proposals prepared by academician S. S. Shatalin and backed by Russian Federation leader Boris Yeltsin, and relatively less sweeping proposals orchestrated by Gorbachev and his advisers, have not only damaged the prospects of the program, but have also made the whole enterprise uncertain.

GOALS OF *PERESTROIKA*

At the earlier stage, the economic strategy of *perestroika* included a drastic shift in economic priorities toward a more social orientation of development; substitution of traditional extensive methods of production by intensive methods based on expedient use of the scientific and technological revolution; and replacement of the old administrative management of the economy with a fundamentally new and comprehensive system of management based on economic methods.[5] Both Aganbegyan (1987 & 1988a) and Gorbachev (1987 & 1988a) proclaimed that *perestroika*'s topmost priority was to promote the social environment so that (1) appropriate sectors of the economy were developed and consumer needs like housing and food were satisfied on a priority basis; (2) productivity of labor and capital were enhanced with scientific and technological progress; and (3) the economic system was rejuvenated by new economic incentives and democratic practices. Indeed, *perestroika*'s goals are vividly expressed in three Russian words—*uskoreniye* (acceleration), *intensifiatsiya* (intensification), and *perestroika* (restructuring).

Table 5.1
Soviet Economic Performance: 1981-90 (Plan)
(percent per annum, unless otherwise indicated)

	1981-85 actual	1986-90 plan	1986-88 actual	1986 actual	1987 actual	1988 actual	1989 plan	1989 actual	1990 plan
National Income Utilized	3.1	4.1	3.0	3.4	1.5	4.2	3.4	n.a	n.a.
National Income Produced	3.6	n.a.	3.6	4.1	2.3	4.4	3.8	2.5	2.0
GNP (Official Soviet)	4.1	n.a	4.1	4.1	3.1	5.0	4.5	3.5	n.a.
Per Capita Income (Official Soviet)	2.1	2.7	2.7	2.5	2.0	2.5	3.1	n.a.	n.a.
Per Capita Consumption (CIA estimate)	0.8	n.a.	0.3	-1.5	1.0	1.5	n.a.	n.a.	n.a
Gross State Investment	3.5	4.3	6.3	8.3	5.7	4.8	2.3	n.a.	n.a.
Industrial Production	—	—	4.7	3.7	4.6	4.8	n.a.	n.a.	n.a.
Agricultural Production	—	—	2.5	2.1	2.7	n.a.	n.a.	n.a.	n.a.
Budget Deficit (billion rubles)	R17.6	n.a.	R65.7	R51.9	R66.2	R79.0	R120.0	n.a.	R60.0
Net Hard Currency Debt (billion dollars)	$12.6	n.a.	$26.6	$21.5	$27.1	$28.2	n.a.	n.a.	n.a.
Debt Service Ratio	0.13	n.a.	0.18	0.17	0.18	0.20	n.a.	n.a.	n.a.

Source: Based on Hewett 1988, 52; 1989b, 56-57.

Perestroika anticipated ambitious growth rates for all major sectors of the economy to catch up with the Western countries. Expected growth rates for the economy were set above 4 percent annually for 1986-90 and over 5 percent for the 1990s. Achievement of such ambitious goals would mean doubling the growth rates of the 1976-85 period and returning to the growth rates of the 1960s and early 1970s (see Table 3.1). Industrial growth during 1986-90 was targeted to double that of the preceding decade and even reach higher during the 1990s (see Table 5.1). Agricultural production was targeted for the 1986-90 period to triple that of the preceding fifteen years. Labor productivity was set to grow at 4.6 percent annually. The Twelfth Plan (1986-90) envisaged a growth rate of 2.7 percent annually in per capita income growth, which was considerably below the growth rates of the early 1970s, but significantly above those in recent years. Real per capita income growth was targeted to move from 2.7 percent during the Twelfth Plan to 3.4–4.7 percent in the 1990s.

Along with a heavy emphasis on the acceleration of growth of investment rates, *perestroika* also sought to alter the nation's economic priorities. The bulk of investment was directed toward restructuring and reequipping existing plants rather than building new ones. To modernize the nation's antiquated capital stock, the Twelfth Plan called for nearly doubling retirement rates and replacing over one-third of the total capital stock by 1990. This gigantic task was to be made possible by an 80 percent increase in the amount of investment directed to the civilian machinery industries, compared to a gain of perhaps 20 percent in the preceding five years. With this investment, machinery industries were to double the growth rate of output and radically upgrade their quality and technological level. By 1990, 90 percent of all machinery was supposed to meet world standards, compared to about 20 percent in 1985.

In subsequent stages, most of these objectives remained not only unfulfilled, in most cases they were either abandoned or drastically revised. By the end of 1988, performance of the economy began to deteriorate so alarmingly that the expectations of the Twelfth Plan appeared impossible. Therefore, revising the earlier objectives, a stabilization program for 1989-90 was initiated that reduced subsidies to loss-making enterprises, defense expenditures, and costs of economic administration (see Ofer 1989). At the third stage, goals of *perestroika* advanced from an "optimal" balance between plan and market, in which the market was expected to help in accomplishing planned objectives, to establishing a "regulated market," which was expected to dismantle the planning apparatus itself. At the fourth stage, the Five Hundred Day program provides broad guidelines for creating preconditions for monetary, financial, credit, and currency policies aimed at switching the economy to market mechanisms. But, as mentioned above, the Five Hundred Day program remains at a state of flux.

PERESTROIKA'S PRESCRIPTIONS AND PERFORMANCES

Economic Reforms

Under the auspices of *perestroika*, numerous laws, decrees, and orders have been passed, and many of these were put into practice during the last six years. Landmark policies include the "Basic Guidelines for Economic and Social Development" adopted by the Plenary meeting of the CPSU Central Committee in 1985; the Guidelines for the Economic and Social Development of the USSR for 1986-90 and for the period ending in 2000, endorsed by the delegates to the Twenty-seventh Congress of CPSU in February 1986; the "Basic Provisions of Fundamentally Reorganizing Economic Management," approved by the Supreme Soviet in June 1987; the Law on State Enterprise passed in June of 1987; and the resolutions of the CPSU Party Conference held in June 1988; the Law on Self-Employment, passed in July 1987; and the Law on Cooperatives, enacted in July 1988; the Law on Property in the USSR, enacted in February 1990; and Basic Guidelines for the

Stabilization of the National Economy and the Changeover to a Market Economy, approved in October 1990. *Perestroika*'s major economic reforms are outlined below.

Reforms in Economic Mechanisms for State Enterprises. The Law on State Enterprises, which came into effect in January 1988, envisaged conversion of public enterprises to the principles of complete fiscal autonomy, self-financing, and self-administration. The enterprises were expected to function as autonomous bodies in working out and elaborating annual and five-year plans on the basis of control indicators, long-term economic normatives, government contracts, and limits (these concepts are differentiated below). The law sought to bring all public enterprises under its provisions by the end of 1989.

This law aimed at freeing public enterprises from day-to-day interference by the central apparatus. The control indicators, economic normatives, and other devices would lose their traditional directive character. On the other hand, public enterprises were expected to cover all their expenses, including wages and investments, from their own revenues. Enterprises were called upon to work in a competitive environment, attract customers for their products, and negotiate with suppliers for their own raw materials. Government was to relinquish its commitments to enterprises, and persistently loss-making enterprises were to face liquidation or bankruptcy. Such a self-financing, self-managing mechanism was expected to enhance labor productivity and improve the quality of products by generating business-like attitudes among enterprises, and by making them more responsive to market demand.

Reversing the traditional practices whereby the central apparatus had authority but no responsibility while enterprises had responsibility but no authority, the law greatly expanded the authority of the enterprises. The only limitation imposed on enterprise decisions was that they were not allowed to run counter to existing legislation. But the law also obligated the enterprises "to strictly observe plan discipline and meet plans and contractual obligations in full," and emphasized that fulfillment of orders and contracts serve "as the most important criterion for evaluating the activities of enterprise and providing material rewards for its employees" (Schroeder 1987, 222).

To lay the foundations for the over-arching goal of establishing the principle of self-financed public enterprises, the law outlined two *khozraschet* (economic accountability) models. The first *khozraschet* model is based on a normative distribution of profit, that is, residual profit was distributed into various funds, and taxes and interest payments were paid from profit. The income of the enterprise in this model is made up from the wage fund and residual profits. Central authorities are legally prohibited from confiscating residual profits of enterprises. A second *khozraschet* model distributed income remaining after deduction of material costs. Under this model taxes and interest payments are paid from income, after-tax income remains at the disposal of the enterprise (as collective income) and then splits into work remuneration, production development, and other funds that are formed according to the normatives prescribed by the law. While the first model more or less guarantees wages, the second model provides no such guarantee; here, the wage fund could go below or rise above usual levels. Therefore, the second model is likely to create hard conditions of self-financing, to put the enterprises on Kornai's "hard-budget constraint," as all expenses must be paid first, and only the remainder would be distributed in the form of wages and other incentives.

Under a third *khozraschet* model, which can be understood as an offspring of the *khozraschet* movement, employees rent the enterprises from the state, where the state collects fixed amount of rent from the employees as specified under the lease agreement, and the remaining income is distributed by the employees according to their own preferences. Another offspring of the *khozraschet* movement is inter-branch state associations or socialist firms (*MGO*), in which producers join in voluntary unions that are independent of ministerial control. Of the four models described above, the first one appears to be overwhelmingly popular. About 60 percent of industrial output was produced under this model in 1988, and the other models are clearly emerging (Shmelev & Popov 1989, 152-53).

Perestroika also called for greater democratization in the management of state enterprises. This drive is particularly manifested in drawing broad sections of workers into management, as the rights of the workers are substantially extended in all sectors of the economy, and public enterprises are required by law to organize elected workers' councils and elect key enterprise personnel, including the manager. The law envisages that top enterprise management are to be elected for a five-year term by a conference of workers in multi-candidate elections. The law entrusts the workers' council with the responsibility of overall performance of enterprises, distribution of funds between long-term goals such as investment, product innovation, and development on the one hand and consumption, such as housing and welfare, on the other.

At the fourth stage, the Five Hundred Day program calls for a substantial increase in enterprise autonomy, and allows enterprise management to operate in the interests of their "employees" and "stockholder-owners" in determining the volume and structure of their production, customers, and suppliers, and directly participating in foreign economic activity in accordance with market conditions.

But as yet prices have not been liberalized, and all these reforms remain within an artificial construct. The existing price mechanism hardly reflects the real economic trade-offs, and in such a constrained environment the principle of self-financing remains unworkable. Moreover, institutional resistance on the part of the central and branch ministries (whose interests are at stake as reforms reduce and challenge their power and control), absence of a developed wholesale trade, relative shortages of labor in some regions, and intrinsic shortcomings associated with operation of enterprises under dual control of market and plan, all critically constrain the success of enterprise reforms. Necessary organizational and institutional changes as emphasized by the Five Hundred Day program must be in place for effective transformation of enterprises into self-financing entities.

Reforms in Central Planning. At the initial stage, central planning, which many think is the root cause of all the troubles of Soviet economy, remained the main instrument for the realization of economic reforms. The emphasis was on improving the central planning mechanism, and efforts were primarily directed at eliminating traditional direct and detailed management through annual plans. New methods of central planning emphasized nonbinding control indicators, (like value of output, profit, foreign currency receipts); long-term normatives (like efficiency and factor productivity); government contracts (like the mandatory bill of state orders of output that represent the state's highest priority needs); and limits (like rationed goods and centralized investment allocations). The *Gosplan*'s responsibility was concentrated more on long-run strategic planning and development of techniques for managing the economy through economic methods like long-run plans and normatives, finance, credit, and prices. With the growing importance of money, credit, and prices, *Gosplan*'s role was expected to decline significantly.

At the second stage, the contradiction of continuation of central planning and simultaneous promotion of economic accountability of enterprises began to surface as "old habits [were] asserting themselves, . . .[and] old assumptions [were] still accepted" (Hewett 1988, 344). During this stage, Gorbachev and his economic advisers did advocate serious surgery on the central planning apparatus, but still insisted on continuing central planning and using market mechanisms to accomplish planned objectives.[6] Reforms in the role and jurisdiction of central planning at this stage were "continuous, consistent and at the same time better-balanced," but redefining the functions of *Gosplan*, *Gossnab* (State Committee for Material-Technical Supply) and *Gosbank* (State Bank) remained problematic and sensitive because it touched "upon the very nature of the Soviet economic system and also upon the vested interests of the higher and intermediate-level economic bureaucracy" (Hohmann 1987, 36).

Therefore, at the third stage, dysfunctional consequences emanating from the simultaneous continuation of central planning and *khozraschet* principles, as well as persistently poor performance of the economy, convinced Gorbachev and his associates that more radical reforms were in order. Consequently, the focus shifted from improving the planning machinery to dismantling it altogether and establishing a regulated market economy. At the fourth stage, the Five Hundred Day program envisages a gradual switch to market institutions and the dismantling of central planning mechanisms. It aims at creating market-based fiscal and monetary institutions and at diminishing the central plan's role by encouraging destatization of resources and enhancing market-based motivational mechanisms, and by decentralizing authority to the republics and local governments.

Changes in Management Structure. Perestroika also drastically revamped the existing organization and management structure of the economy. In order to eliminate duplication and inefficiency, streamline responsibilities, and improve performance, significant rearrangement of economic authority and responsibility was undertaken. By replacing three union-republic food-processing ministries, a new institution, *Gosagroprom* (State Committee for the Agro-Industrial Complex), was created in November 1985. A drive for economic reorganization and creation of superministries were also manifested in the formation of Bureau of Machine-

Building, which integrates functions of eleven formerly operative civilian machinery production ministries. Similarly, by merging four all-Union ministries, *Gosstroi*, a new State Committee for Construction, was created.

Also in 1986, the State Foreign Economy Commission was founded as the coordinating supreme authority on international economic affairs, and the State Committee for Computers and Information Sciences was established. The State Committee for Science and Technology was reorganized to work out state programs for development of science and technology, and to coordinate the activities of intersectoral scientific and technical complexes. The number of ministries were reduced and ministries were relieved of day-to-day responsibilities; sectoral subbranches (*glavki*) were replaced by several thousand large associations and enterprises directly accountable to all-union ministries. Supervision of huge scientific production enterprises remained with the central bodies, but responsibility for supervising medium and small enterprises producing for local markets were transferred to the republican and local organs. Ministries were expected to become the scientific, technical, planning, and economic headquarters of individual industries and be responsible for satisfying the country's demands in their respective branch. The State Committee for Work and Social Problems (*Goskomtrud*) was reorganized for handling labor replacement, released workers, and unemployment problems. At the fourth stage, the Five Hundred Day program called for sharp reduction in central management and emphasized a mutually beneficial relationship based on equal partnership with the republics. It allowed the republics to determine the level of basic taxes and to form their own budgets. All these would constitute a sharp decline in the authority of central management and sweeping organizational and institutional changes in the republics (CDSP, vol. 35, Dec 19, 1990).[7]

Price Reforms. Perestroika, since its early stage, proposed the most sweeping price reforms in Soviet history, but time and again reforms in price structures have been either partially attempted, temporarily postponed, or shelved for an indefinite period. Therefore, price reform remains one of the most sensitive and problematic areas of *perestroika*'s reform package.[8] Procurement prices in agriculture and the prices of natural resources like fuel, energy, and other raw materials have traditionally been kept low by ignoring the cost of rent and underestimating the value of labor. As mentioned above, between 1965 and 1988, state subsidies on wholesale and retail prices increased twenty times, from 3.6 billion to 73 billion rubles, constituting twenty percent of the state budget. Prices of most essential goods and services remained unchanged for decades.

According to the earlier proposals, price reforms were scheduled to be completed by 1990, so that the new prices could be used for developing the Thirteenth Plan (1991-95) and a new regulated market could be launched. Reforms were expected to encompass all forms of prices; wholesale, procurement prices for agriculture, retail prices, tariffs, rates, and fees for services. According to Aganbegyan (1987, 291), reforms in price structure encompassed not only price levels and relative prices, but also the process of price formation, and aimed at reducing reliance on centralized influences on prices, and broadening reliance on contractual and unrestricted prices. Therefore, the share of centrally set prices was expected to go down sharply, and such prices were to be fixed on the basis of socially necessary expenses of production and sale, utility, quality, and effective demand. Contract prices, limit prices, and those set by enterprises were to become more common, and were to be set on the same basic principles as state-set prices.

During this stage, *perestroika* emphasized that many prices would be decentralized, but prices for most essential commodities would be set centrally. The main focus of the price reforms was to reduce or eliminate state subsidies and create an economic environment for promotion of self-financing of public enterprises. Most significantly, *perestroika* sought to do away with the traditional administrative methods of price-fixing that were based on the principle of producer's cost plus a normal profit or average cost plus standard profit. *Perestroika* envisaged a price structure based on "social costs" with due considerations given to "cost effectiveness of production" and world prices (Aganbegyan 1988a, 136). In the agricultural sector, procurement prices for agricultural goods had been geared to create conditions favoring certain key areas of agricultural production and increasing the profitability of farms. A more flexible approach to the marketing of surplus agricultural produce was introduced so that state or collective farms could sell all produce harvested over and above their production targets. Also, in order to bring the level of domestic prices into line with world market prices, wholesale prices of fuel and raw materials were raised significantly.

According to Shmelev and Popov (1989, 157-58), by 1987, *Gosplan* brought down the number of centrally planned industrial products from 123 to 60, and that of centrally allocated resources from 256 to 23. As a result, about 20 percent of all industrial output was planned and distributed from the center, another 30 percent was administered by departments and local authorities, while the rest was not planned at all. Still, prices continue to be controlled by the government.

But gradually Soviet leadership came to realize that comprehensive price reforms were sine qua non for the success of *perestroika*. In the earlier stages, price reforms, including wholesale and retail prices, were postponed or pushed into the indefinite future to avoid exacerbating consumer problems. Many Soviet economists maintained that the reform should be deferred until adequate stability of the consumer market has been achieved, until sufficiently large stocks of consumer goods could offset potential negative events. Prominent economists like Nikolai Shmelev, Leonid Abalkin, and others cautioned that no matter how carefully retail price reforms were engineered, the ensuing situation would be disruptive (see CIA & DIA 1989, 29).[9] Besides, Soviet scholars demonstrate divergence of opinion about the very content of price (Nove 1987).

But since early 1990, incompatibility between central planning and private initiatives, prices and market forces, surfaced more clearly than ever before. As a result, the leadership has moved fairly boldly in terms of price reforms, liberalization of economy, and dismantling the central planning apparatus. In May 1990, a sweeping decision was made to put the economy on market forces, to introduce a "regulated market economy" in which prices of all products, including foodstuffs like bread, meat, and dairy products, would be based on actual cost and profit. These decisions envisaged direct state control over 60 percent of all prices, and indirect state control over 25 percent, leaving 15 percent of all prices outside state control. All these were scheduled to go into effect by early 1991 (*Wall Street Journal*, May 22, 1990).

At the fourth stage, the Five Hundred Day program envisaged that by 1992, price controls would be eliminated for most goods except for a narrow range of essential consumer goods. The program, however, granted the republics and other local bodies the right to enforce price ceilings in cases of excessive rises in decontrolled prices (CDSP, no. 42, Dec. 19, 1990). Implementation of these reforms could constitute a decisive break with the past practices. Although in early 1991 prices of most consumer goods were increased on average 60 percent or more in order to bring consumer prices in line with production costs, simultaneous existence of an overwhelmingly large sector of state-fixed-prices and a smaller sector of market-fixed-prices, together with Gorbachev's cautious approach to the liberalization, still remain problematic for *perestroika*.

Reforms in Banking and Finance. To facilitate fundamental reforms in the price, money, and credit structures, and to switch to new economic methods in price formation, money, and financial systems, *perestroika* also initiated a sweeping transformation of finance and banking. In the past, the credit system was coordinated by central planning; therefore, it was largely an adjunct of the bureaucratic redistributive machinery, an extension of the state plan itself. Under the auspices of *perestroika*, a new banking system is being set up in the Soviet economy. Although establishment of banks was emphasized since the early stage of *perestroika*, in July 1987 six specialized banks were actually established: the *Gosbank* (State Bank), the *Promstroibank* (Industrial and Construction Bank), the *Agroprombank* (Agro-Industrial Bank), the *Zhilsotsbank* (Housing, Social, and Communal Bank), the *Sbirigatelnyi* (Savings and Consumer Credit Bank), and the *Vneshneekonombank* (Bank of Foreign Economic Activity).

Besides such specialized banks, commercial and cooperative banks, are also being established, especially since 1988. All these banks are expected to function as commercial enterprises and compete for their own markets, and enterprises have the liberty to choose their own banks. The banks are expected to promote commercialization of their services, by for instance, becoming more cautious in granting credit for business transactions and offering competitive interest rates and innovative ideas for the capital market.

At the third stage steps were contemplated to introduce checking accounts for individuals, a consumer credit system, stock exchanges, and the financing of joint enterprises with foreign companies. Also, measures were taken to bring the money supply into balance with existing material resources. Money supply in the Soviet economy traditionally outstripped national income. Such imbalances between effective demand and supply of goods resulted not only in chronic shortages, but also stimulated an underground economy, which we have elaborated above. Attempts were made to enhance purchasing power and convertibility of the ruble.

The May 1990 decisions that emphasized an entrepreneur-led, market-driven, profit-motivated orientation also called for a new banking system aimed at attracting savings and capital deposits with higher interest rates and then redeploying those funds more productively.

At the fourth stage, the Five Hundred Day program envisaged immediate transformation of *Gosbank* into a reserve system administered by a Central Council, whose chairman would be appointed by the Supreme Soviet and the directors of the republics' central banks. Like Western reserve banks, the *Gosbank* is expected to enjoy a monopoly on the emission of money and to coordinate banking policies (CDSP, No. 44, Dec. 19, 1990).

Wage Reforms. Perestroika promotes remarkably greater wage differentials than those of other periods of Soviet history since Stalin. Simultaneously, it insists on cutting the work force and achieving other economies, and promotes private activities, although on a limited scale. The intent of *perestroika*'s wage reform is to raise workers' earnings, make bonuses harder to get, and more closely dependent on the efficiency and quality of both firm and worker performance, tighten work norms, and contribute to the more general objectives of enforcing self-finance, eradicating *uravnilovka* (wage-leveling) and encouraging work effort and acquisition of skills.[10]

In sharp contrast to earlier practices, at the initial stages of *perestroika* enterprises have been allowed to increase wages about 20-25 percent on average across the board, with 30-35 percent increases for professionals, such as designers, technologists engineers, and other white-collar workers (Leggett 1988, 30). In addition, enterprise workers' collectives were empowered to grant increases in the pay scales and rates for extra professional skills and for more productive labor. The new wage structure was stipulated to be fully effective by the end of Twelfth Plan. By early 1987 all trade was converted to the new wage system, and by the beginning of 1988, 10 million people were covered by the new structure of salaries and wages, and an additional 70 million were expected to be covered by the end of the Thirteenth Plan period. The new wage structure connects wages more closely with profits, and resulted in layoffs of extra workers. But because of the apparent shortage of labor (which is true at least in the European part of the Soviet Union), laid off workers, according to Shmelev and Popov (1989, 191-93), do not find it difficult to get work elsewhere.

Private and Cooperative Activity. One of the most far-reaching changes initiated by *perestroika* is the bolder and more conspicuous role of and opportunities for private and cooperative economic activities. Overwhelming emphasis was given to the liberalization of the economy because to the new leadership this constituted a significant step toward democratization of economic life. At the earlier stages, *perestroika* strongly endorsed measures to expand the role of producer cooperatives and private individuals in the economy, but particularly emphasized three types of businesses: consumer service, food service, and production of consumer goods. The Law on Cooperatives, passed in November 1986 and effective in May 1987, lowered the extremely high tax rates on income from private work and allowed groups of three or more people to form cooperatives. Under this law, state employees (outside work hours), pensioners, homemakers, and the handicapped were allowed to undertake private initiatives. In August 1986, the "Basic Principles for Development of Cooperative Forms of Production" was approved, which legalized producer cooperatives organized on a voluntary basis. The basic thrust at this stage was to satiate market demand by improving quality and increasing the supply of consumer goods and services, and to increase industrial outputs in selected sectors by mobilizing additional laborers and encouraging individuals and small cooperative enterprises to devote their after-hours to working for additional income.

Further liberalization of the economy was encouraged by the Law on Self-Employment, passed in May 1987. This law widened the sphere of cooperative economic activities by permitting individual activity wherever it is not explicitly prohibited, and granted extensive rights to local authorities to regulate private/cooperative initiatives. *Perestroika*'s priority in the cooperative movement has also been manifested in its efforts to replace the material and technical supply system (*Gossnab*) with a wholesale trade system, so that cooperatives and private businesses could obtain required goods and services from markets according to their choice, and are not forced by *Gossnab* to accept inputs of inferior quality at inflated prices (Leggett 1988, 30).

Initial steps did boost cooperative economic activity in the country. For example, cooperative cafes, taxi cabs, medical care, teachers and tutors, and construction proliferated. Initially such activity was limited to agriculture, then spread to other sectors, such as manufacturing and trade. But provisions for private/cooperative initiatives remained largely circumscribed. These laws simply legalized what had long been practiced illegally, in the underground economy. Moreover, they did not extend substantially the theoretical guarantee of rights of citizens to engage in self-employment activities as prescribed by the Soviet Constitution of 1977 (see Blough, Muratore & Berk 1987, 262). These laws granted the right to participate in private business only to those who were not part of the regular labor force. Moreover, a progressive income tax was levied on private businesses, and the government imposed stiff penalties for failure to register businesses and pay taxes. Taxes were raised up to 90 percent on incomes earned from cooperative enterprise.

In the second stage of *perestroika*, in September 1987, the cooperative law was extended to include privately run shops, and the Law on Cooperation, passed in the spring of 1988, extended cooperative activities to industry, processing of raw materials and semi-finished goods, construction, trade, and service sectors of the economy (Hasbulatov 1989, 11-12). Moreover, a new agricultural policy, adopted in March 1989, abolished district agro-industrial complexes, and instead involved nontraditional forms of agricultural organizations in land cultivation and animal husbandry on a long-term lease basis. Thus, the administrative command system that jeopardized agricultural production for decades was being replaced by administrative support to local cooperative producers.

But still, private and cooperative activities did not constitute a big part of the

Soviet GNP. The number of entrepreneurs increased from 100,000 at the end of 1986 to 300,000 at the beginning of 1988, and constituted only 0.2 percent of all those employed in the Soviet Union. In 1987, the total number of people employed in cooperatives increased to 200,000, and contributed only 0.1 percent to GNP. Soviet experts had expected about 25-30 percent of GNP to come from this sector (see Shmelev and Popov 1989, 270).

At the third stage, *perestroika* called for more fundamental reforms by revising ownership rights and promoting diversified ownership of the means of production. The Law on Property, passed in early 1990, brought forth radical reforms in property relations. It envisaged legal, political, and economic steps in the direction of bolder private ownership and initiative, and even allowed foreign companies the same rights as domestic enterprises to set up industries in the Soviet Union.[11] The law also permitted individuals to, among other things, own residential buildings, plots and lands, means of transportation, money, stocks and other securities, and means of production for peasant farming and other types of labor enterprises and business activities. The law allows hiring of workers other than family members and the inheritance of property; it thereby constitutes a remarkable break with the central tenet of Marxian socialism from Stalin onward that emphasizes the absence of private ownership of means of production in socialist economy (CDSP, April 25, 1990, 21). The law also envisaged a grand change in state ownership of enterprises.[12] In May 1990 government also approved construction and sales of private housing.

At the fourth stage, the Five Hundred Day program called for even greater privatization and liberalization of economy. The program guaranteed the transfer of state property to citizens through "destatization and privatization" and called for creation of special privatization agencies and land reform committees to realize the rights of citizens to own property. It also aimed at creating appropriate market-oriented motivational mechanisms and institutional arrangements to promote private ownership of resources (see CDSP 1990, vol. 35, 5-7). Thus, by allowing greater privatization and revising inheritance laws and employment rights, which extend to industrial and manufacturing sectors as well, Gorbachev also went beyond the Leninist market-mixed economy of early 1920s.

Foreign Economic Relations. Perestroika calls for elimination of the traditional autarchic tendencies in economic policies. Stalin's principle of "socialism in one country" virtually isolated the Soviet economy from the international market, and reintegration of the economy into the world economy remained largely unaccomplished. As a result, while in most capitalist countries the proportion of exports to national income ranged between 40 and 50 percent in 1986, in the Soviet economy the share was 12 percent. Moreover, while the whole structure of international trade changed drastically (i.e., the share of raw materials and traditional industries like textiles, footwear, and steel was falling and the share of high-tech fields like electronics and aerospace industries was rising rapidly), the Soviet Union's exports were still dominated by fuel and electricity (53 percent), raw materials (9 percent), and machines and equipment (14 percent) (Aganbegyan 1988a, 141).

Therefore, improving foreign economic relations constituted a major task of *perestroika* since its inception. Gorbachev repeatedly insisted on taking advantage of international division of labor, integrating of the Soviet economy into the international market, and improving foreign economic relations. At the earlier stages, as mentioned before, organizations concerned with international economic policies and activities were drastically reorganized. As early as April 1985, the Ministry of Foreign Trade's monopoly over international trade was eliminated and rights to operate directly in the international markets were granted to twenty one ministries and institutions. Ultimately, the Ministry itself was abolished and the State Foreign Economic Committee and Ministry of Foreign Economic Relations were set up to oversee all facets of foreign economic activity.[13]

Initially emphasis was given to attracting international joint ventures, and especially to building stronger ties with the Socialist states to create an integrated Socialist economy. But at a later stage, the drive toward ever greater openness of economic relations extended beyond the COMECON (Council of Mutual Economic Assistance) countries, and greater emphasis was attached to joint ventures with foreign countries, including Western firms. According to government decrees in 1987, joint enterprises must satisfy at least three prerequisites: (1) foreign capital's share in the joint ventures cannot exceed 49 percent; (2) Soviet labor laws must be applicable to joint ventures; and (3) joint enterprises have to be headed by a Soviet citizen. Joint ventures are also subject to a 30 percent tax on profits, but the rest can be divided among the partners. An additional 20 percent tax was to be levied if the profit was transferred to foreign countries.

Subsequently, the drive toward greater integration with the international economy and division of labor has been intensified. In December 1988, the Soviet government decided to extend rights to participate freely in international trade to all enterprises and organizations with products that are competitive on the foreign market. Also, the prerequisite of a 51 percent Soviet share in joint ventures has been relaxed, differentiated hard currency coefficients were gradually phased out, and international convertibility of the ruble is being pursued more seriously. Substantial progress in joint ventures has not yet been made.

At the third and fourth stages, both the Law on Property and the Five Hundred Day program encouraged private initiatives by putting international companies on the same level as local enterprises, and simultaneously emphasizing convertibility of rubles and reform of the banking system. These goals, although not yet accomplished, are conducive to attracting more vigorous international finance.[14]

Trading Guns for Bread. Perestroika has emphasized trading guns for bread since its inception. According to many Sovietologists, the increased defense burden emanating from competition with the United States (which has a much bigger GNP and also, during the Reagan era, had a substantially increased defense expenditure), has made it increasingly difficult for the Soviet leadership to sustain nonmilitary economic development. The share of Soviet GNP devoted to military activities, according to the CIA (1989), increased in current ruble prices from between 12 and 14 percent in the early 1970s to between 15 and 17 percent in the early 1980s. The

Soviet economy experienced no growth at all in the late seventies and early eighties, but even in this period military spending kept growing.

Therefore, Gorbachev and his associates have been endeavoring to trade guns for bread. Over the past several years, Gorbachev has succeeded in bringing an end to the cold war, reducing expenditure on armaments, and diverting resources from the defense sector to the consumption sector (although major results have not yet surfaced). Defense spending cuts are carried out primarily in military research, development, testing and evaluation. The redirection is being carried out by converting existing military plants from defense to civilian production, rather than by transferring manpower and equipment from defense plants to civilian enterprises. Former Soviet Premier Nikolai Ryzhkov maintained that the share of civilian goods produced by defense industries would increase from 40 percent currently to 50 percent in 1991 and to some 60 percent by 1995 (CIA & DIA 1989, 21). The report also claims that in 1988, Soviet defense spending grew by roughly 3 percent—in line with the growth rates of the whole economy. At the Nineteenth Party Congress the leadership characterized the threat from the West as declining. In the United Nations in December 1988, Gorbachev made specific promises for unilateral cuts in Soviet military manpower and equipment to be carried out during 1989 and 1990. More substantial cuts in defense spending are expected from future summits between Soviet President Gorbachev and United States President George Bush. In the Twenty-eighth Congress of the CPSU in July 1990, Gorbachev (1990b, 28) identified reconversion of defense production as one of the promising areas for integration of the Soviet economy into the global economy.[15]

Performance of Soviet Economy Under *Perestroika*

Available information suggests that most objectives of the reforms initiated by Gorbachev and his associates have remained so far either largely unaccomplished or in serious jeopardy. Shmelev and Popov (1989, 247-93) provide a meticulous appraisal of the sluggish process of implementation of reforms from 1985 to early 1988. According to these authors, virtually no progress has been made in the agrarian sector, the principle of mandatory plan deliveries still continues, and sweeping bureaucratic authority by RAPO (regional agro-industrial associations) still controls "everyone living in the countryside." Ninety percent of the rural economy is still run by the old administrative methods of command and coercion.

One of the top priorities of *perestroika* is encouragement of cooperatives and private initiatives. But progressive taxation on cooperatives, as of March 1988, imposed a 50 percent tax on monthly earnings of more than 700 rubles, 70 percent on earnings of more than 1,000 rubles, and 90 percent for earnings above 1,500 rubles.[16] Largely as a result of public outcry, this taxation policy was revoked in July 1988 and replaced with a 10 percent tax rate in addition to the usual income tax applicable to the cooperative members (a maximum of 13 percent).

In industry the situation is no better. Because the central plan still dictates, enterprises are caught in between two mutually exclusive demands. The central plan insists on production of planned gross output, while *Gospriemka* (State Quality Inspectorate) insists on meeting its quality standards. While reforms envisaged a sharp drop in state orders to enterprises, in 1987, state orders covered 96 percent of output in light industry, 95 percent in the fuel and energy industry, 87 percent in wood chemistry, 86 percent in metallurgy and machine building, 99.2 percent of the entire volume of production under the Ministry of Instrument Making, and 100 percent of everyday services to the population. In 1987 alone *Gospriemka* sent back goods worth thirteen billion rubles for additional work, and by the first half of 1988, returned goods worth seven billion rubles. As a result, unsold inventories of products grew once again, making the paradox of excessive demand and excessive inventories grow worse. On the other hand, planned targets of meeting world standards for 80-90 percent of goods by 1990 remains unfulfilled. Reforms outlined conversion of 100 percent of the country's industrial output into the *khozraschet* model by the end of 1989, but no substantial progress has been made. One very serious hurdle is the delay in price reforms. If prices do not reflect economic trade-offs, introduction of economic accountability will remain problematic. Economically, therefore, *perestroika* has so far remained largely unimplemented. As a result, a catastrophic or near catastrophic situation has prevailed in the country.[17]

During the early eighties (1980-84), when Gorbachev and his associates believed that stagnation or near stagnation prevailed in the country, the annual average growth rate of the economy was 1.9 percent, equal to that of the United Kingdom and less than that of the United States, but still a respectable figure by Western standards (see Table 5.1). But between 1985-88, according to CIA (1989) estimates, the average annual growth rate of the economy fell to 1.7 percent. The CIA estimates that the Soviet economy grew at a rate of .08 percent in 1985, 4.0 percent in 1986, 1.3 percent in 1987, and 1.5 percent in 1988. Soviet official statistics, on the other hand, show that the actual growth of the Soviet economy was 4.1 percent in 1986, 3.1 percent in 1987, and 5.0 percent in 1988. Disparities between the two estimates are rather glaring. The CIA figures show a 2.26 percent average annual growth of Soviet economy between 1986-88, while the Soviet statistics show a 4.06 percent average growth for the same period. Soviet official statistics also show that the Soviet economy registered 3.5 percent growth during the first half of 1989.[18] During the Twelfth Plan period, the planned growth rate was estimated to be 4.1 percent (see Table 5.1).

The fact that the Soviet economy is lagging behind the planned growth rate is also demonstrated in Table 5.2 in terms of key economic and social indicators. Based on twenty-one key indicators, in 1986, eleven indicators, and in 1987, fifteen indicators fell short by 20 percent or more of the planned growth targets. However, in Soviet economic history actual indicators have satisfactorily matched planned ones only during the 1950s-60s, and in other periods actuals deviated from planned targets by an average of 27-56 percent (see Bergson 1989, 236-43).

Another striking feature of the Soviet economy is the recent explosion of the budget deficit. As Table 5.1 shows, the budget deficit has jumped from 17.6 billion rubles (2.4 percent of GNP) during 1981-85 to 120 billion rubles (13.7 percent of GNP) in 1989. Gorbachev's economic policies, however, are not primarily responsible for this explosion; factors beyond Gorbachev's control, like unanticipated declines in oil prices, the Chernobyl accident, and the Armenian earthquake, contributed heavily to the unprecedented deficit buildup in the Soviet economy (see Ofer 1989, 107-61; Gorbachev 1990b, 3-5).

Table 5.2

Key Indicators of Economic and Social Development in the USSR: Actual and Planned Growth Rates, 1986 and 1987

(in percent)

Indicator	1986			1987		
	Actual (1)	Plan (2)	Ratio (1:2)	Actual (3)	Plan (4)	Ratio (3:4)
National Income Produced	4.1	3.9	105	2.5	4.1	61
Industrial Output	4.9	4.3	114	4.4	4.4	100
Producer goods	5.3	4.3	123	4.8	4.3	112
Consumer goods	3.9	4.4	89	3.4	4.5	76
Gross Agri. Output	5.3	5.3	100	0.2	2.2	9
Prod. Capacity Util.	5.9	14.4	41	-2.7	4.6	-59
Investment	8.4	9.2	91	4.1	6.0	68
Transportation						
Freight Turnover	4.1	1.7	241	3.3	2.4	138
Passenger Turnover	3.9	1.2	325	5.3	3.1	171
Labor Productivity	3.8	3.8	100	2.4	4.0	60
Number of Employees	0.6	0.4	150	0.6	0.7	86
Nationwide Economy	8.8	8.9	101	6.8	7.5	91
Nationwide Wage Fund	3.5	2.7	130	4.2	3.9	108
Average Nominal Wage	2.9	2.3	126	3.5	3.2	109
Wages of Collective Farm						
Workers	6.3	1.5	420	7.3	4.0	182
Payments/Benefits to						
Population from Social						
Consumption Fund	5.4	4.1	132	6.2	4.9	127
Real Per Capita Income	2.5	2.5	100	2.0	2.6	77
Retail Trade Turnover in						
State and						
Cooperative Trade	6.3	5.3	119	-0.3	3.4	-9
-Excluding alcoholic						
beverages	7.2	6	120	4.0	5.9	68
Paid Service to Population	10.2	14.2	72	4.3	9.5	45
Completed Housing	6.0	5.0	120	9.3	7.0	133
Average Deviation of						
Actual from Planned Growth						
Rate (either direction) in						
Percent of Planned Rate			49			43

Source: Shmelev & Popov 1989, 93-94.

A discussion of contemporary Soviet economic performance would remain incomplete without reference to the consumer situation. According to Desai (1989, 106), whether shortages of consumer goods have increased extraneously or *perestroika* has contributed to the problem remain debatable; nevertheless, the Soviet Union has been experiencing chronic shortages of consumer goods. Chastened by years of economic decline and dwindling food supplies, consumers are becoming increasingly disappointed with *perestroika*'s reforms. All these facts clearly substantiate Andrei Sakharov's claim that the Soviet economy is approaching a catastrophic economic situation, and validate Nikolai Shmelev's contention that if the negative trends are not turned around, in two to three years there will be complete destruction of the consumer market (*Los Angeles Times*, May 15, 1989).

Of course, there are many systemic causes, internal and external problems, and strategic, diagnostic, remedial, and temporal shortcomings that one way or the other contributed to the apparent failure of *perestroika*'s economic programs. We shall take up the discussion on the problematics of *perestroika* in greater detail in Chapter 6. But some of the most serious shortcomings of *perestroika* perhaps unavoidably deserve mention here in connection with the performance of the Soviet economy.

First, simultaneous emphasis on increasing economic growth and massive economic restructuring is unrealistic. This is especially true in a situation where both acceleration and restructuring of the economy involve radical, if not revolutionary, transformations of the whole economy and society. Second, despite the exhortations and rhetoric of Gorbachev and his associates, during the initial stages of *perestroika* the Soviet Union continued central planning that dictated blueprints for detailed functioning of the economy. Reform efforts were rather aimed at achieving greater growth rates without changing the economic system and disturbing the internal balance of power. Third, Gorbachev and his advisers mistakenly believed that the main problem of the economy was the use of extensive methods of production, and thus diagnosed that a transition to intensive methods of production, coupled with improvements in central planning apparatus would do. They failed to realize that the old system would not be receptive to any kind of scientific and technological progress, indeed any progress at all (Gorbachev, *New York Times*, June 2, 1990). Fourth, market economy is not automatically self-emergent. It requires institutions and social attitudes that, in Western societies, have emerged over a long period of time. Fifth, during institutional transition, the simultaneous operation of traditional, centralized management systems, and emergent, more decentralized processes conflict and to some extent nullify each other. Sixth, economic reform is powerfully constrained by politics. Up to the end of the third stage, Gorbachev walked a tightrope between his more radical economic advisers and conservative defenders of centralized and authoritarian methods in party, army, secret police, and government and industrial bureaucracy. But at the fourth stage, *perestroika*, with its accompanying *glasnost* and *demokratizatsiya*, has ironically encouraged secessionist tendencies and turmoil in the country, which in turn have polarized both conservatives and radicals. Gorbachev has since distanced himself from the ultra-radicals and sided with the conservative elements in the CPSU and state bureaucracy. As the power struggle continues, whether ultra-radicals, led by Boris Yeltsin, or conservatives, basically Communist Party *apparatchiks*, constitute the greater threat to *perestroika* remains to be seen.

Perestroika's Political Reforms and Performance

Gorbachev and his associates believe that one of the root causes of the failure of most of the previous economic reforms in the Soviet Union was that those efforts were not reinforced by commensurate measures to bolster individual initiative or broad-based public participation in reform programs and processes. Therefore, *glasnost* and *demokratizatsiya* were initiated, in Aganbegyan's (1988a, 193) words, as the "dynamo of *perestroika*."

To Gorbachev and his associates, *perestroika*'s "new thinking," goes far beyond transformation of the Soviet economy. Indeed, putting the economy back on the right track constitutes "not even the most important part of the problem with *perestroika*" (Shmelev & Popov 1989, 271). For them, the three-prong programs, *perestroika*, *glasnost*, and *demokratizatsiya* are inextricably interlinked and interdependent. Gorbachev (1988a, 420) declares, "*Perestroika* implies not only eliminating the stagnation and conservatism of the preceding period, and correcting the mistakes committed, but also overcoming historically limited, outdated features of social organizations and work needs." *Perestroika*, therefore, stands not only for a profound restructuring of the economy, it also envisages a thorough reconstructing of the material, spiritual, and intellectual foundations of Soviet society.

Glasnost, as an instrument of *perestroika*, is expected to expose the underlying causes of the dismal performance of the Soviet economy and polity, and is not merely an instrument of "publicity" as many envisage (see Thom & Regan 1988). Major objectives of *glasnost* include: rejuvenating and reorganizing the masses "who have fallen asleep," stimulating worker morale and breaking taboos that pose threats to changes and reforms; enlisting support for successful implementation of *perestroika*'s economic reforms (Gorbachev 1987, 75-79; Aganbegyan 1988b, 193-202), and creating "a mechanism for two-way communication between government and society" (Lapidus 1989, 134).

Demokratizatsiya, on the other hand, envisages ensuring worker participation in the work place and public participation in political and governmental processes. Major goals of *demokratizatsiya* include strengthening the democratic bases of society; establishing "a genuine control from below" in all levels of administration and economic management of the country (Gorbachev 1987, 36); and developing "socialist pluralism," which in Brown's (1989, 9) words, refers to the "fight against dogmatism and political intolerance." The Stalinist totalitarian system alienated workers from the production processes and ruthlessly suppressed the voice of intellectuals and opposition. Residual elements of Stalinism must be superceded if the broader aspirations of *perestroika* are to be achieved. *Demokratizatsiya*, therefore, aims at shaping a "rule-of-law State" by carefully preserving "the democratic values of mankind," imparting new meaning, and preventing any possibility of "deformation and deviation from the principles of Socialism" (Kudryavtsev 1988, 124-25). While Khrushchev began the process of dismantling Stalinist totalitarianism and Brezhnev ended up with authoritarianism, Gorbachev's *perestroika* aims at making a transition to a democratic state and society. By dismantling the outdated command system, Gorbachev endeavors to build "a humane and democratic socialist society."

The pace of the sweeping changes that have so far occurred in Soviet society and polity under the banners of *glasnost* and *demokratizatsiya* have clearly exceeded both common expectation and the pace of economic reform. Gorbachev, indeed, has made change a value in itself in the contemporary Soviet Union. According to Henry Kissinger (quoted in *Time*, April 10, 1989, 57), Gorbachev has already achieved a herculean task. He has gone "much further, much faster than his countrymen or outsiders ever dreamed possible" (Kaiser 1988, 109). Since the early stage of *perestroika*, changes have been the most dramatic, exciting, and far-reaching in the field of *glasnost*. *Glasnost* has made public opinion a serious force for social change, developing a political and civic culture in the Soviet Union. *Glasnost* has effectively repudiated the mythology of Stalin and his command model of socialism, shattered taboos that dominated the country for generations, and reinstated many prominent dissident activists like Andrei Sakharov, radical writers like historian Roy Medvedev, and revolutionary thinkers, such as Nikolai Bukharin.

The degree of freedom that the media in general enjoy in today's Soviet Union has simply no parallel in its entire history. *Perestroika*, writes Falin (1988, 306), "has already printed once-disgraced books in millions of copies, restored the stature of scores of cultural figures formerly anathematized for different reasons or for no reasons at all." *Glasnost* has literally opened up the Soviet mind; it provided the widest platform in Soviet history for reinterpretation of history itself; exposed long-suppressed ethnic, nationality-oriented, religious, and social grievances and conflicts; and facilitated dauntless expression of ecological, societal, humanitarian, and cultural concerns.

In the field of *demokratizatsiya* changes are no less exciting. *Perestroika* allows Soviet citizens to actually do things that had been beyond their imaginations for decades. Democracy is clearly expanding in many areas of Soviet society. Brzeziniski (1989, 59) remarks that Gorbachev has been "remarkably successful" in creating "a higher degree of individual motivation" and in ensuring greater participation of the masses at all levels of the Party and state machineries.

In 1989, for the first time in Soviet history, 1,500 out of a 2,250-seat Congress of the People's Deputies were freely elected through secret ballots, the rest were chosen by various public organizations. This phenomenon transformed the Congress of the People's Deputies into the most democratic governmental institution in more than seven decades of Soviet rule. Although the CPSU as a party won the election, many individual party officials were defeated. Most importantly, in terms of power and functions, the newly constituted Congress has already buried its conventional rubber stamp role, and instead has been vigorously pursuing a significant role in national and international policy matters (see Hough 1989). Unlike earlier practices, heated discussions and fearless opposition in the Congress floors have become a routine matter in contemporary Soviet Union.

Demokratizatsiya has ushered in a significant process for the transformation of the Soviet society from a centralized, authoritarian structure to a democratic and pluralistic one. In mid-1989, a formal opposition in the nation's parliament, the Interregional Deputies Group led by Boris Yelstin (currently chairman of the Russian republic's parliament) and prominent human rights activist Andrei Sakharov was allowed to operate. A revolutionary turning point in Soviet history occurred in February 1990 when Gorbachev formally brought an end to the political monopoly that the CPSU had enjoyed in the Soviet Union since 1917.[19]

Another step toward democratic institutions, namely, the establishment of a strong executive presidency, in fact, has also begun to erode the CPSU's seven-decade-old monopoly over power.[20] The presidency bill, which was overwhelmingly approved (1,817 to 133, with 61 abstentions) by the Congress on March 12, 1990, moves in the direction of transferring power away from the CPSU to the Government. In the local elections in March 1990, noncommunist candidates outnumbered the Communist Party candidates and won most of the seats throughout the country (*Time*, March 8, 1990).

Like economic reforms, the political reforms of *perestroika*, too, demonstrate an evolutionary character. At the earlier stages Gorbachev and his associates emphasized *glasnost* and *demokratizatsiya*, because earlier reform efforts bogged down in the absence of democratic and political support from below, and they envisioned that popular participation would embolden government's ability to implement reforms. Therefore, many scholars legitimately remarked that *glasnost* and *demokratizatsiya* were largely aimed at building a constituency for new thinking and transformation, not at increasing freedom of expression or political freedom (Hardt & Kaufman 1987, xiv).

The character of *glasnost* and *demokratizatsiya* began to change especially since the spring of 1988 with the emergence of a myriad of informal and unofficial political, social, other kinds of groups and associations. At this stage, which can be considered the second stage of *perestroika*'s political reforms, numerous unofficial and informal organizations with diverse political preferences, programs, and constituencies began to surface (these forces will be identified and discussed in Chapter 7). Lewin (1988, 129-35) described this stage as one-party democracy. One of the major goals of the myriad of social and political groups in this period, Brovkin (1990) points out, was to mount a credible opposition and challenge to the CPSU monopoly on political power. During this period, Richard Nixon (1990) comments, "Gorbachev's strategy for keeping his empire together has been to keep his hands firmly on the reins of central power, while tolerating more protests against it than most of his predecessors would have done." The most radical political reform carried out during this stage in connection with the republics was a Presidential decree (issued in early 1989) that transferred primary authority over managing agriculture and the consumer sector to the republics while retaining the central government's authority over raw materials and heavy industry. The decree also enhanced the republics' authority over their own budgets.

The beginning of the third stage of Gorbachev's political reforms can be traced to early 1990 with the elimination of the CPSU's monopoly of political power, thus, setting the stage for multi-party political pluralism. This stage was also marked by a proliferation of independence movements in the Baltic States, and by Gorbachev's (1990b, 36-37) call for "self-determination" of republics, "harmonizing inter-ethnic relations" and efforts to establish "optimal links" between republics and Union governments. During this period, Gorbachev also consolidated his power as President of the USSR.[21] At the Twenty-eighth Congress of the CPSU, Gorbachev made clear the principle of noninterference of the CPSU in the functioning of the machinery of government and therefore called for complete separation of state and party. Gorbachev asked the CPSU to work within the bounds of democratic process, as a parliamentary party, and to shun its right to control management of enterprises, departments, and other government bodies. Therefore, from now on the CPSU's influence will be primarily determined by the strength of its ideas and their attractiveness to the people.

Therefore, marking the sharpest break in seventy three years of rule by the CPSU, during which the CPSU used state power as the primary motor for the construction of socialism, dramatic and sweeping steps were taken to separate party from the state authority. The Politburo of the CPSU has been reorganized and extended to incorporate leaders from the Soviet Union's fifteen republics and other grassroots organizations; thus, for the first time in Soviet history, representation to the politburo from all corners of the country was ensured.[22] Second, measures were taken to restrict Politburo activity to party matters and stop its direct management of the state and economy. State officials, including the head of government and members of the council of ministers, were excluded from the Politburo.[23]

In the third stage, *perestroika*'s political reforms are also marked by far greater democratization and *glasnost*. While in the initial stages *glasnost* was intended to cautiously relax, the nearly totalitarian control of the state over media and the near monopoly of official Soviet ideology, the third stage marked a virtual disappearance of official censorship or control over the media and the freedom of expression of ordinary citizens. Soviet citizens were virtually free to talk to any news media, foreign or domestic, join any organization, political, economic, or cultural. Newspapers could publish anything, including demands for disintegration of the country, the overthrow of the CPSU from power, or denouncement of Soviet official ideology—indeed, of socialism itself. And the Soviet state-controlled media, including state-run television, radio, and the news agency TASS, gave coverage to dissident and oppositional activities. In the immediate aftermath of the Twenty-eighth Congress of the CPSU, Gorbachev lifted the Communist Party's monopoly over the state-run radio and television system, and opened opportunities for all political movements and organizations to have access to the airwaves, including the right to set up their own television and radio stations (see *Los Angeles Times*, July 16, 1990). In brief, three institutional changes followed the Twenty-eighth Congress of the CPSU. Politburo is now the highest decision-making body of the CPSU, not of the Soviet government. A Presidential Council was formed, including a position of vice-president, and a new Union Treaty was proposed for forming a new Soviet Union consisting of "soverign republics."

At the fourth stage, supplementing the Five Hundred Day program, in November 1990 the Supreme Soviet approved a new Union based on "optimal links" between the weakened center and voluntary cooperation of the "sovereign republics." On March 17, 1991, a nationwide referendum was held in connection with the formation of the new Union. Although six republics (Armenia, Estonia, Georgia, Latvia, Lithuania and Moldavia) boycotted the referendum, Gorbachev won approval of the new Union Treaty (see *New York Times*, March 17, 1991). The treaty seeks, among other things, to establish a Council of Federation, composed of presidents of the constituent republics, to be the highest collective policy-making body of the country, which may replace the Presidential Council. It also calls for a Constitutional Court to resolve disputes between the center and the republics (see Brown 1990).

But the Union Treaty does not solve the mounting problems stemming from age-old ethnic and nationality disputes. Moreover, Yeltsin, chairman of Russian Federation, remains unconvinced that the referendum will help in the recovery from the existing turmoil. These developments at the fourth stage have led to increased emphasis on law and order, and a partial and temporary reversal of the trend toward increased democratization and liberalization (see below).

But if the fourth stage is considered an aberration, it can be argued that *perestroika* provides far greater freedom of expression, publication, association, and other forms of communication than the Soviet people have ever experienced, and more political freedom than the citizens of many authoritarian, even so-called democratic, states enjoy. Moreover, since the advent of Gorbachev to power in 1985, forces of democratization and *glasnost* have persistently weakened the role and power of the CPSU and simultaneously strengthened those of the state relative to the party; a culmination of this process is being demonstrated at the fourth stage. Also, greater enthusiasm with *glasnost* gave birth to many political forums both within and outside the CPSU. These alternative platforms and leadership form the embryonic stage of multi-party pluralism, which, especially in the aftermath of the Twenty-eighth Congress of the CPSU and in early 1991, seems clearly to be emerging.

Interrelationships Between Economic and Political Reforms

Reforming a socialist system, especially the Stalinist model of Soviet socialism, has long been considered a highly arduous, if not an utterly impossible, job. In previous chapters we elaborated how and why many prominent Sovietologists, especially in the fifties and sixties, concluded that Soviet socialism was an unreformable and frozen totalitarian system. It has been believed that political, social, economic, and ideological factors that are systemic to and inseparable in a centrally planned and politically directed economy constrain any "crucial reform" of "real socialism" (Kosta 1989, 9-22).

The first manifestation of reform efforts in the Soviet-type economies can be traced to Yugoslavia. Perhaps because of Yugoslavia's relative success in economic reforms (which will be discussed in details in the next chapter), and many successful efforts at economic rather than political reforms in other Central European countries, such as Hungary and Poland in the fifties and sixties, and also because of the success of China's economic reforms of the late seventies and early eighties, it is commonly believed that economic, rather than political, reforms are easier in socialist economies. It has also been perceived that generally oligarchic political leadership in socialist countries will be more comfortable with economic reforms, because such reforms will be less threatening to their power and position relative to political reforms or restructuring. Also, empirically, it has been demonstrated in all of the above-mentioned countries that ruling authorities found economic reforms to be politically advantageous, and often orchestrated such reforms from above without much popular demand, but held back political reforms, often brutally, a vivid recent example being the incident of Tiananmen Square.

Another corollary of the strategic debate on reforms concerns the appropriate sequence of reforming sectors; whether industry or agriculture should be the point of departure. Reform experience of the socialist countries, especially in Hungary, Poland, and China (which we shall also elaborate in detail in the next chapter), show that agriculture or the rural economy is the more logical step to begin reforms with, and that an "agriculture first" strategy "worked very well" (Hewett, quoted in Aganbegyan 1987, 284) in generating momentum for extending reforms to industrial sector.

Therefore, Gorbachev's reforms, which preferred political to economic reforms as a key strategy, and stressed the industrial rather than rural/agricultural sector as a point of departure, come as a surprise to many. Such strategy and sequential arrangements, so far, have resulted in tremendous success in the political sphere and relatively less progress in the economic sphere. By directing the reforms the other way around, both sequentially and strategically, Gorbachev has been navigating in uncharted waters. The problematics and prospects of such a strategy will be taken up in the next chapter. Here we shall concentrate on the interrelationships of economic and political reforms as Gorbachev's *perestroika* suggests. Whether economic reforms lead to further political reforms or political reforms lead to further economic reforms remains a controversial among scholars and practitioners (see *Soviet Economy*, 1987, vol., 3 & 4). Gorbachev and his associates, however, concluded that one of the crucial reasons for the failure of previous economic reforms in the Soviet Union was that they were not accompanied by political reforms. They also concluded that the economic situation they inherited demanded a completely different strategy and sequential arrangement of reforms than China or Hungary had previously pursued somewhat successfully. The Soviet Union lacked the huge manpower in rural areas that could be transformed into active work forces under a "rural revolution" as done in China. Rather, the Soviet Union has highly educated and skilled manpower that is now ready for a diversified social and political structure. Hungary's New Economic Mechanism (NEM), introduced in 1968, succeeded in boosting agricultural production, but in the field of industry the success is rather limited. Hungarian reforms were more concerned with economic mechanisms, while Gorbachev's reforms encompass social, political, cultural, and economic aspects of the Soviet Union. In Hungary, the standard of living is high relative to growth and the level of the national economy, while in the Soviet Union growth performance of the national economy outstripped the standard of living for decades. Moreover, unlike the Soviet Union, in Hungary, different social and political groups were ideologically acknowledged more easily. Besides, there are many other geographical, historical, political, ideological, social, institutional, and international factors that distinguish the Soviet Union from other socialist countries.

In any event, Gorbachev's unique strategy of simultaneous economic and political reforms, with greater importance given to the political sphere and sequential preference to the industrial sector, resulted in substantial, even fundamental progress in the political arena but far lesser achievements in economic sphere. A careful analysis of this development reveals a kind of dialectic relationship between *perestroika*'s economic and political reforms. At the earlier stage, as mentioned above, Gorbachev initiated *glasnost* in order to elicit public criticism against the bureaucratic apparatus of the centralized, authoritarian state and to mobilize public support for *perestroika*. *Glasnost* granted some latitude to journalists and intellectuals so that the evils of the inherited system could be revealed, and at the same time, forces opposed to reforms could be challenged. *Glasnost*'s freedom and democratization were less than the rhetoric implied, but enough to generating support for *perestroika*.

But *glasnost* generated enormous and unprecedented enthusiasm and rejuvenation in the press and among the masses in the society. Scores of discarded leaders and scholars were rehabilitated and millions of copies of prohibited books and fliers were published and circulated. Gorbachev (1990b, 25) comments that *glasnost* has brought "millions upon millions of working people back into public life." As people became more open-minded, aware and informed of the actual conditions of the existing society, economy, and polity, they became more vocal against evils, oppression, corruption, and official privileges, demanding further extension of *glasnost*. And to accelerate the process of implementation of economic reforms, Gorbachev, up until the end of the third stage, found more *glasnost* to be advantageous for *perestroika*'s overall strategy. Therefore, he actively encouraged and patronized freedom of thought and liberation of mind. Such fuller and deeper political freedom was expected to provide the foundations for more radical economic reforms.[24]

The new stage of society's revolutionary transformation, unprecedented democratization of society, openness to both domestic and international information and events, and spiritual and ideological rebirth of Soviet citizens, together contributed to a paramount challenge of the Soviet citizenry to the monopoly of power and control of the CPSU. The CPSU, on the other hand, remained dominated by conservative forces who believe in orthodox Soviet socialist values and are unwilling to give up the party's supreme authority over the state, society and economy. Facing this situation, Gorbachev is left with two options: either transform the party into a liberal one suited to the needs, concerns and challenges of the changed population, or shift power from the party to the state. Gorbachev is apparently doing both. In the immediate aftermath of the Twenty-eighth CPSU Congress, conservative leader Yagor Ligachev was retired, a new central committee was formed with a larger number of liberals, the politburo was reorganized with its power and control clearly circumscribed, and definitive steps were taken to separate party from state and to let the Communist Party compete for the people's mandate in an environment of multi-party political pluralism. This embryonic stage of political pluralism has been given special momentum with the resignation of maverick political leader Yelstin during the Twenty-eighth Congress of the CPSU.

Up until the third stage, Gorbachev, who began with rather cautious efforts at easing authoritarianism, was rapidly moving toward more radical and widespread democratization. Indeed Gorbachev's democratization went beyond many socialist countries that have been experimenting with market-oriented reforms for decades; it even went beyond many so-called democratic countries. In the case of China, economic reforms stimulated demands for political reforms, and authorities crushed such demands. But in the Soviet Union, political reforms stimulated demands for more radical economic reforms, and authorities not only approved such demands, in fact, they officially orchestrated them. At the fourth stage, Gorbachev, faced by dangers of national disintegration, lawlessness, and leadership turmoil, resorted to a temporary ban on public demonstrations and censorship of the state-controlled media. As the transition of socialist economies still continues, a definitive answer to the question of appropriate strategy and sequential arrangements for reforms lies in the future. But it should be noted that although empirical evidence helps, an appropriate strategy or sequence of reforms depends most importantly on the economy and society in question.

PERESTROIKA COMPARED WITH OTHER DECENTRALIZED APPROACHES TO SOVIET SOCIALISM

The reforms envisaged by *perestroika* have been remarkably reminiscent of the NEP policies and programs. Gorbachev's emphasis on the promotion of market relations such as profits, prices, economic incentives, a greater role for the private sector and private initiatives, an increasing emphasis on international trade and openness to the outside world, encouragement to foreign investments, and so on, clearly resemble Lenin's NEP programs. But it is needless to mention that *perestroika* can not be equated with the NEP. Although the Stalinist drive for rapid industrialization and coercive collectivization of agriculture vividly resembled "the surviving spirit of War Communism" (Tucker 1977, 410), it cannot validly be argued that the Stalinist revolution repeated 1917-21 or that the Stalinist order revived the system of War Communism. In the same way, although Gorbachev (1988a, 410) himself claims that *perestroika* turns "ever more often to the last works of Lenin, to Lenin's New Economic Policy, and strives to extract from it all the valuable elements," it would be an exaggeration to conclude that *perestroika* is simply a revival of Lenin's NEP period.

Many of *perestroika*'s economic and political reforms do have historical, ideological, and intellectual roots in Lenin's NEP period (see Dowlah 1990b, 163-205). For example, *perestroika*'s approval of limited private enterprise goes right back to the NEP period. *Perestroika*'s urge for foreign investment and joint ventures are definitely and strikingly similar to the urgencies of Lenin's NEP. Like the NEP, *perestroika* does envisage at least a partial revival of capitalism, and seeks to establish a "market-mixed" political economy. Politically, at the earlier stages, *perestroika*, like the NEP, encouraged one-party political pluralism. Also, the evolutionary character of *perestroika*'s reforms very convincingly demonstrates how much Gorbachev and his associates adhered to the Leninist principle of the NEP period that demonstrated that the Soviet system "could compromise, twist and turn, retreat and advance, without losing its essential character" (Draper 1988, 292).

Major differences between *perestroika* and the NEP period are both political and economic in character. Lenin's NEP did emphasize dissent, discussion, and political opposition, but allowed it within the Communist Party, not outside it, and indeed, drove open opposition underground. Gorbachev's *perestroika* not only allows dissent and opposition, it encourages and marshalls it from above. It even allows multi-party political pluralism, promoting growth of civic culture within the Soviet Union. Second, the background that compelled Lenin to resort to NEP-type policies was quite different from the background that inspired Gorbachev to embark upon the massive programs of *perestroika*. Like NEP, *perestroika* was also initiated to save the Soviet Union from imminent economic crisis. However, the Soviet Union that Gorbachev inherited was not an agrarian underdeveloped economy. He did not have a hostile capitalist class within the country; he did not find it necessary to give the Communist Party "breathing space," and, internationally, he did not confront the situation that Lenin confronted during and after the civil war. Economically, especially at the third stage of *perestroika*, serious amendments in property rights and open calls for dismantling the central planning apparatus and introducing market economy most certainly lead *perestroika* beyond the NEP period.

The next decentralized approach of Soviet socialism was manifested during the Khrushchev's period. Several of the reforms initiated by Gorbachev's *perestroika* clearly resemble Khrushchev's reforms. For example, *perestroika*'s emphasis on decentralizating authority to the enterprise level, strengthening the role of the trade unions, providing economic incentives for improving the quality of products, establishing economical methods of production, promoting incentives for agricultural production, allowing private initiatives, making wage reforms, extending price and money systems—all these vividly resemble the reforms of Khrushchev. Politically, Khrushchev made a decisive break with the Stalinist totalitarian system, he effectively repudiated the Stalinist personality cult, eliminated the use of terror, and rejected the notion of the inevitability of war between capitalism and socialism. All these are readily echoed in Gorbachev's *perestroika*.

However, there are also crucial differences between Khrushchev's reform efforts and those of Gorbachev. *Perestroika* attempts de-Stalinization by promoting democratization and openness in the society, while Khrushchev wanted to accomplish his goals by administrative orders from above. Moreover, Khrushchev did not intend to repudiate Stalinism completely. Rather, he differentiated between disposable and indispensable elements of Stalinism, and tried to do away with only the disposable part of Stalinism, that is, the personality cult of Stalin and totalitarian rule, but wanted to continue the indispensable part of Stalin's model: domination by the Communist Party over the state and continuation of central planning as opposed to market processes. By contrast, *perestroika* denounces Stalinism in toto, both Stalinist totalitarian rule and the command model of economy that was continued by post-Stalinism.

As proposals and intended reforms, many of *perestroika*'s reforms do resemble Kosygin's efforts to reform Soviet economy. Especially, Kosygin's reforms in enterprise management, efforts to increase the power and responsibility of enterprise management, reduction of indicators dictated by central planning authorities, emphasis on profitability and sales of enterprises, reduction or elimination of subsidies, and efforts to put the enterprises on the *khozraschet* system vividly resemble *perestroika*'s reforms. Moreover, Kosygin raised purchasing prices of agricultural goods, lowered tax obligations of farmers, and sought to reduce detailed administrative interference on collective and state farms, and all of these are similar to *perestroika*'s reforms in agricultural sector. Kosygin also emphasized price reforms that according to Nove (1969, 23), failed to "provide the scarcity signals, or the cash flow to enterprises, required to achieve the intended autonomy of industrial enterprises." But as mentioned above, most of Kosygin's reforms remained on paper; the leadership had neither the commitment nor the capability to carry out the reforms as done under *perestroika*. Moreover, Kosygin's reforms were mainly economic in character, they neither had a comprehensive character nor an economic urgency for reform, as *perestroika* envisages.

CONCLUDING REMARKS

Economic and political reforms initiated by Gorbachev and his associates to dismantle the central planning apparatus, initiate a "government regulated market," and establish a multi-party based political pluralism, a "humane and democratic socialist society," and a federation of sovereign republics, are far-reaching and revolutionary in character and magnitude. Although many of *perestroika*'s reforms have roots in the Soviet past, in terms of whole-hearted commitment and comprehensive character, they have no true parallels or full precedents in Soviet history.

Perestroika has initiated a revolutionary process to transform the traditional and authoritarian economy into a democratic, decentralized, and competitive one. Although sweeping changes have already taken place, still *perestroika* falls short in establishing preconditions for a market-oriented economy. But the process of economic and political development and modernization has the potential to do away not only with the Stalinist, but also with the post-Stalinist models of Soviet economy and polity.

Politically, *perestroika* accomplished a herculean task. It guarantees democracy and freedom to its people and supplements mature socialism with a less authoritarian structure of government. By introducing *glasnost* and *demokratizatsiya*, Gorbachev has not only revitalized Soviet society, he has also brought the country to turmoil and near disintegration. Economically, by initiating measures aimed at the establishment of "preconditions" for transition to market economy, *perestroika* has opened the door for extensive and dominant cooperative, private, and self-employed sectors, and a decentralized public sector. These economic and political possibilities have created both problematics and prospects for *perestroika*, which we shall discuss in the next chapter.

NOTES

1. Perhaps referring to this stage, Schroeder (1988) criticized Gorbachev for "radically implementing Brezhnev's reforms," and many others, including Gunlicks (1987), Hewett (1989a), Bialer (1989), Zemtsov and Farrar 1989 opined that *perestroika* envisaged neither radical change nor reform.

2. Referring to this stage, Gorbachev states:

When we began *perestroika*, we thought that we would be able just to add a certain dynamic to our society, to improve the state of research and development in the Soviet Union, to improve productivity . . . and through that we will be able to get a better Soviet Union. But we found that the old economic system rejected any kind of progress, rejected any kind of scientific and technological progress. It really was not receptive to that . . . there was no incentive, no motivation for people to work (*New York Times*, June 2, 1990).

3. Gorbachev's own remarks quoted above make this clear. Also see Gorbachev's interview with *Time*, June 4, 1990.

4. Referring to this stage, Goldman (1990, 26-34) remarks that Gorbachev came to realize that "instead of being the solution, central planning had become the problem" and it is about time that the Soviet people "step out from underneath the security blanket of the central plan and collectivized farm."

5. Aganbegyan (1987) Gorbachev's chief economic adviser at that time, identified three basic directions of *perestroika* as: a) efforts to enhance the social orientation of economic development; b) commitments to intensify the acceleration of technological progress; and c) radical restructuring and democratization of economic management.

6. As Shmelev & Popov (1989, 175) remark, planning indeed remained "sacred cow, an icon before which we must genuflect no matter what."

7. Along with the structural and organizational reforms, sweeping measures were undertaken to replace, demote, or fire key personnel in various key branches of government. Colton (1987, 145-46) shows that in the government and party hierarchies of economic management, more than 70 per cent of key personnel were replaced, demoted, or fired. Aslund (1989, 116-17) reports that out of 2,560 employees of *Gosplan*, 1,095 of were cut, and about 2,500 people lost their job with *Gossnab* by 1988. According to Shmelev and Popov (1989, 273), in the year 1988 alone, the number of administrators throughout the economy was reduced by 600,000 people.

8. Every year *Goskomtsen* (State Committee on Prices) approves about 200,000 prices and rates on goods and services. Besides, it has to keep track of another 24 million prices and directly sets 42 percent of all wholesale prices in the economy (see Shmelev and Popov 1989, 155-171).

9. At an earlier stage of *perestroika*, Aganbegyan (1988a, 132) even asserted that if market socialism stood for universalization and general spread of the market place, *perestroika* did not anticipate a direction toward it.

10. Kushnirsky (1988, 50-51) summarizes the wage reforms initiated under the banners of *perestroika*:

Revisions of employee position lists (*shtatnoe raspisanie*), introduction of more differentiated piece-work rates for blue-collar workers, lifting of the direct planning of white-collar positions, specification of white-collar positions into a great number of grades, reevaluation of the credentials of white-collar workers, easing the control of average wages for each category of workers, and the cautious letting go of excessive labor.

11. The law, however, carefully avoided the term "private property," using "Citizen's Property" instead.

12. This law, Abalkin (1990, 19) asserts, "stipulates that the enterprise owns, uses and disposes of its property and at its own discretion performs any other operations vis-a-vis this property that are not prohibited by the legislative acts of the USSR and those of the Union Republics."

13. By the end of 1988, most ministries and departments, all union republics, and more than 100 associations and intersectoral scientific and technical complexes were granted rights to carry out international trade directly. Such independent international trade constituted 12 percent of imports and 28 percents of exports in 1987, and 32 percent of imports and 22 percent of exports at the beginning of 1988 (see Shmelev & Popov 1989, 232-33).

14. Also, in January 1990 the Soviet-led trading bloc Council for Mutual Economic Assistance (COMECON, founded in 1949) was dissolved and replaced by the Organization for International Economic Cooperation (OIEC), which aims at greater integration of the Soviet Union and its former satellite countries into the world economy on the basis of market principles rather than central planning.

15. It should, however, be noted that there are observers who think defense spending in the Soviet Union has been going up in recent years (see Buchanan 1991).

16. In contrast, Shmelev and Popov point out that during the NEP period, private entrepreneurs paid only 5.7 percent of their earnings as tax.

17. Measuring the performance of the Soviet economy is problematic. Hewett (1989b, 55) observes that lack of any "simple set of indicators" reflecting the overall condition of the Soviet economy, "questionable quality" of traditional quantitative indicators like national income statistics, and sheer absence of price deflators, make evaluation of Soviet economy's performance "notoriously difficult." Moreover, Bergson (1989, 263-81) maintains, neither the CIA estimates nor Soviet official statistics (TsSU) seem to be fully reliable, both enjoy "relatively privileged status" of reliability in terms of some estimations, and lack the same for other spheres. Our intention here is to try to sketch a reasonably balanced picture of the contemporary Soviet economy.

18. According to the UN sources (1990, 19), the Soviet economy grew at 1.6 percent in 1985, 2.3 percent in 1986, 1.6 percent in 1987, 4.4 percent in 1988, and 2.4 percent (preliminary) in 1989. According to Selyunin & Khanin (1987), the Soviet economy grew at a rate of 0.6 percent during the period 1981-85 (see Aslund 1989, 15).

19. The repeal of Article 6 of the Soviet Constitution that guarantees constitutional monopoly power to the Communist Party was ratified by 1,771 to 264, with 74 abstentions (see *New York Times*, March 14, 1990).

20. However, Gorbachev still serves both as president of Soviet government and leader of the CPSU.

21. Of course, many think this step constituted a backward movement toward authoritarianism (see Kissinger 1990).

22. The old Politburo had 13 full members—11 Russians, 1 Georgian, and 1 Ukrainian; 8 candidate members—7 Russians and 1 Byelorussian; and a 10-member Secretariat with one non-Russian (see Whetten 1989, 7). The newly constituted politburo, in contrast, has 24 full members drawn from the whole country.

23. Referring to the newly constituted politburo, *Pravda* comments, "This is the first time that no one from the Soviet government or the Soviet parliament's [executive] presidium joined the Politburo" (quoted in *Los Angeles Times*, July 15, 1990).

24. Gorbachev (1990b, 22) proclaimed at the Twenty-eighth Congress of the CPSU that without *glasnost*, Soviet society could "scarcely have reached the new stage in society's revolutionary transformation."

6

Crisis of Transition:
The Problematics of *Perestroika*

INTRODUCTION

This chapter examines the roots of the contemporary Soviet crisis and then explores the problematics and prospects of *perestroika* as a strategy for transition from a centrally planned economy to a more decentralized, more democratic, and more market-oriented economy. This chapter builds on the premise that the Soviet economy has been experiencing a profound systemic crisis that goes beyond economic structure and policies, beyond both the general economic and noneconomic environment, and extends well into the structures of the economic and political systems. It is argued that this is a systemic crisis requiring a systemic solution; the longer it takes for recovery from the current crisis, the greater the possibility that the Soviet Union might disintegrate or disappear altogether.

Mikhail Gorbachev inherited a "statist political-economic system" and is struggling to replace it with a "democratic socialist political-economic system" (Sherman 1990), through what he calls a "peaceful revolution" from above and below. *Perestroika* envisaged six preponderant objectives: (1) the dismantling of the centrally planned (Stalinist) economy to make a transition to what Gorbachev and his advisers call a "regulated market economy"; (2) the injection of scientific and technological innovations into the economy—intensifying methods of production, improving worker morale, skill, and productivity; (3) openness in societal and governmental processes—transition from an authoritarian state to a more democratic system of governance characterized by rule of law and consent of the governed; (4) the integration of the Soviet economy into the global economic system, bringing an end to traditional isolationism; (5) the acceleration of economic growth, raising living standards and reinvigorating the potential of Soviet individual and society, overcoming economic stagnation and social apathy; and (6) keeping the Soviet empire together by bringing an end to centralized rule and establishing a "Union of Sovereign States."

Strategically, unlike the experiences of China, Yugoslavia, or Hungary, where economic reforms came first, Gorbachev's strategy of transition began with political reforms as preconditions for economic reforms. Also, in contrast to an "agriculture first" principle followed in these countries, Gorbachev stressed an "industry first" strategy. Moreover, as discussed before, *perestroika*'s programs and policies demonstrate an evolutionary character.

The chapter is organized as follows: Section two examines theoretical expositions on the diagnosis of the import and magnitude of the "crisis" inherited by Gorbachev. Section three explores theoretical and empirical guidance for a "systemic" transition of Soviet socialism into a more decentralized, more market-oriented economy. Section four scrutinizes systemic constraints of *perestroika*.

DIAGNOSTIC PROBLEMS

In the sixty years' history of the centrally planned system, the Soviet economy experienced sustained growth for the first thirty years and a significant slowdown in economic growth in the latter half. Low performance of the Soviet economy began to surface especially in the late seventies. In the early eighties, the slowdown in economic growth reached crisis level and the economic potential of the country came under serious pressure. Indeed economic destabilizers like stagnation, low productivity, lack of initiative and innovations, and technological backwardness plummeted the economy into a serious crisis. Although the new Soviet leadership acknowledge that this economic stagnation has not only shattered the dream to overtake the United States in terms of economic production, but also has threatened the very legitimacy of socialism itself, they first diagnosed the problem as a "pre-crisis" or "near-crisis" situation. Soviet leaders maintained that *perestroika* became necessary to salvage the country from economic stagnation and other associated problems, but the crisis itself was not only conceived as a mere "pre-crisis" situation, it was also believed (erroneously) that a transition from extensive to intensive methods of production—an intra-system reform—would resolve the problem.

But breathtaking events in the socialist countries throughout the tumultuous years of the late eighties have drastically changed, indeed profoundly deepened, both Soviet and Western perceptions of the magnitude, breadth, and depth of the contemporary crisis. In the early eighties, when Gorbachev assumed power, the annual growth rate of the Soviet economy was a little less than 2.0 percent. In the late eighties, the situation worsened. Politically, policies of *glasnost* and *democratizatsiya* have had the side effects of threatening political order and stability. Indeed, lack of timely and appropriately expressed diagnosis of the situation critically circumscribed the prospects of *perestroika* since its inception. Therefore, before embarking on the critical details of *perestroika*'s problematics and prospects, a clear understanding of the character of the contemporary Soviet crisis itself is in order.

Theoretical Expositions of Contemporary Crisis

The fact that the contemporary Soviet economy is passing through a profound crisis is no longer disputable. Sovietologists began to proclaim the existence of such a crisis in the Soviet Union in the early eighties.[1] Since the mid-eighties, most Western economists and political scientists accepted this characterization as an axiom (Gustafson 1990, 4). Soviet leaders and scholars themselves began to acknowledge the proximity or actual existence of a "catastrophic," or "crisis-scale" situation in the country, especially since the late eighties.[2] Gorbachev himself began to use the expression "acute sociopolitical and socioeconomic crisis" since late 1989. Therefore, the question is no longer whether the Soviet economy is in crisis, but rather how deep and acute is the crisis, and whether Soviet socialism and the Soviet Union can survive it. The following discussion sheds light on the character, depth, and magnitude of the contemporary crisis.

Cyclical Crisis. The contemporary crisis has shattered the traditional belief that the socialist economies are immune to business cycles. Marxian economics have traditionally been overwhelmingly concerned with capitalistic, instead of socialist, crisis phenomena. Crises were considered to be necessary and chronic features of capitalist economies, and ex ante planning—existence of central planning in socialist economies—was considered the best guarantee against such anarchic tendencies. Besides, as crisis and depressions were believed to be alien phenomena to socialism, "hidden faults" (explained below) of centrally planned economy were carefully kept "below the threshold of analytical consciousness" (Drewnowski 1982, 76).

But in the early sixties, scholars demonstrated that virtually all Central European socialist countries experienced cyclical fluctuations, periods of overheated growth followed by periods of slowdown or recession (see Bauer 1990; Kalecki 1972). The cyclical crisis tendencies in the socialist economies are analogous to but different from Western business cycles. The two systems are indeed mirror images of each other (see Nee & Stark 1989). In the capitalist system crises tend to result from overproduction and lack of demand; in the socialist economies the major causes and indicators of crisis are overinvestment and excess demand (see Kornai 1980).

Scholars generally agree that the Soviet-type economies have experienced cyclical crises since the Second World War. But the fact that the contemporary crisis in these economies is much deeper and more severe than a cyclical crisis is hardly disputable. It is a crisis of long recession and stagnation, the roots and genesis of which can be traced to the late seventies. Szelenyi (1989, 209) observes that it is "too deep and broad to qualify as just another cycle in socialist economic growth." Besides, in the past such cycles lasted for a short time when growth rates declined and living standards stagnated. But the current crisis poses a credible threat to the very survival of the socialist system itself.

Stagflation Crisis. Some scholars tend to interpret the contemporary situation as a crisis of stagflation. They argue that stagflation in the capitalist economies in the early seventies (caused by changing scarcities, new world market patterns, and changing demand on Western markets) contributed to serious economic crises in the socialist countries. Bechtold and Helfer (1987), for example, argue that stagflation of the seventies called for stimulating flexibility and innovations in the economy in order to guide investments from low-level productivity toward dynamic growth. But subsidies, tariffs, and governmental regulations favored endangered, weakened and old industries at the cost of innovative and young industries, and thereby sabotaged structural change in the economy and prevented a shift toward new structures of production. They argue that these types of culprits of stagflation in Western economies have stronger counterparts in central planning and economic concentration of the socialist countries. Therefore, the crisis of stagflation was manifested even more severely in the socialist economies.[3]

Problems with the applicability of this theory stem from the fact that although governmental interventions or stagnation of the economy can be easily identified, measuring the rate of inflation in a socialist economy is a difficult task. Price levels in these economies do not represent economic opportunity costs or real trade-offs. Inflation is generally hidden or more often deliberately suppressed by government. Moreover, prices of basic necessities such as food and housing have been kept artificially low. That is why switching from suppressed or hidden inflation, through so-called "shock therapy," results in an explosion of prices, which the Soviets have so far feared to do.[4]

Also, stagflation theorists believe that the solution to the crisis lies in the introduction of capital markets undisturbed by governmental interference. They oppose not only a bureaucratic redistributive system as can be seen in a socialist economy, but also Keynesian fiscal management. This theory fails to capture the very essence of the contemporary crisis: This is not a crisis of economic stagnation or suppressed or hidden inflation, or for that matter of incredibly high subsidies or deficits. Recent experiences of Hungary and Yugoslavia show that substantially free movement and development of capital markets, without a major overhauling of systemic factors inherent in a socialist economy, fail to ensure a trade-off between shortages and inflation and eliminate the so-called soft-budget constraints.[5]

Therefore the contemporary crisis cannot be considered a mere cyclical or stagflation crisis. This is a severe systemic crisis. It is a political legitimation crisis that threatens the socialist countries with the possibility of becoming "permanently developing" countries (Winiecki 1989b). Before moving on to systemic crisis, however, the arguments of the transition theorists will be considered.

Transition Crisis. Transition theorists, in contrast to the proponents of cyclical/ stagflation theorists, maintain that the current crises in the socialist economies constitute a "crisis of transition."[6] Transition theorists maintain that these crises reveal exhaustion of existing politicoeconomic institutions and structures, and the solution lies in remaking the institutions and structures to suit the changed needs and demands of the population. Proponents of this theory compare the socialist depression of the 1970s and 1980s with the Great Depression of the 1930s in the capitalist economies. During the 1930s the capitalist system was at the breaking point; so is the socialist system today. In the thirties the capitalist system was challenged by a transition crisis, originating in the transition from the extensive to intensive methods of production, from industrialization to the post-industrialization phase of economic development. The current crisis is fundamentally concerned with an analogous transition. Capitalism survived the crisis of the Great Depression by two means: President Franklin Roosevelt's New Deal Politics and John Keynes's demand-side economics, in other words, by injecting some socialist institutions into the economy.[7] However, the basic institutions of private ownership and market economy remained dominant. Socialist economies, therefore, could survive the present crisis by injecting some capitalist instruments, like fiscal and monetary policies, into the system. Therefore, there is no need to replace the existing system by another (for example, capitalism). What is needed is a transition to a mixed-economy model that does not dismantle the existing system, but is characterized by multiple and crisscrossed arrangements of mutually beneficial and trustable ownership and control of the means of production between state and private initiatives (see Nee & Stark 1989; Karol 1988; Yakovlev 1990).

The optimism of this theory that structural transformation will be sufficient and no systemic transition is needed rests on another mirrored comparison. In the thirties the Soviet Union made tremendous economic progress under Stalin's command model. During the same period, the Western world was caught up in the Great Depression, and was indeed moving toward "paralysis of production, decline and, ultimately, to the danger of revolution" (Karol 1988, 23). Moreover, the simultaneous downturn of the capitalist world and the emergence of the socialist system brought the whole capitalist system to a breaking point. Almost an exactly opposite situation has been prevailing in the contemporary world. Socialist economies are facing either downturns or severe crisis situations while the capitalist economies show recovery from recession and a moderate upswing in economic performance. The current downturns in the socialist economies, like that of the capitalist system in the thirties, do not necessarily manifest exhaustion or uselessness of the system itself. Therefore, what is needed is serious surgery or rejuvenation, not an elimination or replacement of the system.[8]

Transition theorists' apparently convincing theory, however, ignores some important factors. First, socialist economies, except perhaps the Soviet Union and China, did not develop endogenously. Ideology that cements economic and political behavior of individuals in a society was imposed from above. During the Great Depression, the legitimacy of capitalist ideology and institutions was seriously questioned in the United States.[9] But demands for the abolition of capitalism were not as forceful or widespread as contemporary demands for the dismantling of the institutions of centralized state and planning and the monopoly of the Communist Party in political and economic life in Central European countries and the Soviet Union.[10] Moreover, the capitalist crisis of the thirties, at least in the United States, was not accompanied, as is true in the contemporary Soviet situation, by disruptive nationalist and secessionist movements.

Moreover, in terms of organization and mode of operation of economic activities, socialist economies provide a formidable problem. Restructuring the Soviet system would require a thorough overhaul of the whole system, if not its replacement with a new one. Such transformation in socialist economies affects the interests and status of people in all social strata, groups, the party, and government. It involves radical and sweeping transformation of the country's property relations, production mechanism, and distribution structures and patterns. Incorporation of market elements into socialist economy could involve a substantial reduction of the state's share in economic activities and a significant increase in the share of private initiatives. Experience with market and monetary reforms without fundamental transformation of the socialist political and economic structures results, many believe, in the worst of both worlds (see Kornai 1989; Alexiev 1990c; Milanovic 1989).

Most important, tinkering with the system may help to buy time, but it has been amply demonstrated over the years, especially in Hungary and Poland, even in the Soviet Union by now, that tinkering will not make the system work better. Gorbachev himself proclaims that the Soviet Union incurred "tremendous losses by stubbornly clinging" to the administrative-command system for decades, and Soviet history clearly shows "the futility of attempts to get out of the plight" by "patching up" and "putting the brakes on renewal and the transition to new forms of economic life" (*News and Views*, July 12, 1990, 7). Therefore, both Soviet and Western scholars agree to the diagnosis that the Soviet Union is in crisis. Indeed, it is simultaneously a crisis of economic survival, political legitimacy, and the system itself, which "has been in place for long time and has created many disproportions" (Goldman 1983, 5). Gorbachev and his associates rightly conclude that to resolve the contemporary Soviet crisis requires transformation of the system itself. Therefore, *perestroika*'s challenge goes far beyond economic and political spheres. It confronts ingrained cultural values, beliefs, and life patterns of the individual members of the society. Institutions may well be restructured, privatization might well be encouraged openly and officially—all these will require reformed and restructured "new individuals" to take the initiative and actually materialize these reforms. Not only communism but also the communists need to be transformed.

In short, *perestroika* not only denounces the last sixty years of seventy-year-long Soviet history, it also demonstrates that the socialist project itself can be established wrongfully and can be sustained, even somewhat successfully, for more than half a century (see Lapidas 1989). Therefore, it powerfully attacks the social, political, and cultural fabrics of Soviet society.[11] But this is a transitional as well as a systemic crisis. It is systemic crisis because the system itself is in crisis,[12] and it is also a transition crisis in that it involves a transition from one system to another, and therefore, must confront the problems associated with systemic transition.

Systemic Crisis. Systemic crisis theorists postulate that the existing form of socialism, as a system, has exhausted its growth potential and this situation has worsened the loss of legitimacy of the communist regimes throughout the world. These theorists predict that socialism, as it is, will lead to collapse and disintegration of the socialist systems. Three strands of thought can be identified in this context.

First, the contemporary crisis in the Soviet-type economies constitutes a severe systemic crisis that demonstrates that the socialist economic system is not capable of lasting recovery, it cannot grow intensively, and therefore it threatens the project of socialism itself. Birman (1988), for example, argues that the contemporary crisis in the Soviet Union is so systemic, endemic, and alarming that collapse of the Soviet politicoeconomic system is a "distinct possibility." He argues that the Soviet economy is caught in a vicious cycle. Characterized by chronic shortages, Soviet-type economies depend on economic growth for alleviating persistent imbalances, but as growth slows down, shortages grow worse. He maintains that the contemporary decline in growth can even lead to an absolute decline in output, and thereby to the collapse of the system in its entirety. To some of the proponents of this strand of thought the solution to the contemporary crisis lies with the replacement of socialism with capitalism, with no other way in between.[13]

Although many others conclude that the contemporary crisis is a systemic crisis, they hold that the root cause of the crisis lies with the politicoeconomic structure that owes its origin to the Stalinist system.[14] Although not very optimistic of survival of the socialist system, they, do not prescribe outright replacement of the socialist system by capitalism, but emphasize market, monetary, and price reforms of dramatic and sweeping character. To these writers, socialism is the problem, for which such major systemic changes are the solution.

A third strand of thought characterizes the crisis as systemic, but does not imply the automatic or inevitable collapse of socialism. The exponents of this strand of thought believe what is needed is a system-wide, profound, and fundamental reform program capable of overcoming the threat of imminent collapse, through a social democratic model incorporating a blend of plan and market, social and private ownership.[15] According to systemic theorists, Soviet-type economies are actually state-socialist systems. Only a systemic transformation, which goes far beyond structural-functional transformation that transition theorists emphasize and also involves a radical transition of the system into a new system, can help the survival of socialist economies.[16] These theorists believe that the Great Depression was in fact a systemic crisis, and capitalist systems survived that not by replacing capitalism, but by incorporating several socialist elements within the capitalist system, creating thereby a new form of capitalism. Private businesses accepted substantial doses of government intervention, and characteristic features of capitalist system such as market failures and business cycles came under active governmental guidance. Similarly, socialist economies may survive the current crisis by drastically revamping the existing socioeconomic and political system. This might not necessarily involve replacing socialist system, but will essentially require measures much greater in strength and magnitude than what the transition crisis theorists emphasize. What is needed is a Gorbachevian New Deal.

Gorbachev and his associates, as mentioned above, believe that the contemporary crisis of the Soviet economy is indeed a profound systemic crisis. Like those who expose the first strand of thought, they agree that the Stalinist totalitarian model has outlived its usefulness and its politicoeconomic institutions have become dysfunctional. But Gorbachev and his associates carefully differentiate the Stalinist model of socialism from the socialist project in general. For them dismantling Stalinism contributes to a movement toward socialism, not away from it. They do not opt for dumping the socialist project altogether, which could be the case for the proponents of the first strand of thought. Like those of the third strand of thought, Gorbachev and his associates identify the root cause of the crisis with the state-socialist system that was bequeathed to them by Stalin and Brezhnev. But, in contrast to the second strand of thought, Gorbachev and his associates do not believe that the Statist or the Stalinist system can be salvaged by incorporating some capitalist elements in it. They rather believe that the whole system is in deep crisis. For them, the Stalinist model stubbornly rejects any attempt to ameliorate it.

By denouncing Stalinism, Gorbachev accomplishes three far-reaching objectives. He: (1) separates Stalinism from the socialist project, and therefore, efforts to attribute Stalinism's failure to the project of socialism itself are thwarted; (2) demonstrates that a wrong model can be established for a long time and with considerable economic success; and (3) splits up the Soviet history of socialism, therefore challenges the "continuity theory" (discussed in Chapter 4), and isolates the Lenin of the NEP period, which in turn serves two specific purposes—It provides historical, ideological, and intellectual precedents in support of his vision of socialism (see Dowlah 1990b), and it enlists support of both domestic and international forces that are sympathetic to the October Revolution and NEP-Lenin but are critical of Stalinist aberrations.

Roots of Systemic Crisis

Three factors substantially contribute to the systemic character of the contemporary Soviet crisis: overcentralization of economy, overconcentration of political power, and failures of proper and timely action.

Overcentralization of Economy. Most of the problems of the contemporary Soviet economy stem one way or the other from the so-called centrally planned and state-managed economic system.[17] Two fundamental lapses can be identified that symbolize Soviet central planning. First, it was conceived as a substitute (not a complement) to the market system, and was started on a massive scale without any theoretical guidance or empirical experience. Sweezy (1990) remarks that central planning was introduced in the Soviet Union under "economic and social conditions that bordered on the chaotic" and through a "vast increase in the economic role of the state, extreme centralization of decision making, harsh regimentation of the population," it was eventually elevated "to the status of a science, invented in the Soviet Union and available for adoption by the rest of the world." Second, the central plan stressed "material balances" (physical planning) and "target fulfillment" (quantity of output) that strongly and systematically militated against quality of goods and services, worker morale and productivity, and innovation and initiatives.

Evidently, Soviet central planning at first worked exceedingly well. Growth rates of the Soviet economy, till the early seventies, were unquestionably strong. The secret of this overwhelming success, however, lay with the unusually high endowment of raw materials in the country. But since the early sixties, with the exhaustion of surplus manpower and depletion of low-cost raw materials, central planning lost its magic. Extensive methods of production as pursued by central planning became less and less efficient. It became increasingly difficult to mobilize more people from the agricultural to the industrial sector and put more raw materials and capital resources into the production processes. Consequently, the Soviet economy has plunged into a crisis since the late seventies that continued through the eighties, making it the worst stagnation in Soviet history.

Besides playing with abundant resources, orchestrating the minutest details of material balances, and miscalculating production targets and figures, the Soviet central planning apparatus grossly underestimated the impact of technological revolution in the work place and on the overall economic activities of the nation. Indeed, aside from the military sector, the country largely missed the scientific and technological revolution that vastly increased productivity around the globe. By building up a massive bureaucratic machinery, involving its resources in a statistical morass, and wiping out most private initiative and competition, the planners built a dysfunctional edifice that accommodates inefficiency, wastage, and shortage under the same umbrella. Therefore, far from being immune to crisis, the existing socialist economies have shown their susceptibility to it ever since their emergence. Two major schools of thought can be identified pertaining to systemic faults associated with central planning: the theory of shortage economy, and the disequilibrium school.

Theory of Shortage Economy. Theorists of shortage economy maintain that chronic shortage under the existing system of economic management in the socialist countries is systemic; it has its origins in the infinite demand for resources by enterprises, both for current inputs and for investment resources. Essential arguments of shortage theory, as stipulated by Kornai (1984), can be summarized as follows: Under central planning, enterprises are constrained by a "soft budget" in contrast to a "hard budget," and are not responsible for cost and salability of their goods and services. In addition, the central plan not only overwhelmingly emphasizes "target fulfillment," it also sets overambitious targets for enterprises, and assumes responsibility for supplying necessary inputs. Given targets and soft-budget constraints, enterprises, in turn, demand greater and greater amounts of inputs, leading to the insatiable demand for investment goods that Kornai calls "investment hunger," but resources are limited in supply relative to the insatiable hunger of enterprises for investment goods. All these produce a paradox of shortage and underutilization, because resources are scarce relative to the infinite demand of enterprises, not necessarily in absolute terms. Enterprises systematically underreport the amount of inputs to meet future uncertainties to obtain more subsidies, and to extend production capacities further they routinely inflate production figures.[18]

The fundamental contribution of Kornai to the paradox of central planning in a socialist economy lies in the argument that the same mechanism that can overcome initial barriers to rapid socioeconomic change, in the long run, can develop "inflexible economies and general inefficiencies" (Rider 1988) that can result in chronic shortages, hindering further economic growth. Kornai has shown that the simultaneous existence of underutilization and excess demand of resources, soft-budget constraint, and inefficiencies of enterprises produce a self-generating vicious circle of shortages, which are not random but systemic in character, because shortage conditions are expected to reproduce themselves (see Brabant 1990).

Supplementing this line of thought, Winiecki (1989a) argues that even if socialist economies were not economies of shortage, even if they were economies of surplus, central planning will fail to function effectively. Under the existing form of socialist economy, even in a surplus situation microeconomic distortions will prevail. He maintains that central planning and uncertainty are twins; if one exists, the other will also. That means, if uncertainty remains in terms of supply of goods (shortage economy), bureaucratic redistributive machineries will be in place. This happens because central planning perpetuates a dependency relationship between state and enterprise. Kornai (1989) also maintains that central planners, by assuming responsibility for the overall well-being of the economy, tend to develop a kind of paternalism towards enterprises, and are more likely to steer production of enterprises and salvage it in times of difficulty. On the other hand, because of the shortage economy, investment hunger, and soft-budget constraint, enterprises find it conducive to live with, rather than without, the central planning.

Macroeconomic Disequilibrium Analysis.[19] In contrast to Kornai's theory of shortage economy that revolves around "microeconomic agents," Portes'(1978) disequilibrium analysis focuses on aggregate behavior of households as consumers and suppliers of labor. While Kornai sees shortages in centrally planned economies as all pervasive, systemic, and self-generating in character with a propensity to persist for a protracted period, Portes, a mainstream economist, tends to work "in terms of aggregate excess demand and supply concepts instead of distinguishing between shortage intensity and the degree of slack in each market" (Brabant 1990, 165). To Portes, in socialist economies excess demand is not "large and persistent," and disequilibrium is not a "chronic feature." Basically, Portes's analysis focuses on the demand side, ignoring the microfoundations of economic behavior that Kornai emphasizes.

Portes's model postulates a two-sector economy—households and planners—in which three commodities are traded: money, consumption goods and labor. The model assumes that during the plan period the prices of consumption goods and labor remain fixed (sticky prices) and both sectors of the economy compete for consumption goods and labor. During the plan period, either or both markets remain quantity-constrained, and rationed quantity in one market determines effective supply and demand in the other sector. According to Portes, in the socialist economies quantity rationing prevails because relative prices do not adjust quickly to eliminate excess supplies or demands. Quantity-constraint forces the consumers either to raise savings or substitute leisure for labor, but it does not force them to significantly modify their economic behavior. On the other hand, quantity constraint affects planners' expectations for capital stock, inventories, and household assets for next year's plan. Thus, the quantity constrained socialist economy, instead of producing chronic problems, serves as "equiliberating mechanisms in the medium run" (163).

The basic difference between these two approaches does not relate to micro- versus-macro economic analysis, but rather encompasses a whole range of other issues. Brabant (166) remarks that Kornai indeed provides a vision of "how planned economies operate and what should usefully be done to eliminate imbalances and buttress steady economic growth." On the other hand Portes's disequilibrium analysis fails to explain imbalances in markets of goods and services when the macroeconomic "equilibrium" is spurious because it might conceal microeconomic imbalances. Besides, empirically Kornai's theory of shortage economy has been profusely substantiated by the experience of the Soviet Union and other socialist economies.

Overconcentration of Power.[20] One of the root causes of the contemporary crisis lies with the political system of domination that wiped out all legal and judicial control over Communist Party decisions based on the pretext of revolutionary and ideological legitimacies. The Soviet Union is the world's oldest socialist society. Therefore, Soviet values and institutions, although initially imposed from above, have become "uniquely deeply rooted" (Lieven 1989) and the Soviet population (not merely the leaders) has become committed through experience to its own perception and practice of socialism. Stalin consolidated his power as a dictator and, complemented by state-party control, established totalitarian rule over Soviet society. Subsequently, with the course of history and "self-sustaining change" due to industrialization and modernization (Lowenthal 1970, 54), totalitarianism was replaced by a "classic form of authoritarianism" (Migranian 1990a) by Khrushchev. But both the monopoly of the central planning apparatus over the nation's economy and the CPSU's monopoly over the nation's politics were considered indispensable during the post-Stalinist period. Although various institutions resembling Western political pluralism evolved in the post-Stalinist era (see Hough 1982; Skilling 1966), the Soviet system remained "essentially monocratic and highly resistent to change" (Baum 1989, 111-12). Therefore, overconcentration of political power remained as a dominant cause for the systemic failure of the Soviet economy. How did overcentralization of political power cause systemic failure? Three chronic features can be identified in this context.

Suppression of Truth. According to Drewnowski (1982), suppression of truth constitutes the "first cause of degradation" of the Soviet-type economies. Socialist economies, including the Soviet Union, have long been accused of suppressing freedom of speech and free flow of information. Government monopolized its power over truth, and blurred the difference between the truth and official truth. Commensurately, the citizens' right to freedom was seriously circumscribed.[21] Deliberate policies of socialist regimes to prevent free and undistorted flow of information manifested in four serious consequences: (1) official ideology, Marx- ism-Leninism, was claimed as absolute truth—domestically nonbelievers were routinely haunted by the KGB, and internationally, such dogmatism excruciatingly isolated socialist regimes from the rest of the world; (2) restriction of information to the "selected few" resulted in an "endemic dearth" of information available to decision makers at all levels—thus, false perceptions based on official propaganda persisted, exact conditions of the economy remained unknown, and deficient economic decisions led to economic degradation; (3) in the absence of appropriate incentives, not only "truthful and exact" reporting disappeared but also a "compulsion to false reporting" and "planning without facts" proliferated; and finally (4) suppression of truth resulted in the isolation of the people from the Communist Party and the State, because the principle of suppression is based on distrust of the people, not in their strength or support.

Eradication of Dissent. Another inevitable offshoot of overconcentration of power was eradication of dissenting views and meaningful discussions. By actively obstructing dissent or critical interpretation of economic and political situations, socialist regimes encourage "insufficient and grossly distorted information." The best examples of suppression of dissent are Nobel prize winners Aleksander Solzhenitsyn and Andrei Sakharov. Solzhenitsyn and many others voiced their dissent against forced collectivization, and wanted to portray in their works how official versions distorted the truth by concealing terrible injustices and excruciating sufferings. Sakharov, a nuclear physicist turned human-rights activist who developed the first Soviet hydrogen bomb in the early fifties, was virtually an outcast in the country in the seventies because of his campaign for human rights and disarmament. In early 1980 he was exiled to Gorky for his challenge of the Afghan invasion. Besides Nobel prize winners, many other dissidents and dissident works were suppressed in the Soviet Union.[22]

Had the Soviet government allowed these dissident writers and thinkers "the right to disagree," social, political, economic and cultural evils that the Stalinist leviathan bequeathed to present reformers could have been considerably diminished.

Repudiation of Fairness. The third main cause of the "degradation" in the socialist economies, Drewnowski maintains, is the repudiation of fairness manifested in: human relations in general, and appointments and promotion policy in particular. The Communist Party's monopoly over political and economic power resulted in the rule of so-called *nomenklatura*. Managerial positions were reserved for the members of *nomenklatura*, who were recruited and selected on the basis of political criteria. Such a recruitment and selection policy obviously promoted incompetence and favoritism. Even appointments below the managerial positions, which were not officially reserved for *nomenklatura*, were made on the basis of party membership and the confidence of the party apparatus.

Party control goes beyond appointments of key positions. Enterprise managers are subject to duality of control. Besides usual administrative and governmental channels, managers are responsible to the party, for it controls the state administration and the economy. Managers can follow neither administrative directives nor their own judgment, because of party interference. Nor can they rely on their superiors, because they, too, are controlled by party; nor on party officials because they have authority but not responsibility. This situation prevailed for decades and resulted in two systemic behavioral patterns in the Soviet economy: rigid adherence to regulations and fulfilling targets, because strict observance of procedure and fulfillment of targets will presumably provide the managers "immunity against biased and irresponsible criticism"; and lack of initiatives and innovations, because by preventing technically qualified people from exerting their own judgment, the system "rewarded dull conformism."

Inactions and Inappropriate Actions. Failures to rectify aggravating situations at appropriate times and with appropriate measures constitute one of most important systemic causes of the contemporary crisis in the Soviet Union. First, the Stalinist system outlived its usefulness, but no serious efforts were made to replace it until the economy stagnated in the late seventies. This situation could have been averted if necessary measures had been taken in time, presumably during the Khrushchev period. Second, Brezhnev did realize that extensive methods of production were out of joint with real needs, and injecting technological and scientific revolution in the production processes was necessary to check diminishing rates of return, but preferred to continue with the system as it was. Third, the cumulative effect of buck-passing resulted in serious damage to the socialist project and an unbearable burden for the system. Timely measures could have made the system work better, could have prevented problems from taking on a systemic character.

In the category of inappropriate actions three points deserve mention. First, reforms carried out in the pre-Gorbachev period were cosmetic, half-hearted, and piecemeal in character. Second, reforms were misdirected. Sporadic efforts were made to improve the incentive system, central planning, even the economic structure, but the real problem lay in the absence of fundamental human rights and democratic practices. Third, reforms never addressed the "degradation of tissue": faulty information and planning without facts, distorted evaluations and destruction of corrective mechanism, the incompetence and inhibitions of decision makers, and an absurd complexity of procedures and rigidity of targets.

THEORETICAL AND EMPIRICAL GUIDANCE

Perestroika has shifted attention from the debate on whether planning and markets are incompatible to how to blend these apparently opposed elements into an effective, functional mechanism. For *perestroika*, therefore, the issue is no longer, as Lavoie (1990, 72) puts it, "whether socialism needs to come to terms with market forms, but how, exactly, it should do so." But an appropriate mingling of planning and markets under a socialist economic system remains one of the crucially problematic factors for the socialist project itself and for *perestroika* as well. Therefore, a brief account of the theoretical and empirical pursuits directed to establishing a congruous relationship between planning and markets is in order.

Theoretical Models

The theoretical debate over a pragmatic and functional blending of market elements and planning instruments under a socialist setting goes back to the thirties when, as discussed in Chapter 1, the first round of debate, the so-called "great socialist controversy" broke out.

Lange's Market Socialism. Lange's market socialism, as mentioned before, emerged as a formidable challenge to the neo-Austrian critique of socialism. Lange developed the "classic model" of market socialism based on neoclassical methodology and showed that rational and sophisticated economic calculation and social coordination of allocation of resources is possible in a socialist economy. Although Lange accepted the neoclassical contention of the necessity of price systems for economic calculation and coordination, he denied the necessity of a money price system based upon market actions of private resource owners for efficient determination of resource prices.

Lange's model of market socialist economy has three major decision-making units: households, enterprises, and a central planning board (CPB). Households are completely autonomous in the exercise of their choices of consumption, saving, and occupation. Enterprise and industry managers, given market and accounting prices, have autonomy in the determination of level and composition of outputs and inputs within the framework of well-known rules postulated by the CPB. The role of the CPB is confined primarily to macroeconomic direction of the economy, that is, growth rates, investment policies, and so on. The postwar Lange model, however, emphasizes a greater role of the CPB than "mere coordination of public policies," but at the same time insists that the CPB must avoid getting into details of economic life of the nation Lange's CPB must accomplish at least two tasks: dividing national income between accumulation and consumption, and distributing investments among the different branches of the economy. He cautions, however, that economic means must be pursued whenever possible, even when the plan is realized by administrative measures.

No socialist country ever claimed to have followed Lange model. Many Western writers, for example Gregory and Stuart (1980, 299), believe that the Lange model has been a source of inspiration for Hungarian reforms; but many others, including Kornai (1989), remain unconvinced that the Hungarian New Economic Mechanism resembles the Lange model of market socialism. None of the contemporary Soviet reforms come close to Lange's prescriptions. But for its theoretical soundness and especially for its neoclassical methodology, the Lange model remains a heuristically important contribution to the blending of planning and markets in a socialist setting.

Four reasons can be cited for the "unsuitability" of the Lange model in a contemporary situation. First, Lange's dual economy emphasized a predominant role for the public sector and a relatively smaller and weaker role for private sector. Moreover, it is preponderantly concerned with public ownership and control, and with the mechanisms for rational allocation of resources under the CPB. In all socialist countries, including the Soviet Union, central planning (although it has no connection whatsoever with Lange's CPB, is considered to be the root cause of the contemporary crisis. Second, as Kornai (1989, 85) points out, living in the "sterile world of Walrasian pure theory" Lange failed to consider the "sociopolitical underpinning of his basic assumptions." The Lange model restricts the CPB's role in the determination of prices based on market signals as demonstrated by movements in prices and excess demand. But the CPB that Lange envisions consists of "reincarnations of Plato's philosophers, embodiments of unity, unselfishness and wisdom," which never "existed in the past and will never exist in the future" (84). We have seen above how bureaucratic unresponsiveness, selfishness, and paternalistic interventions reproduce chronic shortages and mounting wastage in a centrally planned socialist economy. Moreover, even for determining prices based on market signals the CPB would require an army of bureaucrats, who are considered to be the prime beneficiary, and therefore, arch defender of central planning.

Third, in Lange's model enterprises are expected to follow rules "designed by the system engineer" without taking recourse to conflicting interests between the regulators and the enterprise managers. The assumptions that Plato's "philosopher kings" will make the best decisions and enterprises will dutifully carry them out in the national interest contradicts the whole experience of central planning for last six decades. Fourth, the emphasis in contemporary socialist societies, including the Soviet Union, is not in improving the rational allocation or calculation of resources by the CPB, but in dismantling it altogether. If calculation is the only problem, the need for borrowing capitalistic elements in socialist system simply disappears—computers can easily accomplish the job.[23]

On the other hand, the Lange model(s) still contains insights and potential applicability to contemporary reforms under the banners of *perestroika*. First, in Lange's argument, relationship between households and enterprises are integrated essentially through market processes (consumer goods markets and labor markets) in the normal institutional sense of the term. In the Soviet Union, the intended scope for market processes is, of course, greater than this. But it is also true that developing market relations should be easier in interactions between households and firms than elsewhere because the basic foundations already exist. Second, in other areas—land, capital, intermediate goods, money— Lange proposes that the CPB function as a sort of market, raising and lowering prices in response to supply and demand conditions, modified by social aims (such as social costs and benefits, anticipation of effects of interdependencies in the economy, for example that an increase in the demand for automobiles will tend to increase the demand for oil). This notion of quasi-market relations accords reasonably well—in principle if not in precise form—with Gorbachev's concept of a "regulated market economy," that is, markets, but subject to special governmental supervision.

Third, the Lange model includes a government sector where goods are financed by taxation and provided to the citizenry collectively. No doubt, this sector will be substantial in the future Soviet economy. Relative to resources, Soviet provision of such collective goods as health and education is among the largest in the world.

Because this is important for the leadership's legitimacy in a socialist society, it will presumably continue. In addition, new public institutions, such as those to enable monetary and fiscal policy, will be necessary as part of the economic restructuring. Moreover, the public sector will need to face and to some extent meet demands arising from adverse distributive effects emanating from reforms. Fourth, Lange's original model of the thirties envisages that the CPB determine the overall level of investment. In his postwar analysis, Lange (1958) extends the role of central planning authorities to include the allocation of investment resources, though not construction of micro plans for sectors or enterprises. As long as the Soviet economy retains public ownership as the dominant mode in a mixed economy and resists complete marketization of the economy, including determination of overall patterns of economic growth and income distribution, these kinds of decisions will be integral to the new role for (indicative or macro) planning in a reformed Soviet setting.

In the context of market and democracy-oriented socialist economic system two other theoretical models deserve attention: Radoslav Selucky's (1979) "democratic socialism" and Alec Nove's (1983) "feasible socialism."[24]

Selucky's Democratic Socialism. Selucky (1979) uses the expression "labor" self-managed rather than "worker" self-managed model of socialism. By rejecting Marx's suggestion that the working class constitutes a "universal class," Selucky's democratic socialism denounces hegemony as well as the dictatorship of proletariat and allows all working people (not only the laboring class) equal access to management and control of the economy. Selucky's democratic socialism envisages: separation of economic and political power; central planning as an instrument of social regulation and social control over the market; decentralized decision-making; free consumer, occupational, and educational choice; competition and pursuit of self-interest; and self-management in microeconomics. Such a model, Selucky claims, will retain the most valuable socialist principles such as the absence of exploitation, the absence of private ownership of land and capital; representative democratic control over the macroeconomic direction of the economy; and, by blending economic calculation with maximization of social welfare, maximum freedom, and liberty for all people.

Selucky's democratic socialism guarantees individual self-interest, curtails central authorities' detailed planning, provides market mechanism with a greater role, and politically ensures democratic representation in work places and governmental bodies. Moreover, Selucky's model emphasizes "pluralistic political superstructure," that is, multi-party political system. As Howe (1988, 518) points out, Selucky's model presupposes "the flourishing of 'civil society' and its autonomous 'secondary institutions' (such as trade unions, political groups, fraternal societies), apart from and, when necessary, in opposition to the state."

Wherein does this model seem suitable to the expectations of *perestroika*? In many respects, *perestroika*'s programs resemble Selucky's model. These include emphasis on political pluralism, individual self-interest, decentralization of power and dismantling of central plan's authority, emphasis on socially regulated market, and separation of economic and political power. On the other hand, *perestroika*'s drive for private ownership extends well into land, capital and credit (which Selucky's model preserves in the social sector), and *perestroika* envisages diversified ownership involving private and cooperative control over macroeconomic sectors of the economy (which Selucky's model preserves for societal control). Moreover, *perestroika*'s direction is more toward a market-oriented economy than Selucky's model would presumably emphasize.

Nove's Feasible Socialism. Nove's "feasible socialism" also envisages a decentralized market model of socialism. Nove's model emphasizes diversification of ownership of means of production and democratization of economic management and mechanisms of a socialist economy. Nove emphasizes five categories of ownership and management: (1) state enterprises, which would involve large-scale therefore, technologically viable, economies, and would be state-owned and centrally controlled and administered; (2) socially-owned enterprises, or enterprises not centrally controlled or administered, but owned and operated by the enterprise workers autonomously. In this case management presumably will be elected by and responsible to the work force, not to the central plan authorities; (3) cooperative enterprises—the difference between socially-owned enterprises and the cooperatives is that cooperatives would be solely responsible for success or failure of the enterprise, they can even liquidate business, of course within socially regulated directions; (4) small-scale private enterprises, which would allow limited hiring of a few people as decided democratically and work within the limits set by the society (limits could be "on numbers employed, or on the value of capital assets, and could be varied by sector"); and (5) individuals, who would have freedom of occupation and education. Nove's (1983, 207) feasible socialism provides "no provision for any class of capitalism; our small private entrepreneur works, even when employing a few others. There is no unearned income, arising simply from ownership of capital or land."

Nove's model emphasizes market socialism based on private incentives and profit motives, diversification of ownership that allows the state to own most of the means of production and entrusts the state to rely on market forces to set prices. The principal argument of Nove's model is that all kinds of incentives that have traditionally been offered under a market system are not essential for ensuring "socially beneficial efforts"; what is required is to eliminate the "duke" who extorts money because of his ownership rights. The main problem with Nove's model is that state agents themselves may become "powerful extortionists" (Lavoie 1990, 77). Moreover, Nove's model came under fire for deducing generic "human acquisitiveness" from scarcity, basing arguments on Soviet experience of centralized bureaucracy and for claims such as "socialism without commodity production" is impossible to realize (Mandel 1986).

But a comparison of Selucky's democratic socialism and Nove's feasible socialism can be useful at this point. Compared to Selucky's model, Nove's socialism seems to have emphasized more centralized control. In Selucky's model, more decentralization and more democratization occupies a central position. In

Nove's model diversification of property ownership appears to be the core element. Is it possible to combine Selucky's stress on workers' self-management with Nove's stress on diversification of property? Howe (1988, 520) believes that might be asking for "the best of all possible worlds, something actuality is chary of providing." But isn't that what Gorbachev wants to accomplish—political pluralism characterized by a multi-party system (as Selucky emphasizes), and a socially regulated market characterized by diversification of property and democratically decided limits on private ownerships (as Nove proposes)?

These theoretical models provide significant insights for a democratic, decentralized version of socialist economy. At the same time, there are important problems. First, none of them provide a perfect fit. *Perestroika*'s aspirations extend beyond Lange's market socialism, Nove's economic incentives, and Selucky's political pluralism. Second, these models provide general insights, but little operational guidance. Notably, these theoretical perspectives concentrate on the end-state of alternative versions of socialist economy and society; they say little about practical methodologies for making a transition to such states from the present partially reformed, but still heavily centralized, Soviet system.

Reformed Planned Economies (RPEs) and *Perestroika*

Is there any empirical example that can guide *perestroika*'s strategies for transition? The following section sheds light on the experience of the reformed planned economies of Hungary, Poland, and China, to explore guidance for overcoming transitional turmoil in the Soviet Union. Although all socialist economies began with Soviet-type central planning,[25] over the course of last forty years, three substantially reformed socialized economies have emerged where "serious attempts were made to reintroduce market and monetary relations" (Bechtold & Helfer 1987, 18). The experience of these RPEs may provide a guidance to *perestroika*'s efforts to establish a democratic and decentralized socialism in the Soviet Union.

Yugoslav Model of Workers' Self-Management. After breaking away from Stalin and the Soviet bloc, Yugoslavia embarked on an "independent path" of market-oriented, worker managed model of socialism in the early 1950s. The main characteristics of the Yugoslav model include social ownership of means of production, a market mechanism for allocation of resources, worker self-management of enterprises, and decentralization of economic management. Politically, the Yugoslav model operated under one-party rule. Although recently marked by high inflation and unemployment rates, economic performance of the Yugoslav model throughout the last forty years has been no less satisfactory overall than that of the other socialist countries.[26] The history of Yugoslav worker self-managed socialism, however, has had twists and turns. Although basic characteristics, namely social ownership and workers' self-management, remain unchanged, Yugoslav socialism has passed through five distinctive periods: (1) administrative socialism (1945-52), basically a Soviet-type centrally planned economy; (2) administrative market socialism (1953-62), characterized by massive decentralization of the economic mechanism; (3) market socialism (1963-73), marked by institutional changes directed to a greater role of market and monetary forces; (4) contractual socialism (1974-80), characterized by stricter central control and interference; and (5) reintroduced market socialism (since 1982), marked by the introduction of a "Long Run Stabilization Program."

Table 6.1

Performance Indicators of the Yugoslav Economy, 1946-85

	1946-52	1952-62	1963-73	1974-79	1980-85
Rates of Growth					
Gross Domestic Product	2.3	8.3	6.5	3.5	0.8
Industrial Production	12.9	12.2	8.6	5.4	3.0
Agricultural Production	-3.1	9.2	3.1	2.3	0.3
Employment	8.3	6.8	2.4	3.6	2.4
Exports (U.S. dollars)	-3.1	12.0	14.0	11.3	6.5
Imports (U.S. dollars)	3.6	10.1	16.6	10.3	-2.0
Fixed Investments	---	11.5	5.3	0.7	-8.9
Private Consumption	---	6.5	6.4	2.2	-1.0
Retail Sales Prices	---	3.6	13.0	33.3	48.7
Ratios					
Investment/GNP Rate		41.99	38.87	35.21	28.60
Capital/Output Ratio		2.28	2.23	2.64	2.82
Employment/Output Ratio		3.87	2.42	1.86	1.84
Unemployment Rate		5.01	7.58	13.29	14.24
Export/Import Rate		64.66	69.96	63.96	74.81

Source: Mencinger 1987, 103.

The average rate of growth of GDP of Yugoslav economy was the highest (8.3 percent) during the period of administrative market socialism (see Table 6.1). The growth rate was the lowest (0.8 percent) in the fifth period (immediately before and in the immediate aftermath of the reintroduction of market socialism). Growth rates were 2.3 percent during the period of administrative socialism, 6.5 percent in the third period, and 3.5 percent in the fourth period. The highest rate of industrial production (12.9 percent) was achieved during the first period and the rate dropped to 3.0 percent in the fifth period. The first period was characterized by almost full employment, but the rate of unemployment consistently moved upward since 1952 when Soviet-type central planning was abolished. The unemployment rate reached 5.0 percent in the second period and sky-rocketed in the fifth period (14.2 percent).

What are the lessons for *perestroika*? Yugoslav experience demonstrates four specific lessons. First, periods of decentralization (third and fourth, from 1952-73)[27] were marked by a high level of economic growth (averaged 7.4 percent) and the periods of centralization (first and fourth) attained very low growth rates (averaged 2.8 percent). Thus, Yugoslav experience demonstrates a positive correlation between decentralization and economic growth, and a negative correlation between centralization and economic growth. Second, the Yugoslav economy achieved high economic growth without sacrificing the standard of living of the people, demonstrating that there is no necessary trade-off between growth and the standard of living. Third, the Yugoslav model demonstrates that the principal dogma of Stalinist model (that rapid industrialization and central planning are unavoidable twins) need not be accepted unquestionably. Fourth, the Yugoslav economy demonstrates that social ownership of the means of production is not necessarily incompatible with market elements.[28] Fifth and finally, the Yugoslav model demonstrates that a high degree of democratic participation and institutions (i.e., workers' self-management) can be possible without adversely affecting economic growth.[29]

Hungary's Third Way. Hungary also began with a Soviet-type centrally planned economy, but since the early fifties three factors have bothered the Hungarians: poor functioning, even malfunctioning, of central planning and management; deteriorating performance of the economy; and other systemic irrationalities of the Soviet-type economy like disincentive for initiative and innovation. But Hungarians apparently remained convinced that planning is superior to spontaneous market forces and therefore, intensively searched for a "third way" between "preserving and abandoning socialist planning" that would presumably include the key features of planning but still allow "for money, market, flexible prices, and local initiative" (Bauer 1990, 104-05). The beginning of Hungary's "third way" can be traced to the reform movement of 1956, especially the abolition of compulsory deliveries in agriculture in 1956-57 (Kornai 1989, 33).

Three rounds of reforms can be identified in the uninterrupted experiments of Hungarian reforms: the first round began with the famous New Economic Mechanism (NEM) introduced in 1966. The second round can be traced to the late seventies, and the third round began in the late eighties. The first round of reforms substantially curtailed the central plan's authority and jurisdiction by replacing centralized resource allocation by free trade in material inputs and by freeing enterprises from mandatory plan targets and supply quotas. The NEM, however, did not bring any change in formal ownership rights, that is, no significant change took place in the arena of private ownership. The most significant accomplishment of the NEM was that enterprises began to operate on the basis of market principles, that is, prices, opportunity costs, interest rates, and so forth.

As mentioned above, Hungarian experience demonstrates a smooth and progressive movement without major setbacks toward market economy. In the second round of the reforms, therefore, emphasis was shifted to reform the system more fundamentally; the central plan's residual control over enterprises was again curtailed, state monopolies were broken up, the capital market was diversified, private ownership rights were significantly extended, especially in agriculture and housing, and efforts were made to make prices exogenous both to the enterprises and central authorities. With the third round of reforms, more decisive steps are being taken to free market forces from the interference of government authorities. While the first and second round of reforms brought a decisive end to "direct bureaucratic control," they made room for "indirect bureaucratic control" (Kornai 1989). The third round of reforms, characterized by disappearance of the belief in the supremacy of planning, is essentially directed to replace indirect bureaucratic control by market regulation. In the third round, as Bauer (1990, 112) remarks, instead of "the organic combination of planning and market" the idea of a "socialist market economy" or even "market economy without any attribute" gained momentum. Recent developments in Hungary show an unmistakable direction towards what Bauer calls "market economy without any attribute."

Table 6.2
Indicators of Growth in Hungary, 1956-84
(Average annual growth rates in percent)

Indicator	1956-67	1967-73	1973-78	1978-84
National Income	7.2	6.1	5.2	1.3
Investment	10.4	7.0	7.8	-3.0
Average Wage	3.9	3.1	3.2	-1.4
Consumption (Per Capita)	4.4	4.6	3.6	1.4
		1971-73	1973-78	1978-81
Gross Convertible Currency Debt (at current prices)				
On Forint base		13.8	20.0	9.1
On U.S. $ base		23.8	26.8	2.6

Source: Kornai 1989, 78.

The average annual growth rates of the Hungarian economy were 7.2 percent between 1956-67, 6.1 percent during 1967-73, 5.2 percent during 1973-78, and 1.3 percent during 1978-84 (see Table 6.2). As the Hungarian reform process has been relatively smoother, economic performance of different periods cannot be correlated with processes of centralization or decentralization (as could be done, prima facie, in the context of other RPEs). Also, looking at the growth figures of the fifth period, it cannot be argued that progressive intensification in market-oriented reforms contributed to a progressive decline in economic growth. The late seventies and early eighties saw recession around the globe. Moreover, the Hungarian economy has been dismantling one system and building another at the same time, while its economic performance was never very disappointing. Inflationary and unemployment pressures, however, remain problematic for Hungary. The rate of inflation was 1.0 percent to 3.0 percent in the early seventies, 3.9 percent between 1973-78, 7.5 percent between 1978-84, and over 15.0 percent in 1988-89 (see Kornai 1989; Wolf 1990).[30]

What are the lessons for *perestroika*? The Hungarian experience of reforms provides a notable example of a transition from a centrally planned socialist economy to a market economy.[31] It provides three lessons for *perestroika*. First, abolition of mandatory planning is viable even without a fully developed market mechanism. Second, dismantling a traditional central planning system and building a new, more market-oriented system has worked simultaneously in practice. That means a dual economy can function effectively; prevailing structures and institutions do not first have to be totally dismantled. Third, from the vantage point of Hungarian reforms, Gorbachev's reforms, even at the third stage, can be located in between the first and second rounds of Hungarian reforms. Therefore, the obstacles and opportunities that Hungarian reformers are confronting now and faced during the transition from the first round to the second round of reforms may be instructive for *perestroika* at the current stage.[32]

The Four Modernizations of China. China's reform movement, known officially as "four modernizations," which covered the sectors of agriculture, industry, science and technology, and national defense as priority areas for development, can be traced to the immediate aftermath of the crisis of stagnation that followed the so-called Cultural Revolution (1966-76).[33] Chinese reforms have two phases: agricultural reforms (1979-84) and industrial reforms (since 1984).

Sweeping reforms were carried out in the agricultural sector. Agriculture was literally decollectivized and marketization for agricultural products was introduced. Collective lands were leased to the peasants, though ownership of lands remained with the society. Peasants were allowed, however, to sell their land with the permission of local collectives, to own agricultural capital such as small and medium-sized tractors, livestock, trucks, and to sell their produce in open markets, after contractual obligations are met. Beginning in 1984, the drive for partial privatization and marketization was extended to the urban sector. Also, some medium-sized industries were denationalized and transferred to the cooperative sector. During 1978-87, the share of state enterprises in the gross output value of industry declined from 80 to 60 percent, while the share of cooperative industry rose from 19 to 27 percent (see Prybyla 1990, 117).

Other prominent reforms in China include: (1) strengthening enterprises' positions by freeing them from the control and supervision of superior institutions; (2) allowing small-scale enterprises in the private sector, mainly engaged in retail trade and catering; (3) giving a greater role to price and market forces compared to the planning apparatuses; (4) introducing stock exchange; and (5) opening the economy to international markets, especially by establishing four Special Economic Zones in 1980, and opening fourteen coastal cities to foreign capital. The Chinese open-door strategy also envisaged expansion of enterprises on three counts: sole foreign proprietorship, joint ventures, and looser forms of cooperation between Chinese and foreign companies (see Harding 1987; Costa 1987).

Performance of the Chinese economy during the Dengist reform period was dramatically superior to that of pre-reform China. As Table 6.3 shows, average annual economic growth rates in China were 6.0 percent during 1953-78, and 8.3 percent during 1979-84. Growth of national income is indeed dramatic if looked at in annual figures; for example, the rate was 4.9 percent in 1981, then jumped to 8.3 percent in 1982, 9.8 percent in 1983, 13.9 percent in 1984, and 16.2 percent in 1985. The average growth in per capita income was 3.9 percent during 1953-78, but increased to 7.0 percent during 1979-84. In the field of agriculture, performance is particularly notable. Average annual growth in gross agricultural output was 3.3 percent during 1953-78, but jumped to 9.4 percent during 1979-84.

Table 6.3
Average Annual Growth in China, 1953-85

Indicator	Total		Per Capita		
	1953-78	1979-84	1953-78	1979-84	1979-85
National Income	6.0	8.3	3.9	7.0	9.1
Gross Industrial Output	11.3	8.9	9.1	7.6	10.9
Heavy Industry	13.6	6.6	11.4	5.3	9.9
Light Industry	9.1	11.7	7.0	10.3	12.1
Gross Agricultural Output	3.25	9.4	1.2	8.1	10.9

Source: Kosta 1987, 160.

But as demonstrated in Tiananmen Square in 1989, the Chinese reforms lacked a fifth modernization: democratization and political freedom. Besides, as Prybyla (1990) points out, both goals of modernization—marketization of the price system and privatization of property rights—were carried less than half way, and inflation and unemployment accompanied the four modernizations as ugly brothers. The inflation rate was 2 to 3 percent in the late seventies and early eighties, but jumped to almost 30 percent in 1988. However, by 1989 inflation was brought down to less than 10 percent (Wolf 1990). The speed of Chinese reforms slowed in the latter half of eighties; in the industrial sector it proceeded rather slowly, and in the agricultural sector the growth rates began to decline, especially since 1985. Western scholars tend to blame half-hearted efforts and piecemeal reforms for the bleak picture of the late eighties.

What lessons can be derived for *perestroika* from the Chinese experience? We elaborated before on the constraints of the Soviet Union with respect to China. Keeping those in mind, we can identify four specific lessons for *perestroika*: (1) What is important is not "the color of cat, but whether it can catch mice"; (2) Agriculture can be decollectivized, agricultural lands and equipments can be transferred to the peasants, and thereby agriculture (that has been dragging the Soviet economy ever since 1930s) can be turned into a productive sector; (3) An "agriculture first" principle for reforming planned economies is less risky and less painful, because it creates fewer enemies. Agricultural reforms in China indeed resulted in inequality in income distribution, but not in reduction in the standard of living. There have been few big gainers, but not significant losers; and finally (4)

Chinese experience demonstrates eloquently that systemic reform in a planned economy is unlikely without political reforms. Therefore, Chinese experience suggests that by introducing political reforms as preconditions of economic reforms, Gorbachev has indeed facilitated the process of transition.

SYSTEMIC CONSTRAINTS OF *PERESTROIKA*

The preceding discussion demonstrates two things very clearly: blending markets and planning remains a problematic in all the RPEs, both theoretically and empirically; and in all the RPEs market-oriented reforms are associated with inflationary pressures and unemployment. All these remain problematic for *perestroika*, too. But in the context of the Soviet Union, three major systemic constraints are identified that we believe *perestroika* must confront in order to make a transition from a centrally planned economy to a democratic polity and decentralized and market-oriented economy— blending markets and planning, keeping the Soviet empire together, and ideological renovation.

Blending Markets and Planning

Two broad strands of thought can be identified in the context of blending planning and markets in socialist economies. One strand of thought is that planning and markets are incompatible; they represent two different systems having their own internal logic and coherence; therefore, one cannot be superimposed on the other. Proponents of this strand of thought maintain there is nothing like "market socialism or a socialist market," rather there is a market system or a system of central planning and therefore, blending markets and planning creates a non-system in which neither markets nor planning works (Prybyla 1990, 116). They identify three main reasons for the incompatibity of planning and market institutions: (1) the ex ante versus ex post method of pricing in the two systems; (2) the antithetical relation of mandatory instructions and economic freedom; and (3) the inability of state capital to compete successfully with private capital (see Popkova-Pijasheva 1990).

This strand of thought, therefore, emphasizes what can be called an extra-systemic solution to the contemporary crisis in socialist economies. Instead of blending planning and markets or moving to market socialism, they stand for a straightforward transition to either what Bauer (1990) calls "market economy without any attribute" or what Mandel (1986) calls "democratically centralized planning and self-management." They prescribe specific measures that might facilitate transition to either a market or a centrally planned economy.

A second strand of thought envisages an appropriate blending of planning and markets. They believe that plans and markets are not only compatible, but also that "there is nothing specifically capitalist about the market" and "there is nothing specifically socialist about planning" (Selucky 1979, 181). They argue that even in the capitalist countries planning is extensively used.[34] The proponents of this strand of thought view economic systems as a spectrum with the most centralized at one end and pure market economy at the other. Marketization and economic liberalization is a movement away from the planning axis toward the other end. For them, however, neither pure plan nor pure market is desirable. Within this strand of thought, some believe choosing a point along the spectrum, from the pure command economy to fully decentralized market economy, "is independent of other changes in the economy" (Ickes 1990, 55). Still others believe commensurate changes in other fields of economy are equally important for success of such a movement (see Kowalik 1989). Apparently Gorbachev and his associates endorse the latter viewpoint. All decentralized theorists and practitioners and the empirical experience of Hungary, Yugoslavia, and China, as explained above, vividly demonstrate that planning and markets did and can work together, and also, it has been demonstrated that disjointed reforms lead nowhere.

Experience in the RPEs demonstrates that for an appropriate blending between the planning apparatus and market elements in the context of the Soviet Union, reformers will need to confront the following sets of constraints: establishment of required institutions, recasting ownership and control, and controlling unemployment and inflationary pressures.

Institutional Problems. Marketization and central planning have different logics of economic coordination requiring and facilitating their own sets of institutions. Therefore, blending these methods of economic coordination and management poses formidable institutional problems. First, organizational structures suited to a planned economy might not be well-suited for market economy. For example, central planning is essentially hierarchical in character. In order to overcome the problems associated with informational requirements and reduce coordination and transaction costs, central planners tend to encourage vertical integration and larger conglomerations of enterprises. On the other hand, a market economy would, presumably, encourage a movement in opposite direction; numerous small enterprises would compete horizontally for goods and services, both in consumer and product markets. Moreover, as organizational forms in a socialist economy are exogenous in character (imposed by central plan or the state), introduction of market elements affect only the coordination and transaction costs, not the organizational structure. Economic reforms tend to eliminate some hierarchical flows of information, so enterprise managers continue to make decisions on the basis of hierarchical relations because they have to depend on their superiors for both inputs and outputs, and their own welfare.

Second, ideal market economy requires free exit and entry of enterprises, whereas under central planning both entry and exit are imposed from above. Central planning, by emphasizing larger and fewer enterprises, reinforces sellers' markets, that in turn elicit low-quality goods and services and lack of innovation. Greater decentralization of authority to enterprises, in the absence of competition from new entries, might not result in improvement in the quality of goods or introduction of new innovations. Thus, efficacious, market-oriented reforms require provisions to foster entry of new firms. Otherwise, the result of reforms might be unregulated monopoly. Even exit is not based on economic performance of enterprises under central planning. Even if enterprises are proved to be losing concerns, no process exists to ensure exit of the bankrupt enterprise from the market, unless central planners themselves decide to that effect. A redistributive bureaucracy, because of its paternalistic obligations, may continue to bail out inefficient enterprises. In the absence of decontrolled prices, it is hardly possible to measure *khozraschet* (economic accountability) of enterprises. Therefore, in the absence of bankruptcy procedures, marketization might not result in an efficient allocation of resources. Conversely, market-oriented reforms must include bankruptcy institutions and procedures.

Third, marketization in planned economies have resulted in huge inflationary pressures. Also, as demonstrated in the Soviet Union, price reforms are delayed and at the same time enterprises are asked to be economically accountable, ministries are held responsible for overall production of the sector, while enterprises are granted larger autonomy in terms of reduction of central control and planning their own inputs and outputs. Therefore, market-oriented institutional changes must be undertaken to replace central plan's direct control, and to put the economy on indirect, regulatory kinds of economic mechanisms.

Also, one should keep in mind that introduction of market economy in a centrally planned economy does not begin with a clean slate. Neither can such a beginning be delayed until all the remnants of central planning are abolished once for all. The process has to be a simultaneous one: dismantling of central planning and replacing it with market elements. Also the objective would be to ensure state direction in regard to macroeconomic decisions, while leaving market processes to play not only a larger, but also a relatively uninterrupted, role in the microeconomy. What are *perestroika*'s constraints in this regard? *Perestroika* wants to dismantle central planning, and it has already traveled a great distance toward accomplishing this goal; but how far has it laid the foundations for market economy? And what exactly are the market institutions that *perestroika* must institute in order to make a transition to a "regulated market economy"?

For transition to a regulated market economy, according to Brus (1973), a centrally planned system while taking care of fundamental macroeconomic decisions must satisfy two prerequisites: the seller's market phenomena (administrative restrictions and physical allocation of resources) must be done away with. That is, the administration must turn loose of the "second group of decisions" involving the size and structure, sources of supplies and direction of sales, personnel and financial decisions that can be delegated to the enterprises. Second, enterprises must be given "alternatives of choices" in which prices, wages, and interest rates will play "parametric roles" so that physical proportions can be translated into monetary terms, and the structure of output can be translated into the language of price relations. Brus's prescriptions do not seem quite appropriate for *perestroika*'s "regulated market." Emphasizing state ownership of all means of production, Brus, in fact, envisages a model of planned economy with a built-in regulated market mechanism. Such a market mechanism would be rather a mere instrument for adjusting enterprise behavior to the "general preferences expressed in the plan" and for "directing the economic process in a pre-determined manner" (Kowalik 1989, 60). *Perestroika*, as we elaborated elsewhere, has increasingly been taking a radical character that would envisage not the use of market for plan purposes, but use of plans for market purposes.

Perestroika's "regulated market" seems rather more similar in some aspects to Walter Eucken's paradigm of "social market economy." Eucken's model has been "put to test" in postwar West Germany and is believed to have been successful in developing a synthesis between the "people's appetite for material gain and their desire for economic security" and in combining a "functionally competitive economy" with "the Welfare State" (Krasten 1985, 178). If we believe *perestroika*'s "heart" lies in making a transition to such a "functional social market economy" as Karsten (1990, 8) suggests, then Eucken's "structural" and "regulating" principles can provide heuristic guidance to find out how far *perestroika* has proceeded and what now needs to be done.[35]

Eucken's "functionally competitive" social market economy has eight "structural principles" designed to give structure to the economic processes, and five "regulating principles" concerned with providing necessary momentum to the structure. For Eucken, the "structural" and "regulating" principles are complementary; they need to be integrated in a "unified approach." Another important feature of Eucken's model is that unlike Adam Smith, who saw competitive market economy as a spontaneous process characterized by almost noninterference by government, Eucken envisages guidance by government for combining advantages of competitive market with concerns for social justice and equity.[36]

With respect to Eucken's first structural and regulating principles that envisage the state's commitment to a competitive social market economy and reduction and control of monopoly, *perestroika* has made significant progress. Enterprises are being placed on a *khozraschet* (economic accountability) model. They are now responsible for acquiring inputs and selling outputs, for their wages and costs, profits, losses and investments—in other words, enterprises are increasingly facing competition. However, because of delays in price reforms, the *khozraschet* models remain problematic.

In terms of reduction and control of monopoly, no appreciable progress has been made so far. With increasing emphasis on diversification of ownership of means of production and a rapidly growing private, especially cooperative, sector, it can be argued that the process is moving in that direction. But two substantial problems remain: First, no progress has been made in disintegrating many large conglomerates of enterprises where, in the absence of specialization and assurance of supply of necessary inputs, the drive for self-dependency has led to production of all kinds of goods, and therefore monopolization of both inputs and outputs. These large conglomerates, such as Khrunichev Machine Building Enterprise in Moscow, which produces everything from rockets to bicycles, should be divided into separate and more manageable enterprises. Also, legal arrangements should be made for joint-stock companies so that once big conglomerates are dissolved, they could be converted into joint-stock companies in which government might retain some share (see Hewett & Hornik 1990). Breaking up of such gigantic enterprises into many would presumably promote: specialization, freer markets for inputs and outputs, private initiative, and more competitiveness and productivity increases. Second, reduction or control of monopoly would require immediate anti-monopolistic, anti-collusive legal measures akin to the Sherman Act (1890), Interstate Commerce Commission Act (1887), Clayton Act (1914), and Federal Trade Commission Act (1914) in the United States.

Eucken's second set of structural and regulating principles envisages the primacy of monetary and income policies pertaining to stabilization of the value of money, and other legal measures for banking and credit, tax and welfare administration, industrial management, and labor relations. *Perestroika*'s problems are monumental in this respect. The existing bank and credit system in the Soviet Union is simply an adjunct to the state plan. Commercial banks are regulated by the state bank, which in turn is regulated by the state. Those mechanisms of central planning have to be replaced by a new banking system in which the central bank will regulate commercial banks through controls over discount rate, open market operations, reserve requirements, and interest rate manipulations. Such a banking system would envisage the independence of the central bank from state interventions, and commercial banks' operations free from direct interventions by central bank or government bodies or party organs. Such a system can introduce personal checking accounts for average citizens, and thus promote greater and smoother financial transactions and freedom, bring an end to supplying credit to losing enterprises. It could foster the free operation of finance capital in a responsible manner. Establishment of a central bank along the lines of the Federal Reserve Bank in the United States would allow commercial banks to operate on the basis of economic accountability, and extend credits to entrepreneurs to rejuvenate the economy.

By dismantling central planning and introducing market elements, the Soviet government is also resorting to giving up central planning's most sacred contribution: guarantee of full employment and a high level of state-financed welfare. Both will be under fire under market forces. Putting enterprises on economic accountability will result in the closure of inefficient enterprises, rising unemployment, and therefore, poverty for many. Currently, the country hardly has any institutional remedies to such a situation. Therefore, an immediate need would be to create a safety net—unemployment insurance or negative income tax kind of arrangements—as a necessary condition for transition to market economy. Also, legal measures should be in place for fiscal policies pertaining to personal and corporate income taxes. Social regulation of economy would involve not only safeguarding the underprivileged, but also taxing private business and corporations. The Soviet Union hardly has anything like this. Inexperience and indecisive stands on taxes in the context of cooperative enterprises resulted in discord and confusion in the late eighties. Also, with the dismantling of central planning institutions and greater decentralization of power and responsibility to enterprises, existing regulations of business–labor relationships must be recast. Workers' participation and grievance management would require new kinds of industrial democracy and bargaining suited to the needs of a regulated market economy.

Eucken's third structural and regulating principles call for open competitive markets based on prices that reflect true economic costs. These principles would envisage an end to restraints on the demand and supply of goods and services, irrespective of domestic or foreign. Implementation of such principles would mean an elimination of state subsidies to inefficient enterprises and putting enterprises on "hard budget constraint," and abolition of the central plan's directives, mandatory targets, and manipulation of supply of inputs and sale of outputs. This will require a reorientation in production decisions that means bringing an end to sellers' markets and making enterprises responsive to consumer demands. Evidently, the Soviet economy is still far from such a fundamental transition in the behavior of state enterprises, including agricultural collectives. Although *perestroika* emphasizes "full self-accounting," price reform remains unaccomplished. Second, very few enterprises have moved to the first *khozraschet* model, which ensures financial accountability. *Perestroika* allows most enterprises to enter into contracts with foreign agencies and businesses, but still the ruble remains unconvertible. Moreover, the central plan's considerable control remains in force in most of enterprises and products.

Eucken's fourth structural and regulating principles envisage stable and predictable economic policies, which are essential for long-term decisions, and "an integrated countercyclical policy approach" to control short-term economic instability. Clearly, *perestroika* envisages economic policies aimed at a greater role for market economy, but still central planning is needed because market economy, even in principle, is far from stable. As mentioned before, *perestroika*'s economic policies demonstrate an evolutionary character. Also, there have been some twists and turns, as demonstrated in bolder initiative to introduce market economy and price reforms in February 1990, then backing off in fear of the "Polish therapy" in the end of the year, and later in early 1991 again raising prices for some essential consumer goods. Eucken's integrated countercyclical policy approach refers to the fact that pressures from interest groups, or problems like unemployment and inflation cannot be addressed separately, but rather should be addressed synergistically, by exploring the problems in the context of the whole society. *Perestroika*, since its emergence, clearly demonstrates an indecisive position as regards price reforms. Gorbachev and his advisers plainly are worried about the explosive inflation and unemployment that might accompany such reforms.

Eucken's fifth structural principle, that envisages private ownership of the means of production, has clearly been an area of priority for *perestroika*. In the initial stages, initiatives for privatization were relatively mild, but subsequently bolder steps, even sweeping changes, in ownership rights have been made. Clearly, *perestroika* envisages private ownership that extends from private land and plots to manufacturing industry. Gradually, greater and greater concessions are being made for international capital, and reduction of taxes on private business, both foreign and domestic. But still, the Soviet Union lacks special economic zones, has made hardly any headway in terms of sole foreign proprietorships and joint ventures as done in China and central European countries, especially Poland and Hungary. Eucken's fifth regulatory principle calls for depoliticizing and stabilizing the supply of money by linking it to a "basket of commodities." Soviet progress in this regard is essentially disappointing. The Soviet Union continues to "create" money and pump it into the economy as subsidies and credit extensions. That has resulted in "billions of unspent—now largely unspendable—rubles lurking in the shadows of the economy" that can anytime explode as a "giant monster" (Hewett & Hornik, 1990). To stop money printing, the current status of *Gosbank* as an integral organ of the state needs to be replaced by a central bank with independent legal status and constitutional responsibility.

The sixth and seventh structural principles of Eucken's paradigm pertain to fostering greater freedom of entry and exit for enterprises. As mentioned above, central planning not only eliminated all kinds of competition, it also blocked the entry of new enterprises and exit of inefficient enterprises. According to Gorbachev (1987, 105-9), as many as 30,000 national normative acts were in place to control and regulate the activities of public enterprises in the economy. *Perestroika* has made substantial headway in tearing down of many of those cumbersome central plan directives, and for encouraging self-financing of enterprises. But bailing out inefficient enterprises still remains the rule rather than the exception. Also, legal measures for treating bankrupt enterprises still need to be developed.

Recasting Ownership and Control. An important corollary to the problems associated with the blending of planning and markets in the Soviet Union involves recasting of ownership and control that had been absolute monopoly of the CPSU for last seven decades. As mentioned above, by concentrating power and privileges under the guise of a multi-level hierarchical command system and overemphasizing plan fulfillment, party *apparatchiks* and the central planners built up what Winiecki (1990) calls a "strikingly nonexclusive structure of property rights."[37] According to him, the party *apparatchiks* and economic bureaucracy maximized their rents in two interconnected ways: through the principle of *nomenklatura*, and through protracted interference in a shortage economy. The principle of *nomenklatura* allows the CPSU to recommend and approve all appointments for managerial positions. As elaborated before, these appointments and subsequent promotions and placements had always been based primarily on loyalty to the CPSU, not on competence and merit. Second, an economy of chronic shortage allows the central planners to patronize and punish enterprise managers through providing or denying various kickbacks as explained above. Therefore, introduction of market elements into the economy directly challenges the vested interests of both the party *apparatchiks* and the economic bureaucracy. The market not only challenges the party *apparatchiks'* monopoly of over the distribution of privileges, it also threatens discretion associated with higher positions and salaries. The fundamental challenge of market will be against the economic bureaucracy that does not depend "upon the creation of wealth but upon interference in the wealth creation process" (67).

Therefore, recasting ownership and control will require: (1) giving up state's monopoly ownership of the means of production and encouragement of, among things, private ownership; (2) separating the party from the state, thus curbing the privileges of party *apparatchiks* and eliminating the principle of *nomenklatura*; and (3) establishing institutions and legal measures to protect property rights. Steps are being taken to meet all these objectives. But problems remain because dismantling central planning and eliminating *nomenklatura* help neither the ruling class nor the economic bureaucracy. For example, private ownership denounces interference of the state and party *apparatchiks*, market forces are destined to disconnect the bloodline of the principle of *nomenklatura*, separation of party from the state will bring an end to the practice of distributing well-paid jobs to the card-carrying cronies of the CPSU, and market coordination is destined to exterminate economic bureaucracy and, therefore, privileges associated with the shortage economy.

Controlling Inflationary and Unemployment Pressures. Another corollary of the problems associated with the introduction of market elements will be tremendous pressures on inflation and unemployment. As mentioned above, in all the RPEs, market-oriented reforms are almost invariably associated with open inflation, unemployment, and large external imbalances. In 1989, as mentioned before, inflation rates soared to 15 percent in Hungary, 200 percent in Poland, almost 30 percent in China, and well over 1,000 percent in Yugoslavia. Mainly to avoid such a "shock therapy," Gorbachev and his advisers repeatedly have delayed price reforms. As explained before, such inflationary pressures do occur in the reformed planned economies because: (1) actual reforms have been less thorough and comprehensive than initially contemplated; (2) enterprises began to take advantage of increased prices without changing long-ingrained attitudes resulting from central planning; and above all (3) inadequate institutional development has occurred for indirect regulation based on financial instruments like credit, interest rates, and fiscal and monetary policies as explained above. As the Soviet Union hardly has developed such institutional and infrastructural arrangements for financial discipline, similar inflationary and unemployment pressures and large-scale imbalance in payments might occur.

Some scholars assert that such pressures for inflation, unemployment, and imbalance of payments need not be either systemic or a serious threat to market-oriented reforms. Price reforms in a planned economy, Wolf (1990) argues, should result in a "once-and-for-all" increase in the price level because of either reduction or elimination of an already existing excess demand problem. Fundamental reforms aimed at tightening macroeconomic policies, creating financial institutions for strengthening competition and financial discipline, can help control the situation. Therefore, given the experiences of the RPEs, the Soviet Union's cautious strategy to move to price reforms seems logical. At the Twenty-eighth Congress of the CPSU, Gorbachev denounced the idea that market-oriented reforms have to begin with price reforms. Instead, he argued that an appropriate institutional framework, as mentioned above, must be in place before price reforms are initiated. By backing away from the Shatalin's Five Hundred Day program, once again, he demonstrated the same commitment.

This is again a matter of sequencing reforms: RPEs have preferred price reforms before creating financial institutions. Gorbachev prefers financial infrastructure over price reforms. Obviously Gorbachev's strategy is to avoid the "Polish therapy." Some say the Polish therapy worked for Poland. Once the shock of price reforms receded, economic conditions began to improve. Many observers believe an economy riddled by a systemic crisis often is not given enough time for rational sequencing of reforms, and perhaps delay in price reforms is substantially responsible for the continued faltering of the Soviet economy.

Is there an intermediate position, in between large-scale price increases and delays of price reforms? If so, its implementation would help *perestroika* in the transition process of moving toward more decentralized and market-oriented processes. To continue to delay the price reforms leaves unresolved many instances of excess demand, shortages, queues, and prices that are misleading for purposes of rational calculation and efficient resource allocation. To impose massive price reforms, as in the Polish therapy, on the other hand, generates other problems.[38]

One possible intermediate strategy is to undergo the price reforms, but to do so more gradually than in, for example, Poland, and in moderate doses. No doubt this strategy has its disadvantages. Gradual and moderate price reforms postpone the day of marketization. Moreover, moderate price increases, in a regime in which future price increases are expected, might elicit speculation of continued price rises, and therefore foster greater inflation over time than that which might have occurred if big increases were imposed with one clean, fell swoop. The economic disruption of massive price increases, however, and their accompanying provision of windfall distributive effects for some, provide support for an intermediate strategy. In any event, such a strategy might be the only politically acceptable route.

Keeping the Soviet Empire Together

The Soviet Union is a multi-national, multi-ethnic and multi-cultural society of 280 million people which has been tightly controlled and hierarchically administered from the center since the early twenties.[39] Amalgamation of nations, cultures, and ethnic and religious segments has remained a deep-rooted problematic for the Soviet Union since its inception. The 1922 agreement that serves as the basis for the Soviet federation forced integration of various nationalities and cultural entities. The situation was further aggravated by Stalinist policies that deprived several national minorities of their territories and established many nationalities without any cultural and historical links. As a result, interethnic tensions and an enduring sense of dislocation has haunted many of the nationality and cultural-religious groups. Therefore, *glasnost* has unleashed a "veritable Pandora's box in the form of reawakened national identities and unprecedented opportunities" (Clark 1989, 12) for resurgence of dormant feelings and aspirations. And nationalistic movements have gone so far, especially in the third and fourth stage of *perestroika*, that the country itself is virtually on the verge of disintegration.

Consequently, safeguarding the integrity of the Soviet Union constitutes one of the most important systemic challenges for *perestroika*. In 1985, when Gorbachev assumed power, the country was on the verge of economic crisis. Now, after six years of *perestroika*, not only have economic conditions further deteriorated but also the very integrity of the country is at stake. Most of the dramatic events that powerfully threaten the integrity of the country, however, have their genesis in *Perestroika*. In that sense *perestroika* has created its own nemesis, its own monster—the "nationality problem."

Perestroika itself is responsible for amplifying demands for dramatic reduction of central power and greater autonomy on the part of republics and regional bodies. Its economic reforms have called for greater decentralization. This means: (1) recasting of Union-republic relationship so that more and more decision-making powers are shifted away from the center to the republics and regional authorities; (2) republics and regional bodies, having both authority and responsibility, are now better able to address local economic and social needs, and thereby can enhance their credibility and legitimacy; and (3) while central planning was suitable for centralized authority of the Union government, market relations and private initiatives as emphasized by *perestroika*, will be better served by local bodies.

Politically, *glasnost* allows recovery of indigenous art and literature, language and history, exposure of nationality, minority, and religious problems, and ecological and cultural concerns. By revitalizing national consciousness, it helps resurgence of nationalist movements and aspirations. That, in turn, has amplified cries for independence, which, in turn, carries seeds for potential shrinkage or outright disintegration of the country. By denouncing traditional coercive measures and supplementing this with six years of persistent "delegitimization of ideological, political and institutional" structures, *perestroika* has resulted in an all-pervasive crisis of "governance in all important spheres of social activity" (Migranian 1990b). At the initial stages, Gorbachev and his advisers hardly realized that the magnitude of nationalistic, ethnic, religious, and territorial conflicts and resentments would critically contain *perestroika*'s reforms. But at the third stage, with the elimination of the CPSU's monopoly power, declaration of independence or legal precedence of local laws over the Union government in many republics, deterioration of economic conditions, and worsening of ethnic and nationality-oriented violence, *glasnost* and *democratizatsiya* were transformed into a real challenge threatening the survival of Gorbachev and the country itself.

As noted, the nationality issue has its roots in the 1922 agreement that brought non-Russian republics from the Ukraine to Central Asia into the USSR. The mechanism of the agreement remained questionable. Many believe these republics were forcibly welded into the Soviet Union. The republics of Estonia, Latvia and Lithuania were incorporated into the Soviet empire in 1940 following the signing of the Molotov-Ribbentrop pact, and the peoples of these republics believe it was a forced incorporation. Besides fifteen republics, the Soviet Union has numerous ethnic and religious groups. Resentments and conflicts among these groups, which have surfaced under *perestroika* have already taken hundreds of lives.

The nationality question, according to Lapidus (1990), embraced six "structurally distinct" problems stemmed from different "configurations of socioeconomic and cultural cleavages" in the Soviet Union. First, powerful and cohesive national movements in the Baltic republics challenged the legitimacy of Soviet rule over their territories. Second, long-simmering territorial, religious and political rivalries—for example, struggles between Armenia and Azerbaijan over Nagro-Karabakh—fueled conflict with central government. Third, in Central Asian republics interethnic violence having broader socioeconomic and demographic roots, erupted as a spillover of economic grievances into communal violence. Fourth, nonrepublic national groups and other minorities (like Tartars, Bashkirs, and Abkhazians) demanded upgrading of their status to republic level. A fifth problem stemmed from communities (like the Crimean Tartars, Checken Ingush, and Volga Germans) who were forcibly relocated during the Stalinist era. These people demanded historical rehabilitation and restoration of their homelands, requiring redrawing of the map of the Soviet Union. A sixth problem stemmed from the rise of Russian nationalism. Growing intensity of ethnonationalism and anti-Russian sentiment prompted questions involving fusion of Russian nationalism and Soviet imperialism and stimulated chauvinistic and anti-Semitic forms of Russian nationalism. Under *glasnost*, nationality problems have confounded so alarmingly that every sphere of the country and society is profoundly affected.

Perestroika's accomplishments to quell the nationality crisis remain at best modest. The Twenty-eighth Congress accomplished three important objectives. Gorbachev's nationalization policy called for greater economic and political freedom for the republics and redesigning of an agreement for a "Union of sovereign nations." Second, the reconstituted Politburo incorporated members from all fifteen republics; thus, the republics' representation to the center was broadened. And third, new political and legal institutions were created for resolving center-republic conflicts and ethnic disputes. Also, a legal framework was created to allow concerned republics to secede in an orderly manner.

Immediately after the Twenty-eighth Congress, revoking the 1922 agreement, Gorbachev proposed an eight-point program to create a new Union based on voluntary agreement and greater powers for local authorities. This program restricted central government's control to defense, borders, and the KGB; foreign policy and foreign trade; coordination of transport; coordination of market relations, that is, unified monetary policy; personal legal rights and the creation of a national institution to prevent ethnic conflicts; environmental regulation; and guarantees for energy supply to all republics and scientific and technological progress. Local governments were expected to handle the rest autonomously (*Los Angeles Times*, July 21, 1990).

At the fourth stage, revising and upgrading the earlier proposal, in November 1990 Gorbachev outlined a draft proposal for a "Union of Sovereign Soviet Republics," in which each republic was expected to enjoy full authority over its territory as a "sovereign state." Approved by the Supreme Soviet later the same month, the proposal provided for voluntary signing of the treaty by the republics, but denied free exit from the Union. The treaty guaranteed wider access and voice in many policy areas to the sovereign republics but vested ultimate control in the center. It also allowed the republics to form their own budget, determine their own taxes and settle their disputes with the center at a constitutional court. Besides, the treaty provided for a Federation Council composed of fifteen republican leaders and headed by the President of the federation.

Supplementing the provisions of the treaty, the Five Hundred Day program guaranteed the republics "economic sovereignty"; besides their own budget and taxes, republics were allowed to decide forms and methods of privatization, regulate prices for most goods, and restrain center's discretion in financing programs within the republics (CDSP, vol. 35, 1990, 7). In a nationwide referendum held in March 1991, 76 percent of Soviet people approved the draft Union treaty. As mentioned above, six republics boycotted the referendum to press on their demand for independence. Although the referendum strengthened Gorbachev's ability to handle the nationality issue, many republics, that either had declared independence or wanted a new deal remained openly critical of central government's role. To Russian leader Boris Yeltsin the referendum constituted a ploy to strengthen central control over the republics (*Time*, March 25, 1991). Gorbachev insisted on a "transition period" of five years for an orderly secession, but many republics deemed this a tactic to buy time.[40]

Scholars debate the magnitude and depth of the nationality question and the consequent misfortune of the Soviet Union. Some predict that in the face of ethnic hatreds, economic deterioration and political turmoil, the country will either disintegrate or return back to totalitarianism (Kissinger 1991); some believe it will settle down as a small and more stable USSR (editorial of *Los Angeles Times*, May 27, 1990); still others believe a diverse, loose confederation of the USSR could still be established in which the center will be responsible for only defense and foreign policy, some republics could be run from the center, and some (like the Baltic republics) could be given "associated status" that will guarantee them virtual independence (Malashenko 1991). Gorbachev is unwilling to preside over the Soviet Union's disintegration; therefore, his position comes closer to the last option. Yeltsin is willing to settle for a smaller USSR; therefore, the second position conforms to his standpoint. Only the conservatives would like to return to the Stalinist totalitarianism; to both Gorbachev and Yeltsin this option remains unacceptable (more on this issue in the next chapter).

But much depends on whether the Soviet Union can reverse the decline in living standards and improve the consumer goods situation; and workout a confederation in which a sufficient degree of autonomy can guarantee aspirations of republics and nationalistic forces. Economically, the nation is passing through a severe recession and consumer dissatisfaction has reached nadir. Politically, especially at the current stage, with Yeltsin's rise to popularity and sharp decline in Gorbachev's credibility, turmoil and lawlessness has reached the zenith since the inception of *perestroika*. Therefore, at the fourth stage of *perestroika* both economic recovery and political stability of the country remain a formidable challenge to Gorbachev and his associates.

Ideological Constraints

Although the socialist project was distorted and deformed by Stalin for three decades, it accomplished two major objectives: it transformed a backward Soviet economy into an economic and military superpower; and it provided an alternative ideological path for economic development. The contemporary crisis threatens both these accomplishments. Gorbachev, as discussed in Chapter 4, intends to redefine and renovate socialism, to remake the "entire social edifice—from its economic foundations to its superstructure." His ideological reconstruction not only denounces the bulk of Soviet history, but also opens a Pandora's box of ideological questions that are systemic in character.

The Soviet Union has been caught up in a severe crisis at a time when it has already traveled a substantially long distance in its transition to communism.[41] Sweezy (1990) says "the puzzling question is why the regression set in after so many years of social progress and impressive achievements." Because Gorbachev denounces both Stalinism and post-Stalinism as aberrations of the socialist project, he actually discards much of what the Soviet people have done since the October Revolution. To Gorbachev, the War Communism was a period of "war and dislocations," "civil war and intervention from outside" (Gorbachev 1988a). Therefore, Soviet history that conforms to his vision of socialism is relatively short, namely, the period of the NEP (1921-28). Although the NEP provides rich precedents of various elements of multi-sectoral market-mixed economy model of socialism, Gorbachev is indeed starting it all over.

Second, ideological dogmatism of the past, by proscribing economic crisis, depression, business cycles, and so on, as alien phenomena to socialism, undermined and seriously discouraged study and research on the possibilities of such crisis tendencies in socialist economies. Socialist economy was considered a political society par excellence, a society in which politics, not economics, rules. Economics as a discipline generally played a subordinate role in the design and operation of the economy. Also, study of sociology was seriously neglected prior to the arrival of Gorbachev. Zaslavskaya (1988) maintains that not only was the study of sociology as a discipline seriously discouraged, all the previous leadership in the Soviet Union almost completely ignored public opinion and social responses, and hardly emphasized social and economic levers of success.

Therefore, redefining socialism, reorienting ideology to incorporate larger doses of market elements, establishing the rule of law, that is, making a transition from authoritarianism to democracy, and above all, shelving the tantalizing dream of establishing communism for an indefinite period and convincing Soviet people that the whole Stalinist project was not only antidemocratic but also antisocialistic, will remain a systemic constraint. That would require, Gorbachev claims, "remaking of the entire social edifice," remaking of Soviet man and mind, and remaking of socialist institutions.

CONCLUDING REMARKS

The Soviet Union is passing through a crisis of transition; a profound systemic crisis. The magnitude and intensity of the crisis entails systemic transition—a fundamental overhauling of all aspects of the Soviet Union—and thorough transformation of its social, economic, and political spheres, —its base and superstructure—that demands *raskreposhchenie* (emancipation of society and the individual), not *perestroika*. By initiating this process, Gorbachev is trying to manage a revolution, which may be initiated, as he did, but cannot be managed easily, as recent experience indicates. In a sense, Goldman (1987, 9) rightly remarks that Gorbachev's task might be easier if he were starting anew. By embarking on a revolution to dismantle the Stalinist model, Gorbachev has stepped in a number of traps simultaneously.

Economically, he has to dismantle central planning, but he has to accomplish it in the absence of institutions and forces of market economy. He cannot wait until the existing system is abolished or market institutions are created. Second, massive economic restructuring essentially involves dislocations and disruptions. Therefore, a slowdown, even negative economic growth, could result. But he can hardly afford that. He is presiding over a population whose hunger for food is stronger than for democracy. Therefore, he has to accomplish two contradictory jobs simultaneously: growth of the economy and dismantling of the existing economic system.

Politically, *perestroika* aims at a transition to a democratic and humane society, but Gorbachev is not willing to preside over even a partial disintegration of the Soviet Union. But the Soviet Union neither has a democratic society nor the democratic institutions (as will be discussed in the next chapter) to channel the spontaneous feedback of the people. It lacks democratic legal and political institutions. At the same time, in many parts of the country *perestroika* has been misconstrued as a chance for secession. As Gorbachev champions the values of freedom and democracy, he cannot resort to repression and coercion to quell the secessionist movements. Therefore, both politically and economically, dismantling the old system plunges the country into a vacuum, where neither the old system nor the new system under *perestroika* works.

NOTES

1. For example, Goldman (1983, 9) maintains that the Soviet Union, both politically and economically, was in deep crisis, especially since the late seventies, and warned that "the longer economic and political change is postponed, the more violent it is likely to be when it eventually comes." Similarly, Bialer (1986) argued

that in the late seventies the Soviet Union was passing through a "crisis of effectiveness" that, in the absence of immediate and effective measures, could result in a profound "crisis of survival." Soviet sociologist Zaslavskaya (1984) proclaimed the pervasive and systemic character of the crisis in the Soviet Union in her so-called *Novosibirsk Document* in the early eighties.

2. For early reports on crisis see Sakharov, quoted in *Los Angeles Times*, May 15, 1989; Abalkin, quoted in *Wall Street Journal*, July 7, 1989.

3. Making a stagnationist argument, Menshikov (Galbriath & Menshikov 1988) also maintains that international trade patterns (for example, the oil crisis), and changing demand patterns in Western markets are partially responsible for the contemporary crisis of Soviet economy.

4. In late March 1991, however, as mentioned before, the Soviet Union increased the price of a large number of essential consumer items.

5. Kornai (1989, 6-32) has shown that introduction of market and monetary relations in a basically unreformed socialist economy facilitates the ability of the firms to boost prices without effecting a fundamental change in their behavior.

6. Crisis of transition, as defined by the transition theorists, can be understood as a structural crisis—an intra-system crisis that involves a transition from one structure to another within the system (see Szelenyi 1989).

7. It is notable, however, that these measures were ultimately successful in overcoming depression only through the massive government expenditure and controls of the war economy. This leaves unresolved the question of whether a capitalist society in deep crisis can recover under normal peacetime circumstances merely by moderate, intra-systemic reforms.

8. Soviet conservatives (whose position will be discussed in the next chapter) presumably also subscribe to this kind of explanation. For them the contemporary crisis has to do with the economic structure and policies, with the economic and noneconomic environment. Therefore, associating it with the system and rocking the system itself constitutes "thoughtless radicalism." It is an intra-system crisis requiring gradual but determined improvement of the system, not its displacement.

9. Classic examples are the Wobblies and the American Communist Party—both forcibly repressed —who called for capitalism's dismantling. Even President Roosevelt spoke of "male-factors of great wealth" and, in his Philadelphia speech, linked the Great Depression with slavery. But political turmoil in the USSR today is far deeper, more intense, and more complex than in the United States of the thirties

10. However, as Zaslavskaya (FBIS, Jan 19, 1989) points out, increasingly the entire Stalinist and post-Stalinist periods are being reevaluated as "antidemocratic and antisocialistic."

11. Wilhelm (1990, 322) writes:

With the information that has been emerging from the Soviet Union since the advent of *glasnost*, can there really be any doubt that the Soviet economy is in crisis and that the crisis is as severe as Birman [elaborated below] has implied? And can there really be any doubt, given the persistence and severity of the difficulties encountered with Soviet-type economies and their reformed versions, from Beijing to Budapest and Belgrade, that the problem is systemic?

12. Systemic crisis can be understood as an all-pervasive crisis that endangers the system itself. It is a general crisis that cripples the system's viability by affecting its structures, policies, and environment (Montias 1973), its "institutional setting," and "the rules for its functioning" (Drewnowski 1982).

13. See Popkova-Pijasheva (1990). Liberal critics like Fukuyama (1989) and Heilbroner (1989), who conclude that the current crisis represents a "clear capitalist victory" in the competition between socialist and capitalist systems, can also be categorized in this group.

14. Like Hewett 1988; Bialer 1986 & 1987; Colton 1987; Hauslohner 1987; Ofer 1989; and Goldman 1983 & 1987.

15. Prominent systemic theorists that can be categorized in this group include, Kornai 1980; Winiecki 1989a; Staniszkis 1989; Milanovic 1989; Nee & Stark 1989; and Brus 1989.

16. The new system might not be necessarily capitalism, but it must denounce Stalinism, which has outlived its usefulness, must involve a decisive move toward incorporation of some market elements, and must lead to the creation of a market-mixed model.

17. There are scholars who would consider this as a sweeping conclusion. Sweezy (1990), for example, maintains that blanket condemnation of central planning as "intrinsically inefficient" and arguing that it has "outlived its usefulness" constitutes sweeping generalizations. For him, what led to the present plight of the Soviet economy is precisely those aspects that are peculiar to the Soviet experience and not any inherent characteristics of planning as such. Grossman (1987) also points out that the planning apparatus itself was not developed adequately enough to be able to counter the contemporary Soviet crisis.

18. The soft budget constraint imposes uncertainty because the degree and extent of state assistance is decided randomly, and is routinely manipulated by a redistributive state based on subjective judgment. The more enterprises are optimistic that excess expenditure will be covered and additional input demands will be met by the state, the greater will be the impact of the soft-budget constraint (also see Kornai 1986).

19. The credit for the conception of disequilibrium analysis in the context of the socialist economies goes to Richard Portes (1978).

20. Overconcentration of power is understood as the absence of basic democratic and human rights caused by concentration of power in the hands of an authoritarian state and all-pervasive control of one-party rule over the state and the economy.

21. Korotich (1990) compares Soviet citizens' freedom with the freedom of submarine crew members to breathe below water.

22. A short list of other works that remained suppressed for long and only recently came to light because of *glasnost* include: Chinggiz Aitmatov's *The Executioners Scaffold*, Mikhail Shatrov's *Dictatorship of Conscience*, and Boris

Pasternak's *Doctor Zhivago*.

23. The contemporary problems lie elsewhere. As Lavoie (1990, 76) writes: "Markets are not, as Lange thought, primitive precursors to present-day computers, which we can expect to be replaced, eventually, by a centralized computopia. On the contrary, present-day computers can be seen as primitive, central-planning approaches to computation, to be replaced, eventually, by decentralized market approaches."

24. In this connection two other models deserve mention: James Yunker's (1979 & 1986) "rational socialism" and Ernest Mandel's (1986, 1981 & 1979) "democratically centralized planning and self-management socialism." Discussion on Yunker's model has been avoided because it shares many of Lange's assumptions and methodology, and may be subject to the same kind of criticisms. Mandel's model defends centralized planning, which seems to be out of joint with contemporary needs in socialist countries

25. Of course, Soviet-type central planning could not be implanted in toto in all of the Central European countries. For example, in Poland the agricultural sector remained largely beyond collectivization, and Yugoslavia abandoned Soviet-type planning within a couple of years to pursue its independent path.

26. The annual growth rate of the Yugoslav economy was 7.0 percent for 1965 to 1973, and 5.6 percent for 1973 to 1980. During 1971 to 1983, average overall unemployment rate in the country was 9.26 percent (see Mencinger 1987). Inflationary pressures often took chronic proportions: in the early seventies, the inflation rate was less than 20 percent, but during 1986-88, the rate rose to well over 100 percent, and in 1989, the rate accelerated to over 1,000 percent (see Wolf 1990).

27. The fifth period, which shows a near stagnation situation, also incorporates a part of the reintroduced market socialism. We exclude this period for consideration, because the roots of this stagnation might lie with the centralization of the previous period, a point that we shall discuss in a moment.

28. But it should also be noted that the Yugoslav economy has persistently been whipped by inflationary pressures and in the early eighties was plunged into a stagnation crisis. Scholars tend to argue that systemic factors like prevention of the entry of efficient economic units, savings and investment balance, monopolistic economic structure, and government interventions still pose serious threat for the transition to market economy.

29. For details on Yugoslav economy see Horvat 1982; Kowalik 1989; Mencinger 1987.

30. Another significant problem of the Hungarian economy of the eighties is the burden of foreign debt. Between 1981 and 1988, Hungary's foreign debt doubled from $6 billion to $12 billion, which, in terms of per capita debt made it the most indebted nation among the socialist economies (see Schoflin, Tokes & Volgyes 1988). The debt figures are considerably higher in the late eighties and early 1990.

31. Three points deserve mention here. First, Hungary might be at the final stage of such a transition now; therefore, the transition is not yet achieved. Second, transition to a market economy might not be a goal for all socialist economies now

undergoing transition. Third, many scholars, including Kornai (1989), believe that Hungarian enterprises still operate in a condition of dual dependence; vertically they depend on bureaucracy and horizontally on suppliers and customers. Therefore, the soft-budget constraint and weak price responsiveness continue to plague the economy's performance.

32. Of course, no suggestion is made here to the effect that the Soviet Union should follow Hungarian experience. No country should imitate another. The author has analyzed elsewhere how the Soviet Union differs from Hungary and also discussed Soviet leaders' perceptions on Hungarian reforms.

33. It was also marked by the defeat of the so-called 'Gang of Four' in the fall of 1976 and the eventual triumph of Deng Xioping as the new Chinese leader by 1978.

34. For example, capitalist corporations plan (see Galbraith 1979; Murrell 1983), and the capitalist state intervenes into the economy (see Zysman 1983). Similarly, so-called command economies do experience a great deal of bargaining within the system- among the central planners, the branch ministries, and the enterprises (see Wolf 1990). The problem of central planning lies not with the absence of bargaining, but with the absence of competition that results in inefficient use of information (Bergson 1967, 657-58), and irresponsible and undemocratic behavior (Mandel 1986), on the part of central planners.

35. No claim is made here that Gorbachev is contemplating the establishment of an Euckenian "social market economy." As discussed in Chapter 4, Gorbachev's model is a unique one, which has similarities with many empirical and theoretical models, but remains very distinct. For heuristic purposes Eucken's model has been adopted here to facilitate a discussion on the constraints and prospects of *perestroika*.

36. Indeed, "justice" and "equity" are words having controversial meanings and ramifications. Karsten (1985) believes that by striking a synthesis between "negative liberty and positive freedom" Eucken's model conforms to John Rawl's (1971) and Robert Nozick's (1974) theories of justice.

37. The logic and crucial justification of such property structure is simple enough: means of production belong to the state, the state belongs to the working class, the working class is led by the Communist Party; therefore, the Communist Party controls the means of production.

38. This is illustrated by this Polish joke: Under the old regime, ordinary working people couldn't buy the goods because they weren't there (in sufficient quantity relative to market demand); under the new regime, ordinary working people can't buy the (now abundantly available) goods because they are so expensive.

39. The Soviet Union, with 8.6 million square miles area, covers one-sixth of the earth's land and spreads over eleven time zones. It has fifteen union republics, twenty autonomous republics, eight autonomous provinces, and ten autonomous regions, organized hierarchically in terms of powers and responsibilities with the USSR (federal government) at the apex of the pyramid.

40. Such suspicion of the republics stems partly from the fact that the 1977 constitution of the Soviet Union granted broad secessionist rights to its republics,

but because of the central government's overwhelming control those rights remained only on paper.

41. Of course, if Stalinist and Brezhnevian periods are considered periods of "antisocialism," as Gorbachev, his supporters, and academicians like Zaslavskaya and others contend, and therefore, are not incorporated in the Soviet Union's "eternal path to Communism" (O'Brein, 1990), the distance traveled will be extremely short: Lenin's NEP period (1921-28), and Gorbachev's (1985-onward).

7

Crisis of Transition:
Factors and Forces for and
against *Perestroika*

INTRODUCTION

This chapter examines contending perceptions of *perestroika* from both the Western and Soviet perspectives, and then explores the forces and factors within the Soviet Union that foster or impede the processes of Mikhail Gorbachev's economic and political reforms. Gorbachev's vision of democratic, decentralized, and market-oriented socialism, which intends to dismantle the Stalinist command model without making a straightforward transition to Western-style market economy, generated highly controversial perceptions. Consequently, since its emergence in April 1985, *perestroika* has faced both strong support and staunch opposition around the globe. These challenges and opportunities, in turn, have not only graced or hindered the progress of *perestroika*, but have also conditioned its programs and strategies throughout the contemporary transitional crisis in the Soviet Union. Contending perceptions of *perestroika*, in the context of both the Soviet Union and the Western world, are elaborated in Section two. Section three explores the forces for and against *perestroika*.

CONTENDING PERCEPTIONS OF *PERESTROIKA*

Conceptions of *perestroika* range from no reform to radical reform to comprehensive radical reform; from revolutionary process to revolution to counter-revolution (see Dowlah 1990b, 21-29).[1] Amazingly, different and even sharply opposing arguments often lead observers to surprisingly similar conclusions. Such divergent views naturally represent contrasting standpoints of the observers. Moreover, many observers have changed their positions, thanks to the tumultuous events over the course of the last six years. But each one of these strands of thought enriches our understanding of *perestroika*.

Western Perceptions

Western writings on contemporary Soviet Union reveal at least three alternative interpretations. According to the first interpretation, *perestroika* is "only a palliative, a half-measure" that amounts to "an impressive-appearing but, in reality, only partially and largely ineffective policy of liberalization" (Zemtsov & Farrar 1989, xi). As the Soviet Union under previous leaderships largely missed the technological revolution and failed to move from the industrial to the post-industrial phase of modernization, the new leader Gorbachev, by emphasizing accelerated intensification in the economy, has actually been trying to reform the economic system by changing national priorities and "making the [economic] system work better" (Hardt & Kaufman 1987, xi). According to this interpretation, Gorbachev neither intends to change the Soviet socialist system, nor endeavors to usher in a revolution for its overall transformation. The goal of *perestroika* is rather modest, designed to effect changes within the system, to inject some flexibility and dynamism into the stagnant Soviet economy. As Brezezinski (1989, 59) claims, what Gorbachev plans to accomplish is "not to overturn the system but to rationalize it."

According to these writers, *perestroika* hardly envisages a fundamental break with the previous reform efforts in Soviet history. They emphasize that although Gorbachev has been struggling to open-up the Soviet society and has been making rather desperate attempts to decentralize highly centralized management of the economy, *perestroika*'s reforms fall far short of a revolution because they "retain or enhance strong central control over the general structure and direction of economic activity" (Hewett 1989a, 16). These writers are suspicious about the lasting impact of *perestroika*, and contend that in the Soviet Union party and state leaderships were often associated with similar efforts in the past. The previous reform attempts, they argue, "left behind a sense of frustration and disillusionment" (Jermakowicz 1988, 111) within three to four years of their initiation.

According to some writers, *perestroika* could even be found wanting as an attempt at genuine reform aimed at establishing a socialist market economy. Hohmann (1987, 31) maintains that Gorbachev's reform sharply differs from the concept of a socialist market economy; he rather envisages a "relaxed and rationalized planned economy which attempts to make more use of market mechanisms." Although Gorbachev has gone further than any Soviet reformer before him, his reforms have been "restricted to the relatively subordinated instrumental sphere of activity, which revolves around changing or improving economic mechanisms" (Lenches 1990). Gorbachev's reforms, writes Issacson (1989, 57), "while radical, are nonetheless, carefully circumscribed." Similarly, analyzing *perestroika* from a Marxian view of revolution, some writers maintain that in Gorbachev's rhetoric, "revolution" need not be taken literally. Draper (1988, 292) asserts that if *perestroika* stands for revolution, from a Marxist point of view, its efforts should be directed toward overthrowing the existing ruling class and replacing it with another class. As Gorbachev does not intend to replace the existing ruling class by another class, these writers argue that *perestroika* does not constitute a revolution.[2]

A second strand of thought conceives the phenomenon of *perestroika* in the context of Soviet history. This view, emphasizing the revolutionary undercurrents implicit in Gorbachev's reforms, affirms *perestroika* as a revolutionary process of transformation. These writers characterize Gorbachev's reforms as "substantially more comprehensive" than earlier reform efforts, conclude that *perestroika* is "much more radical," and postulate that it stretches far "behind economic mechanisms into associated processes of power and participation" (Elliott 1989, 35) in Soviet society. This view deems that Soviet society is undergoing a serious transformation that challenges traditional political rigidity, intellectual petrification, and ideological dogmatism. To them, Gorbachev's reforms are "really tantamount to sudden revolutionary change" (Galbriath & Menshikov 1988, 52) that strives to build a new system instead of preserving the old one.

Some writers of this strand of thought believe that *perestroika*'s challenge goes beyond Stalinism or post-Stalinism, and encompasses Leninist legacies. They maintain that *perestroika* redefines the socialist project itself, that *perestroika* constitutes a revolutionary phenomenon (see Lapidas 1989; Scanlan 1989). Although they firmly believe that *perestroika* connotes a revolutionary process, or at least marks the genesis of a revolutionary transformation, they underscore that such processes are aimed at consolidating socialism, not replacing it by capitalism. As Issacson (1989, 57) remarks, "Gorbachev is not marching headlong to capitalism but is attempting to reinvent Marxism by creating socialist markets, socialist competition and cooperative ventures."

A third group contemplates that *perestroika* constitutes nothing less than a counterrevolution. They tend to argue that if *perestroika* stands for a revolution, then certainly it negates the October Revolution. Essentially this interpretation presumes that there cannot be another revolution in the Soviet Union without negating, or at least challenging, the October Revolution. These writers, mainly Western non-Marxist writers, especially journalists, anticipate that Gorbachev is moving away from socialism (Heilbroner 1989). Accepting Gorbachev's claim of revolution at face value, they conclude that *perestroika* stands for a counterrevolution in the Soviet Union.[3] Swayed by the unprecedented opening up of Soviet society, unflappable liberalization of the economy, and unflinching dismantling of the centralized-bureaucratized system since the assumption of power by Gorbachev, these writers believe that socialism as an ideology has "proven illusory" and that the ambitions of the socialist world are "anachronistic in the modern world" (Kaiser 1988, 112). These writers believe *perestroika* marks the "end of a cycle of history" (Unger 1989), if not "the end of history" (Fukuyama 1989).

Within this strand of thought another group conceives of *perestroika* as a counter-revolution, but builds their reasoning on a different foundation. The former group characterizes *perestroika* as a counterrevolution because it is moving away from socialism and toward capitalism. The latter group, on the other hand, defends Stalin's command model of socialism, and, by equating Stalinism and socialism, accuses Gorbachev of repudiating Stalinism, and therefore repudiating socialism itself. These writers postulate that *perestroika* manifests a negation of socialism, and that by throwing away Stalin's command model, Gorbachev is actually trying to abandon socialism itself. Here again are those who argue that the failure of the Soviet socialist system actually represents failure of Stalinist socialism, which, in their opinion, instead of freeing workers from exploitation and alienation, actually constitutes a travesty of socialism, and under a highly organized elitist leadership depoliticized and alienated workers from the production and governmental processes (see Harrington 1989; Howe 1988).

Of course there are Soviet observers according to whom Gorbachev is not really a reformer at all. They find no evidence whatsoever that the new leadership's attitude toward the classical Stalinist economic system and the post-Stalin political system contains criticism of its foundation (see Gunlicks and Treadway 1987). These writers, however, acknowledge that Gorbachev is making determined efforts to revitalize the country's stagnant economy, and indeed trying to restructure it. They surmise that Gorbachev's intention is to achieve that transformation by combining new leadership with more effective policies. These efforts, they assert, do not constitute a reform or a revolution, because these reforms neither intend to overthrow the Stalinist model, nor aim at dismantling the superstructures of bureaucratic administrative and economic machineries. There is, indeed, a large disparity between *perestroika*'s rhetoric and actual accomplishments.[4]

This strand of thought enjoyed little support until the end of 1989, but especially since early 1990, at the third and fourth stages of *perestroika*, their arguments have intensified and apparently gained momentum. At this stage disparities between the rhetoric and the realities, fueled by Gorbachev's antisecessionist policies, economic failures, and increasingly closer association with authoritarian elements, brought about the sharpest criticisms to date for *perestroika*'s policies and programs. The prime issue at this stage is whether *perestroika*, or for that matter Gorbachev, has outlived its usefulness. Scholars differ here, too. According to Reddaway (1990), Gorbachev's vision has increasingly proved uninspiring or off-target to many Soviet people, and, combined with some apparent mistakes on his part, has led to an irreversible decline in his authority, which, in turn, makes the success of *perestroika* tremendously difficult, if not entirely impossible. Brown (1990), on the other hand, argues that although a one step back, two steps forward strategy resulted in confusion, ambiguities, and uncertainties, Gorbachev still possesses political acumen, tactical flexibility, and international prestige, which could be of great use for transforming the command economy and monist polity into a market economy and pluralist democracy.

Soviet Perceptions

As *perestroika* struggles to dismantle the Stalinist model and introduce a market-mixed economy, quite expectedly it has generated mixed feelings and controversial perceptions within the Soviet Union. Indeed, the Soviets are now in the grip of profound and widespread changes.

Essentially pro-reform intellectuals, whom Shlapentokh (1988, 146-148) calls liberal-Marxists, view *perestroika* as a genuinely revolutionary phenomenon.[5] They believe under the auspices of *perestroika* a "genuine psychological revolution" has already occurred in the country. The conservatives, whom Shlapentokh calls Brezhnevian, defend the existing political order, fear destabilization of the state and party in the success of *perestroika*, and therefore challenge its reforms. Conservatives look at *perestroika*'s programs as deviations from socialism, and frighten Soviet people "with visions of anarchy, the resurrection of capitalism, and total collapse." Neo-Stalinists, who otherwise represent dynamism and stand for rejuvenation of society, criticizes *perestroika*'s reforms. They want protection of the political system and public ideology, and therefore specifically denounce *perestroika*'s thrust to challenge the system and weaken the legitimacy of Soviet ideology. They argue that exposing societal flaws hurts Soviet patriotism, weakens feelings of pride in Soviet society and significantly undermines Soviet prestige in the world. They argue that by publicizing negative phenomena as being endemic to Soviet society, *perestroika* encourages further deformation of Soviet society and ideology. They emphasize a "businesslike approach" to solving the problems of inefficiency, low productivity, alcoholism, and corruption without resorting to fundamental transformation of Soviet society and polity. Therefore, their position is largely similar to that of the conservatives.

Until the Twenty-eighth Congress (held in July 1990), two extreme perceptions of *perestroika* prevailed within the CPSU. Conservative leader Egor Ligachev emphasized less radical reforms for improving the economic mechanism, tightening discipline, fighting corruption and alcoholism, and so on. Ligachev championed traditional Marxist values; to him, so-called "black spots" in Soviet history do not cancel out the USSR's glorious past or the importance of Stalin's contributions. Ligachev strongly opposed *perestroika*'s efforts to end the CPSU's monopoly power, the trend toward a multi-party political system, extension of private property rights, and separation of political institutions from the administrative apparatus of the country. Ligachev, who was also a member of the Politburo until 1990, believes *perestroika* discards many of the Soviet institutions that are fundamental for Marxism-Leninism.[6] For him, *perestroika* envisages a movement away from socialism. It should, however, be noted that Ligachev does not oppose reform of the system or party as such; he emphasizes the orthodox Soviet Marxist tradition and wants to press ahead with careful reforms that do not challenge such an orientation.

Another extreme perception of *perestroika* is championed by Boris Yeltsin, who represents the radical viewpoint. Yeltsin, who remained critical mainly of the momentum of change initiated by *perestroika*, dramatically resigned from the CPSU itself at the end of the Twenty-eighth Congress of the CPSU. To Yeltsin, who was elected chairman of the Russian Federation's parliament in June 1990, *perestroika*'s programs and policies fall short of the challenges and demands of contemporary Soviet society. Yeltsin, an outspoken opponent of Communist Party privileges, challenges orthodox Marxist-Leninist values as represented by Ligachev and conservatives. Yeltsin stands for transition of the Soviet economy into a market economy, and transformation of the Soviet political system into a multi-party political pluralism. Yeltsin accuses Gorbachev of "indecisiveness," "continuous compromise and half-measures" (*Time*, June 11, 1990). He considers *perestroika* as not radical enough given the desperate situation in the country. Indeed, until the end of 1990, his concern was not with the vision of *perestroika*, but more with the pace of its change and implementation. He believes that if democratization of Soviet society does not proceed very rapidly, political developments within the country may lead to a fate similar to that of the Central European communist parties.

Yeltsin, however, has gradually intensified his position and distanced himself from Gorbachev and his policies. In February 1991, in yet another dramatic move he accused Gorbachev in a nationally televised program of deceiving the Soviet people by failing to implement radical economic reforms boldly and decisively. Yeltsin is also critical of Gorbachev for accumulating enormous personal power, which he believes is indicative of an imminent dictatorship, and therefore, threatens burgeoning democracy and decentralization in the Soviet Union (see *Time*, March 4, 1991).

Such polarization of opinions is also taking place among the conservatives. Hardline members of the CPSU, senior military and civil officials including KGB, and nationalist forces that stand for national integration and continuation of past privileges and power, are also marshalling their strength and influence. With growing disorder and tensions in center-republic relations, proliferation of lawlessness, and secessionist tendencies, the position of the conservatives has also further solidified.

Polarization of these countervailing forces, along with overall deterioration in economic and political situations within the country, also provoked sharp questions among the Soviet people about the usefulness of *perestroika* and Gorbachev. Until the end of 1990, Gorbachev stood at the center, walking a tightrope between his more radical economic advisers and conservative defenders of centralized authoritarian methods in the party, army, secret police, and government and industrial bureaucracy. The need to placate the conservatives has increased recently because of tendencies toward conflict and secession in several of the republics. Migranian (1990a) argues that by initiating political reforms first and economic reforms next, Gorbachev indeed committed a blunder, but although that sequence cannot be reversed, Gorbachev's usefulness has not finished yet. At this stage of the transition, Gorbachev would be very useful in preventing the transition from being violent, and facilitating marketization and democratization processes by orchestrating a partial dissolution or a confederation of the Soviet Union.

Beyond such controversies and approaches, especially due to the policies of *glasnost*, the entire Soviet history is currently being reinterpreted more vigorously than ever before. Especially in late 1990 and early 1991, political processes like elections, processions and movements, as initiated under *perestroika*, are directed to organize populist protests against specific political incumbents at all levels of government; ideological trends are being polarized into contending streams of conservatism, liberalism, and radicalism; and these populist movements and ideological polarizations are being gradually transformed into political parties and electoral coalitions. The next section highlights how these standpoints translate into challenges and opportunities for *perestroika*.

FRIENDS AND FOES OF *PERESTROIKA*

By envisaging a sweeping transformation of all aspects of Soviet society and polity, *perestroika* affects everyone everywhere in the Soviet Union. From the men on the street to the men who run the nation, commonly known as *apparatchiks*, none is immune to *perestroika*'s changes. Quite naturally, it does not affect everyone equally and evenly; it has (or has created) its friends and foes, supporters and adversaries.

Zaslavskaya (1988, 255-80) identifies eight different perceptions of *perestroika* in the Soviet Union based on their group affiliations. The first group, which she calls ideologists and movers of *perestroika*, conceive of *perestroika* as a radical revolutionary program, which, they think, is both necessary and timely for the country. Gorbachev and his supporters, pro-reform intellectuals, journalists, liberal politicians, and so on, can be categorized in this group. Their viewpoints are similar to Gorbachev's as we have highlighted above. A second group, the followers of *perestroika*, is composed of "the most progressive, energetic, and creative part of Soviet society" who conceive *perestroika* as a democratic and humanitarian vision aimed at establishing "socialist justice." A third group, the social allies, looks at *perestroika* essentially as a reform process aimed at making the existing system work better. A fourth group, quasi-supporters of *perestroika*, is composed of "leading cadres of the country," who are ready to "support any master." This group views *perestroika* neither with enthusiasm nor resistance. A fifth group, the watchers, essentially views *perestroika* as just another reform effort in their country. "Each tangible success [of *perestroika*] reduces their skepticism, each failure [of *perestroika*] refuels it." A sixth group, the neutrals, distinguished by their "social passivity," have developed no opinion about *perestroika*. A seventh group, the conservatives, who mainly defend the Stalinist command system, brand *perestroika* as "antisocialist," but do not necessarily imply a counterrevolutionary phenomenon. An eighth group, the reactionaries, is composed of orthodox dogmatic socialists, who are "basically alienated from Socialist and humanist values," and try to portray *perestroika* as a counterrevolutionary phenomenon.

Alexander Bovin (1989) identifies three groups that are resistent to *perestroika*: (1) those blinded by ideological blinders, a small segment of Soviet population who think Gorbachev is moving away from socialist path; (2) those who stand to lose personal power and privileges, a wider segment of the population whose high material standard of living is based on authority, not on responsibility; and (3) those too stupid to restructure themselves, a small segment of Soviet population who because of their "ingrained habits" are incapable of working in a new way. Zaslavskaya (1990, 194-95) identifies officials nominated by the CPSU and working in the political administration, and workers in the distributive and service sectors, as the main enemies of *perestroika*.

The following subsections examine the strength and weakness and respective positions and constituencies of major organizations and institutions, interest groups, and clubs that either amplify or defy *perestroika*'s economic and political reforms.

Communist Party *Apparatchiks*

At the initial stages, as Gorbachev sought to make the system work better, emphasis was on decentralization, on freeing enterprises from the control and interference of central ministries and local party *apparatchiks*. Therefore, the local level *apparatchiks* were directly affected; they largely lost their "petty tutelage" in controlling appointments of enterprise personnel and incurred an unprecedented loss in status and privilege that emanated from intervening in the operation of enterprises. Naturally the losses made them unhappy about *perestroika*'s reforms, but Gorbachev had the rest of party with which to build his constituency. With the elimination of Article 6 of the constitution that guaranteed the CPSU monopoly over power, and with bold actions taken in the aftermath of the Twenty-eighth Congress, *perestroika*'s challenge even extended more decisively throughout the party.

The Twenty-eighth Congress, as elaborated before, brought a formal end to the CPSU's direct control over state-machineries; the CPSU has been thrown wide open to competition for power on the basis of persuasion and ideological acceptance by the people. Thus, the *nomenklatura* principle that allowed the CPSU to control appointments of managerial positions came to a formal end. Also, as a result of the Twenty-eighth Congress, the CPSU Politburo lost its direct control over the administration of government. Therefore, those who want to sustain their traditional rights and privileges (the conservatives) characterize *perestroika* as "blind radicalism."

Conservatives oppose *perestroika* because they do not think the Soviet Union was struck by as severe a crisis as Gorbachev and his advisers envisaged. From the conservatives' point of view, the decline of the early eighties required "new tactics rather than new strategy" and *perestroika*'s strategies are "necessarily destabilizing" (Borcke 1989, 21). They threaten not only the socialist project but also the integrity of the Soviet Union itself.[7] Of course, radicals, led by Yeltsin, on the other hand, find that still the CPSU still occupies a huge amount of real estate[8] and still commands *nomenklatura* privileges and benefits not earned by a person's own labor, and thus they demand elimination of *nomenklatura* principles and privileges, nationalization of CPSU properties and more radical economic and political reforms aimed at multi-party political pluralism and market economy. Both conservatives and radicals stayed within the CPSU until the Twenty-eighth Congress.[9] But at the end of the Congress, both conservatives and radicals began to openly oppose *perestroika*. Thus, the doors for real multi-party political pluralism have been opened.

The Twenty-eighth Congress has accomplished three helpful objectives for *perestroika*: (1) it has given a clear mandate for Gorbachev's programs and policies; (2) the Communist Party Politburo was reconstituted by incorporating fifteen new members (taking one from each republic), and electing a central committee with more pro-*perestroika* forces;[10] and (3) this Congress began the historic process of separating the party from the state administration.

Since the Twenty-eighth Congress, three important institutional developments have furthered political pluralism and democratic establishments in the Soviet Union, and thereby diminished the importance of the Communist Party *apparatchiks*. A new treaty for the Union based on voluntary membership of the constituent "sovereign republics" has been enacted; the treaty proposes a new office, the "Council of the Federation" composed of the presidents of the republics and vested with the power of the central policy-making body of the Union; and a presidential council, which replaced the former council of ministers under the prime minister, directly appointed by and responsible to the president of the Union. While the presidents of the republics may be elected directly by the citizenry or indirectly by the legislatures of the republics, the president and vice-president of the Union have to be elected by the citizenry (see Brown 1990, 151-152).

The Intelligentsia and Informal Organizations [11]

Gorbachev's policies, especially *glasnost*, have a very profound appeal among the members of the intellectual and scientific community. *Glasnost* allows them greater criticism of the Soviet past and present, openness to the outside world, and freedom of press, speech, and publication. Above all, absence of censorship and elimination of restrictions on associations and assemblies allow them to mobilize opinions, organize movements and influence governmental processes. *Glasnost* has shattered the traditional taboos and reconstituted the relationship between the regime and the society. It has fundamentally challenged the traditional instruments of control—ideology, propaganda, coercion, and censorship—and has already laid the foundations for legitimation of democratic governmental processes and institutions. Therefore, the members of the intelligentsia were initially enthusiastic supporters of *perestroika*. But at a later stage, *glasnost* turned into "a genuine public opinion in the original sense of the word—a controlling agency of society" (Borcke 1989, 37) and resulted in greater diversity of intellectual opinions.

Such diversification, in turn, found expression in a myriad of informal organizations and associations. Brovkin (1990) believes that formation of informal organizations was sparked by the conservative challenge to *perestroika* as manifested in Nina Andreeva's letter.[12] Tarasulo (1989, 128-29) identifies three principal reasons for the sprouting of informal organizations during the Gorbachev era: (1) during previous regimes party leadership seriously neglected ecological concerns, and industrial development led to serious environmental problems; (2) the official Communist youth group (*Komsomol*) and other official organizations have been thoroughly discredited in the eyes of Soviet youth;[13] and (3) under *glasnost*, liberalized conditions allowed the people to organize without fear of oppression. Among a myriad of informal organizations, associations and clubs, the following deserve mention.

Federation of Socialist Clubs (FSC). The FSC's agenda is reminiscent of the Mensheviks' political programs of the twenties. It represents informal organizations committed to antibureaucratic and anti-KGB attitudes, widespread and genuine democratization, and a workable combination of democracy in politics and socialism in economics. They demand market socialism, emphasizing regulations to safeguard workers' interests. Among diverse opinions and interests, members of this federation share one thing in common: they believe that the system created by Stalin has nothing to do with true socialism. To them, like the Mensheviks in the 1920s, democracy and socialism are inseparable. Since Soviet socialism is not democratic, it is not socialism, either. The FSC acknowledges *perestroika* as the beginning of a revolutionary process aimed at the establishment of democratic principles of socialism. But FSC is against a "liberal interpretation" of the reforms and is concerned with widening of social inequality and privileges for the technical elite. Therefore, FSC's support to *perestroika* is conditional; reforms are all right as long as they are circumscribed. They are opposed to widespread privatization and marketization.

Popular Front (PF). Popular Front champions demands for radical reforms and national autonomy, and stands for a liberal interpretation that the FSC detests. Their demands include the following: massive democratization, exposure of Stalinist crimes and widespread peoples' participation in the local governmental processes. They also demand a quickening of the pace of economic reforms and profound democratization of Soviet society. They emphasize establishment of a rule of law, institutions and mechanisms to hold government accountable to the people, abolition of the principle of *nomenklatura* and the vestiges of Stalinism, introduction of multi-party political pluralism, and dismantling of the Communist Party's monopoly power and other privileges. Initially the PF constituted a rather radical wing of *perestroika*, but with Yeltsin's resignation from the CPSU at the Twenty-eighth Congress and subsequent distancing from *perestroika*, the PF is gradually acquiring capabilities to organize Union-wide political opposition under Yeltsin's leadership.

Moscow Tribune. Moscow Tribune Club forms what Brovkin (1990) calls "loyal opposition" to Gorbachev's *perestroika*. Among others, historian Roy Medvedev, human rights activist Andrei Sakharov, populist leader Yeltsin, and sociologist Zaslavskaya belong to this group. Their preponderant preoccupation is with democratizing electoral law, broadening the rights of nationalities, disengaging bureaucracy from economic management, and passing specific legislative proposals relating to ecological concerns.

Memorial Society. Memorial society is similar to Popular Front in its basic intellectual outlook and political views, but it is devoted to profound de-Stalinization and to commemorating the victims of Stalin's repression. Major objectives of this society include the following: establishment of a monument, a library, and an archive depicting the memory of victims of Stalinist rule. The society wants to create an oral history library, based on interviews on collectivization, the purges, the war, and executions. Memorial's main concern is to reveal the truth about the past, to rethink and rediscover not only Soviet but also Russian history.

Democratic Union (DU). Democratic Union, like the PF, stands for a transition to a market economy, the rule of law, and a multi-party system. For DU, *perestroika* is indecisive, full of half-measures and uncertain standpoints. For them *perestroika* stands for restructuring, but what is required is replacement of the system itself. They criticize the totalitarian state and centrally planned economic system as established after the October Revolution as an "omnipotence of the *nomenklatura*" and deprivation of the common masses of their political and economic aspirations. While *perestroika* denounces the Stalinist project of socialism, the DU condemns the whole project of socialism and rejects the entire Soviet system of government and economy. It reflects the views of frustrated young people and intellectuals who believe that little has been changed so far and little can be done under existing conditions.

Pamyat (Memory). *Pamyat* represents a sharply different organization known for its antisemitic thrust. Also known as Russian Patriotic Organization, this group differentiates itself from other parties by its attacks on: (1) nationalistic demands of other Soviet peoples, (2) Western influences and Western orientation of Soviet foreign policy; and (3) underrepresentation of Russians in Soviet government and culture. Earlier, its demands included preservation of Russian historical monuments, Russian villages and customs, dialects, and traditions; but gradually, it has intensified in the direction of Russian chauvinism, xenophobia, and rabid antisemitism. *Pamyat* condemns communists and Jews for the "misfortune" of Russia, and attacks the whole project of Soviet socialism as a Marxist-Jewish conspiracy. *Pamyat* has followings in many big cities in the country. *Pamyats* are extremists; to them, their "motherland is in danger," and only antisemitism and Russian chauvinism can save the country (Petrov 1989, 148-49). Gradually *Pamyat*'s attack has been shifted more and more to antisemitism.[14] *Pamyat* endorses *perestroika* partially, but both *Pamyat* and *perestroika* are skeptical of each other.

Islamic Democratic Party. Islamic Democratic Party (IDP), formed by the Muslim militants[15] of southern republics of the Soviet Union, surfaced in August 1990. Essentially a religious-ethnicity-based organization, IDP demands a "completely sovereign state [based on Muslim law], politically, economically and culturally" (Dadakhan Hassanov, chief of IDP, quoted in *Los Angeles Times*, August 6, 1990). Other Muslim groups, including the Islamic Revival Party (IPR) based in the Volga basin, demand greater autonomy, but IDP, based in Turkestan,[16] seeks a coordinated, nonviolent Islamic revolution in all Muslim areas. IDP's strategy is to unite all Muslims of the Soviet Union and then train them in the "spirit of Islam," and through a peaceful revolution establish a separate Muslim state in Central Asia. IDP, basically a secessionist movement, constitutes yet another threat to Gorbachev and *perestroika*.

All the organizations mentioned above, especially after the Twenty-eighth

Congress, seem to be moving in the direction of formation of political parties.[17] In late 1990 and early 1991 such polarization resulted in consolidation of power and support bases for both conservatives and radicals. The conservatives, that is, Communist Party members, civil and military bureaucracy and reactionaries, capitalized on the issue of possible dissolution of the Soviet Union and called for strict maintenance of law and order and economic stabilization. The radicals, mainly led by Yeltsin, demanded bolder legalization of private property including land, rapid transition to a market economy, and are willing to grant independence to some republics and form a loose confederation of the rest of the Soviet Union (*Time*, March 25, 1991).

Economically, by withdrawing his support from the five hundred day program and opting for piecemeal reforms in October 1990, and politically, by increasingly leaning toward the conservatives since the early 1991, Gorbachev has entered into another stage of his tumultuous career. As in previous stages of *perestroika*, Gorbachev's mission is fraught with powerful challenges and obstacles. Although his primary concerns at this stage—safeguarding national integrity and restoring order in the country—come closer to the standpoint of the conservatives, because of his radical policies at the earlier stages of *perestroika*, conservatives find it increasingly uncomfortable to trust him. On the other hand, radicals obviously conceive Gorbachev's current position as a betrayal to their aspirations and are increasingly getting hostile to his leadership. This disappointment is rapidly being translated into support for Yeltsin, who holds Gorbachev responsible for the current economic and political disarray of the country.[18] Moreover, Yeltsin obtained huge support for a directly-elected presidential position for the Russian republic during the referendum held on March 17, 1991. According to media reports, Yeltsin has a great chance to be elected to this position, and such election would definitely enhance his leadership ability, and compared to the appointed position of the president of the Soviet Union, will give him wider credibility. But again, it should also be noted that Yeltsin is still far from uniting the splintered and squabbling opposition forces within the country to organize a credible opposition to the CPSU. On the other hand, Gorbachev's current alliance with the conservatives might be a tactical maneuver: It is an alliance that might have led to postponement of his more radical agenda. From his handling of secessionist movements in the Baltic republics and selection of top leaderships in the early 1991, it seems clear that he is not following the conservative agenda in toto. A truthful following of the conservative agenda could have resulted in a massacre in Vilnius, and presence of more conservative elements in the leadership (see *Time*, March 25, 1991).

Second, since Gorbachev has sided with the conservatives, although perhaps temporarily, threats to *perestroika* from the side of the conservatives have diminished, at least for the time being. While threats from the radical side have increased so much that even the whole process of democratization may be in danger, at this stage the main problems that *perestroika* face are related to nationality and political stability issues. In both respects Yeltsin's position is sharply different from that of Gorbachev. The contemporary situation gives Soviet leaders four options: (1)

accept a total breakup of the Union; (2) roll back to Stalinism; (3) settle for a smaller USSR by letting defiant republics go; and (4) form a loose confederation. Obviously to Gorbachev, the first three are impossibilities. He is reluctant to preside over the liquidation, even partial liquidation, of the Soviet Union. His primary concern at the current stage is to form a loose confederation, presumably along the lines we discussed in the previous chapter. Yeltsin is opposed to Stalinist totalitarianism but is willing to settle for a smaller USSR, while the conservatives still stand for rolling back *perestroika* and returning to Stalinism. Therefore, differences among the radicals and conservatives continue to create impediments for *perestroika*.

Economic Bureaucracy and Enterprise Managers

Introduction of market elements threaten the power and privileges of the economic and administrative bureaucracy most decisively.[19] Greater decentralization results in substantial increases in the power and responsibilities of enterprises vis-a-vis the central planning agencies and central ministries. The more market elements are introduced, like banking and credit systems, price reforms, and enterprise autonomy, the more bureaucracy shrinks in terms of power and privileges, size, and credibility. Therefore, bureaucrats, whether administrative or economic, want a continuation of status-quo, and support neither political nor economic reforms. Many Sovietologists conclude that the success of *perestroika* lies in "neutralizing" the bureaucracy, the most organized force that so far powerfully, somewhat successfully, resisted the processes of implementation of reforms.

Under *perestroika* enterprises are given greater autonomy from central direction. But initially, central ministries were held responsible for the overall output of each sector. Enterprises were thus actually trusted with contradictory responsibilities: to demonstrate initiative (which requires creativity and freedom) and to show obedience to the ministry (which requires submission to central direction). Moreover, enterprise managers are not well accustomed to hard work and imaginativeness that *perestroika* envisages. Therefore, few did indeed take up the challenge. According to Zaslavskaya (1988), this partially explains why implementation of *perestroika*'s reforms fell short of expectations. Zaslavskaya also observes that *perestroika* envisages honesty and competition in the trade and consumer sectors, but as the economy is characterized by shortages of consumer goods; *perestroika* could hardly earn supporters or allies among these officials to whom black market trading remains more profitable.

In contrast to these trading and consumer service officials, *perestroika*, has strong support among the members of small cooperatives. Zaslavskaya, however, maintains that this support might disappear with bolder private initiatives of *perestroika*. But members of creative professions, doctors, teachers, and artists, and members of scientific and technical intelligentsia, as mentioned above, although belonging to the civilian bureaucracy, are typically strong supporters of economic and political reforms.

Workers and Peasants

According to Soviet official classification, the working class includes both industrial and agricultural workers employed on state farms, they number 61.8 percent of the Soviet population, and constitute the largest group in Soviet society. As *perestroika* emphasizes meritocracy, that is, skill and productivity, those workers having higher levels of skills and initiative most certainly favor *perestroika*'s economic reforms, because they can expect rewards based on their skills. But less skilled workers, who are accustomed to obeying orders and are unable to improve their skill level, will certainly find Gorbachev's wage differentiation proposals as contradictory to their interest. The working class was also affected by Gorbachev's initial crackdown on worker discipline and alcoholism. Moreover, as the persistent miners' strike demonstrates, workers are also cynical about the prospects of *perestroika*. Like previous reforms, Gorbachev also demands patience and help from the workers, but they find empty shelves in the consumer markets. Intellectuals can wait ten or twenty years for liberalization, but workers, remarks Nikolai Shmelev, need to see "some real, tangible betterment in their day-to-day conditions" (*Newsweek*, Jan 2, 1989). Moreover, price reforms, which unavoidably will result in increases in consumer prices, including housing, cannot be a welcome change for workers. In addition, *perestroika*'s processes of intensification, renovation, and modernization, coupled with private enterprise and competition, will inevitably result in unemployment of overemployed and unskilled workers. Zaslavskaya, therefore, concludes that the unskilled, the old, and workers having problems in relocating are unlikely to support Gorbachev's political and economic reforms.

Peasants (employed in collective farms, *kolkhozies*), with 12 percent of population, constitute the second largest group in the Soviet society. Here again, the enterprising and creative part of the farmers will find *perestroika* conducive to their interests of freedom from official control and interference. But a bigger part of the peasants who are accustomed to guaranteed income, and who fear liquidation of farms because of inefficiency and low productivity, find little incentive to support *perestroika*'s economic policies. But Zaslavskaya believes that increased freedom of what to plant, how much to produce, other measures like transferring ownership of land to peasants, and opportunities for small-scale business, might result in a potential "true social base" among the leading stratum of peasantry, while the rest might remain allies to *perestroika*.

Military Bureaucracy

The military bureaucracy deserves mention especially because *perestroika*'s policies and programs have already accomplished sweeping changes in this sphere and are aimed at far-reaching and fundamental changes in the Soviet economy having repercussions in other sectors as well. The military is by nature a conservative and authoritarian force, which favors discipline and patriotism. The Soviet military is not an exception.

But *perestroika* envisages trading guns for bread. The defense burden of the Soviet Union has been enormous. Until the sixties, the Soviet economy was growing fast, and it was possible (although at the cost of consumer goods industries) to channel increasing proportions of Soviet GNP to the development of the military-industry sector. Although the Soviet GNP[20] was even less than half of that of the United States, superpower rivalry compelled the Soviet Union to indulge in armaments requiring defense budgets equal to those of the United States.[21] Richard Nixon (1990)[22] remarks that the Soviet Union is indeed a superpower militarily, but is economically a third world nation.[23]

With decline in economic growth, especially since the late seventies, it became harder for the Soviet leaders to divert larger and larger proportions of GNP to the military sector. The situation worsened further with the Ronald Reagan era's Strategic Defense Initiative, which demanded channeling a far greater proportion of Soviet GNP to military buildup in order to counter U.S forces. As the economy continued to worsen, all these economic reasons led the Soviet leadership to reassess the limited political value of military power and reject traditional "zero-sum-conflict view of the world" with a doctrine of "reasonable sufficiency" (Borcke 1989, 27-29).

But *perestroika*'s policies also demanded diversion of funds from the military sector to the civilian sector. Although the military establishment is not opposed to economic efficiency and modernization, it is particularly affected by cuts in the military budget. As mentioned before, in 1988 Gorbachev made sweeping proposals for unilateral reduction in Soviet military manpower in the United Nations.[24] Subsequently, Gorbachev announced public exposure of the military budget and up to a 14.2 percent cut in the military budget by 1991. Also, Gorbachev pulled out military forces from Afghanistan, and later, from Central European countries, thereby, causing serious psychological impacts on,[25] and potential economic problems for the Soviet military.[26] On the other hand, growing nationality and ethnicity problems all over the Soviet Union compel Gorbachev to turn to the military forces to quell the situation. All these could produce dissatisfaction for *perestroika*'s policies in the military. But military officers do understand that a declining economy can hardly afford to sustain a military complex that demands as much as one fifth of its GNP. Second, the military got a blow in the March 1989 elections when some top military commanders failed to be elected. In sum, the military up until the end of 1990 maintained a largely apolitical character.[27]

Economically, reduction in defense spending constitutes a promising aspect for *perestroika*. It reverses priorities of national development by diverting funds to the consumer sector, which was squeezed for decades by the military buildup. Coupled with the disappearing threats of cold war and eagerness of Western nations to help Gorbachev build the Soviet economy, defense cuts might result in greater integration of Soviet economy into the world economy and therefore, greater access to technological and scientific advancements. That in turn, can help the military, because it, too, needs sophisticated technology to remain competitive. With greater integration in world economy, technology will cost less and an economically developed nation can afford such technology more easily. Therefore, in the final analysis, *perestroika* may not constitute a threat to a potentially renovated, technologically sophisticated Soviet military. Perhaps that is why discontent in military has not resulted in serious problems for *perestroika* so far.

CONCLUDING REMARKS

By waging a war against Stalinist and post-Stalinist system, *perestroika* has created its friends and foes. Those who stand to lose from *perestroika*'s reforms, mainly the traditional bureaucracy and party *apparatchiks*, are destined to oppose, while those who stand to gain, skilled workers, intellectuals, and a new breed of entrepreneurs, are willing to support it. The latter group also incorporates those who are impatient with the pace of *perestroika* and are increasingly taking stands against it. Such polarizations, on the one hand, enhance political pluralism, a major objectives of *perestroika*, but on the other hand create incredible challenges and obstacles for its success as is demonstrated at the current stage.

Management of a transition of this magnitude is an enormously difficult, if not impossible, job. Tumultuous events of the last six years indicate that both friends and foes of *perestroika* changed their positions, often diagonally and diametrically, and Gorbachev has survived many predictions and possibilities of demise or downfall, and masterfully managed and overcomed many apparently unsurmountable obstacles.[28] Talbott (1991, 33) observes that Gorbachev specializes in the politics of impossible and still remains, in the Soviet Union, the only acceptable figure among the "tribes and factions that hate one another even more than they hate him." No doubt, Gorbachev's mission to establish a regulated market economy and a carefully circumscribed political pluralism or a Union of sovereign republics remains fraught with powerful challenges and obstacles, but his success (or even failure) will constitute an extraordinary chapter in the history of mankind.

NOTES

1. The concept of revolution was defined earlier. A counterrevolution can be understood as an attempt to restore the status quo ante. In this instance, counterrevolution would constitute the restoration of capitalism and reversal of the effects of the Bolshevik Revolution. Reform, on the other hand, stands for partial, piecemeal, sporadic efforts to transform a system, change a policy or program, or restructure institutions, so on and so forth. Reforms, however, can well be either sweeping or rapid or fundamental, or a combination of all or some of these elements in different degrees. According to Cohen (1980, 13), reform is attributable to "those policies, which seek through measured change to improve the existing order without

fundamentally transforming existing social, political and economic foundations or going beyond prevailing ideological values." The distinction between comprehensive and partial reforms, in the words of Hewett (1988, 14), "implies that economic systems can be separated into discrete parts and that some can be changed while others are not."

2. Of course, if one contends that the political-bureaucratic elite itself constitutes a social class characterized by centralization and concentration of power and wealth in Soviet society, then its genuine displacement might be regarded as a revolutionary phenomenon from a Marxian perspective (unless they are the ones who capture the benefits of privatization).

3. An almost similar interpretation was made when Lenin introduced NEP in 1923 and Khrushchev initiated his destalinization campaign in the late fifties (see Howe 1988; Adams 1972).

4. Milanovic (1989) shows how the reform calculus of Gorbachev falls far short of expectations, while in Poland and Hungary more progress has been made toward economic restructuring.

5. Soviet sociologist Tatyana Zaslavskaya (1987; 1988; 1990), poets Andre Voznesensky 1989; Yevgeny Yevtushenko 1989; Aleksander Solzhenitsyn 1989; economists Aganbegyan (1988; 1989; 1990), Shmelev and Popov 1989; to name a few, belong to this group.

6. At the Twenty-eighth Congress of the CPSU, Ligachev blasted five years of *perestroika* as "blind radicalism," aimed at "collapse of socialism" within the CPSU and in the Soviet Union. For him, private ownership "indisputably causes social stratification" and the purpose of "revealing of the possibilities inherent in the socialist system" (which Gorbachev claims to be an objective of *perestroika*), cannot be achieved by "sale of enterprises into private hands." Strongly denouncing the separation of power between the state and the CPSU, he asserted, "With the party, and only with the vanguard party can we move forward on the way of socialist renewal. Without the party of Communists, *perestroika* is a lost cause" (*New York Times*, July 4, 1990). Above all, Ligachev and conservatives accuse *perestroika* of "abandoning the ideological heritage of Marxism-Leninism," of "slipping toward a capitalist type market economy," of giving up the socialist regimes in the Eastern Europe and of ensuring the disintegration of the Soviet Union itself.

7. See Ligachev's address at the Twenty-eighth Congress, *New York Times*, July 4, 1990.

8. *Time* (July 23, 1990) reports this to be worth $12 billion.

9. At the end of the Congress Yeltsin resigned from the party and in the immediate aftermath of the Congress Ligachev was relieved from the Politburo of the Communist Party.

10. The Central Committee of the Twenty-seventh Congress had 49 percent members who were office holders, 9 percent peasants, and 42 percent workers. The Central Committee as elected by the Twenty-eighth Congress, in contrast, is composed of: 5.4 percent peasants, 6.0 percent military and KGB officials, 11.6 percent workers, 17.0 percent office holders and 43.0 percent party officials (*Los*

Angeles Times, July 6, 1989)

11. The intelligentsia in the context of the Soviet Union is understood as the whole of the Soviet educated society: students, professors, journalists, writers, lawyers, engineers and other professional people. Informal organizations are understood as organizations having no legal registration and no formal connection with the state

12. The letter was published in *Pravda* on April 5, 1988. It is widely believed to be an organized effort by the conservatives to roll back *perestroika*'s reforms.

13. Criticism of *Komsomol* sparked again with the recent appearance of *Dictatorship of Conscience*, a play by Mikhail Shatrov, which was banned before the *glasnost* era

14. The Soviet Union has about 2 million Jews. In 1989, 70,000 left, and in 1990, 150,000 were expected to leave the country. According to Shalin (1990), if this trend continues, by the end of the century Soviet Jewish population will drop to tens of thousands.

15. Currently 55 million ethnic Muslims constitute 19 percent of the Soviet population. By the end of this century, the percentage is expected to grow to 25 percent.

16. Turkestan is the old name of the Central Asian region that embraces present-day Kazakhstan, Tadzhikstan, Kirghizia, Turkmenia, and Uzbekistan, an area half the size of the United States.

17. Besides these, a large number of local organizations have sprung up in many republics (see *London Economist*, 26 May, 1990).

18. In the immediate aftermath of the nationality referendum, Yeltsin, addressing the Russian Republic's Congress, proclaimed the existence of two opposing camps in the country: one composed of those who "want to drastically renew the USSR and transform in into a union of sovereign republics" and the other, composed of those who want to "preserve and even enhance the economic monopoly of the center" and thus bring economic catastrophe. Situating Gorbachev in the latter group, he claimed "what we have been witnessing for last six years is not *perestroika*, but rather the last phase of the period of stagnation" (*New York Times*, March 30, 1991).

19. As of 1987, the Soviet economic bureaucracy consisted of 38 state committees, 33 union ministries, 28 union-republican ministries, and more than 300 regional ministries and authorities. It manages 1.3 million production units composed of 43,000 state enterprises, 26,000 construction enterprises, 47,000 farming units, 260,000 service establishments, and more than 1 million retail trade establishments (see Gregory 1990, 2-3).

20. CIA estimates show that Soviet GNP is half of the United States' GNP. But recent reports show that both Bergson's estimates and CIA calculations overestimated Soviet GNP and underestimated the Soviet GNP share to military build up (also see Brzeski 1987).

21. That means if the United States spends 5 percent of its GNP for military buildup, the Soviet Union has to spend 10 percent of its GNP just to compete on

equal financial terms. That is exactly what happened. In 1970, Soviet defense expenditures amounted to 11 to 13 percent of GNP, and even in the late eighties the rate has been 14 to 17 percent, while the United States spent in average 4 to 5 percent for these periods (see Naylor 1988; Brzeski 1987; Bergson 1988).

22. According to Nixon (1990), the Soviet Union spends 20 percent of its GNP on military, while the United States spend only 6 percent.

23. Becker's (1982, 22) remark in this context is worth quoting, "The USA *has* a military-industrial complex, the USSR *is* a military industrial complex."

24. Gorbachev proposed a unilateral cut in military by 500,000 men and 10,000 tanks.

25. Psychological problems are mainly associated with the withdrawal from Afghanistan. The military believes it was deprived of victory. Economic problems are obvious: nearly half a million military men will be brought back to the Soviet Union, who, according to Soviet chief of the general staff, "lived relatively well abroad" and are "coming back to nothing" (*Time*, April 9, 1990).

26. See statements of military leaders in the Twenty-eighth Congress, reported in *New York Times*, July 2-4, 1990.

27. It should however be noted that since late 1990 and early 1991, military and other security forces, along with conservative elements within the society, continue to be more vocal in the political processes and show remarkable resistance to *perestroika*'s programs. This development forces Gorbachev, during this period, to placate the conservatives, and in turn, to subject himself to sharp criticisms of radicals.

28. Referring to Gorbachev's unusual survivability, Brown (1990, 141) remarks, "It is clear, too, that there are big dangers ahead for Gorbachev, although salutory to recall that he has surmounted a great many already."

8

Conclusion

Existing socialist economies are currently experiencing severe and large-scale difficulties. The magnitude and critical character of these problems, the advent of *perestroika*, apparently ailing socialism, and worldwide demands for freer and more democratic economic and political systems, have provoked many to infer the demise of socialism and its replacement by capitalism. Such claims are partially true and partially false. Soviet society, in the course of its development and evolution, has experienced different stages or empirical models, as different, for example, as the New Economic Policy of the twenties and the Stalinist variant of centralized state socialism that followed. In each instance, advocates of that particular empirical model have claimed affinity with or inspiration from Marxian socialist theories or texts.

We conclude that characterizations of the Soviet economy, society, and politics as being "in crisis" are essentially correct. But the claim that socialism is being replaced by capitalism is substantially exaggerated, at least in the Soviet Union. The contemporary Soviet crisis has two main aspects: systemic and transitional. It is a systemic crisis because contemporary problems are deeply rooted in the basic institutions and modes of living in the society, requiring for their resolution substantial changes in the foundations of the society and, indeed, transformation to a different system (which need not necessarily be capitalism). It is also a transitional crisis, because the process of changing to the new system is itself filled with uncertainty and problems.

Mikhail Gorbachev and his advisers, however, believe that the contemporary problems in the Soviet Union are critical enough to require dramatic, perhaps revolutionary changes to prevent extreme disorder and to ensure politicoeconomic survival. Gorbachev claims that *perestroika*'s programs embody "more socialism, not less," and that he is looking within socialist theory and practice, not outside it, for solutions to problems of the contemporary Soviet economy. The evidence, drawn from Marxist theories and real-life experience, largely supports Gorbachev's claim. Greater decentralization, a larger role for market economy and private initiative, and enhanced democratization and citizen participation in public and industrial life do not necessarily constitute a movement away from socialism, as is often claimed.

As Chapters 1 and 2 demonstrated, Marxian thought from the time of Karl Marx to the present provides strong theoretical ideas pertaining to both relatively more centralized (and, typically, authoritarian) and relatively more decentralized (and, typically, democratic) versions of socialism. The centralized strand of socialist thought has been elaborated from the perspectives of Vladimir Lenin, Leon Trotsky, Maurice Dobb, Paul Sweezy, Paul Baran, Charles Battleheim and M. Kalecki. The decentralized strand of socialist thought has been explored through the writings of Edward Bernstein, Nikolai Bukharin, Karl Kautsky, Rosa Luxemburg and Oscar Lange. The decentralized and democratic strand of Marxian thought demonstrates not only the compatibility of democracy with socialism, but also the need for democracy to realize a socialist economy and society.

Also, as the preceding discussion shows, existing socialist economies have been characterized by diversity in their economic and political organization. We have seen that Soviet society since 1917 has experienced several distinct models or forms of centralization/authoritarianism and decentralization/democracy. The periods of the New Economic Policy, Nikita Khrushchev and Aleksei Kosygin demonstrated relatively more decentralized and democratic approaches to socialist economy and society, compared to the relatively more centralized approaches and practices of socialism as demonstrated during the War Communism, Joseph Stalin and Leonid Brezhnev periods.

It should be noted, however, that the centralized socialists' emphasis on plan and deemphasis on market clearly conform to a part of Marx's vision. The decentralized socialists' emphasis on developed economy and greater worker participation also conforms to Marx's view of socialism as a model for the post-capitalist democratic society. Although Marx emphasized the importance of planning, he never gave sovereignty to planners as some centralist socialists envisaged. Although Marx tended to associate markets with capitalism and their abolition with socialism, strictly identifying markets with capitalism or plan with socialism is parochial. Second, the dichotomous use of centralization and decentralization is another problematic dimension of the whole debate. No economic system can be totally command-oriented or purely competitive. Every system combines these elements in different degrees. Market elements can be introduced into a planned economy and, similarly, elements of planning can be well-placed in a capitalist economy. Indeed, pressures for planning in capitalist markets are as striking as the urgency for market elements in socialist economies.

Most scholars, therefore, emphasize a rational, democratic organization of socialist economies that blends central planning and market-based resource allocation. But the fact remains that although socialist scholars have long sought to work out an optimal combination of centralization and decentralization, to combine market processes and democratic elements in a rational socialist society, theoretical and practical difficulties involved in such a comprehensive mechanism remain largely unresolved.

As regards the practice of socialism, it has been observed that the Soviet Union started with an extremely centralized and nonmonetary socialist economy, and gradually moved toward greater decentralization. This movement was neither unidirectional nor smooth, however. There have been twists and turns; bold initiatives for reform were often reversed, and often left midway. But in general, economic reforms contributed to further decentralization, softening the controls of central planning.

It has also been demonstrated that, in the context of the Soviet Union, no correlation can be established between the degree of decentralization and better/ poor economic performance or centralization and poor/better economic performance. The growth of the Soviet economy demonstrates that waves of reforms— centralization and decentralization—shaped and influenced structure and performance of the economy. Although the growth rate was very high in the fifties, no correlation between greater degrees of decentralization and higher growth rates of the economy can be generated. The growth rate was much higher during the Stalinist period, when economic administration was extremely centralized, and it was extremely low from the late seventies through the eighties, when the economy was greatly decentralized. Again, the rate of growth during the relatively more centralized Brezhnevian period was lower than that of the Khrushchevian period, which was characterized by relatively greater decentralization.

We have seen, however, that relatively more decentralized and democratized periods in the Soviet Union not only worked reasonably well, but were generally associated with higher standards of living and better fulfillment of the higher ideals of socialism. In terms of democratization of work-places, public participation in the governmental processes, liberation of the human mind, creativity and enthusiasm, decentralized approaches have outperformed centralized approaches, while their performance in terms of lower ideals of socialism, such as economic growth, have occasionally exceeded and, in any event, not lagged far behind that of the centralized models.

Chapter 3 examined the immediate background of *perestroika*. Based on the economic, social, and political parameters of the early eighties, we conclude that Gorbachev's claim that he inherited the Soviet economy and society in serious troubles requiring radical remedy is hardly an exaggeration. The economic downturn of the late seventies was indeed a powerful threat to the legitimacy and authority of the Soviet government, and created a formidable problem for the exercise of authority by the CPSU. On the other hand, there has been a substantial change in the demand structure and levels of aspiration of the industrialized, urbanized, and modernized Soviet population in the eighties. Ironically, the expertise of such a skilled and educated population has not been utilized properly in a political setting dominated by authoritarian one-party rule, and an economic setting dictated by central planning. Organization of production and employment/occupational patterns have not kept pace with educational and cultural advancements.

Consequently, the Soviet system has failed to meet the altered demands and modern challenges of a qualitatively changed population. Although Gorbachev's predecessors recognized the critical nature of the problems that were causing degradation in the tissues of the society and economy, they took no significant measures to remedy the situation. With the advent of Gorbachev as general secretary of the CPSU, the problems that had accumulated for years came to the forefront of national attention. The new leadership in particular, and the population at large, came to realize that the existing system was utterly failing to deliver goods and services as expected, and that the system itself could not continue without major surgery.

Chapter 4 explored Gorbachev's critique of Soviet socialism and his own vision of socialism. The chapter also described the Soviet and the non-Soviet critique of Soviet economy and society. We conclude that Gorbachev's socialism is a unique model among various versions of existing socialist systems, and constitutes a revolutionary phenomenon in Soviet history comparable only to the October Revolution in its significance and magnitude. It is also observed that Gorbachev strives to redefine socialism, remake the Soviet man and mind, apply and extend democracy, and restructure the Soviet Union's social, economic, cultural and political bases to suit the needs and challenges of post-industrialized society. His socialism visualizes a complete replacement of Stalinist command model, emphasizes profound restructuring of the economy to bolster workers' morale and participation in public enterprises, and envisages sweeping measures to liberalize the state economy, encourage private, individual and cooperative sectors, and allow international economic cooperation.

Therefore, we conclude that *perestroika* ushers in a genuinely revolutionary process of social, economic, and political transformation in the Soviet Union. *Perestroika* not only challenges Stalinism and post-Stalinism; in its direction and progression it even goes beyond orthodox Soviet Marxism-Leninism. By blending plan and market, private and public activities, *perestroika* would establish institutions and processes that retain major benefits of a socialist economy, but within a more market-oriented, privatized, and democratic setting. Still, there remain significant impediments both to the theory and the practice of such a blend.

Chapter 5 examined the economic and political reforms by which Gorbachev and his associates sought to dismantle the central planning apparatus, initiate a new system of "government regulated market," and establish a multi-party system based on political pluralism and a "humane and democratic socialist society." These reforms are radical and far-reaching in their character and magnitude. Although many of *perestroika*'s reforms have historical, ideological, and intellectual roots in the Soviet past, they have no true parallels or precedents in Soviet history. The policy prescriptions of *perestroika* clearly indicate an intention to transform the traditional, administrative, and authoritarian economy into a democratic, decentralized, and competitive one. *Perestroika* still falls short of establishing preconditions for a market-oriented socialism. But there is no doubt that it goes far beyond any earlier decentralized approaches to economic management in the Soviet Union.

Politically, *perestroika* has already accomplished a herculean task. It has extended democracy and freedom to the people and has supplemented mature socialism with a less authoritarian government. By extending *perestroika* far beyond the restructuring of the economic sector, and by simultaneously introducing the programs of *glasnost* and *demokratizatsiya*, Gorbachev has embarked on a vigorous revitalization of the whole Soviet society. Economically, by diversifying the existing forms of property ownership and putting them on an equal footing, *perestroika* might end up creating an economy composed of an extensive and dominant cooperative and self-employed sector and a large but decentralized public enterprise sector. Such an economy also presumably does away with the traditional state monopoly in many industries. Thus, increasingly, state-regulated competition might emerge to rejuvenate the Soviet economy.

Challenged by the needs of a mature economy, the socialist ideology is being transformed and redefined. Gorbachev's claim that *perestroika* is not a movement away from socialism, but rather a movement within socialism, a movement toward a more democratic and more market-oriented socialism, is legitimate. Just as capitalism incorporated many socialist principles after the Great Depression, the contemporary crisis will force the Soviet people to interject some capitalist medicines into their economy and polity. In his sweeping political and economic programs, Gorbachev is not forcing the Soviet Union to drop socialism and central planning and embrace capitalism and its market relations. We believe *perestroika* aims at eradicating the last vestiges of the outdated political and economic order of the Stalinist and post-Stalinist periods.

The Soviet Union is passing through a systemic crisis. The magnitude and intensity of the crisis entails systemic transition—the replacement of the existing system by another system, not merely restructuring of the existing one. And that involves a sweeping and fundamental overhaul of all aspects of the Soviet Union—a thorough transformation of its social, economic, and political structures, and a reorientation of each citizen's worldview and mental frame. It demands *raskreposhchenie* (the emancipation of society and the individual), not mere *perestroika*.

The Soviet economic crisis could be compared to the Great Depression, which was resolved by Franklin Roosevelt's New Deal; its political and nationality crisis could be compared to the American Civil War, which was resolved by Abraham Lincoln. But even if Gorbachev combined the qualities of both Roosevelt and Lincoln, the obstacles that face *perestroika* would remain severe. Gorbachev's main problem is that he is trying to manage a revolution. A revolution can be initiated, as he did, but it cannot be easily managed, as history amply demonstrates. It is a spontaneous process; some may take credit for sparking it off, but none can control its destiny.

By embarking on a revolution aimed at dismantling the Stalinist and Brezhenevian models, Gorbachev has already surmounted a great many formidable obstacles, but he still must confront a number of challenges. Economically, he has to dismantle central planning, but he has to accomplish it in the absence of institutions and forces of market economy. He cannot wait until the existing system is abolished or institutions of the market have been created. Second, massive economic restructuring essentially involves dislocations and disruptions. Therefore a slowdown, even negative economic growth, may result. But Gorbachev can hardly afford that. He presides over a population whose hunger for food is stronger than that for democracy. Therefore, he must accomplish two possibly contradictory jobs simultaneously: growth of the economy and dismantling of the existing economic system.

Politically, *perestroika* aims at a transition to a democratic and humane society. But the Soviet Union has neither a democratic society nor democratic institutions to channel the spontaneous feedback of the people. It even lacks democratic legal and political institutions to deal with demonstrations and ethnic clashes that have become routine matters under *perestroika*. Moreover, at the current stage, with sharp polarization of Soviet society, the emergence of Yeltsin as a formidable radical leader and Gorbachev's temporary alliance with the conservatives, the support bases of *perestroika* have eroded alarmingly.

So, both politically and economically, dismantling the old system plunges the country into a vacuum, where neither the old system, nor the new system that *perestroika* strives to build, functions. Every revolution involves a period of destruction and then a prolonged period of reconstruction. Gorbachev has to manage both at the same time and, worse still, remain committed to the people in doing so. Indeed, one of the crucial problems of *perestroika* is that it is running short of time.

Optimistic prospects for *perestroika*, however, lie with the fact that Gorbachev not only came to power at a historically momentous time, he has also been masterfully steering the wheel of history. Hardly ever in history has any single leader led a nation all the way through transition. Brown (1990) remarks that it would be an astounding political feat if Gorbachev were to lead his country all the way from a highly authoritarian system through the transition period toward a pluralist democracy and market economy. By utilizing his superb qualities and skills, political acumen, tactical maneuvering, and above all, highly remarkable pragmatism, if Gorbachev succeeds in improving the nation's economic condition and can keep the country together, both he and *perestroika* will survive. As recent events demonstrate, both these aims remain seriously problematic. Moreover, they seem to be interdependent: if economic conditions improve, secessionist movements might lose momentum; on the other hand, if economic conditions deteriorate, secessionist movements might accelerate further. If secessionist movements succeed and Gorbachev presides over even a partial liquidation of the Soviet empire, the whole question of economic recovery will be redundant. Gorbachev has already accomplished the most important requirement of any change, however; the awakening of the masses. He has changed the Soviet man and mind forever. *Perestroika* might falter, Gorbachev might be replaced, but the Soviet people have only one option open—to move forward. They and their nation will never be the same. Here lies Gorbachev's accomplishment and, ironically, *perestroika*'s future.

References

Abouchar, Alan. (1979). *Economic Evaluation of Soviet Socialism.* New York: Pergamon Press.

Adams, Arthur E. (1972). *Stalin and His Times.* New York: Holt, Rinehart, and Winston.

Adirim, I. (1989). A Note on the Current Level, Pattern and Trends of Unemployment in the USSR. *Soviet Studies* 41:449-61.

Adoratsky, V. (ed.). (1935). *Karl Marx: Selected Works in Two Volumes.* Moscow: Cooperative Publishing Society.

Aganbegyan, Abel. (1987). Basic Directions of Perestroika. *Soviet Economy* 3:277-97.

—. (1988a). *The Economic Challenge of Perestroika.* Bloomington: Indiana University Press.

—. (ed.). (1988b). *Perestroika 1989.* New York: Charles Scribner's Sons.

—. (1989). *Inside Perestroika.* New York: Harper and Row.

Albert, Hans. (1987). Is Socialism Inevitable? Historical Prophecy and the Possibilities of Reason. In *Socialism: Institutional, Philosophical and Economic Issues,* ed. Svetozar Pejovich (1987). Boston: Kluwer Academic Publishers. 55-88.

Alexiev, Alex. (1990a). Unrest Reaches Moscow as Communism Unravels. *Los Angeles Times.* January 21:M2-4.

—. (1990b). Life-Death Struggle for the Soul and Center of Soviet Union. *Los Angeles Times.* March 25:M2.

—. (1990c). Gorbachev has met his match: History. *Los Angeles Times.* April 22:M1-2.

Alexiev, Alex, Archie Brown, Mark Kramer, Adam Ulam, Marshall Shulman, and Dimitri Shalin. (1990d). Soviet Disunion: When the Costs of Empire Outweigh Its Benefits. *Los Angeles Times.* May 27:M1.

Almond, Gabriel A., and Laura Roselle. (1989). Model Fitting in Communism

Studies. In *Politics and the Soviet System*, ed. Thomas Remington (1989). New York: St. Martin's Press, 170-224.

Altvater, Elmer. (1981). The Primacy of Politics in Post-Revolutionary Societies. *The Review of Radical Political Economics* 13: 1-10.

Aptheker, Herbert. (ed.). (1965). *Marxism and Democracy: A Symposium*. New York: Humanities Press.

Arendt, Hannah. (1966). *The Origins of Totalitarianism*. New York: Harcourt, Brace.

Aslund, Anders. (1989). Soviet and Chinese reforms-why they must be different. *The World Today*. November: 190-91.

—. (1989). *Gorbachev's Struggle for Economic Reform*. Ithaca, N.Y.: Cornell University Press.

Asselain, Jean-Charles. (1984). *Planning and Profits in Socialist Economies*. London: Routledge and Kegan Paul.

Attewell, Paul A. (1984). *Radical Political Economy Since the Sixties*. New Brunswick: Rutgers University Press.

Avidar, Yosef. (1983). *The Party and the Army in the Soviet Union*. Jerusalem: The Magnes Press.

Balinky, Alexander. (1970). *Marx's Economics*. Lexington, Mass.: Heath Lexington Books.

Baran, Paul A. (1980). *Post-Revolutionary Society*. New York: Monthly Review Press.

—. (1957). *The Political Economy of Growth*. New York: Monthly Review Press.

Baran, Paul A., and Paul A. Sweezy. (1966). *Monopoly Capital*. New York: Monthly Review Press.

Barghoorn, Frederick C. and Thomas F. Remington. (1986). *Politics in the USSR*. Boston: Little Brown.

Barone, Enrico. (1935). The Ministry of Production in the Collectivist State. In *Collectivist Economic Planning*, ed. Frederick Hayek (1935). New York: Augustus M. Kelley. 245-90.

Baum, Richard. (1989). Beyond Leninism? Economic Reform and Political Development in Post-Mao China. *Studies in Comparative Communism*. Summer/Autumn:111-23.

Bauer, Tamas. (1987). Economic Reforms Within and Beyond the State Sector. *AEA Papers and Proceedings* 452-56.

—. (1990). Reforming the Planned Economy: The Hungarian Experience. *Annals of the American Academy of Political and Social Sciences*. January: 103-12.

Bechtold, Hartmut, and Andreas Helfer. (1987). Stagflation Problems in Socialist Economies. In *Crisis and Reform in Socialist Economies,* eds. Peter Gey, Jiri Kosta, and Wolfgang Quaisser (1987). Boulder, Colo.: Westview.

Becker, Abraham C. (1987). *Ogarkov's Complaint and Gorbachev's Plan: The Soviet Defense Budget and Party-Military Conflict*. Santa Monica, Calif.: Rand Corporation.

Bergson, Abram. (1967). *Planning and Productivity under Soviet Socialism*. New

York: Columbia University Press.

—. (1989). *Planning and Performance in Socialist Economies*. Boston: Unwin Hyman.

Bergson, Abram, and Herbert Levine. (eds.). (1983). *The Soviet Economy: Toward the Year 2000*. London: Allen and Unwin.

Berki, R. N. (1975). *Socialism*. New York: St. Martin's Press.

Berliner, Joseph, S. (1981). The Prospects for Technological Progress. In *The Soviet Economy: Continuity and Change*, ed. Morris Bornstein (1981). 293-312.

—. (1987). Organizational Restructuring of the Soviet Economy. In *Gorbachev's Economic Plans*, Joint Economic Committee (1987). Washington D.C.: U.S. Government Printing Office. 1:70-83.

Bernholz, Peter. (1987). Information, Motivation, and the Problem of Rational Economic Calculation in Socialism. In *Socialism: Institutional, Philosophical and Economic Issues*, ed. Svetozar Pejovich (1987). Boston: Kluwer Academic Publishers. 147-74.

Bernstein, Edward. (1909). *Evolutionary Socialism: A Criticism and Affirmation*. New York: B. W. Huebsch.

—. (1986). Evolutionary Socialism. In *Essential Works of Socialism*, ed. Irving Howe (1986). New Haven, Conn.: Yale University Press. 131-35.

Bettleheim, Charles. (1976). *Class Struggles in the USSR*. New York: Monthly Review Press.

—. (1981). Stalinism as the Ideology of State Capitalism. *The Review of Radical Political Economics* 13: 40-54.

—. (1975). *The Transition to Socialist Economy*. Atlantic Highlands, N. J.: Humanities Press.

Bettleheim, Charles, and Paul Sweezy. (1971). *On the Transition to Socialism*. New York: Monthly Review Press.

Bialer, Seweryn. (1986). *The Soviet Paradox: External Expansion, Internal Decline*. New York: Knopf.

—. (1987). The Soviet Union in a Changing World. In *The Soviet Union in Transition*, ed. Kinya Niiseki (1987). Boulder, Colo.: Westview. 4-17.

—. (ed.). (1989). *Politics, Society, and Nationality Inside Gorbachev's Russia*. Boulder, Colo.: Westview.

Bideleux, Robert. (1985). *Communism and Development*. New York: Methuen.

Birman, Igor. (1988). The Imbalance of the Soviet Economy. *Soviet Studies*. April: 210-21.

Blough, Roger, Jennifer Muratore, and Steve Berk. (1987). Gorbachev's Policy on the Private Sector: Two Steps Forward, One Step Backward. In *Gorbachev's Economic Plan* (Vol. 2), Joint Economic Committee (1987). Washington D. C.: U.S. Government Printing Office. 261-71.

Borcke, Astrid von. (1989). Gorbachev's Perestroika: Can the Soviet System be Reformed? In *Gorbachev's Agenda*, ed. Susan L. Clark (1989). Boulder, Colo.: Westview. 13-56.

Bornstein, Morris. (1969). *Comparative Economic Systems: Models and Cases*.

Homewood, Ill.: Richard D. Irwin.

—. (1985). Improving The Soviet Economic Mechanism. *Soviet Studies* 37:1-30.

—. (1987). Soviet Price Policies. *Soviet Economy* 3:96-134.

Bottomore, T. B. (1964). *Karl Marx: Early Writings.* New York: McGraw Hill.

Brabant, Jozef M. van. (1990). Socialist Economics: The Disequilibrium School and the Shortage Economy. *Journal of Economic Perspectives* 2:157-76.

Bregante, Nieves. (1989). Nationalist Unrest in the USSR and the Challenge to the Gorbachev Leadership. In *Gorbachev's Agenda*, ed. Susan Clark (1989). Boulder, Colo.: Westview. 85-108.

Breslauer, George W. (1980). Khrushchev Reconsidered. In *The Soviet Union Since Stalin*, ed. Stephen Cohen et al. (1980). Bloomington: Indiana University Press. 50-70.

Brezezinski, Zbigniew. (1989). An Increasingly Sterile System. In *Perestroika: How New is Gorbachev's New Thinking?*, ed. Ernest Lefever, and Robert Lugt (1989). Washington D. C.: Ethics and Public Policy Center. 55-62.

Brovkin, Vladimir. (1990). Revolution From Below: Informal Associations in Russia 1988-1989. *Soviet Economy* 2:233-57.

Brown, Archie. (1989). Ideology and Political Culture. In *Politics, Society, and Nationality Inside Gorbachev's Russia*, ed. Seweryn Bialer (1989). 1-40.

—. (1990). Gorbachev's Leadership: Another View. *Soviet Economy* 6:141-54.

Brown, Neville. (1990). Perestroika in Perspective. *World Today* 6:115-17.

Brundy, Yitzhak M. (1989). The Heralds of Opposition. *Soviet Economy* 2:162-200.

Brus, Wlodzimierz. (1972). *The Market in a Socialist Economy.* London: Routledge and Kegan Paul.

—. (1973). *The Economics and Politics of Socialism.* London: Routledge and Kegan Paul.

—. (1989). Evolution of the Communist Economic System: Scope and Limits. In *Remaking of Economic Institutions of Socialism*, eds. Victor Nee and David Stark (1989). Stanford, Calif.: Stanford University Press. 255-77.

Brus, Wlodzimierz and Tadeusz Kowalik. (1983). Socialism and Development. *Cambridge Journal of Economics* 7:243-55.

Brzeski, Andrzej. (1987). The Case of Central Planning in the USSR. In *Socialism: Institutional, Philosophical and Economic Issues*, ed. Svetozar Pejovich (1987). 209-38.

Buchanan, Patrick J. (1991). Its the Best Army Money Can Buy. *Los Angeles Times*, January 20:M2.

Buck, Trevor, and John Cole. (1989). *Modern Soviet Economic Performance.* Oxford: Basil Blackwell.

Bukharin, N. I. (1982). *Selected Writings on the State and the Transition to Socialism.* Ed. Richard B. Day. Armonk, New York: M.E. Sharpe.

—. (1964). *The Politics and Economics of the Transition Period.* Ed. K. J. Tarbuck. London: Routledge and Kegan Paul.

—. (1967). *The Path to Socialism in Russia: Selected Works.* Ed. S. Heitman. New

York: Omicron.

—. (1966). *Imperialism and World Economy*. New York: Howard Fertig.

—. (1986). Organized mismanagement in Modern Society. In *Essential Works of Socialism*, ed. Irving Howe (1986), 226-38.

Bukowski, Charles, and J. R. Walsh. (eds.). (1990). *Glasnost, Perestroika, and the Socialist Community*. New York: Praeger.

Burganov, Agdas. (1990). *Perestroika and the Concept of Socialism*. Moscow: Novosti Press.

Burkitt, Brian. (1984). *Radical Political Economy: An Introduction to the Alternative Economics*. New York: New York University Press.

Burlatsky, Fyodor M. (1988). Khrushchev, Andropov, Brezhnev: The Issue of Political Leadership. In *Perestroika 1989*, ed. Abel Aganbegyan (1988b). New York: Charles Scribner's Sons. 187-216.

—. (1989). Brezhnev and the End of the Thaw: Reflections on the Nature of Political Leadership. In *Gorbachev and Glasnost: Viewpoints from the Soviet Press*, ed. Issac Tarasulo (1989). Wilmington, Del.: SR Books. 50-62.

Cameron, Kenneth Neill. (1985). *Marxism: The Science of Society*. Massachusetts: Bergin and Garvey.

Campbell, Robert W. (1989). The Soviet Future: Gorbachev and the Economy. In *Gorbachev and the Soviet Future*, eds. Lawrence Lerner and Donald Treadgold (1989). Boulder, Colo.: Westview, 44-64.

Carr, E. H. (1952). *The Bolshevik Revolution, 1917-1923, Volume Two*. New York: Macmillan.

—. (1958). *Socialism in one Country Vol.1*. London: Macmillan.

CDSP (Current Digest of the Soviet Press). (1987). Gorbachev Addresses Party on Change-I. February 25. 4:1-8.

—. (1987). Gorbachev Addresses Party on Change-II. March 4. 5:8-12.

—. (1990). The Law on Property in the USSR. April 25. 12:21-25.

—. (1990). Gorbachev-Yeltsin, Ryzhkov Plans Weighed. October 3. 35:1-4.

—. (1990). Shatalin's Economic Program Summerized. October 3. 35:4-6.

—. (1990). Gorbachev Comments on Iraq, reform Plans. October 3. 35:6-9.

—. (1990). USSR Supreme Soviet Mulls Reform Plans. October 17. 37:1-7.

—. (1990). Reform Guidelines Adopted Amid Rancor. November 21. 42:1-7.

—. (1990). Guidelines for Stabilizing the Economy-II. December 5. 44:17-19.

—. (1990). Shatalin, Others Attack Reform Compromise. December 12. 45:1-3.

—. (1990). Gorbachev Tries to Assess USSR's Crisis. December 19. 46:1-6.

CIA & DIA (Central Intelligence Agency and the Defense Intelligence Agency). (1989). *The Soviet Economy in 1988: Gorbachev Changes Course*. Washington D. C.: Directorate of Intelligence.

Clark, Susan L. (ed.). (1989). *Gorbachev's Agenda*. Boulder, Colo.: Westview.

Cliff, Tony. (1974). *State Capitalism in Russia*. London: Pluto Press.

—. (1978). *Lenin, Volume Three: Revolution Besieged*. London: Pluto Press.

—. (1979). *Lenin, Volume Four: The Bolsheviks and World Communism*. London: Pluto Press.

Cohen, Carl. (ed.). (1972). *Communism, Fascism and Democracy: The Theoretical Foundations*. New York: Random House.

Cohen, Stephen F. (1974). *Bukharin and the Bolshevik Revolution: A Political Biography 1888-1938*. New York: Alfred-A-Knopf.

—. (1977). Bolshevism and Stalinism. In *Stalinism: Essays in Historical Perspective*, ed. Robert Tucker (1977). New York: Norton and Company. 3-29.

—. (1980). The Friends and Foes of Change: Reformism and Conservatism in the Soviet Union. In *The Soviet Union Since Stalin*, eds. Stephen Cohen, Alexander Rabinowitch, and Robert Sharlet (1980). Bloomington: Indiana University Press. 11-31.

—. (1985). *Rethinking the Soviet Experience. Politics and History Since 1917*. Oxford: Oxford University Press.

Cohen, Robert S. (1965). Marxism and Democracy. In *Marxism and Democracy*, ed. Herbert Aptheker (1965). New York: Humanities Press. 1-17.

Cohn, Stanley H. (1987). Soviet Intensive Economic Development in Perspective. In *Gorbachev's Economic Plans*, Joint Economic Committee (1987). Washington, D.C.: U.S. Government Printing Office. 1:10-26.

Colton, Timothy J. (1987). Approaches to the Politics of Systemic Economic Reform in the Soviet Union. *Soviet Economy* 3:145-70.

Conot, Robert. (1990). A Red Square Reformation. *Los Angeles Times*. March 11:M1-3.

Connor, Walter D. (1986). Looking Backward, Looking Forward: Lessons of the Brezhnev Era. *Studies in Comparative Communism* Winter: 261-69.

Corrigan, Philip, Harvie Ramsay, and Derek Sayer. (1978). *Socialist Construction and Marxist Theory*. New York: Monthly Review Press.

Crick, Bernard R. (1987). *Socialism*. Minneapolis: University of Minnesota Press.

Dahl, Robert A. (1982). *Dilemmas of Pluralist Democracy*. New Haven, Conn.: Yale University Press.

Dhal, Robert A., and Charles E. Lindblom. (1953). *Politics, Economics and Welfare*. New York: Harper Torchbooks.

Dallin, Alexander, and Condoleeza Rice. (eds.) (1986). *The Gorbachev Era*. Stanford, Calif.: Stanford Alumni Association.

Davis, R. W. (1990). Gorbachev's Socialism in Historical Perspective. *New Left Review*. January/February:5-27.

Day, Richard B. (1973). *Leon Trotsky and The Politics of Economic Isolation*. Cambridge, England: Cambridge University Press.

Desai, Padma. (1989). *Perestroika in Perspective*. Princeton, N.J.: Princeton University Press.

Deutscher, Issac. (1960). *Russia in Transition*. New York: Grove Press.

—. (1967). *The Unfinished Revolution: Russia 1917-1967*. New York: Oxford University Press.

Dickinson, H. D. (1933). Price Formation in a Socialist Community. *Economic Journal* 43:237-50.

—. (1939). *Economics of Socialism*. Oxford, England: Oxford University Press.

Dietrich, M. (1986). Organizational requirements of a socialist economy: theoretical and practical suggestions. *Cambridge Journal of Economics* 10:319-32.

Djilas, Milovan. (1969). *The Unperfect Society*. New York: Harcourt Brace Jovanovich.

—. (1955). *The New Class*. New York: Praeger.

—. (1990). Why Perestroika Cannot Succeed. Interview with *Time*. February 19:18-27.

Dobb, Maurice. (1966). *Soviet Economic Development Since 1917*. London: Routledge and Kegan Paul.

—. (1955). *On Economic Theory and Socialism*. London: Routledge and Kegan Paul.

—. (1970). *Welfare Economics and the Economics of Socialism*. Cambridge, England: Cambridge University Press.

Dowlah, A. F. (1990a). *Perestroika: Soviet Political Economy in Transition*. Ph.D. Dissertation. University of Southern California.

—. (1990b). *Perestroika: An Inquiry Into Its Historical, Ideological and Intellectual Roots*. Stockholm, Sweden: Bethany Books.

Draper, Hal. (1977). *Karl Marx's Theory of Revolution: Volume 1, State and Bureaucracy*. New York: Monthly Review Press.

Draper, Theodore. (1988). Soviet Reformers: From Lenin to Gorbachev. *Dissent* 287-301.

Drewnowski, January (1961). The Economic Theory of Socialism: A Suggestion for Reconsideration. *Journal of Political Economy*. August. In *Comparative Economic Systems*, ed. Morris Bornstein (1969). Homewood, Ill.: Richard D. Irwin. 110-27.

—. (ed.). (1982). *Crisis in the East European Economy*. London: Croom Helm.

Dunn, John. (1984). *The Politics of Socialism, An Essay in Political Theory*. Cambridge, England: Cambridge University Press.

Eckstein, Alexander. (1976). *Chinas Economic Development: The Interplay of Scarcity and Ideology*. Ann Arbor: University of Michigan Press.

Economist. Guide to Soviet Democracy. May 26:2.

Eisenhower, Susan and Ronald Sagdeev. (1990). Communisms Crucible: Whose Party Will It Be? *Los Angeles Times*. July 3:B7.

Elliott, John E. (1976). Marx and Contemporary Models of Socialist Economy. *History of Political Economy* 151-84.

—. (1980). Marx and Engels on Communism, Scarcity, and Division of Labor. *Economic Enquiry* 275-92.

—. (1981). *Marx and Engels on Economics, Politics and Society*. Santa Monica, Calif.: Goodyear.

—. (1984). Contending Perspectives on the Nature of Soviet Economic Society. *International Journal of Social Economics* 11:40-61.

—. (1985). *Comparative Economic Systems*. Belmont, Calif.: Wadsworth.

—. (1989). Gorbachev's Perestroika. *Contemporary Policy Issues* 35-52.

Elliott, John E., and Joanna V. Scott. (1986). Marx, Yugoslavia, And Self-

Governing Socialism: A Social and Political Economy Approach. *Research in Political Economy* 9:157-217.

Ellman, Michael. (1986). The Macroeconomic Situation in the USSR- Retrospect and Prospect. *Soviet Studies* 38:530-42.

—. (1989). *The USSR in the 1990s. Struggling out of Stagnation.* London:EIU Special Report. No 115.

Engels, Frederick. (1939). *Anti-Duhring.* New York: International Publishers.

—. (1935). *Socialism: Utopian and Scientific.* In *Karl Marx: Selected Works in Two Volumes*, ed. Adoratsky, V. (1935).

Erlich A. (1960). *The Soviet Industrialization Debate.* Cambridge, Mass.: Harvard University Press.

Evans, Alfred Jr. (1986). The Decline of Developed Socialism? Some Trends in Recent Soviet Ideology. *Soviet Studies* 38:1-23.

Fainsod, Merle. (1953). *How Russia is Ruled.* Cambridge, Mass.: Harvard University Press.

Falin, Valentin M. (1988). Glasnost: Getting at the Roots. In *Perestroika 1989*, ed. Abel Aganbegyan (1988b). New York: Charles Scribner's Sons. 281-308.

FBIS (Foreign Boradcasting Information Service). (1989). Academician Zaslavskaya on Restructuring. January 19:75-78.

—. (1989). Text of Gorbachev Speech to Agriculture Plenum. March 16:29-49.

—. (1989). Gorbachev's Closing Speech at 25 Apr CPSU Plenum. April 27:34-44.

—. (1989). Gorbachev's Concluding Speech at 18 Jul Session. July 21:76-79.

—. (1989). Text of Gorbachev 11 Jul Leningrad Discussion. August 21:39-51.

—. (1989). Gorbachev Defends Perestroyka in 9 Sep Address. September 11:27-29.

—. (1989). Gorbachev Opens CPSU Party Plenum. September 19:40-42.

Field, Mark G. (ed.). (1976). *Social Consequences of Modernization in Communist Societies.* Baltimore: Johns Hopkins University Press.

Frank, Peter. (1989). Perestroika in Crisis. *The World Today.* November:184-88.

—. (1990). The End of Perestroika. *The World Today.* May:87-89.

Franklin, Bruce. (ed.). (1972). *The Essential Stalin: Major Theoretical Writings, 1905-52.* New York: Doubleday.

Freidberg, Maurice, and Heyward Isham. (eds.). (1987). *Soviet Society Under Gorbachev: Current Trends and the Prospects for Reform.* New York: Sharpe.

Friedrich, Carl J., and Zbigniew Brezezinski. (1956). *Totalitarian Dictatorship and Autocracy.* Cambridge, Mass.: Harvard University Press.

Fukuyama, Frank. (1989). The End of History. *National Interest.* Summer: 1-17.

Gabrisch, Hubert. (ed.). (1989). Economic Reforms in Eastern Europe and The Soviet Union. Boulder, Colo.: Westview.

Galbraith, John Kenneth. (1979). *The New Industrial State.* New York: New American Library.

Galbraith, John Kenneth, and Stansilav Menshikov. (1988). *Capitalism, Communism, and Coexistence.* Boston: Houghton Mifflin.

Gay, Peter. (1952). *The Dilemma of Democratic Socialism.* New York: Columbia University Press.

Gey, Peter, Jiri Kosta, and Wolfgang Quaisser. (eds.). (1987). *Crisis and Reform in Socialist Economies*. Boulder, Colo.: Westview.

Goldman, Marshall I. (1983). *U.S.S.R. In Crisis: The Failure of an Economic System*. New York: Norton and Company.

—. (1987). *Gorbachev's Challenge: Economic Reform in the Age of High Technology*. New York: Norton and Company.

Goldman, Marshall, and Merle Goldman. (1988). Soviet and Chinese Economic Reform. *Foreign Affairs* 551-73.

Gooding, John. (1990). Gorbachev and Democracy. *Soviet Studies* 42:195-231.

Gorbachev, Mikhail S. (1987). *Perestroika: New Thinking For Our Country and the World*. New York: Harper and Row.

—. (1988a). Document: The Revolution and Perestroika. *Foreign Affairs* 410-25.

—. (1988b). *Gorbachev at the Summit: Speeches and Interviews, February 1987-July 1988*. New York: Richardson, Steirman and Black.

—. (1990a). *Towards A Humane and Democratic Socialist Society*. Moscow: Novosty Press.

—. (1990b). Gorbachev Addresses Party Conference. *News and Views From the USSR*. June 21:1-24.

—. (1990c). The Full Report Given By Mikhail Gorbachev at the 28th Congress of the Communist Party of the Soviet Union. *News and Views From the USSR*. July 5:1-46.

— . (1990d). Gorbachev's Concluding Remarks at the 28th Communist Party Congress. *News and Views From the USSR*. July 12:1-17.

Gregory, Paul R. (1989). Soviet Bureaucratic Behavior: *Kohzyaistvenniki* and *Apparatchiki*. *Soviet Studies* October:511-25.

—. (1990). Restructuring the Soviet Economic Bureaucracy. New York: Cambridge University Press.

Gregory, Paul R., and Robert C. Stuart. *Comparative Economic Systems*. Boston, Mass.: Houghton Mifflin.

—. (1986). *Soviet Economic Structure and Performance*. New York: Harper and Row.

—. (1990) *Soviet Economic Structure and Performance*. New York: Harper and Row.

Griffith, William E. (ed.). (1989). *Central and Eastern Europe: The Opening Curtain*. Boulder, Colo.: Westview.

Grossman, Gregory. (1977). The Second Economy in the USSR. *Problems of Communism* 26:25-40.

Gunlicks, Arthur B., and John D. Treadway. (eds.). (1987). *The Soviet Union Under Gorbachev: Assessing the First Year*. New York: Praeger.

Gustafson, Thane. (1990). *Crisis Amid Plenty: The Politics of Soviet Energy Under Brezhnev and Gorbachev*. Princeton, N. J.: Princeton University Press.

Hanson, Philip. (1987). The Soviet Twelfth Five Year Plan. In *The Soviet Economy: New Course?*, ed. Reiner Weichhardt. (1987). Brussels: NATO Economics Directorate. 10-28.

Harding, Harry. (1987). *China's Second Revolution: Reform after Mao*. Washington D. C.: Brookings Institution.

Hardt, John P., and Richard F. Kaufman. (1987). Gorbachev's Economic Plans: Prospects and Risks. In *Gorbachev's Economic Plans*, Joint Economic Committee (1987). Washington D.C.: U.S. Government Printing Office. 1:vii-xix.

Harrington, Michael. (1989a). Toward a New Socialism: Beyond the Limits of Present. *Dissent*. Spring:153-63.

—. (1989b). Markets and Plans: Is the Market Necessarily Capitalist? *Dissent*. Winter:56-70.

—. (1989c). *Socialism: Present and Future*. New York: Arcade Publishing.

Harris, Chauncy D. (1970). *Cities of the Soviet Union*. Chicago. University of Chicago Press.

Hasbulatov, Ruslan. (1989). *Perestroika as seen by an Economist*. Moscow: Novosti Press.

Hauslohner, Peter. (1989). Politics Before Gorbachev: De-Stalinization and the Roots of Reform. In *Politics, Society, and Nationality Inside Gorbachev's Russia*, ed. Seweryn Bialer (1989). 41-90.

—. (1987). Gorbachev's Social Contract. *Soviet Economy* 1:54-89.

Havel, Vaclav. (1990). The Revolution Has Just Begun. *Time*. March 5:14-15.

Havlik, Peter. (1989). Gorbachev's Reform Course Confirmed. In *Economic Reforms in Eastern Europe and the Soviet Union*, ed. Hubert Gabrisch (1989). 89-98.

Hayek, Friedrich von. (ed.). (1935). *Collectivist Economic Planning*. New York: Augustus M. Kelley.

—. (1969). Socialist Calculation: The Competitive Solution. In *Comparative Economic Systems*, ed. Morris Bornstein (1969). Homewood, Ill.: Richard D. Irwin.

Haynes, Michael. (1985). *Nikolai Bukharin and the Transition from Capitalism to Socialism*. Kent: Croom Helm.

Hazan, Baruch A. (1990). *Gorbachev and His Enemies*. Boulder, Colo.: Westview.

Heilbroner, Robert. (1989). A Vision of Socialism. *Dissent*. Fall:562-63.

Heller, A., and Ferenc Feher. (1988). Khrushchev and Gorbachev: A Contrast. *Dissent*. Winter:6-10.

Hewett, Ed A. (1988). *Reforming The Soviet Economy: Equality versus Efficiency*. Washington D.C: The Brookings Institution.

—. (1989a). Economic Reform in the USSR, Eastern Europe, and China: The Politics of Economics. *AEA Papers and Proceedings*. 16-20.

—. (1989b). *Perestroyka* and the Congress of Peoples Deputies. *Soviet Economy* 1:47-69.

Hewett, Ed A., and Richard Hornik. (1990). Hurry, Doctor! *Time*. May 7:84-87.

Hilferding, R. (1971). State Capitalism or Totalitarian State Economy? In *Essential Works of Socialism*, ed. Irving Howe (1979). New York: Bantam Books. 411-17.

Hoffman, Erik P., and Robbin F. Laird. (1982). *The Politics of Economic Modernization in the Soviet Union*. Ithaca, N. Y.: Cornell University Press.

Hohmann, Hans-Hermann. (1987). Gorbachev's Approach to Economic Reforms. In *The Soviet Economy: A New Course*, ed. Reiner Weichhardt (1987). 29-46.

Hook, Sidney. (1955). *Marx and the Marxists: The Ambiguous Legacy*. Princeton, N.J.: D. Van Nostrand Company.

Horvat, Branko. (1964). *Towards a Theory of Planned Economy*. Belgrade: Yugoslav Institute of Economic Research.

—. (1982). *The Political Economy of Socialism*. Armonk, N. Y.: Sharpe

Hough, Jerry F. (1982). Pluralism, Corporatism and the Soviet Union. In *Pluralism in the Soviet Union*, ed. Susan Gross Solomon (1982). New York: St. Martin's.

—. (1989). The Politics of Successful Economic Reform. *Soviet Economy* 1:3-46.

Howe, Irving. (ed.). (1986). *Essential Works of Socialism*. New Haven, Conn.: Yale University Press.

—. (1988). Thinking About Socialism: Achievements, Failures and Possibilities. *Dissent*:509-25.

Hutchison, T. W. (1980). *The Limitations of General Theories in Macroeconomics*. Washington, D. C.: American Enterprise Institute for Public Policy Research.

Ickes, Barry W. (1990). Obstacles to Economic Reform of Socialism: An Institutional-Choice Approach. *Annals of the American Academy of Political and Social Sciences*. January:53-64.

International Monetary Fund (1990). *World Economic Survey 1990*. Washington D. C.: The Fund.

Isaacson, Walter. (1989). A Long, Mighty Struggle. *Time*. April 10:49-59.

Jameson, Kenneth P., and Charles K. Wilber. (1981). Socialism and Development: Editors' Introduction. *World Development* 9:803-11.

Jasny, Naum. (1972). *Soviet Economists of The Twenties*. Cambridge, England: Cambridge University Press.

Jermakowicz, Wladyslaw. (1988). Foundations and Prospects for Soviet Economic Reforms: 1949 to 1987. In *Gorbachev's New Thinking: Prospects for Joint Ventures*, ed. Ronald Libowitz (1988). Cambridge, Mass.: Ballinger Publishing Company. 111-46.

Johnson, Chalmers. (ed.). (1970). *Change in Communist Systems*. Stanford, Calif.: Stanford University Press.

Jones, Anthony T. (1983). Models of Socialist Development. *International Journal of Comparative Sociology* 26: 86-99.

—. (1976). Modernization Theory and Socialist Development. In *Social Consequences of Modernization in Communist Societies*, ed. Mark Field (1976). 19-49.

Juviler, Peter, and H. Kimura. (eds.). (1988). *Gorbachev's Reforms: U.S and Japanese Assessments*. New York: Aldine De Gruyter.

Kagarlitsky, Boris. (1990a). The Intelligentsia and the Change. *New Left Review*. July-August: 5-26.

—. (1990b). *The Dialectic of Change*. London: Verso.

Kaiser, Robert G. (1988). The U.S.S.R in Decline. *Foreign Affairs* 97-113.

Kalecki, M. (1971). *Selected Essays on the Dynamics of the Capitalist Economy*.

Cambridge, England: Cambridge University Press.

—. (1986). *Selected Essays on Economic Planning*. Cambridge, England: Cambridge University Press.

Karol, K. S. (1988). Gorbachev and the Dynamics of Change. In *Socialist Register*, eds. Ralph Miliband, Leo Panitch, and John Saville (1988). London: Merlin Press. 12-36.

Karsten, S. G. (1985). Eucken's Social Market Economy and Its Test in Post-war West Germany. *The American Journal of Economics and Sociology* 44:169-83.

—. (1990). Gorbachev as a Social Market Economist. Presented at the 65th Annual Conference of Western Economic Association International held in San Diego, Calif., July 2, 1990.

Katz, Abraham. (1972). *The Politics of Economic Reform in the Soviet Union*. New York: Praeger.

Kaufman, Richard F. (1987). Industrial Modernization and Defense in the Soviet Union. In *The Soviet Economy: A New Course?*, ed. Reiner Weichhardt (1987). 247-62.

Kautsky, Karl. (1964). *The Dictatorship of the Proletariat*. Michigan: University of Michigan Press.

—. (1971). *The Class Struggle*. Trans. W. E. Bohn. New York: Norton.

—. (1986). The Commonwealth of the Future. In *Essential Works of Socialism*, ed. Irving Howe (1986). 95-118.

Kautsky, John. (1972). *The Political Consequences of Modernization*. New York: John Wiley and Sons.

Kellogg, Robert L. (1988). Modeling Soviet Modernization: An Economy in Transition. *Soviet Economy* 4:36-56

Kemme, David M. (1989). The Chronic Shortage Model of Centrally Planned Economies. *Soviet Studies*. July:345-64.

Kimura, Hiroshi. (1987). Gorbachevism-Simply Old Wine in a New Bottle? In *The Soviet Union in Transition*, ed. Kinya Niiseki (1987). Boulder, Colo.: Westview.

Kirkpatrick, Jeane. (1989). Return to Leninist Orthodoxy. In *Perestroika: How New is Gorbachev's New Thinking?*, eds. Ernest Lefever and Robert Lugt (1989). 47-54.

Kissinger, Henry. (1990). New World Acoming- and a new peril, too. *Los Angeles Times*. March 4:M2-8.

—. (1991). The Soviet Union Searches for Its New Order. *Los Angeles Times*. March 31:M1

Kolakowski, Leszek. (1977). Marxist Roots of Stalinism. In *Stalinism: Essays in Histroical Interpretation*, ed. Robert Tucker (1977). New York: Norton and Company. 283-98.

—. (1978). *Main Currents of Marxism (Vol. II)*. Oxford: Clarendon Press.

Kontorovich, Vladimir. (1987). Labor Problems and the Prospects for Accelerated Economic Growth. In *Soviet Society Under Gorbachev*, eds. Maurice Friedberg and Heyward Isham (1987). 30-51.

Korotich, Vitaly A. (1990). Happiness is Hard Work. *Los Angeles Times*. February 18:M1.

Kornai, Janos. (1957). *Overcentralization in Economic Administration*. London: Oxford University Press.

—. (1980). *Economics of Shortage*. Amsterdam: North-Holland.

—. (1984). Adjustment to Price and Quantity Signals in a Socialist Economy. In *The Economics of Relative Prices*, eds. Bela Csikos-Nagy, Douglas C. Hauge, and Graham Hall (1984). London: Macmillan. 60-77.

—. (1989). The Hungarian Reform Process: Visions, Hopes, and Reality. In *Remaking the Economic Institutions of Socialism*, eds. Victor Nee and David Stark (1989). Stanford, Calif.: Stanford University Press. 32-94.

—. (1990). *Vision and Reality, Market and State*. New York: Routledge.

Kosta, Jiri. (1987). The Chinese Economic Reform: Approaches, Results and Prospects. In *Crisis and Reform in Socialist Economies*, ed. Peter Gey et al. (1987). 145-72.

—. (1989). Can Socialist Economic Systems Be Reformed. In *Economic Reforms in Eastern Europe and The Soviet Union*, ed. Hubert Gabrisch (1989). 9-22.

Kostakov, Vladimir G. (1988). Employment: Scarcity or Surplus? *Soviet Review* 20-36.

Kowalik, Tadeusz. (1989). On Crucial Reform of Real Socialism. In *Economic Reforms in Eastern Europe and The Soviet Union*, ed. Hubert Gabrisch (1989). 23-59.

Kramer, Mark. (1990a). Let Reforms Take Hold Before Aid Flows. *Los Angeles Times*. July 16: M1.

Kuhne, Karl. (1972). *Economics and Marxism (Vol. 2)*. New York: St. Martin's.

Kushnirsky, Fyodor I. (1988). Soviet Economic Reforms: An Analysis and a Model. In *Reorganization and Reform in the Soviet Economy*, eds. Susan Linz and William Moskoff (1988). Armonk, N. Y.: Sharpe. 44-72.

—. (1989). The New Role of Normatives in Soviet Economic Planning. *Soviet Studies* 526-42.

Kurtzweg, Laurie. (1987). Trends in Soviet Gross National Product. In *Gorbachev's Economic Plans*, Joint Economic Committee (1987). 1:126-65.

Lane, David . (1985). *Soviet Economy and Society*. Oxford: Basil Blackwell.

—. (1986). *Labor and Employment in the USSR*. Brighton: Wheatsheaf Books.

Lange, Oscar. (1958). *The Political Economy of Socialism*. The Hague: van Keulen.

—. (1969). The Role of Planning in Socialist Economy. In *Comparative Economic Systems*, ed. Morris Bornstein (1969). Homewood, Ill.: Richard D. Irwin. 169-83.

— and Fred M. Taylor. (1938). *On The Economic Theory of Socialism*. Minneapolis: University of Minnesota Press.

Lapidus, Gail W. (1989). State and Society: Toward the Emergence of Civil Society in the Soviet Union. In *Politics, Society, and Nationality Inside Gorbachev's Russia*, ed. Seweryn Bialer (1989). 121-48.

— . (1990). Gorbachev and the National Question: Restructuring the Soviet

Federation. *Soviet Economy* 3:201-50.

Latey, Maurice. (1989). The General Crisis of Socialism. *The World Today*. August-September:128-34.

Lavigne, Marie. (1974). *The Socialist Economies of the Soviet Union and Europe*. White Plains, New York: International Arts and Sciences Press.

Lavoie, Dan. (1990). Computation, Incentives, and Discovery: The Cognitive Function of Markets in Market Socialism. *Annals of the American Academy of Political and Social Sciences*. January: 72-79.

Legget, Robert E. (1988). Gorbachev's Reform Program: Radical or More of the Same? In *Reorganization and Reform in the Soviet Economy*, eds. Susan Linz and William Moskoff (1988). Armonk, N. Y.: Sharpe.

Lenches, Elizabeth T. (1990). Soviet Ideology and Soviet Reforms. Presented at the 65th Annual Conference of WEAI, San Diego, Calif., July 2.

Lenin, V. I. (1967). *What is to be Done*. In *Selected Works in Three Volumes*, New York: International Publishers. 91-256.

—. (1974). *The State and Revolution*. In *Selected Works, One Volume Edition*. New York: International Publishers. 264-352.

Lerner, Abba P. (1934). Economic Thoery and Socialist Economy. *Review of Economic Studies* 2:51-61.

Leung, Hanson C. K. . (1985). The Role of Leadership in Adaptation to Change: Lessons of Economic Reforms in the USSR and China. *Studies in Comparative Communism* 18:227-46.

Lewin, Moshe. (1974). *Political Undercurrents in Soviet Economic Debates: From Bukharin to the Modern Reformers*. Princeton, N. J.: Princeton University Press.

—. (1977). The Social Background of Stalinism. In *Stalinism*, ed. Robert Tucker (1977). New York: Norton and Company. 111-36.

—. (1988). *The Gorbachev Phenomenon: A Historical Interpretation*. Berkeley, Calif.: University of California Press.

Liberman, E. G. (1971). *Economic Methods and the Effectiveness of Production*. White Plains, New York: International Arts and Sciences Press.

Liebowitz, Ronald D. (1988). *Gorbachev's New Thinking: Prospects for Joint Ventures*. Cambridge, Mass.: Ballinger Publishing Company.

Lieven, Dominic. (1989). Crisis in the Soviet Union - the Historical Perspective. *World Today* 5:90-93

Lindemann, Albert S. (1983). *A History of European Socialism*. New Haven, Conn.: Yale University Press.

Linz, Susan, and William Moskoff. (eds.). (1988). *Reorganization and Reform in the Soviet Economy*. Armonk, N. Y.: Sharpe.

Lippit, Victor D. (1987). *The Economic Development of China*. Armonk, N. Y.: Sharpe.

Little, Daniel. (1986). *The Scientific Marx*. Minneapolis: University of Minnesota Press.

Littlejohn, Gary. (1984). *A Sociology of the Soviet Union*. London: Macmillan.

Los Angeles Times. (1989). Soviet Union Near Economic Catastrophe, Sakharov

Warns. May 15. Part 1:6.

—. (1990). Soviet Propose Mixed Economy, Private Property. By Michael Parks. February: A1-13.

—. (1990). Soviet Union at 'Danger Point', Ligachev Says. By Michael Parks. March 26:A1-7.

—. (1990). Soviet Economic Shift to Double Food Prices. By Michael Parks. May 23:A1-9.

—. (1990). A Smaller U.S.S.R.? A More Stable One? Editorial. May 27:M6.

—. (1990). Soviet Disunion: When the Costs of Empire Outweigh Its Benefits. May 27:M1-2.

—. (1990). Kremlin Old Guard Swept Out of Central Committee. By John-Thor Dahlburg. July 14:A1-15.

—. (1990). New Politburo Drops Kremlin's Key Ministers. By Michael Parks. July 15: A1-14.

—. (1990). Gorbachev Lifts Party Monopoly on Radio, TV. By Michael Parks. July 16:A1-9.

—. (1990). Gorbachev Advances Plan for Decentralizing Nation. By John-Thor Dahlburg. July 21:A11.

—. (1990). Muslims in Soviet Central Asia Seek Sovereignty, Form an Islamic Party. By Doyle McManus. August 6:A4.

—. (1991). Soviets Vote in Unity Showdown. By John-Thor Dahlburg. March 18:A1-13.

Lovell, David W. (1984). *From Marx To Lenin: An Evaluation of Marx's Responsibility for Soviet Authoritarianism.* New York: Cambridge University Press.

Lowenthal, Richard. (1970). Development vs. Utopia in Communist Policy. In *Change in Communist Systems*, ed. Chalmers Johnson (1970). Stanford, Calif.: Stanford University Press.

—. (1976). The Ruling Party in Mature Society. In *Social Consequences of Modernization in Communist Societies*, ed. Mark Field (1976). 81-120.

Luxemburg, Rosa. (1961). *The Russian Revolution and Leninism or Marxism?.* Ann Arbor: University of Michigan Press.

—. (1969). *Social Reform or Revolution.* Colombo: Young Socialist.

—. (1972). *Selected Political Writings.* Ed. R. Looker. London: Cape.

—. (1986). The Conquest of Political Power. In *Essential Works of Socialism*, ed. Irving Howe (1986). New Haven, Conn.: Yale University Press.

Malashenko, Igor. (1991). The Third Way. *Time*. April 8:39.

Mandel, Ernest. (1979). *Trotsky: A Study in the Dynamic of his Thought.* London: NLB

—. (1981). The Laws of Motion of the Soviet Economy. *The Review of Radical Political Economics.* 13: 35-39.

—. (1986). In Defense of Socialist Planning. *New Left Review*. September-October: 5-37.

Marcuse, Herbert. (1958). *Soviet Marxism: A Critical Analysis.* New York: Columbia University Press.

Marschak, Thomas A. (1973). Decentralizing the Command Economy: The Study of a Pragmatic Strategy for Reformers. In *Plan and Market*, ed. Morris Bornstein (1973). New Haven, Conn.: Yale University Press. 23-64.

Mastny, Vojtech. (1989). *Soviet/East European Survey*. Boulder, Colo.: Westview.

Marx, Karl. (1973). *Critique of the Gotha Program*. In *Seleeted Works in Three Volumes, Volume 1*, Karl Marx and Frederick Engels (1973). Moscow: Progress Publishers. 1:9-25.

—. (1975-82). *Collected Works*. London: Lawrence and Wishart.

—. (1977). *Capital: A Critique of Political Economy. Vol 1*. Introduced by Ernest Mandel. New York: Vintage Books.

Karl Marx and Frederick Engels. (1848). *Communist Manifesto*. New York: International Publishers.

Maynes, William. (1990). A Revolutionary Turning Point: As Soviet Socialist Myth Ebbs, What will Take its Place? *Los Angeles Times*. February 11:M1.

Mazlish, Bruce. (1984). *The Meaning of Karl Marx*. New York: Oxford University Press.

Mazlish, Bruce, Arthur D. Kaledin, and David B. Raltson. (eds.). (1971). *Revolution: A Reader*. New York: Macmillan.

Medvedev, Roy. (1979). *On Stalin and Stalinism*. Oxford: Oxford University Press.

—. (1981). *Leninism and Western Socialism*. London: Verso.

—. (1988). Soviet Restore Stalin's Victims. *Los Angeles Times*. February 21: V1-2.

—. (1989). The Sources of Political Terror. *Dissent*. Summer:318-22.

Medvedev, Zhores. (1990). Soviet Power Today. *New Left Review*. January/February: 65-80.

Meissner, Boris. (1987). Implications of Leadership and Social Change for Soviet Politics. In *The Soviet Union in Transition*, ed. Kinya Niiseki (1987). Boulder, Colo.: Westview. 48-71.

Mencinger, Joze . (1987). The Crisis and the Reform of the Yugoslav Economic System in the Eighties. In *Crisis and Reform in Socialist Economies*, eds. Peter Gey et al. (1987). 99-120.

Mesa-Lago, Carmelo and Carl Beck. (eds.). (1975). *Comparative Socialist Systems: Essays on Politics and Economics*. Pittsburgh: University of Pittsburgh Center for International Studies.

Meyer, Alfred G. (1957). *Communism*. New York: Random House.

Mezhenkov, Vladimir and Eva Skelly. (eds.). (1988). *Perestroika in Action. Soviet Scene 1988*. London: Collets.

Migranian, Andranik. (1990a). As Gorbachev Matches Pace to Change, Soviet Union Hurries to Open Politics. *Los Angeles Times*. February 11:M1.

—. (1990b). The Snares of Democracy: Lithuanian Resolve Tests Soviet Reforms. *Los Angeles Times*. April 1:M1-2.

—. (1990c). *Perestroika: As seen by a Political Scientist*. Moscow: Novosti Press.

—. (1990d). Gorbachev's Leadership: A Soviet View. *Soviet Economy* 6:155-59.

Milanovic, Branko. (1989). *Liberalization and Entrepreneurship: Dynamics of Reform in Socialism and Capitalism*. Armonk, N.Y.: Sharpe.

Miliband, Ralph, Leo Panitch, and John Saville. (eds.). (1988). *Socialist Register 1988*. London: Merlin Press.

Mill, John Stuart. (1985). *Principles of Political Economy*. Harmondsworth, Middlesex, England: Penguin Books.

——. (1986). Socialism and Liberty. In *Essential Works of Socialism*, ed. Irving Howe (1986), New Haven, Conn.: Yale University Press.

Miller, David. (1989). *Market, State, and Community: Theoretical Foundations of Market Socialism*. Oxford: Clarendon Press.

—— and Saul Estrin. (1989). A Case for Market Socialism: What does it mean? Why should we favor it? *Dissent* 359-67.

Miller, Robert F. (1987). The Soviet Economy: Problems and Solutions in the Gorbachev View. In *Gorbachev At The Helm: A New Era in Soviet Politics?*, eds. Miller et al. (1987), London: Croom Helm. 108-35.

——. (1989). Theoretical and Ideological Issues of Reform in Socialist Systems: Some Yugoslav and Soviet Examples. *Soviet Studies* 430-48.

Miller, James R. (1981). The Prospects for Soviet Agriculture. In *The Soviet Economy: Continuity and Change*, ed. Morris Bornstein (1981), 273-92.

Mises, Ludwig von. (1935). Economic Calculation in the Socialist Commonwealth. In *Collectivist Economic Planning*, ed. F. A. Hayek (1935). New York: Augustus M. Kelley. 1-40.

——. (1951). *Socialism: An Economic and Sociological Analysis*. New Haven, Conn.: Yale University Press.

Montias, John Michael. (1973). A Framework for Theoretical Analysis of Economic Reforms in Soviet-type Economies. In *Plan and Market*, ed. Bornstein (1973). 65-122.

——. (1975). A Classification of Communist Economic Systems. In *Comparative Socialist Systems: Essays on Politics and Economics*, eds. Carmelo Mesa-Lago and Carl Beck (1975). 39-51.

Moore, Barrington Jr. (1967). *Social Origins of Dictatorship and Democracy*. Boston: Beacon Press.

Munting, Roger. (1982). *The Economic Development of the USSR*. London: Croom Helm.

Murrell, Peter. (1983). Did the theory of market socialism answer the challenge of Ludwig von Mises? A reinterpretation of the socialist controversy. *History of Political Economy* 15:92-105

Myrdal, Gunner. (1969). *The Political Element in the Development of Economic Theory*. New York: Clarion Book.

Naylor, Thomas H. (1988). *The Gorbachev Strategy: Opening the Closed Society*. Toronto: Lexington Books.

Nee, Victor and David Stark. (eds.). (1989). *Remaking the Economic Institutions of Socialism: China and Eastern Europe*. Stanford, Calif.: Stanford University Press.

Nelan, Bruce W. (1990). The Soviet Empire Lashed by the Flags of Freedom. *Time*. March 12: 26-51.

New Left Review. (ed.). (1983). *Western Marxism: A Critical Leader*. London: Verso.

News and Views From the USSR. (1990). Gorbachev Addresses Party Conference. June 21: 1-24.

—. (1990). The Full Report given by Mikhail Gorbachev at the 28th Congress of the Communist Party of the Soviet Union. July 5:1-46.

—. (1990). Gorbachev's Concluding Remarks at the 28th Communist Party Congress. July 12:1-17.

New York Times. (1989). Shakarov in Britain: Jab at Gorbachev. June 6:A3.

—. (1990). Parliament Votes Expanded Powers For Soviet Leader. March 14:A1-6.

—. (1990). Excerpts from Gorbachev's Remarks at Breakfast with U.S. Lawmakers. June 2:Y6.

—. (1990). Excerpts from Speeches at the Communist Party Congress. July 4:A5.

—. (1990). Gorbachev Wins Fight on Leadership of Party. July 10:A5.

—. (1990). Excerpts from News Conference With Bush and Gorbachev. June 4: A12.

Nixon, Richard. (1989). Challenge and Response. In *Perestroika: How New is Gorbachev's New Thinking?*, (ed.), Ernest Lefever and Robert Lugt (1989). 23-38.

— . (1990). Were Not Cold War Victors -Yet. *Los Angeles Times*. April 15:M1.

North, Douglas C. (1981). *Structure and Change in Economic History*. New York: Norton and Company.

Nove, Alec. (1964). *Economic Rationality and Soviet Politics or Was Stalin Really Necessary?* New York: Praeger

—. (1969). *An Economic History of the USSR*. London: Penguin Press.

—. (1980). *The Soviet Economic System*. London: George Allen and Unwin.

—. (1983). *The Economics of Feasible Socialism*. London: Allen and Unwin.

—. (1987). Radical Reform: Problems and Prospects. *Soviet Studies* 39:452-67

—. (1989). The Problems of Perestroika; Portrait of an Economy in Transition. *Dissent*. Fall:462-68.

Nozick, Robert. (1974). *Anarchy, State, and Utopia*. New York: Basic Books.

Nuti, D. M. (1986). Michal Kalecki's contribution to the theory and practice of socialist planning. *Cambridge Journal of Economics* 10:333-53.

O'Brien, John C. (1990). The Eternal Path to Communism: From Marx via Lenin and Stalin to Solzhenitsyn and Gorbachev. Presented at the 65th Annual Conference of WEAI, San Diego, Calif., July 2, 1990.

Ofer, Gur. (1989). Budget Deficit, Market Disequilibrium and Soviet Economic Reforms. *Soviet Economy* 2:107-61.

Palei, L. V and K. L. Radzivanovich . (1990). How to Carry out Economic Reform: Points of View and Reality. *Soviet Studies* 42:25-37.

Parchomenko, Walter. (1986). *Soviet Images of Dissidents and Nonconformists*. New York: Praeger.

Petrakov, Nikolay. (1987). Prospects for Change in the Systems of Price Formation,

Finance and Credit in the USSR. *Soviet Economy* 3:135-44.

Petrov, Vladimir. (1989). Pamyat and Others. In *Gorbachev and Glasnost: Viewpoints from the Soviet Press*, ed. Issac Tarasulo (1989). Wilmington, Del: SR Books. 143-53.

Pitman, Riitta H. (1990). Perestroika and Soviet Cultural Politics: The Case of the Major Literary Journals. *Soviet Studies* 42:111-32.

Polan, A. J. (1984). *Lenin and the End of Politics*. London: Methuen.

Popkova-Pijasheva, Larissa. (1990). Why is the Plan Incompatible with the Market. *Annals of the American Academy of Political and Social Science*. January:80-90.

Portes, Richard. (1978). The Demand for Money and for Consumption goods in Centrally Planned Economies. *Review of Economics and Statistics* 60:8-18

— . (1981). The Theory of Macroeconomic Equilibrium and Disequilibrium in Centrally Planned Economies. *Economic Inquiry* 19:559-78

Post, K., and P. Wright. (1989). *Socialism and Underdevelopment*. London: Routledge.

Poznanski, Kazimierz Z. (1987). *Technology, Competition, and the Soviet Bloc in the World Market*. Berkeley, Calif.: University of California Press.

Preobrazhensky, E. A. (1965). *The New Economics*. Oxford: Oxford University Press.

Prybyla, Jan S. (ed.). (1969). *Comparative Economic Systems*. New York: Appleton-Century-Crofts.

—. (1987). *Market and Plan under Socialism: The Bird in the Cage*. Stanford, Calif.: Hoover Institution Press.

—. (1990). Economic Reform of Socialism: The Dengist Course in China. *Annals of the American Academy of Political and Social Science*. January: 113-22.

Raiklin, Ernest. (1990). On the Causality of Great Personalities and Great Events Exemplified by Lenin and the October Revolution. Presented at the 65th Annual Conference of WEAI, San Diego, Calif., July 2.

Rakovski, Marc. (1978). *Towards an East European Marxism*. New York: St. Martin's.

Rawls, John. (1971). *A Theory of Justice*. Cambridge, Mass.: Harvard University Press.

Reagan, Ronald. (1989). The Perils of Imposed Perfection. In *Perestroika: How New is Gorbachev's New Thinking*, eds. Lefever and Lugt (1989). 15-22.

Reddaway, Peter. (1990). The Quality of Gorbachev's Leadership. *Soviet Economy* 6:125-40.

Remington, Thomas F. (ed.). (1989). *Politics and the Soviet System*. New York: St. Martin's. 29-55.

Rider, Christine. (1988). Market Reforms in a Shortage Economy. *Review of Radical Political Economics*. 20:138-42.

Rigby, T. H. (1977). Stalinism and the Mono-Organizational Society. In *Stalinism*, ed. Robert Tucker (1977). 53-76.

Rigby, T. H., and Ferenc Feher. (eds.). (1982). *Political Legitimation in Communist States*. New York: St. Martin's.

Rizzi, Bruno. (1985). *The Bureaucratization of the World. The USSR: Bureaucratic Collectivism*. London: Tavistock.

Roberts, Paul Craig. (1971). *Alienation and the Soviet Economy*. Albuquerque: University of New Mexico Press.

Roberts, Paul Craig, and Mathew A Stephenson. (1973). *Marxs Theory of Exchange, Alienation and Crisis*. Stanford, Calif.: Hoover Institution Press.

Roeder, Philip G. (1988). *Soviet Political Dynamics*. New York: Harper and Row.

Rossiter, Clinton. (1962). *Conservatism in America*. New York: Random House.

Rostow, W. W. (1978). The Uses of Ideology. In *American Appraisals of Soviet Russia, 1917-1977*, ed. Eugene Anschel (1978). Metuchen, N. J.: Scarecrow Press. 59-62.

Roucek, Libor. (1988). Private Enterprise in Soviet Political Debates. *Soviet Studies*. 60:46-63.

Rumer, Boris. (1987). The Problems of Industrial Modernization in the USSR. In *The Soviet Economy: A New Course?*, ed. Reiner Weichhardt (1987). 229-46.

—. (1989). Soviet Estimates of The Rate of Inflation. *Soviet Studies* 298-317.

Sakharov, Andrei. (1989). The Inevitability of *Perestroika*. In *Gorbachev and Glasnost*, ed. Issac Tarasulo. (1989). Wilmington, Del: SR Books. 321-27.

Samuels, Warren J. (ed.). (1989). *Fundamentals of the Economic Role of Government*. New York: Greenwood Press.

Samuelson, Paul A. (1976). *Economics*. New York: McGraw Hill.

Scanlan, James P. (1985). *Marxism in the USSR: A Critical Survey of Current Soviet Thought*. Ithaca, N.Y.: Cornell University Press.

—. (1988). Ideology and Reform. In *Gorbachev's Reforms*, eds. Peter Juviler and H. Kimura (1988). New York: Aldine De Gruyter. 49-62.

Schapiro, Leonard. (1960). *The Communist Party of the Soviet Union*. New York: Random House.

—. (1966). *The Origins of the Communist Autocracy*. Cambridge, Mass.: Harvard University Press.

Schmidt-Hauer, Christian. (1986). *Gorbachev: The Path to Power*. London: I. B. Tauris.

Schneider, G. (1989). Perestroika of Ideology. In *Western Perceptions of Soviet Goals: Is Trust Possible?*, ed. Kalus Gottstein (1989). Boulder, Colo.: Westview. 24-39.

Schroeder, Getrude E. (1987). Anatomy of Gorbachev's Economic Reform. *Soviet Economy*. 3:219-41.

—. (1988). Organizations and Hierarchies: The Perennial Search for Solutions. In *Reorganization and Reform in the Soviet Economy*, eds. Susan Linz and Moskoff (1988). 3-22.

—. (1990). Economic Reform of Socialism: The Soviet Record. In *Annals of the American Academy of Political and Social Sciences*. January:35-43.

Schumpeter, Joseph A. (1950). *Capitalism, Socialism and Democracy*. New York: Harper and Row.

Schwartz, Harry. (1965). *The Soviet Economy Since Stalin*. Philadelphia: J.B.

Lippincott Company.

Seiful-Mulyukov, Farid. (1989). *The Soviet Economy: A Look Into The Future*. Moscow: Novosti Press.

Selbourne, David. (1985). *Against Socialist Illusion*. New York: Schocken Books.

Selucky, Radoslav. (1979). *Marxism, Socialism, Freedom: Towards a General Democratic Theory of Labor-Managed Systems*. New York: St. Martin's.

— . (1972). *Economic Reforms in Eastern Europe*. New York: Praeger.

Selyunin, Vasily. (1989). Sources. In *Gorbachev and Glasnost*, ed. Issac Tarasulo (1989). Wilmington, Del.: SR Books. 11-27.

Shalin, Dimitri N. (1990). Perestroika's Ugly Brother, Anti-Semitism. *Los Angeles Times*. July 25:B7.

Shapiro, Leonard. (1985). *1917: The Russian Revolutions and the Origins of Present-day Communism*. Harmondsworth, Middlesex, England: Penguin.

Sherman, Howard J. (1970). The Economics of Pure Communism. *Soviet Studies* 22:450-58

—. (1990). The Second Soviet Revolution or the Transition from Statism to Socialism. *Monthly Review*. March:14-23.

Shlapentokh, Vladimir. (1988). *Soviet Ideologies in the Period of Glasnost*. New York: Praeger.

Shmelev, Nikolai, and Vladimir Popov. (1989). *The Turning Point: Revitalizing the Soviet Economy*. New York: Doubleday.

Shoup, Paul A. (1975). Indicators of Socio-Politico-Economic Development. In *Comparative Socialist Systems: Essays on Politics and Economics*, eds. Carmelo Mesa-Lago and Carl Beck (1975). 3-38.

Sik, Ota. (1967). *Plan and Market under Socialism*. New York: International Arts and Sciences Press.

—. (1976). *The Third Way: Marxist-Leninist Theory and Modern Industrial Society*. London: Wildwood House.

Sites, Richard. (1989). *Revolutionary Dreams: Utopian Vision and Experimental Life in the Russian Revolution*. Oxford: Oxford University Press.

Skilling, Gordon. (1966). Interest Groups and Communist Politics. *World Politics* 18:435-51.

Skocpol, Theda. (1979). *State and Social Revolutions*. Cambridge, Mass.: Cambridge University Press.

Slaughter, Cliff. (1985). *Marx and Marxism: An Introduction*. New York: Longman.

Smith, Gordon. (1988). *Soviet Politics: Continuity and Contradictions*. London: Macmillan.

Solo, Robert A. (1967). *Economic Organizations and Social Systems*. New York: Bobbs-Merrill Company.

Sonnenfeldt, Helmut. (ed.). (1985). *Soviet Politics in the 1980s*. Boulder, Colo.: Westview.

Sorokin, G. (1987). Growth Rates of the Soviet Economy. *Soviet Review* 9-26.

Spechler, Dina and Martin Spechler. (1989). The Economic Burden of the Soviet Empire: Estimates and Reestimates. In *Limits of Soviet Power*, eds. Rajan Menon and Daniel Nelson (1989). Lexington, Mass.: Lexington Books. 27-48.

Stalin, Joseph. (1973). *The Essential Stalin*. London: Croom Helm.

—. (1952). *Economic Problems of Socialism in the U.S.S.R*. New York: International Publishers.

Staniszkis, Jadwiga. (1989). The Dynamics of a Breakthrough in the Socialist System: An outline of Problems. *Soviet Studies* 560-73.

Stark, David. (1989). Coexisting Organizational Forms in Hungary's Emerging Mixed Economy. In *Remaking the Economic Institutions of Socialism*, eds. Victor Nee and David Stark (1989). 137-68.

Stephen, White. (1989). The Soviet Political Leadership and Soviet Power. In *Limits of Soviet Power*, eds. Rajan Menon and Daniel N. Nelson (1989). 49-68.

Stone, Lawrence. (1971). Theories of Revolution. In *Revolution: A Reader*, eds. Bruce Mazlish et al. (1971). 44-56.

Stojanovic, Svetozar. (1988). *Perestroika: From Marxism and Bolshevism to Gorbachev*. Buffalo, N. Y.: Promethus Books.

Sweezy, Paul M. (1949). *Socialism*. New York: McGraw Hill.

—. (1980). *Post-Revolutionary Society*. New York: Monthly Review Press.

—. (1990). Perestroika and the Future of Socialism. *Monthly Review*. March: 1-14 and April: 1-17.

Sylos-Labini, Paolo. (1984). *The Forces of Economic Growth and Decline*. Cambridge, Mass.: MIT Press.

Szelenyi, Ivan. (1989). Eastern Europe in an Epoch of Transition: Toward a Socialist Mixed Economy. In *Remaking the Economic Institutions of Socialism*, eds. Victor Nee and David Stark (1989). 208-32.

Szymanski, Albert. (1979). *Is the Red Flag Flying? The Political Economy of the Soviet Union*. London: Zed Press.

Talbott, Strobe. (1987). Gorbachev. *Time*. July 27:28-34.

—. (1989). Fighting the Founders. *Time*. June 5:16-19.

—. (1990). Undoing Lenins Legacy. *Time*. February:29-31.

—. (1991). The Conductor of Discord. *Time*. March 25:33.

Tarasulo, Issac (ed.). (1989). *Gorbachev and Glasnost: Viewpoints from the Soviet Press*. Wilmington, Del.: SR Books.

Taylor, Fred. M. (1929). The Guidance of Production in a Socialist State. In *On the Economic Theory of Socialism*, ed. Benjamin E. Lippincott (1964). Minneapolis: University of Minnesota Press.

Teague, Elizabeth. (1987). Gorbachev's Human Factor Policies. In Joint Economic Committee, *Gorbachev's Economic Plans*. 2:224-39.

—. (1989). Perestroika: Who Stands to Gain, Who Stands to Lose?. In *Gorbachev's Agenda*, ed. Susan Clark (1989). Boulder, Colo.: Westview. 57-84.

Theen, Rolf. (1988). Hierarchical Reform in the Soviet Economy: The Case of Agriculture. In *Reorganization and Reform in the Soviet Economy*, eds. Linz and Moskoff. (1988). 73-87.

Time Magazine. (1988). Travellers to a Changing Land. By John Greenwald. February 16:34-35.

—. (1989). Russia's Prophet in Exile. By Paul Gray. July 24: 56-60.

—. (1989). His Vision Thing. By Bruce W. Nelan. October 2:22-23.

—. (1991). Boris Vs. Mikhail. By Bruce W. Nelan. March 25:26-31.

—. (1990). Red Army Blues. By Bruce W. Nelan. April 9:46-48.

—. (1990). The Eye of the Storm. By John Kohan. June 4:24-34.

—. (1990). Fighting the Founders. June 5:17-19.

—. (1990). But Back Home... Yeltsin Wins Power. By Bruce W. Nelan. June 11:28-31.

Treadgold, Donald W. (1976). *Lenin and his Rivals*. Westport, Conn.: Greenwood Press.

Trotsky, Leon. (1936). *The Revolution Betrayed*. New York: Pathfinder Press.

—. (1962). *The Permanent Revolution*. London: New Park Publications.

—. (1965). *The New Course*. Ann Arbor: University of Michigan Press.

—. (1980). *The Challenge of the Left Opposition, 1926-27*. New York: Pathfinder Press.

—. (1986). Stalinism and Bolshevism. In *Essential Works of Socialism*, ed. Irving Howe (1986). 202-12.

Tucker, Robert C. (ed.). (1977). *Stalinism: Essays in Historical Interpretation*. New York: Norton and Company. 77-110.

Tudor, H and J. M. Tudor. (1988). *Marxism and Social Democracy*. New York: Cambridge University Press.

Ulam, A. B. (1973). *Lenin and Bolsheviks: The Intellectual and Political History of the Triumph of Communism in Russia*. London: Fontana.

Unger, David C. (1989). European Marxism, 1848-1989: History Completes a Cycle of Central Europe. *New York Times*. December 4:A22.

United Nations. (1990). *World Economic Survey*. New York: United Nation's Department of Economic and Social Affairs.

Vanek, Jaroslav. (1970). *The General Theory of the Labor-Managed Market Economy*. Ithaca, N.Y.: Cornell University Press.

Wall Street Journal. (1989). Gorbachev Announces Spending on Soviet Military for First Time. May 31:A12.

Ward, Benjamin N. (1967). *The Socialist Economy: A Study of Organizational Alternatives*. New York: Random House.

Weichhardt, Reiner, (ed.). (1987). *The Soviet Economy: New Course?*. Brussels: NATO Economics Directorate.

Whetten, Lawrence L. (1989). *Interaction of Political and Economic Reforms within the East Bloc*. New York: Crane Russak.

White, Stephen. (1990). Democratization in the USSR. *Soviet Studies* 42:3-25.

Wilczynski, J. (1970). *The Economics of Socialism*. Chicago: Aldine Publishing Company.

Wiles, Peter. (1962). *The Political Economy of Communism*. Cambridge, Mass.: Harvard University Press.

—. (1982). The Worsening of Soviet Economic Performance. In *Crisis in the East European Economy*, ed. Jan Drewnowski (1982). London: Croom Helm. 143-63.

Wilhelm, John Howard. (1985). The Soviet Union Has an Administered, Not a Planned Economy. *Soviet Studies* 37:118-30.

—. (1990). Crisis and Collapse: What are the Issues? *Soviet Studies* 42:317-27.

Winiecki, Jan (1986a). Are Soviet-type Economies Entering an Era of Long-Term Decline? *Soviet Studies* 38:325-48.

—. (1986b). Soviet-Type Economies: Considerations For the Future. *Soviet Studies* 38:543-61.

—. (1989a). *The Distorted World of Soviet-type Economies*. London: Routledge.

—. (1989b). CPEs Structural Change and World Market Performance: A Permanently Developing Country (PDC) Status? *Soviet Studies*. July:365-81.

—. (1990). Obstacles to Economic Reform of Socialism: A Property Rights Approach. *Annals of the American Academy of Political and Social Science*. January: 65-71.

Wolf, Thomas A. (1990). Reform, Inflation, and Adjustment in Planned Economies. *Finance and Development*. March.

Woody, Sylvia. (1989). *Gorbachev and the Decline of Ideology in Soviet Foreign Policy*. Boulder, Colo.: Westview.

Yakovlev, Alexander N. (1988). The Political Philosophy of Perestroika. In *Perestroika 1989*, ed. Abel Aganbegyan (1988b). New York: Charles Scribner's Sons. 33-72.

—. (1989). *Development of Democracy is Imperative for the Renewal of Society*. Moscow: Novosti Press.

—. (1990). *Socialism: From Dream to Reality*. Moscow: Novosti Press.

Yeltsin, Boris. (1990). *Against the Grain*. New York: Summit Books.

Yunker, James A. (1979). *Socialism in the Free Market*. New York: Nellen Publishing Company.

—. (1986). A Market Socialist Critique of Capitalisms Dynamic Performance. *Journal of Economic Issues* 20:63-81.

Yevtushenko, Yevgeny. (1987). A Poet's View of *Glasnost*. *Time*. February 9: 32-33.

—. (1988). We Humiliate Ourselves. *Time*. June 27:30-31.

Zaslavskaya, Tatyana. (1988). Friends or Foes? Social Forces Working for and Against *Perestroika*. In *Perestroika 1989*, ed. Aganbegyan (1988b). New York: Charles Scribners Sons. 255-80.

—. (1990). *The Second Socialist Revolution*. Bloomington: Indiana University Press.

Zaslavsky, Victor. (1987). Soviet Reforms in the 1980s: Current Debate. In *Gorbachev At The Helm*, eds. R.F. Miller et al. (1987). London: Croom Helm. 136-60.

Zemtsov, Ilya, and John Farrar (1989). *Gorbachev: The Man and the System*. New Brunswick: Transaction Publishers.

Zysman, John. (1983). *Governments, Markets and Growth: Financial Systems and the Politics of Change*. Ithaca, N.Y.: Cornell University Press.

Index

About the Author

A. F. DOWLAH is an Assistant Professor of Economics and Political Science at the State University of New York, Canton. Formerly he taught at the University of Southern California, California State University at Fullerton and at Los Angeles. He authored a number of papers and a book entitled *Perestroika: An Inquiry Into its Historical Ideological, and Intellectual Roots* (1990).